REVOLUTION FROM ABROAD

The Soviet Conquest of
Poland's Western Ukraine
and Western Belorussia

EXPANDED EDITION

WITH A NEW PREFACE BY THE AUTHOR

JAN T. GROSS

PRINCETON UNIVERSITY PRESS
PRINCETON AND OXFORD

Copyright © 1988, 2002 by Princeton University Press

Published by Princeton University Press, 41 William Street,
Princeton, New Jersey 08540

In the United Kingdom: Princeton University Press, 3 Market Place, Woodstock,
Oxfordshire OX20 1SY

Library of Congress Cataloging-in-Publication Data

Gross, Jan Tomasz.
Revolution from abroad : the Soviet conquest of Poland's western Ukraine and
western Belorussia / Jan T. Gross. — Expanded ed. / with a new preface by the author.
p. cm.
Includes bibliographical references and indexes.
ISBN 0-691-09603-1 (pbk. : alk. paper)
1. Poland—History—Occupation, 1939–1945. 2. Ukraine, Western—History—
Soviet occupation, 1939–1941. 3. Belarus—History—1917–1991. 4. World War,
1939–1945—Personal narratives, Polish. 5. Soviet Union—Foreign relations—
Poland. 6. Poland—Foreign relations—Soviet Union. I. Title.
DK4415 .G76 2002
943.8'053—dc21   2001058838

British Library Cataloging-in-Publication Data is available

This book has been composed in Linotron Sabon

Printed on acid-free paper. ∞

www.pupress.princeton.edu

Printed in the United States of America

1 3 5 7 9 10 8 6 4 2

REVOLUTION FROM ABROAD

For A.M.

A ragged urchin, aimless and alone,
Loitered about that vacancy; a bird
Flew up to safety from his well-aimed stone:
That girls are raped, that two boys knife a third,
Were axioms to him, who'd never heard
Of any world where promises were kept
Or one could weep because another wept.

W. H. AUDEN, "The Shield of Achilles"

CONTENTS

LIST OF ILLUSTRATIONS

(following page 176)

(Unless otherwise noted, all illustrations are reproduced courtesy of the Arthur L. Waldo Collection in the Hoover Institution, Stanford, California)

PREFACE TO THE EXPANDED EDITION

SINCE THE first edition of this book was published, the Soviet Union has ceased to exist. An important event in its own right, for social scientists interested in the Stalinist era, the demise of the USSR has been a true watershed: suddenly they were given access to official documents of the period that were never meant to be scrutinized by independent scholars. As a result, the field of Soviet history is open. New works are proliferating. The history of the period has to be written anew. And most extant studies will have to be significantly revised in the light of new evidence.

I am pleased to note that *Revolution from Abroad* survived the revolution in availability of archives. Newly available Soviet documents — which by their official nature provide a "top-down" view of the regime — offer a supplement and do not supersede the empirical basis of this study. In the book I reconstructed the workings of Soviet totalitarianism from the bottom up, so to speak; I presented "the phenomenon of the Soviets' seizure of power and imposition of their regime as it was experienced by ordinary people" (p. 225). Someone will still have to write a detailed study of Soviet institutions in the Western Ukraine and Western Belorussia and combine it with an analysis of the impact they had on the local society. But a social history of sovietization as sketched in *Revolution from Abroad* remains valid, and what I have added to this expanded edition grows out of the evolution of my thinking about the historiography of the war period rather than out of newly discovered sources.

Since this book first appeared in 1988, I have indicated in the introduction to *Neighbors* (Princeton, N.J.: Princeton University Press, 2001) that I view "standard historiography of the Second World War, which posits that there are two separate wartime histories — one pertaining to the Jews and the other to all the other citizens of a given European country subjected to Nazi rule" (pp. 7–8) as untenable. The story depicted in *Neighbors* — that of Polish inhabitants of a small town who murder their Jewish fellow-citizens — was a striking illustration of why it is so. The expanded edition of *Revolution from Abroad* is therefore supplemented by a long essay entitled "A Tangled Web," addressing stereotypes concerning relations between

Poles, Germans, Jews, and Communists, which, I believe, the readers will find indispensable for a better understanding of the period.

Finally, I would like to include a factual correction. On the basis of newly available Soviet data—which are incomplete but, researchers agree, fundamentally correct—the number of people who had been arrested in and deported from the Western Ukraine and Western Belorussia from 1939 to 1941 has to be significantly scaled down from previous estimates. The best count of the total number of deportees in this period now runs between 309,000 and 327,000 rather than around half a million or, according to some earlier Polish estimates, as many as 1 million people. And the number of the arrested during this period can now be narrowed to 110,000 to 130,000, as opposed to up to 440,000, as previously considered.* This still represents a staggering toll of human suffering, but one that is more comparable to what went on at the time under the Nazi occupation than I previously indicated in the concluding chapter.

New York City, December 2001

---

* Stanisław Ciesielski, Wojciech Materski, and Andrzej Paczkowski, *Represje sowieckie wobec Polaków i obywateli polskich* (Warszawa: Ośrodek Karta, 2000) 11–16.

PREFACE

THIS STUDY was made possible by an accidental discovery in the Hoover Institution on War, Revolution and Peace. Looking for materials pertinent to the history of the German occupation of Poland during World War II, I found handwritten statements describing individuals' experiences under the Soviet occupation of the eastern half of the country, starting in September 1939. The Hoover Institution archives, as I later realized during my deliberate search for further information about this subject, contains many thousands of such personal testimonies, allowing for a close study of Soviet policies in occupied Poland. I have since investigated archival collections in England, France, Germany, and Israel[1] and interviewed numerous witnesses to these events in Europe, Israel, and the United States. Still, the Hoover holdings offer the richest materials, and I use them as a constant reference in this study. Since the sources are not only unique but also highly personal, the reader should know as much about these documents as I did, in order to understand and evaluate the subsequent narrative.

In September 1939 the Soviet Union, bound by treaty with Hitler's Germany, occupied over 50 percent of the territory of the Polish state. During their twenty-one months of rule in the area—from the Red Army's aggression against Poland on September 17, 1939, to the outbreak of war between the USSR and Germany on June 22, 1941—the Soviet authorities deported about 1.25 million Polish citizens (roughly 9 percent of the local population) to many parts of the Soviet Union. Then, following Hitler's attack on the USSR, Polish-Soviet diplomatic relations were re-established and a pact was signed between the two countries. The agreement called for the "amnesty" (i.e., release) of all Polish citizens detained in the Soviet Union and the establishment of a Polish army on the territory of the USSR. In 1942 about 120,000 people—soldiers of the newly created Polish army and their families—were evacuated to Iran. These were the people who were asked for depositions about their experiences under the Soviet regime. About 20,000 of the original protocols are preserved in the Polish Government Collection, the Anders Collection, and the Poland. Ambasada (USSR) Collection in the Hoover Institution. "A Note about the Collection and Analysis of Source Materials Concerning Soviet Russia," written in wartime London with the date November 20, 1943, penciled in, recognizes the value of the sources: "Polish citizens who went through Russia are the first large group of people in about 20 years who were exposed to life in the Soviet Union, who know from experience the nature of the Soviet regime, and who were then allowed to leave Russia's borders. Their testimonies may constitute a precious source enabling us to reveal to world opinion the truth about Russia."[2]

This task, as it turned out, could not be accomplished at that time. The climate of opinion then was cool toward evidence casting doubt on the character or intentions of amiable "Uncle Joe" Stalin. But the Polish authorities who were assembling evidence about the Soviet Union had something more concrete in mind than merely enlightening the world about the nature of Soviet communism. Some 15,000 Polish officers on duty and in the reserves had mysteriously disappeared after Soviet authorities sent them to POW camps in 1939. They were needed two years later to staff the Polish Army in the East, which was being put together on Soviet soil. Yet they could not be found after the resumption of Polish-Soviet diplomatic relations, and civilian and military authorities kept inquiring about them at all levels of the Soviet hierarchy. All that the Poles succeeded in obtaining were repeated assurances that everyone was being released from confinement. Stalin himself during a conversation with the Polish prime minister, General Władysław Sikorski, guessed that the officers must have escaped to Manchuria.[3]

As it became apparent that the Soviet authorities were either helpless or stonewalling on the issue, the missing men's comrades-in-arms (and then comrades in detention or exile) were asked to help. The initiative to collect evidence came from the newly appointed Polish ambassador to Moscow, Professor Stanisław Kot, an eminent historian and a close confidant of Prime Minister Sikorski.[4] A survey was distributed to the personnel of the Polish Army in the East asking ten questions: about the time and circumstances of the respondent's arrest and detention, about fellow prisoners, about attitudes of prison or camp personnel toward the inmates, about morality among prisoners, about contacts with prisoners' families and the outside world, and finally about the circumstances of the respondent's release. Everyone supplied biographical information—name, date of birth, sex, marital status, profession, and place of residence in Poland before the war. About 10,000 of these questionnaires are now stored in the Anders Collection at the Hoover Institution.

The second most pressing issue concerning Polish-Soviet relations had to do with the status of the eastern half of Poland, occupied by the Soviets in 1939. The Polish-Soviet agreement of 1941 (the so-called

Sikorski-Majski agreement) included a clause abrogating the 1939 Soviet-German treaties concerning Poland. But the agreement did not pronounce directly on the status of the Western Ukraine and Western Belorussia, which the Soviets had annexed, allegedly with the people's mandate given in an October 1939 election. The pros and cons of committing Poland to an agreement with the Soviet Union that did not guarantee Poland's territorial integrity within its prewar borders were hotly debated at the time but never resolved. General Sikorski wanted to save the lives of Poles who were slowly dying in Russia and to normalize relations with the Soviet Union as soon as possible. His decision to sign the document despite its ambiguity on this most important issue led four of his senior cabinet ministers to resign. Needless to say, the Polish authorities did not give up claim to sovereignty over the Soviet-occupied area by signing the agreement. And prudently, they decided to prepare arguments in case the issue came before some diplomatic forum in the future. Hence the origin of another important source of data for the period—a survey of Polish army personnel and their families covering in seven questions the circumstances of the Red Army's entry into the town or village where each respondent lived in September 1939, the ensuing takeover by the Soviet-sponsored administration, and the sequence of events up to and including the so-called plebiscite held on October 22, 1939. As with the earlier questionnaire, personal data were collected from the respondents, who can therefore be identified today by name, sex, marital status, profession, and place of residence in Poland. Approximately 10,000 such questionnaires are preserved at the Hoover Institution archives in the Polish Government Collection.

The quality of the material collected in these two surveys is uneven. Frequently, one comes across no more than a page of laconic answers that merely reproduce a "standard" version of what happened and add little to our knowledge. But fortunately, the questions more often served as a jumping-off point for a narrative full of detail and information of personal significance to the respondent quite beyond what was solicited by the questionnaire. The point is that only a small fraction of those who had to answer these questions were used to filling out forms. Certainly the majority could not write correctly. Some were illiterate.[5] The fact is, most of the respondents still belonged to the oral tradition. So, when asked to fill out questionnaires, they put their stories on paper as they would have told them—literally so, as for the most part they even used phonetic spelling. "I will tell you how it was"—this invocation from one of the documents could appropriately have been placed at the beginning of many.[6]

The Polish authorities had the good sense to encourage this free form of expression. In his order of March 13, 1943, the commander of the Polish Army in the East, General Władysław Anders, said it explicitly:

> Work with the questionnaires [about three different ones had already been distributed] must be considered one of the most important current assignments. All our energy and attention must be devoted to its completion. . . . The questionnaire concerning the plebiscite ought to be understood as a guideline only. The development of each topic and its presentation in the form of a free-flowing narrative is highly desirable. . . . Because this initiative is of such superior importance higher commanders ought to designate especially well-qualified officers to coordinate the surveys in each unit.[7]

What has been preserved in the Hoover Institution is only a fraction of the documentation collected on the subject. One archive shipped to London from the USSR sank in transport. Many loads of documents were confiscated by the Soviet secret police during the evacuation of the Polish army from Russia in 1942. Indeed, the Soviet authorities tried to intercept the archives accompanying the Polish ambassador as he was boarding a ship to Iran. This loss was prevented only by the determination of a junior officer escorting the ambassador's luggage, Lieutenant Ksawery Pruszyński, a famous writer, who drew a gun in defense of the papers in his custody.[8]

In fact, Polish authorities began compiling evidence from the moment they were reconstituted in Russia and came in touch with the Polish citizens being released from Soviet camps and forced settlement. Each person was asked to give information about other Polish citizens whom he or she knew were still kept in confinement. Many volunteered memoirs or diaries that they had been writing all along.[9] But the first evidence of systematic data gathering by questionnaire appears in a January 19, 1942, order by Colonel Leopold Okulicki, Anders's chief of staff.[10] He initiated a detailed, eleven-point survey about people's activities in the underground prior to their arrest including a query about other members of the Association for Armed Struggle (zwz, later Home Army [ak]) whose names, pseudonyms, or whereabouts the respondents knew. The point was to pressure Soviet authorities for release of yet unaccounted-for members of the underground who had been deported to Russia.[11]

In addition to the three surveys already mentioned, I found evidence of another six that were conducted among the Poles evacuated from the Soviet Union in 1942–1943: a survey eight items long about religious life in the USSR; a survey about women, including fifteen questions concerning the female respondents' experiences and an additional eight questions about Soviet women; thirty-three questions about Jews; a twenty-item survey comparing working conditions in Poland under the Soviet occupation and in the Soviet interior; a thirteen-point questionnaire distributed by the Office of the Catholic Chaplain of the Army (Szefostwo Duszpasterstwa Katolickiego); and finally, a detailed eighteen-point survey, "Gold" about gold mining in the Soviet Union. Unfortunately, except for a specimen or two, only the blank questionnaires can be found in the Hoover archives.

All documentary materials originally came under the jurisdiction of the military authorities. They were handled first by the Independent Historical Section (Samodzielny Referat Historyczny) directed by Dr. Walerian Charkiewicz; from April 15, 1943, the Bureau of Documents of the Polish Army in the East, established on Anders's order, took over under Colonel Kazimierz Ryziński. On May 12, 1943, the Historical Section was once again set apart from the Bureau of Documents. Almost a year later, on February 4, 1944, the Bureau of Documents was integrated with the Intelligence Department of the army as the Intelligence Archives Section, and Lieutenant Bohdan Podoski was put in charge.[12]

Back in April 1943 an agreement had been reached with the civilian authorities to transfer to their custody the completed questionnaires concerning the October elections.[13] Six months later, in London, Professor Wiktor Sukiennicki received some 12,000 of those protocols for his newly established Research Section. The questionnaires were in pristine condition; they had not even been sorted. When in January 1944 the Red Army once again crossed the prewar Polish borders, Sukiennicki's section started to produce county reports for areas that were being occupied by the Red Army for the second time since the beginning of the war. The reports consisted of quotations from individual depositions, arranged thematically into four broad sections: entry of the Red Army; occupation until the October elections; the elections; and sovietization of the occupied territories following the elections. Sukiennicki's intention was to make clear what the local population would likely experience when the Soviets reoccupied the country. His office, as he states in the "Report of the Activities of the Research Section of the Ministry of Information and Documentation," could not keep pace with the speed of the Red Army's offensive.[14] These are the county reports I refer to throughout this book, from sixty-three counties of the eight voivodeships;* they are stored in the Polish Government Collection. Each report is preceded by a brief statistical description of the county's prewar conditions, and it also gives the number of individual protocols used in the preparation of the report and breaks them down by the social category of the respondents and their place of residence (*gmina*, or township). I have frequently found direct quotations in Sukiennicki's reports corresponding to the text in the original documents I have consulted. This brings us to a sensitive point concerning the Internal Archives of the Bureau of Documents.

The bureau was established to serve several purposes. Its mandate was not only to collect evidence with historical value and immediately applicable intelligence but also to produce materials that could be used for political purposes—to influence public opinion and the Western allies in ways favorable to Polish claims vis-à-vis the Soviet Union. How to best serve the Polish cause in these circumstances was not at all clear even to the small team employed in the bureau, and a dispute arose that spilled over into at least two internal memoranda, written on the 8th and on the 15th of May 1943.[15] At stake was nothing less than the falsification of documents in the bureau's custody. Lieutenant Telmany, author of the May 8 note, described a "pernicious" tendency of the then de facto chief of the bureau, Major Święcicki, to conceive of their work as strictly historical. Telmany strongly disapproved.

> This results in treating all accumulated questionnaires as documentary historical material which has to be faithfully copied just as it is written. This is an unreasonable, impractical, and even pernicious position to take. . . . It should result in the end that in our own materials, prepared and publicized by us, evidence would be found to undermine our own theses and arguments. Because there is not a single protocol where at least one episode could not be found, or a paragraph or a sentence, conveying anti-Ukrainian or anti-Semitic sentiments or describing how some segments of our population opted for the Reds in October 1939. The only sensible solution is to impose political censorship and eliminate voices that could be harmful. We have been working with these considera-

* For purposes of administration, the territory of Poland was divided into seventeen voivodeships, voivodeships were divided into counties, and counties into gminas. The highest official in a voivodeship, appointed by the government, was a voivode (the closest equivalent is a French prefect). A starosta was in charge of a county, and a voyt in charge of a gmina. Villages elected their own sołtys and towns their own mayors. Several larger cities were granted status of separate counties.

tions in mind. About 300 typewritten pages of the protocols (in four copies) have been already suitably edited and prepared—I stress that this was done in accordance with the historical truth and our vital interests.

Then Telmany responds to "strong objections" made by the head of the bureau when he found out about these procedures. The lieutenant concludes by restating his point that "the Bureau of Documents . . . must be a creative unit and not a worthless archive of documents unfit to print, or a workshop where compromising materials are being typed."

This is precisely the kind of creativity that a historian can do without. Regrettably, Major Święcicki seems to have yielded to Telmany's arguments. In his report about the bureau's activities, dated May 15, 1943, he states matter-of-factly that in the already completed volumes, as well as in the volumes of source materials planned for the future, the editors at the bureau would take into consideration both "the historical truth" *and* "our [i.e., Polish] vital interests."

How weak the relative merits of the Polish case must have seemed to these misguided defenders of the Polish "vital interest" who were ready to commit forgery for its sake! The Soviet claims to the Western Ukraine and Western Belorussia were founded on lawlessness and outright lies. No doctoring of the original testimonies was necessary to make the point. But since the quality of the historical sources rather than the mentality of hurrah-patriots is under scrutiny here, three observations are in order. (1) The sources used in the present study are the original protocols, not typewritten copies. Indeed, it is often possible to identify markings on the originals indicating passages to be omitted by the typist. (2) The only typed sources quoted in the book are county reports prepared under Sukiennicki's supervision in London. He would have been appalled (though probably not surprised) to know about the doctoring practiced by the Bureau of Documents. An ongoing feud divided military (i.e., the Army in the East) and civilian (i.e., the embassy) authorities, and, rather suspicious by nature, Sukiennicki was certainly not aloof from it. But foremost, he was a scholar to the bone, not a propagandist. In any case, the Bureau of Documents where Telmany worked and the Research Section, originally headed by Sukiennicki, were two completely distinct units. (3) Most important, I find Telmany's memorandum reassuring. The attitude of the bureau's employees inadvertently provides an independent evaluation of the surveys' worth. That the Polish authorities were uncomfortable with the answers to their questionnaires is an important confirmation of their worthiness. The sources' major limitation is that the overwhelming majority of the respondents were Polish.[16] Therefore, the bureau's concern that their reminiscences did not fit into a narrowly construed idea of Poland's "vital interests" is unintended testimony to their spontaneous authenticity and comprehensiveness.

Yet, even though we can find some comfort in Telmany's worries, the ethnically skewed character of the sources is a serious problem for this study. Membership in one or the other ethnic group determined to a large extent one's experiences as well as one's perception of the Soviet occupation. In addition, hostility between ethnic groups prevented each from seeing objectively, across nationality lines, how the others fared. In order to overcome this imbalance, I have interviewed Ukrainians and Jews, as well as communists and former communists, who lived in the area in 1939–1941. I have read in the Yad Vashem archives in Jerusalem and consulted memorial books, both Ukrainian and Jewish, prepared by the inhabitants of these communities (now mostly non-existent) who found themselves in exile after the war.

To compound the difficulty, official sources from the period are not available either. The Germans confiscated loads of Soviet documents and shipped them to Berlin during their military offensive in the summer of 1941;[17] these records either burned in the destruction of the security headquarters in Berlin in 1945 or disappeared into the mounds of as yet uncatalogued captured German archives. The only relatively complete official source I managed to obtain was the daily *Czerwony Sztandar* (*Red Banner*) (with only a few issues missing), put out in Lwów by the Soviet authorities from September 1939 to June 1941. Thus, we have a better grasp of at least the sequence in which official policies were implemented in the Western Ukraine. Yet, even though the timing and character of these policies were no different in Western Belorussia (*Pravda* and *Izvestia* testify to that), I have much less knowledge about the local conditions in Białystok and Western Belorussia in general.

In conclusion, the most detailed information at our disposal is, so to speak, clustered: it comes predominantly from the Poles; it focuses mostly on the early period of the Soviet rule as well as on prison conditions, deportations, and life in POW camps; and it is complemented, most systematically, by a daily published in the Western Ukraine. Yet, however limited, the wealth of data is still extraordinary due to the social diversity of the respondents.* People who are often written

* A Polish Ministry of Foreign Affairs memorandum entitled "Computation of the Polish Population Deported to the USSR between 1939 and 1941" (HI, PGC, Box 588,

about but rarely heard from have here left detailed accounts of their lives. We have testimonies from peasants describing the organization of Soviet rule in their villages and hamlets, the confiscation of large landholdings and their distribution to the village poor, the taxation imposed on everyone, and the attempts at collectivization. Craftsmen of all sorts and small merchants tell how they fared under the new regime; civil servants, policemen, foresters, schoolteachers, and other petty officials tell what happened to their jobs after the revolution; workers describe new employment conditions in the workers' state. Even when the respondents are barely literate and have no stimulating insights to offer, they still know the names and biographies of their neighbors, they know who did what and sometimes can also tell why, and they remember trivial details, gossip, and scraps of conversation. Through these biographies we can observe the application of Soviet power to what it can do best: carry out a social revolution. Thus, because of the strengths and weaknesses of the sources I was able to assemble, the book I have written is a study of the communist revolution rather than a straightforward history of the origins of the Soviet regime in the westernmost borderlands of the Soviet Union.

The book concentrates on five broad topics—conquest, elections, socialization, prisons, and deportations—treated in separate chapters and grouped in two parts: seizure and confinements. The choice, in a way, was imposed by the quality of the available material. With respect to four of my five topics, I could draw on a rich documentation incomparably more detailed and intimate than data on other subjects that one ideally would want to include in a comprehensive study of sovietization of the Western Ukraine and Western Belorussia. The middle chapter on socialization of youth is included because of the special place given to the young in the blueprint of communist revolution. It serves as a convenient steppingstone in the analysis from the process of subjugation to that of social control. I intend it to illustrate a particular form of confinement, that of the mind and soul rather than of the body.

MSZ, London, Mar. 15, 1944) offers a statistical breakdown of the deportees, compiled on the basis of 120,000 personal files from the Polish Red Cross in Teheran: clergy of all denominations, 0.5%; university professors, scientists, 0.6%; judges and prosecutors, 0.8%; journalists, artists, writers, 1.2%; defense attorneys, 1.3%; doctors and qualified medical personnel, 3.1%; white-collar private employees, 3.2%; workers, 3.3%; employees of the Forestry Service, 3.7%; police and border guards, 4.0%; primary- and secondary-school teachers, 4.0%; merchants, 4.4%; engineers, technicians, agronomists, 4.7%; white-collar state and local government employees, 5.0%; professional military, 8.0%; artisans, 24.6%; peasants, 27.6%. Poles made up about 52% of the deportees, Jews about 30%, and Ukrainians and Belorussians about 18%.

Surely economic policy, collectivization, propaganda, policies vis-à-vis various nationalities, organized resistance, the role of indigenous communists and of the creative intelligentsia, as well as many other subjects, would be of great interest to students of communist regimes and revolution, and I have placed much of this material in the footnotes. But because the data on these topics are, in a way, inferior to those we have concerning elections, prisons, and deportations, and because their bearing on the process of imposition of the Soviet regime is indirect, the analytical unity of the manuscript would have to be sacrificed for the sake of including them.

The following chapters group data thematically. The division into parts reflects an analytical distinction: one moves in temporal sequence from seizure to confinements. In addition, Part One presents the experiences of the entire society, while Part Two concentrates on selected segments of the population. To be sure, these were groups selected by the Soviet authorities, not by me, for special treatment, and they constituted large chunks of the local society. Also in these two parts I attempt to capture two distinct underlying principles of the policies of Sovietization.

I WISH to acknowledge the financial support of Yale University's Griswold Fund and that of the National Council for Soviet and East European Research, which allowed me to collect data. A John Simon Memorial Guggenheim Foundation Fellowship and a Rockefeller Humanities Fellowship supported me at the time of the writing. I am also indebted to the Hoover Institution for a summer research grant and to Emory University for a leave of absence. Florence Stankiewicz, selflessly and with wonderful skill, edited the first draft of this manuscript; Maggie Stephens patiently entered and re-entered it on a word processor. To both of them I am most grateful. I owe special thanks to Włodzimierz Brus, Irena Grudzińska-Gross, Gustaw Herling-Grudziński, Patricia Hilden, Tony Judt, Frank Lechner, André Liebich, Maciej Sikorski, Helen Solanum, and Sarah M. Terry for their help and comments on early drafts of the book.

Atlanta, March 1986

REVOLUTION FROM ABROAD

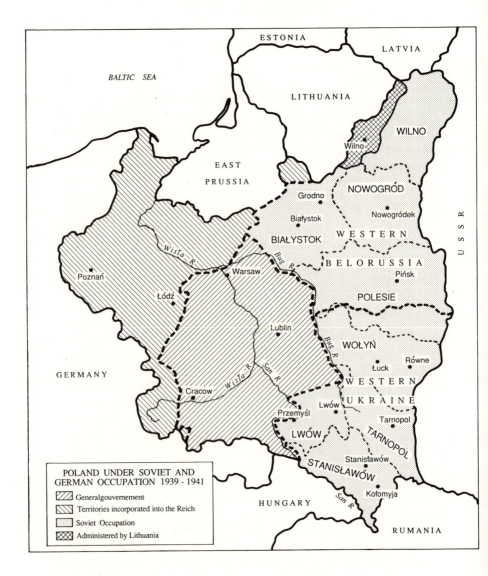

BALTIC SEA

ESTONIA

LATVIA

LITHUANIA

EAST
PRUSSIA

Wilno

WILNO

Grodno

NOWOGRÓD

Białystok

Nowogródek

BIAŁYSTOK

WESTERN

Poznań

Wisła R.

Warsaw

BELORUSSIA

Łódź

Bug R.

Pińsk

POLESIE

Lublin

WOŁYŃ

Bug R.

Łuck

Równe

GERMANY

Wisła R.

San R.

Cracow

WESTERN
UKRAINE

Przemyśl

Lwów

Tarnopol

LWÓW

TARNOPOL

STANISŁAWÓW

Stanisławów

San R.

HUNGARY

Kołomyja

RUMANIA

U S S R

POLAND UNDER SOVIET AND
GERMAN OCCUPATION 1939 - 1941

Generalgouvernement

Territories incorporated into the Reich

Soviet Occupation

Administered by Lithuania

INTRODUCTION

THE CONTEXT

POLAND, once a great European power, was gradually carved into nonexistence by its neighbors during the last thirty years of the eighteenth century. Three successive partitions by Russia, Prussia, and Austria took the country off the map of Europe for well over a century. Only as a result of World War I, which ended, most unexpectedly, in simultaneous defeat of all the partitioning empires, was Poland's independence re-established. Then its survival was threatened again by the October Revolution. The changing fortunes of a protracted Polish-Bolshevik war first brought Poles into Kiev and then the Red Army to the outskirts of Warsaw. Only Marshal Józef Piłsudski's rout of overextended Soviet troops—the "miracle on the Vistula"—on August 15, 1920, saved the country and turned the tide of war once again in the Poles' favor. Yet Polish claims to the reconquered lands were by no means unambiguous. Following the Treaty of Riga with the Soviet Union, signed on March 20, 1921, Poland had to wait almost two more years for the Council of Ambassadors and the international community (with the notable exception of Lithuania) to recognize its sovereignty over the area from Eastern Galicia in the south to Wilno and the adjacent area in the north.

The revolution that came from abroad, the subject of this book, took place here: in the territory of eight southern and eastern voivodeships of interwar Poland. The time was roughly from September 17, 1939, when the Soviets invaded Poland, to June 22, 1941, when the Germans in turn invaded the Soviet Union.[1] The area encompassed almost exactly 200,000 square kilometers (approximately 77,500 square miles) and was populated in 1939 by a little over 13 million inhabitants. Geographically it was a flat country of low elevation, already turning toward the interior of the Euroasian landmass, with two of its main rivers, the Prypeć and the Dniestr, flowing into the Black Sea. At the southern edge it rested on the foothills of the Carpathian Mountains. Cut in the middle by the impassable marshes of the sparsely populated Polesie, it then rolled northwards toward the Baltic, never reaching it though, and ending northeast of Wilno in a picturesque postdiluvial landscape with hundreds of lakes. True to its collo-

3

quial name—"Poland B," as opposed to "Poland A,"—it was the backward half of a backward European country.*

This eastern half of the Second Republic, as Poland was called between the wars, presents a picture puzzle of historically and geographically distinct entities, including Eastern Galicia, Western Ukraine, Wołyń, Podole, Polesie, Belorussia, and Lithuania. The complications of historical geography in the area might seriously challenge even an accomplished toponymist, particularly since names frequently carried for the local inhabitants an avowal of identity or, worse, a denial of someone else's claims. Thus, for example, in the official jargon of the *bien-pensants* and of the Polish administration, Galicia was called Eastern Little-Poland (Małopolska Wschodnia). The Ukrainians poked fun at this newspeak designation. To say "Little-Poland" is an exaggeration, they insisted; this territory is "not-Poland" at all. The truth lay somewhere in between, but the joke had a valid point: Ukrainians made up a clear majority in the total population of the Stanisławów, Tarnopol, and Lwów voivodeships constituting Eastern Galicia. Add the contiguous territory of Wołyń voivodeship (70 percent Ukrainian), and the Ukrainian majority in the area becomes overwhelming.

Poles were a minority in the territory where our narrative is situated. They accounted for roughly one-third of the total population.[2] Another one-third was Ukrainian, while the remainder (discounting a small minority of Germans, Russians, and Lithuanians who were visible because they were compactly settled, maybe 3 percent in all) was more or less evenly split between Jews, Belorussians, and a backwards Orthodox peasantry (mostly residents of the Polesie) which lacked a clear sense of national identity and described itself as being "local." National groups clustered geographically, except for the Jews, who also clustered, but in cities dispersed throughout the area. Not only place of residence but also religion was determined by ethnicity: Jews adhered to Judaism; Poles almost without exception were Roman Catholic; Ukrainians in Eastern Galicia were Greek Catholic, though in Wołyń they were Orthodox (an inheritance of the tsarist policy of Russification from the late 1830s on), as were the Belorussians and the inhabitants of Polesie.[3]

The eastern half of Poland could be divided into three zones from north to south. A clear Ukrainian majority resided in the south, except in some areas where Poles more or less equaled their Ukrainian neigh-

* Statistical yearbooks of the period list Poland under "Agricultural Europe," together with Spain, Portugal, Hungary, Rumania, and the Balkan states.

4

bors; in the central part, in Polesie and Wołyń, a small Polish minority (14 and 16 percent, respectively) faced a mostly Orthodox peasantry (Ukrainian to the south, then "local," and finally, on the northern fringe, increasingly Belorussian); and in the northern part, in Białystok, Wilno, and Nowogródek voivodeships, Poles were in the majority, confronted by a numerically strong Belorussian minority. Jews constituted the principal counterpart of the Poles in urban areas. Almost half of Polish Jewry lived in towns with over 20,000 inhabitants;[4] about 30 percent of Lwów's and Wilno's populations, for example, were Jewish, and in numerous smaller towns Jews were actually in the majority.

Upon this mosaic of religious, ethnic, and linguistic differences was grafted a socio-economic structure that offered little chance to satisfy material needs. But for the oil-extracting and timber- and wood-processing industries, stone and potassium quarries, and food processing there were few employment opportunities for the local population. Consequently, while rural inhabitants made up 72 percent of Poland's total population, in the soon to be Soviet-occupied area the proportion rose to a staggering 81 percent.[5] Rural was synonymous with poverty and backwardness, and with the onset of the Great Depression and the opening up of "price scissors" between industrial and agricultural goods, the material predicament of the countryside became overwhelming. Furthermore, in the east of Poland every conceivable indicator of well-being (or rather the lack thereof) fell beneath the national average.[6] Over two-thirds of the buildings in the area lacked sewer lines, water pipes, electricity, and gas (the national average for these, still not very complimentary by comparison with other countries, was over ten percentage points better than this dismal score), while the population density, as measured by the number of residents per room, was higher than the national average in all but Białystok voivodeship.[7] Consequently, the already paralyzing overpopulation of the Polish countryside (according to some estimates, 42 percent of the rural population was "superfluous")[8] was even more incapacitating in the eastern half of the country. And, of course, the crisis-ridden economy of the 1930s offered no employment opportunities for the under- and unemployed rural poor, especially since they had no skills to sell. About one-fourth of the Polish population could neither read nor write in 1931. The number rose to about 50 percent in Polesie and Wołyń, hovered around one-third of the total population in Tarnopol, Stanisławów, and Wilno voivodeships, and just reached the national average only in Białystok and Lwów voivodeships.[9] There was in addition the small-town poverty of the self-employed; eking out a living from a family business, they for the most part could not afford hired labor even in the depressed market of the 1930s. These countless starving merchants, craftsmen, and itinerant salesmen were mostly Jewish.

I need not dwell on the sorry record of successive Polish administrations' policies vis-à-vis the national minorities. The only possible point of dispute is the extent of official discrimination, never its existence. And all the wrongdoings perceived by the national minorities became an especially important component of the socio-political climate in those territories where the minorities were actually in the majority—that is, in the area occupied by the Soviets in 1939. But despite the injustices, despite the terrorism by the Organization of Ukrainian Nationalists (OUN) and the counter-terror resorted to by the Polish state,[10] despite the systematic Polonization of the school system and conversion of Orthodox churches into Roman Catholic ones under phony pretexts, despite *numerus clausus* and the exclusion of Jews from the professions—despite all of this and more, the material, spiritual, and political life of the national minorities in interwar Poland was richer and more complex than ever before or after. A wonderful testimony to this vitality can be found in a source conceived, sadly, in the spirit of mourning and remembrance of things past: the Jewish and Ukrainian memorial books.[11]

The national minorities lived in interwar Poland supported by a comprehensive network of political, economic, cultural, religious, and community-oriented institutions. Not only were these organizations numerous; they were also bitter competitors—a sure sign of plurality and robustness. Zionists, Bundists, assimilationists, and Agudas Israel fiercely vied for support within the Jewish community; loyalists from the largest Ukrainian political party (UNDO) tried to check the growing popularity of the Organization of Ukrainian Nationalists; in the Belorussian countryside the ideas of the Communist Party of Western Belorussia, especially as put forward by a legitimate front organization, Hromada, found a captive audience.

Just as there were many minority parties and organizations openly engaged in the political life of the country, so were there also alternatives in the illegal or semi-loyal opposition. One could pick a communist or a nationalist organization to suit one's temperament. For Jewish youth, Zionism offered an opportunity to pursue national emancipation but, in principle, beyond the borders of the Polish state. For those who did not want to emigrate but yearned instead for more equal status and recognition among their fellow citizens, the parties of social protest were a natural choice, such as the Bund or the Communist party. Nationalism remained altogether undeveloped among Belorussians; hence their relatively greater attraction to the communist option.[12] Simultaneously, in Eastern Galicia the Ukrainian nationalist underground enrolled ever more adherents.*

Besides politics, which, after all attracts only those most aware and motivated, there was also religious life, in which almost everybody joined. For the Jews, religious instruction opened up an entirely new language, providing also the basis of an alternative, secular (through Zionism) national identification. One can also cite public schooling, numerous publications in the native languages of the minorities, voluntary associations of all sorts, and economic self-help societies (by 1938, 600,000 Ukrainians had joined the cooperative movement, for instance).[13]

Statistics concerning publications nicely illustrate many aspects of the minorities' situation. Jews, as was to be expected, proved the most literate. In Poland in 1931, 920 nonperiodical publications (i.e., primarily books) came out in Yiddish and 211 in Hebrew. Characteristically, not a single nonperiodical publication in Yiddish or Hebrew was issued by a government office or an agency of local administration (as, in contrast, about every seventh book in Polish was); there were only four such government-issued publications in Ukrainian. All but 30 of the 342 Ukrainian nonperiodical publications during this year came out in Eastern Galicia (264 of them in Lwów voivodeship alone). All 33 Belorussian publications were issued in Wilno voivodeship, which was also the second most lively center of Jewish publishing (182 books) after Warsaw (674). In the eight voivodeships occupied by the Red Army in 1939, 40 Jewish (Yiddish and Hebrew), 80 Ukrainian, 9 Belorussian, and 366 Polish periodicals, including daily newspapers, were published in 1931.[14] In 1932 there were 83 Ukrainian-language periodicals in Poland, 9 periodicals in Belorussian, 136 in Yiddish, and 13 in Hebrew. To get a better grasp of the richness and variety of com-

* Changes in the organizational profile of the underground as well as political developments in Poland and in the Soviet Union contributed to this outcome. In 1929 the OUV (Ukrainian Military Organization) became the OUN (Organization of Ukrainian Nationalists), reflecting in name the shift from a cadre to a mass-based organization. The increasing repressiveness of the Polish regime and the more aggressive nationalism in the society at large made accommodation a less likely prospect, which of course worked to the advantage of Ukrainian nationalists. And then came broken illusions about emancipation under communism. Following the government-induced starvation in the Soviet Ukraine and the deportations accompanying forced collectivization in the early 1930s, the appeal of the Soviet Ukraine model of life ("national in form and socialist in content") rapidly waned. Hence, in addition to its historical roots, the unique strength and militancy of Ukrainian nationalism in prewar Poland.

munity life in the territories soon to be occupied, we may consider, instead of aggregate numbers, how many periodicals some towns in this area could sustain: 10 in Białystok, Grodno, and Kolomyja; 13 in Brześć; 18 in Stanisławów and Równe; 79 in Wilno; and a staggering 218 in Lwów.[15]

Much can be read into the distribution of these publications—about the compact geographic settlement and relative isolation of the ethnic groups, as well as about their neglect by the Polish government and their attempt to seek cultural exchange and support and inspiration beyond Poland's borders in Russia or in Germany.* But the most revealing information, I believe, is conveyed by the volume of linguistically varied reading materials. When considering the degree of emancipation accorded to non-Polish ethnic groups under Soviet policies in the Western Ukraine and Western Belorussia in 1939–1941, one should remember that in the year 1931 thirty periodicals were published in the city of Wilno in Belorussian, Yiddish, Hebrew, Russian, and Lithuanian and that sixty-eight were published in Lwów in Ukrainian, Yiddish, and German.

RUSSO-GERMAN RAPPORTS IN THE WAKE OF THE INVASION

The fate of east central Europe was decided far beyond Poland's borders. Ever since the Munich agreements, the Soviets had begun to reorient their foreign policy to find accommodation with Nazi Germany; and Stalin's speech on March 10, 1939, at the Eighteenth Party Congress established the opening for a pact with Germany. Thus, after a long period of freeze, relations between Stalin's Russia and Hitler's Germany bloomed in the spring and flourished in the summer of 1939, as if the two dictators, having discovered their commonality of interests, decided to make up quickly for time lost. The German-Soviet Treaty of Non-Aggression, drafted by the Soviets on August 20, was approved by Hitler on the very same day and signed in Moscow on August 23, 1939.[16] The pact simplified Germany's options by removing haunting thoughts of a revived Entente in response to Hitler's planned military aggression against Poland. The secret protocol

---

* Not a single book written in Ukrainian was translated into Polish in 1931, an indication of indifference fully reciprocated by the Ukrainians (no Ukrainian translations of Polish books were recorded). Yet 7 books were translated from German into Ukrainian. Three books originally written in Yiddish came out in Polish translation in 1931, while 6 Polish works were translated for the Jewish audience (4 into Hebrew and 2 into Yiddish). In the same year 29 Russian books appeared in Yiddish translation. There were no translations into or from Belorussian at all.

attached to the pact set the price the USSR charged for its benign neutrality in the forthcoming war: Bessarabia, Estonia, Latvia, and the better part of Poland, up to and including half of its capital, Warsaw.* Drafted in haste, apparently without adequate maps at hand, the suggested Soviet-German frontier left a gap of several kilometers where the river Pisa was mistaken for the upper reaches of the Narew. A few days after the signing ceremony, at Molotov's insistence (Soviet diplomats spotted the mistake), the Pisa's name was inserted into the provisions of point two of the Secret Additional Protocol.[17] Yet, while meticulous in carving the map of Poland, Soviet leaders left to the Wehrmacht the actual task of military conquest.

In the last week of August, immediately preceding the outbreak of the Polish-German war, the Soviet Union offered little assistance to Hitler in his final preparations. It merely agreed to deny rumors circulating in the Western press about an alleged Soviet withdrawal of troops from the Polish border. "Any appearance of Poland being threatened from the Russian side too ... might ... bring about a remarkable reduction in the readiness to help Poland," cabled State Secretary Weizsäcker to Schulenburg in Moscow, instructing the ambassador to make sure that the Russians rescinded any such redeployment order if indeed they had issued one. "Molotov laughed heartily," when informed by the German ambassador about these reports. "So much nonsense was published in the press nowadays that one could not concern oneself with all of it," he said.[18] But, prompted by the Germans, TASS published an official denial of these rumors on August 30. According to the communiqué, instead of withdrawing troops from the western frontier of the USSR, the Soviet command had decided to increase the numerical strength of its garrisons there. At the same time, a Soviet military delegation, five officers strong, was dispatched to Berlin and arrived there on September 2 in secrecy.[19]

---

* The first draft includes a *Postscript* that, in rather Aesopian language, stakes the Soviet claim to Poland: "The present Pact shall be valid only if a special Protocol is signed simultaneously, covering the points in which the Contracting Parties are interested in the field of foreign policy" (*DGFP*, 7: 151). Thus the supplementary protocol, as Hitler stated in his reply to Stalin, was "desired by the Government of the Soviet Union" (*DGFP*, 7: 157). "In the event of a territorial and political transformation of the territories belonging to the Polish State," read point two of the Secret Additional Protocol, "the spheres of interest of both Germany and the USSR shall be bounded approximately by the line of the rivers Narew, Vistula, and San" (*DGFP*, 7: 247). The most thoughtful political and diplomatic analysis of the Soviet-Nazi pact, as well as of the subsequent relationships between the two powers, remains the book by the then Rumanian foreign minister and later ambassador to Moscow, Grigore Gafencu, *Prelude to the Russian Campaign*.

Tacit military cooperation between the two regimes began on the first day of the war, September 1, with the exchange of very polite telegrams:

> The Chief of the General Staff of the Luftwaffe would be very much obliged to the People's Commissariat for Telecommunications if, for urgent navigational tests, the Minsk Broadcasting Station could, until further notice and commencing immediately, send out a continuous dash with intermittent call sign "Richard Wilhelm 1.0" in the intervals between its programs, and introduce the name "Minsk" as often as possible in the course of its program.

Schulenburg promptly transmitted the Soviet reply:

> The Soviet Government are [sic] prepared to meet your wishes in such a manner that the Minsk Broadcasting Station will introduce as often as possible the word "Minsk" during the course of its program, which could be extended by two hours for this purpose. Please advise whether any definite periods are particularly required for this. The Soviet Government would prefer to omit the addition of a call sign so as to avoid attracting attention[20]

As with the issuance of the TASS communiqué on August 30, the Soviet government was most obliging to the Germans. But at the same time, it feared being overtly identified with Hitler's war effort; hence its request for secrecy concerning the arrival of the Soviet military delegation in Berlin.

The Germans, on the other hand, were anxious to make their collaboration with the USSR "official." Already on September 3, while expressing his anticipation of the rapid defeat of the Polish army (though, coincidentally, this was also the day when France and England declared war on Germany), von Ribbentrop inquired whether the Soviet Union thought it "desirable" to occupy militarily the part of Poland conceded to it in the secret protocol. Not yet, replied Molotov, though in the future the Soviet Union would of course take "concrete action." "It is possible that we are mistaken," he continued in an unusually diffident phrase for a Soviet statesman, "but it seems to us that through excessive haste we might injure our cause and promote unity among our opponents."[21]

The following week of heavy fighting on the Polish-German front saw a lull in Soviet-German diplomatic transactions. Little more than occasional courtesies passed between them, such as Molotov's congratulations to the Reich government after Wehrmacht troops reached the outskirts of Warsaw. In the meantime, the Soviet government watched the rapid German progress in awe and took steps to field the Red Army weeks earlier than originally expected. It also chose a political justification for its impending military crossing of the Polish border: the Red Army would enter Poland in order to aid Ukrainians and Belorussians threatened by Germany. "This argument was to make the intervention of the Soviet Union plausible to the masses," Molotov told Schulenburg during a September 10 conference, "and at the same time avoid giving the Soviet Union the appearance of an aggressor." Four days later Molotov pleaded with Schulenburg to be informed when the Germans anticipated the capture of Warsaw; to give credibility to the political motivation of the Soviet action, it was important not to cross the border until the Polish capital had fallen.[22] But on that day the Soviets had already shown their hand: an editorial appeared in *Pravda* that spelled imminent doom for Poland's future.*

In a long telegram dated September 15th, von Ribbentrop instructed Schulenburg to finalize the arrangements for Soviet military intervention and proposed a joint communiqué articulating the reasons. Unless the Soviet army moved quickly, von Ribbentrop argued, a political vacuum might occur to the east of the German zone of influence, and "new states might possibly be formed there." He was also taken aback by the Soviets' intended justification of their action. A threat to national minorities was "directly contrary to the true German intentions," and Soviet intervention on that basis would be "in opposition to the desire for friendly relations expressed on both sides, [and] make the two States appear as enemies before the whole world." Finally, he suggested that Soviet liaison officers be dispatched to Białystok to coordinate German and Soviet military operations.[23]

Von Ribbentrop's arguments made sense, of course, even to Molotov. But Soviet leaders attributed too much importance to propaganda to abandon the convenient line about national liberation in favor of vague assertions about "natural spheres of influence"—*Lebensraum* rhetoric—as proposed in von Ribbentrop's letter. So, while conceding that the projected argument "contained a note jarring

---

* According to the editorial, Poland would owe its defeat less to the technical and military superiority of the German army than to the country's own multinational structure. National minorities, which according to *Pravda* constituted 40% of Poland's population, were ruthlessly oppressed by Poland's "leadership circles," especially in the Western Ukraine and Western Belorussia. The Polish government's record there was no better than that of the tsarist government in prerevolutionary Russia. Precisely like tsarist Russia twenty years earlier, Poland disintegrated now during its confrontation with Germany.

11

to German sensibilities," Molotov asked German leaders "in view of the difficult situation of the Soviet Government not to stumble over this piece of straw. The Soviet Government unfortunately saw no possibility of any other motivation since . . . [it] . . . had to justify abroad, in some way or other, its present intervention."[24]

And the Soviets stuck to their point obstinately, though at the very last moment they did show some flexibility. At 2 A.M. on September 17 the German ambassador was received by Stalin, Molotov, and Voroshilov. He was informed that the Red Army would cross the Polish-Soviet border at 6 A.M., and he was read a note that was about to be handed to the Polish ambassador. "The draft read to me contained three points unacceptable to us," reported Schulenburg later that morning in a most urgent telegram to Berlin. "In answer to my objections, Stalin, with the utmost readiness, so altered the text that the note now seems satisfactory to us."[25] Thus, the diplomatic note that Deputy Commissar Potemkin handed to Ambassador Wacław Grzybowski at 3 A.M. was, just like the Non-Aggression Pact of August 23 that made it possible, jointly drafted by German and Soviet statesmen.[26]

Only now, with the joint military presence of the Wehrmacht and the Red Army on Polish soil, did Stalin consent to issue a joint Russo-German communiqué. Once again he rejected the German draft of the document ("since it presented the facts all too frankly") and wrote the communiqué himself.[27] Six weeks later the Soviets would no longer weigh their public utterances with so much caution. "One swift blow to Poland, first by the German Army and then by the Red Army, and nothing was left of this ugly offspring of the Versailles treaty," boasted Molotov in his October 31 keynote speech before the Supreme Soviet of the USSR.[28]

The Soviet side, its lesser military contribution notwithstanding, was the main author of *all* Russo-German documents sealing Poland's fate in the late summer and early autumn of 1939. Indeed, the final frontier between the USSR and Germany, quite different from that originally proposed in the August Pact of Non-Aggression, was drawn in the end according to Stalin's new wishes.[29] Presumably unwilling on second thought to split ethnically Polish territories, and having changed his mind about the desirability of allowing the existence of a rump Polish state between Russia and Germany (because either might lead to undesirable Soviet-German friction), Stalin proposed that the Lublin voivodeship and the rest of the Warsaw voivodeship extending to the Bug River be added to the German share of Poland. In exchange, he wanted Lithuania.[30] Their coming to terms may have been facilitated by von

Ribbentrop's desire for a particular forest area near Augustów reputed for its fine game.*

Whether he was concerned about the consolidation of his empire or worried that the Wehrmacht's advance far beyond the originally agreed upon demarcation line would mean difficulty in recovering those occupied territories, Stalin drew the frontier eastward and firmed his grip on the Baltic states by bringing Lithuania, as well as Latvia and Estonia, into his domain.[31] The new territorial arrangements were finalized in the German-Soviet Boundary and Friendship Treaty signed by von Ribbentrop in Moscow on September 28. Its Confidential Protocol allowed for ethnic Germans to resettle into the Reich and for Ukrainians and Belorussians to settle in the Soviet Ukraine and Belorussia. Two Secret Additional Protocols were also included. The first one amended the boundaries of the spheres of interest agreed upon in the Secret Additional Protocol of August 23, 1939. The second, barely two sentences long, annihilated for two years the anti-Nazi communist underground all over Europe:

> Both parties will tolerate in their territories no Polish agitation which affects the territories of the other party. They will suppress in their territories all beginnings of such agitation and inform each other concerning suitable measures for this purpose.[32]**

It took one more year of Central Boundary Commission meetings (until August 17, 1940) to smooth out all territorial disagreements between the two partitioning powers.[33]

---

* Stalin said that "the region should be awarded to Germany for her Foreign Minister because of its fine stags." But the red deer, it turned out, were only migrating through the Augustów forest, and "the Minister was naturally very disappointed" (*DGFP*, 8: 323). "The Foreign Minister now requests you," continues this lengthy and rather amusing telegram from Chief of Protocol Dornberg to Ambassador Schulenburg, "to tell either Mr. Molotov or Mr. Stalin himself that there are no stags at Augustów."

** The strength of this commitment, at least as interpreted by the Soviet side, extended beyond the Polish case. Stalin went so far as to return to Hitler self-exiled German-Jewish communists who had sought refuge in the USSR during the 1930s. See memoirs by Aleksander Weissberg-Cybulski (*The Accused*) and Margarete Buber-Neumann (*Under Two Dictators*).

PART I
SEIZURE

PART I
SECTION I

ONE

Conquest

FRONTIER DEFENSE CORPS AGAINST THE RED ARMY

THE SOVIET CAMPAIGN against Poland in September 1939 was not complicated militarily. The Polish armed forces, routed on the western front by mid-September and surprised by the Soviet move, were incapable of organized resistance to the Red Army. Before escaping to neighboring Rumania with the rest of the Polish government, the supreme commander issued orders not to resist the Soviets. It made little difference: the chain of command and the lines of communication were already broken, and senior officers who found themselves in the Red Army's theater of operations had no choice but to improvise and go by rumors rather than orders. Indeed, the two-week campaign that brought the USSR 200,000 square kilometers of territory, 13.5 million new subjects, and 250,000 prisoners of war cost it, according to Molotov, fewer than 3,000 casualties—737 dead and 1,862 wounded Red Army soldiers.[1]

As defeated Polish army detachments fled the Germans, redeployed, or tried to cross the frontiers of Rumania, Hungary, or Lithuania to reach safety, only one military group remained relatively intact and able to confront the Soviets: the Frontier Defense Corps (Korpus Obrony Pogranicza, KOP). The KOP had been deployed since the 1920s along Poland's border with Latvia, Lithuania, and the USSR. In 1939 an additional regiment was fielded along the Hungarian border and part of the Rumanian border. During the 1930s the KOP's numerical strength increased to about 11,000. Its mission was to police the frontier in peacetime, and it was equipped, trained, and deployed accordingly.[2] It had no artillery, and the few antitank guns received shortly before the war—as the events of September were soon to demonstrate—could not pierce Soviet armor.[3]

Because Polish authorities had not anticipated hostilities on the Soviet border, many KOP officers were assigned in the summer of 1939 to other duties with the army in the west. During the first weeks of the war with Germany the KOP was further weakened when entire detachments were transported west.[4] General Orlik Rückemann was given KOP's command on August 30, 1939, and the order appointing him to this position was the only one he received from his superiors throughout the entire September campaign. To his subordinates, in turn, Rückemann gave a relatively free hand. In early September, before the Soviet invasion, regiment commanders were granted considerable autonomy in the disposition of their forces. "We were ordered to approach the Corps command only in especially important matters," wrote Colonel Kazimierz Kardaszewicz, then in charge of KOP's Lithuanian border section.[5]

When news of the Soviet crossing of the Polish frontier reached him, Rückemann ordered his troops to fight. The KOP's effectiveness was by this time even further diminished: just hours before launching the invasion, the Soviets had sent heavily armed groups to attack KOP guardposts along the entire Polish-Soviet frontier.[6] With communication sporadic or non-existent, confusion soon prevailed. Rumors even began to circulate that the Soviets had entered Poland as allies to help in the war against Germany and that the supreme command had given orders not to oppose the Red Army. In Wilno, while its defense was being prepared, orders came on September 18 not to fight the Soviets. To compound the ensuing confusion, the local radio station announced in the afternoon that Hitler had been killed in a coup, that Germany was engulfed in a revolution, and that Italy and Japan had joined the Allies.[7] Apparently a one-page edition of a Wilno newspaper carried this same later that evening. Similar rumors spread also in Włodzimierz Wołyński and in Pińsk.[8]

But even though they were unable to mount a serious challenge to the Red Army's advance, many KOP detachments did offer armed resistance.[9] Some were quickly destroyed or captured; others meandered for days, sometimes weeks (e.g. Rückemann did not dissolve his KOP group until October 1) between Soviet and German lines, periodically bouncing off superior enemy forces and always heading hopefully toward the Rumanian or Hungarian frontier. Inconsequential as these skirmishes were for the military fortunes of either side—Soviet victory was not in doubt for a moment—they contributed significantly to an atmosphere of civil war, which was later nurtured in the area for some time by the newly installed Soviet authorities. This came about because, in the first place, the Polish-Soviet military hostilities of September 1939 literally involved civilians as active participants.

PRELUDE TO CIVIL WAR

The violence in which the local civilian population participated during the early stages of the Soviet invasion is commonly attributed to two sources: the invading Red Army, obviously, and the so-called ethnic minorities—Ukrainians and Belorussians in particular—who reportedly ambushed small groups of Polish soldiers as they wandered through the area after the rout on the German front and who assaulted local Polish communities and functionaries of the now defunct state administration. Both of these points need refinement. But, more important, to fill in the picture we must also uncover the Poles' contribution to a brief civil war that was waged in the area.

The Polish contribution to violence involving civilians occurred in two contexts. First, civilians (mostly Poles, I presume) joined elements of the Polish army and actively fought alongside them against the Soviets. There were many instances of this sort,[10] and, if nothing else, they must have facilitated the Soviets' subsequent treatment of a certain part of the local population as outlaws. Furthermore, the mixing of Polish civilians with the military must have confirmed a Soviet prejudice about this war. Among the documents captured following a victorious skirmish with a Soviet detachment, General Rückemann found battle orders in which KOP detachments were designated as "bands of Polish officers."[11] The phrase would soon become a staple of official propaganda and, as such, meaningless. But we see that from the initial hostilities, the Soviet military, in *internal* communication, regarded the Polish army as only guerrilla detachments ("bands") with a specific class character ("officers"). To the extent that volunteers did join regular Polish military units in armed combat against the invading Red Army, this a priori rationale for Soviet action was ironically justified ex post facto. And the armed resistance of certain members of recognized groups led the victors to differentiate their treatment of segments of the local population. They would have done so anyway, but it was so much easier to instigate a kind of civil war later if it was immediately preceded by an actual war with clearly identifiable categories of civilians.

Second, and much more important, elements of the Polish army wandering through the eastern voivodeships—several hundred thousand soldiers in all[12]—on numerous occasions turned against the unsympathetic local population. Thus, the last battles of the Polish army in these territories were fought against Ukrainians, Belorussians, Jews, and "locals." Since groups of volunteers frequently joined detachments of the Polish army, civilians sometimes fought on both sides. It may already be impossible to assess the scale or spread of these hostilities with precision, but they were frequent enough to leave numerous memories among those who had no ax to grind against the Polish army. Thus, Wacław Kurzempa, a railroad employee in

Wołkowyska, recalls "a small pogrom" against Jews "by our army units.... I mean that six Jews were killed from among local merchants for their behavior toward the Poles."[13] What these merchants did to deserve their fate we are not told, but the circumstances of similar episodes are not as mysterious. "Two days after the triumphal arch [to greet the Red Army] was erected, the Polish army passed through Trościaniec [Wołyń voivodeship] and it fought a brief battle, killing about ten Ukrainians. Part of the village was then burned down."[14] Jan Wszędobył of Nowa Ruda (Grodno county) observed how "Belorussian bands" that kept ambushing passing Polish soldiers "were on a few occasions deservedly punished by shooting and hangings."[15] "We march at night, there is no contact with the enemy," recalled Captain Romuald Galicki from a KOP battalion. "On the way Ukrainian bands in villages Stepan, Maniewicze, and Ratno were liquidated."[16] "Every night there is shooting," remembered KOP Lieutenant Stanisław Kronak of the last days of the September campaign in Polesie.

> Soldiers are afraid to march in the rear guard. Poleshchuks [the local inhabitants of Polesie] shoot at rear end detachments. A special navy company performs executions in villages. Often fires mark the path of the army's march. Large groups of civilians, Polish civil servants from neighboring towns, join the army on its march.[17]

General Rückemann also recalls, though in more restrained language, that when he found triumphal arches in the village of Bereźne, he ordered KOP gendarmerie "to conduct a quick investigation and punish the guilty." It does not take much imagination to guess the measures of military justice that were dispensed under such circumstances.[18]

It is not unusual, I hasten to add, for an army to use firepower when it is ambushed or for hard-pressed but still armed defenders of a fatherland to turn with deadly force against those who openly sympathize with and support the enemy. Traitors are commonly shot during wartime. And though in reality the issues involved here were more complex and subtle, appearances were as simple as that, and as simpleminded was the response.

Yet the foremost cause of these multiple tragedies was not a flaw of character, whether disloyalty or excessive pride, but simply bad luck, chaos, and confusion. The local towns and villages had already prepared for life under new masters and were surprised by the appearance of Polish army remnants. This is important to note, for it means that the triumphal arches and peasant militias were not meant to spite or challenge the old regime, but rather to welcome or ingratiate with the new. One must wonder at how deeply alienated the local population must have been from the Polish state, which had structured and embraced much of its life for the past twenty years, when it could shed that old life with such precious few regrets. But after the Soviet invasion there occurred no Ukrainian uprising against the remnants of Polish authority that was comparable to the uprising in this area twenty-one months later, against the Soviets after the outbreak of the Russo-German war.

Ukrainian peasants had a telling expression to describe outsiders who periodically came into their country, whether to civilize or to liberate, but in the end always to exploit. They called them *zajdy*: those who "came by" or "strolled in."[19] There is temporality built into the word, a sense of exit as well as of entry. In September 1939 one *zajda* was definitely departing, while another was coming in. The local people prepared for the new arrival with mixed feelings. The zealousness of a small fringe combined with the prudence of the great majority to produce some welcoming ceremonies. But the old *zajdy* had no fixed itinerary on the way out and thus repeatedly stumbled upon communities that had already braced themselves for the future. Bloody encounters followed, with the local population—there is no doubt about this—accounting for most of the victims. These episodes were unwanted and accidental, inasmuch as the Polish army was not trying to pacify the Ukrainian or Belorussian countryside; nor had the local peasantry risen against the Polish authority. Yet the scattered violence added significant injury to the insults the local population had suffered under the Polish interwar administration, and it is in the light of these experiences that one must view the brutalities committed in turn by the local peasantry against Poles during the following days.

Initial Chaos

Anna Gimzewska, who lived in Nowogród voivodeship near Baranowicze, listened to war news on the radio in September 1939 until the last broadcasting station went off the air. Then, she later recalled,

> We were plunged into the mist of insecurity, and various most fantastic rumors became facts for us around which we spun interpretations and forecast the future. The entering Soviet authorities caught us in this state of mind. So, when one misty September morning on the Moscow-Warsaw road tanks, armored cars, cavalry, and infantry in combat gear appeared moving westward, we suddenly faced a number of questions for which we had no

answers. Where was this gray army decorated with red stars going? Was it bringing us assistance or final defeat? What was the meaning of all this? At first we were completely bewildered and taken by surprise. Crowds that lined up the streets and roads in villages and towns were trying in vain to solve this burdensome puzzle.[20]

Nor were the "simple folk" of rural villages alone in their confusion. Polish administration officials still in the area, as well as the military, were equally lost. "After the Bolsheviks invaded, the situation of local administrations in gminas and counties and of the KOP was especially tragic," wrote a school principal from Ostapie (Skałat county). "Without any instructions whatsoever—what to do and how to behave—they were lost in chaos. The most tragic was that nobody had warned the local community and the authorities that a Bolshevik invasion was possible and what to do in case it occurred."[21] As another eyewitness put it, "Nobody from the civilian authorities or the military knew in what capacity the Soviets marched across the frontier."[22]

And appearances could be very confusing indeed! "Around eight or ten in the morning on September 17, Stanisław Żurakowski, the mayor of a frontier town, Ostróg, called the county seat in Zdołbunów," according to Władysław Ogoński, a civil servant from Zdołbunów. "He informed us about the Soviet army approaching the town on the road coming from the border. Ahead of the army a small band was coming playing the 'March of the First Brigade.' "[23] Imagine the reaction of a German mayor in some frontier town near Alsace to the spectacle of French soldiers coming from behind the Maginot Line to the tune of the "Horst Wessel Lied" at a time when Germany was fighting a losing war with Poland! Symbolically, the "March of the First Brigade" and the "Horst Wessel Lied" are as close to national anthems as one can come, each song commemorating the heroic exploits of selfless youth who helped to lay the foundations for the new shape of their fatherland. Both tunes were in fact the private anthems of the ruling establishments. But the use of the Polish song proves that there was deliberate deception on the part of the Soviets, which certainly added to the confusion.*

* Upon learning of the Soviet entry into Poland, the commanding officers of the Lwów garrison, then engaged in defensive combat against the Wehrmacht, assembled in Gen. Langner's headquarters and agreed not to surrender the city to the Germans (GSHI, Collection 88, File B, Col. Kazimierz Ryziński, "Rejestracja faktów i spostrzeżeń dotyczących przygotowań i działań wojennych," p. 10). On the following day Langner told Lwów's mayor, Stanisław Ostrowski, that he would surrender Lwów to the Bolsheviks, who were Slavs and who would assist the Poles in their war against Germany (GSHI,

So it is no wonder that the order not to oppose the arriving Soviet troops with military force somehow became an instruction to greet heartily, as one would allies coming to help in time of trouble. In Tarnopol, county prefect Majkowski urged the population through loudspeakers to give a friendly welcome to the entering Soviet army. Posters signed by the mayor of Stanisławów and appealing for a calm, friendly reception were put up throughout the city on the morning of the eighteenth. In Równe, the county prefect came out personally with a retinue of local officials to greet the spearhead of the Soviet column. He thanked the Red Army profusely for bringing help to Poles locked in combat with the German invaders. In Kopyczyńce, a city official spoke from the town hall balcony, "Gentlemen, Poles, soldiers, we will beat the Germans now that the Bolsheviks are going to help us," while Red Army commanders embraced Polish officers and Polish soldiers threw flowers into the Soviet ranks. Soviet columns marched through Tarnopol and Łuck side by side with detachments of the Polish army, each giving way to the other at intersections or not paying much attention to the other's presence.[24]

This peaceful coexistence did not last long, we are told—one or two days in Łuck and barely an hour in Kopyczyńce. But before local officials were finally arrested and soldiers disarmed and taken prisoner, the friendly encounter must have fed the confusing rumors that traveled fast and wide before they were replaced by other rumors. Truly, for two or three days following the Soviet invasion, only a few had answers to the questions asked by Anna Gimzewska.

In fact, confusion was almost total, for it affected even the perception of the invading army. Soviet soldiers entering Tarnopol are reported to have shouted to a passing Polish army detachment that they were on their way to fight "the krauts," and they might have actually believed that.[25] Indeed, the original, official Soviet justification for the Red Army's invasion of Poland contained references to a German threat that the Soviet government felt compelled to avert. Schulenburg had succeeded in deleting the most jarring points from the

Collection 88, File B, Dr. Stanisław Ostrowski, "Lwów walczy we wrześniu 1939," pp. 3, 4). In fact when Col. Kazimierz Ryziński, Langner's chief of staff, went to Winniki on Lwów's outskirts to discuss with the Soviet colonel Ivanov the cease-fire and eventual surrender of Lwów's defenders, the following conversation ensued between the two officers: " 'What do you know about us?' Ivanov had asked, 'We know that you came, that you have reached Lwów, but we don't know why you came,' we answered. 'So you know nothing from the radio or the newspapers?' 'We have no time to listen to the radio and newspapers do not get here anymore,' we said, knowing that he had in mind Molotov's speech [of September 17]. Then he stated that they would fight the Germans together with us, but that they wanted first to enter the city" (GSHI, Ryziński, p. 10).

official announcement, but what the Soviet soldiers were told by political officers (politruks) and commanding officers before they were ordered to march is anybody's guess. The new agreement with Hitler and fascist Germany (the bête noire of Soviet propaganda for years) was certainly not yet so thoroughly absorbed as to make the ordinary Soviet soldier skeptical about his mission to protect the "blood brothers" in the Western Ukraine and Western Belorussia from a German war. A shoemaker from Drohobycz remembered that, immediately after the occupying Germans peacefully withdrew from the town to make room for the Soviet forces, to whom this territory belonged in accordance with the Nazi-Soviet pact, the Soviets called a meeting "where the Polish population was informed that it had been sold out to the Germans and that the Soviets came to liberate it."[26]

One can understand the general confidence in Soviet good intentions in view of the residual propaganda from past years, the ambiguous formula justifying the military move, and the wishful thinking of Poles, who certainly preferred to hear that the Soviets came as friends rather than as enemies. Indeed, this optimistic interpretation of Soviet presence on Polish soil circulated in two versions. According to the "hard" version, the Soviets came to help Poland in its war *against* Germany. In the milder version, they only came to offer protection *from* the Germans.[27] The shift in people's minds from a *from* to an *against* was easy enough, given their tension, the lack of communication or news, and the general excitement. Besides, the first claim was not without merit, for in the end, where the Soviets came the Germans did not. And this either/or, whether one liked it or not, was the only available option for Polish citizens residing in the country during this ominous September.

The entering Soviets also used slogans of national liberation and class emancipation, which caused considerable confusion.[28] Indeed, a term already in use in Soviet propaganda from the time of the 1920 Polish-Soviet war—*polskie pany* (Polish Pans)*—united the two types of slogans. Thus, in a feat of simultaneous class emancipation and national liberation, Belorussians and Ukrainians were to be rescued

---

* The word *Pan* has been used in English translations (see, for example, books by Isaac Babel and Nikolai Ostrovski). The meaning of the word in Polish is "mister" and "master" simultaneously. It is a polite, commonly used form of address to strangers. Soviet propaganda locked on to the second meaning: Pan epitomizes the class enemy of peasants and workers. Pan is different from a capitalist; there is a clear aristocratic component of status differentiation in the concept. It includes a notion of superiority and therefore contempt toward "the people," reciprocated with hatred. It is an emotionally charged notion embedded as well in the stereotyped (superior/inferior) national animosity between Poles and Russians.

from Polish domination. Excited crowds of Ukrainian peasants who took these claims literally were immediately disappointed. When they hoisted flags in the blue and yellow Ukrainian national colors in joyful celebration of the long-awaited collapse of the Polish state, they were brought back to their senses by the first Soviet official for whom their greeting was intended. Indignantly they were told to put away their "rags" and to put up instead a red banner.[29]*

THE CITIZENS' GUARD

News of the Red Army's entry into Poland ultimately undermined the will and authority of the local Polish administration. In eastern Poland it was overwhelmed and disorganized by the eastward push of defeated army detachments from the German front and the accompanying masses of refugees. Also, it was left without guidance after the central ministries were evacuated from Warsaw and kept on the run. This administration finally disintegrated under the impact of the Soviet invasion.[30]

A power vacuum spread rapidly *in front of* marching Red Army detachments. As a stopgap measure the Citizens' Guard (Straż Obywatelska), a volunteer formation, was called into existence in many cities and villages to assist the depleted and rapidly dissolving local administrations in keeping order, if not exactly law. After the final departure of local officials, the Citizens' Guard usually continued its mission with no great reluctance, since it was recruited from among local residents who did not want to, or could not, move anywhere else. Sergeant Józef Tryjankowski, while wandering all over the Wilno voivodeship throughout September 1939 in the company of a few soldiers, met Citizens' Guard groups in virtually every village.[31] Thus, in an already complex configuration of ethnic and class cleavages and animosities, we have yet another group of people who got hold of weapons and assumed the prerogative of using coercion. Episodes that I recounted previously, where Polish army detachments were assisted by groups of civilians, must have involved some outfits of the Citizens' Guard.

The Guard's loyalty as well as its tasks focused on the local community; its mission was to protect its village or town rather than to

---

* Similarly, eager inquiries from young Zionists about prospects for emigration to Palestine invariably drew a Soviet reply that the new authorities would create Palestine for Jews "right here." "One of them, himself a Jew, said to us, 'You want to go to Palestine? Fine l'shana Habaah Biyerushalayim—next year we shall all be in Jerusalem. The Soviets will be there too' " ([Hashomer Hatzair], *Youth Amidst the Ruins*, pp. 88, 90).

defend the fatherland. But because the Guard's authority derived from the old regime—in several places it was created by local initiative, but as a rule it had been sponsored by the earlier Polish administration—both its ethnic and its class composition, as well as its perception of the worst threats, were somewhat skewed. The mainstays of the Citizens' Guard were patriotically inclined Polish citizens—the so-called settlers (*osadnicy*) in the countryside, petty officials, or, as in Lwów, members of the Association of Reserve Officers who were too old to be conscripted into the army.[32] Their mission, as they perceived it, was to protect their communities against the surrounding countryside—to deny Ukrainian, Belorussian, or "local" peasants an opportunity to loot, rob, and kill.[33]

This threat was not an imaginary one, as events were to demonstrate. Nevertheless, it must be stated that, in the guise of the Citizens' Guard, Poles armed themselves against ethnic minorities predominant in the area. In turn, the peasantry and communist sympathizers in towns and cities, in the guise of newly formed militias, armed themselves against Poles and Polish sovereignty over the area. A full-scale civil war was averted only because the Soviets stepped in quickly and mitigated the violence that was ready to explode, channeled it in one direction, and simply disarmed one side in the conflict.

The establishment of the Citizens' Guard was the final symptom of the inability of the Polish state to carry on its responsibilities, merely an unstable solution to the power vacuum created by undeclared Polish-Soviet war and the brewing intra-ethnic civil war. One could look upon it as a rear-guard action of the old regime. But it was also the first stage in the process of transition to the new order: the community took upon itself responsibility for its own welfare (since the Guard was, to a degree, a volunteer formation, spontaneous and supported by a network of locally vested interests). It was, or could be, an opening up to the future; it was tuned to the needs of the community, and by virtue of its membership and improvised mode of operation it could achieve its mission of providing security by using more imaginative procedures than would a police or an army detachment. It could, for example, in the rapidly radicalizing atmosphere or at the request of Soviet military authorities, transform itself into a militia. Such was the case in Lwów, in Augustów, and to a degree in Chomsk.[34]*

* The episode in Chomsk must have been similar to events in many other localities, and it renders well the atmosphere of these days. Chomsk was situated in Drohiczyn county of Polesie voivodeship, and Henryk Haake, the teacher from Chomsk who left this account, was in charge of the town's Citizens' Guard. "Before the Red Army entered

In Lwów, for example, a few days after the outbreak of the war a Citizens' Guard was organized by officers retired from active service, and Soviet military authorities allowed it to continue after they occupied the city. It expanded somewhat by incorporating spontaneously formed armed groups of Ukrainians and communist sympathizers (mostly Jewish), and its name was changed; but not until the end of September were its leading officers, including at least two retired generals, arrested. Soviet supervisors were added at the precinct level, but the overall reorganization was slow. It was October 10, for example, three weeks after the occupation, before a professional NKVD operative, Captain Rudenko, was appointed to command the fifth borough (Zielona Street).[35]

The most illuminating story about the Guard is told by Jan Węgrzyn, head of the Welfare Department in the local administration of Baranowicze (Nowogród voivodeship). After news of the Soviet invasion reached him, he consulted with the deputy mayor and they agreed that a Citizens' Guard ought to be established. Węgrzyn took charge of the task.

Within two hours I organized a Citizens' Guard exclusively from Poles I knew personally; I armed 186 people with rifles left at the police station; they put on blue armbands. A crowd was gathering in front of the City Hall and in its vicinity, shouting down with the Polish government. Around ten o'clock armed workers from the Socialist party arrived, led by Machaj, who requested that I immediately pull back the militia with the blue armbands. We came to terms with Machaj, agreeing that people I called into the militia would stay, except that they would put red armbands on. I hadn't yet managed to issue this new instruction when about thirty communists ran into the City Hall, led by a certain Rajski,

our town, but already following the departure of our military detachments, police, and the local administration, the situation in town was rapidly deteriorating. From surrounding hamlets crowds of peasants, Poleshchuks, were pouring in ready to rob. For a few days I managed to persuade them to disperse, but when in the neighboring gminas fires, robberies, and killings began, peasants gathered in the town square—armed, drunk, and insolent—just waiting for somebody to begin. The guard hid somewhere. Alarmed that isolated robberies had already begun or might begin at any moment, I went into the town square, where I realized how dangerous the situation had become. I arranged then for a few of the more reliable peasants, still of rather pro-Bolshevik convictions, to organize a temporary 'revolutionary committee.' And they took the situation in hand. I took off my red-and-white armband and went to sleep, as I was dead tired. Until the Red soldiers came, and even after, gmina Chomsk was rather peaceful. There were no killings or robberies here, while in the neighboring gmina, Motoł, about 250 people were murdered . . ." (HI, PGC, 4106).

shouting enough of your government, get out!!! After a longish discussion we agreed that the city must be defended against robberies and excesses until the Soviet authorities arrived. Machaj, however, was arrested on Rajski's orders.[36]

Here is a replay of modern revolutions—from Mirabeau to Robespierre, or Kerensky to Lenin—all in one morning. Baranowicze Anno Domini 1939, its inhabitants quickly found out on this September day, was not suitable for the display of civic-minded duty by responsible citizens or for reform-minded socialists to come to power. The winds of history, blowing from the east, were too strong for either.

A FRIENDLY RECEPTION

Even though the Soviets had had little time to prepare for the invasion, and although the actual timetable was dictated mostly by the pace of the Wehrmacht's advance on the western front, important propaganda work among Red Army soldiers had been carried out *before* September 17th. That pep talks had been given to Soviet soldiers before they were allowed to go abroad is quite certain. The very monotony of their answers in later conversations with local residents—"u nas vsio est' " (we have everything), "u nas etogo mnogo" (we have plenty of this), "we produce this in factories"—so incongruent with their awe at the abundance of consumer goods and their feverish buying up of everything, is convincing proof that they must have been cued beforehand. Indeed, Red Army soldiers arrested for desertion or some other crime and kept in regular jails of the Western Ukraine and Western Belorussia along with everybody else later told their fellow inmates about "special courses" they had received in the summer of 1939.[37]

It was to be expected that the Soviet authorities would take care to prepare their subjects ideologically for a confrontation with the demoralizing and pernicious consequences of witnessing everyday life in a bourgeois state. It is more striking, however, that Red Army soldiers were also financially prepared for this occasion. As soon as the Red Army invaded Poland, the Soviet ruble was declared legal tender in the occupied area on parity with the Polish złoty, and inhabitants of the Western Ukraine and Western Belorussia noticed with some curiosity that the Soviets always paid for everything without haggling over prices.[38] And they were buying a lot. It seems that they had been given money before the Red Army marched into Poland. Whether each soldier received an allotment or how much, we cannot tell exactly. One source informs us that every soldier received 300 rubles. According to

another, Red Army soldiers were given money with instructions to distribute it among the local population of the Western Ukraine and
Western Belorussia to show Soviet opulence and generosity but they
failed to do so and spent it on personal purchases instead. Yet another
person heard that the soldiers received three months' wages in
advance.[39] All this was told to our informants by Red Army soldiers,
who, despite orders not to engage in any transactions or conversations
with the local population,[40] often befriended the local people and were
quite frank in conversations with them.

For the record it must be stated unambiguously: throughout the
Western Ukraine and Western Belorussia, in hamlets, villages, and
towns, the Red Army was welcomed by smaller or larger but, in any
case, visible, friendly crowds. These were largely composed of young
people from the so-called ethnic minorities—Belorussians, Jews, and
Ukrainians. But since ethnic minorities were a majority in these lands,
such welcoming committees were truly scattered all over the invaded
territory.[41] The crowds had built triumphal arches and put up red banners (it was enough to cut off the white stripe from the Polish national
flag to make one) or yellow-and-blue ones; in Kleck a mixed crowd
came out hoisting church banners, and "in the confusing elation communist songs mixed with religious hymns." Entering troops were
sometimes showered with flowers, embraced, and kissed; even tanks
were kissed (Jews seemed to have a predilection for kissing tanks;
somehow no one mentions Ukrainians or Belorussians doing this).
They were greeted sometimes with bread and salt, a traditional gesture
of hospitality.

Wherever it went on the first day of the offensive, September 17th,
the Red Army was met by beautifully dressed peasants: it was a
Sunday, and crowds coming from church and gaping at the passing
soldiers must have looked very presentable indeed. Peasants in Ogolec
(Kosów Poleski county) were ordered by their Belorussian neighbors
from Blizna hamlet to line the road and wear red bow ties, while
women in Komarnica (Słonim county)—presumably on orders from
the local militia, which was established after the withdrawal of the
Germans—had to put on red kerchiefs and their worsted dresses.
When there was enough time between the entry of the spearhead forces
and that of the main army contingent, making it possible to prepare a
reception more carefully, residents of a city were told to decorate their
houses with red banners. In Kostopol, "a day after they came, the Bolsheviks erected triumphal arches at the city gates themselves."[42]

The Soviet invasion planners undoubtedly regarded it as essential
that the Red Army be greeted warmly as it moved into the newly con-

quered lands, and the early progress reports from the front published daily in *Pravda* allow us to gauge the importance attached to the enthusiastic welcome. The Soviets needed to prove the correctness of their political justification of the invasion. A warm reception was a prelude to, indeed an integral part of, the imminent plebiscite that would finally articulate the political will of the local people. Joyful celebration was, then, a political component of an otherwise military plan of invasion that Red Army commanders had to carry out. And they tried to fulfill the planners' desires as best they could, including staging such innocently fake events as the one in Kostopol promised to be.

Indeed, the Soviets loaded the dice a trifle to make sure of the outcome. Prior to September 17, Soviet agents were activated or sent ahead of the troops to organize friendly receptions for the incoming Soviet army. I would not overestimate the importance of these advance parties, but it cannot be doubted that they were despatched frequently. For one thing, local inhabitants here and there (especially the minorities) seemed to know ahead of time about the forthcoming Soviet invasion. Omeljan Pritzak, a Lwów University student vacationing at home in Tarnopol, remembers hearing radio broadcasts from the Soviet Union that made it clear the Soviets would invade Poland in a few days. One might say that rumors, deductions, and intuitions were transformed through hindsight into firm knowledge. But there was more, and the experience of Byteń (Słonim county) inhabitants was certainly not unique: "Just before the Soviets entered into Byteń their agents simply terrorized inhabitants to put up red banners and to come out and greet the Soviet army. They threatened the unwilling ones. It is not surprising, therefore, that the Soviet army was met by a large crowd, which was nevertheless terribly frightened deep in its soul."[43]

Many a welcoming ceremony was not truly spontaneous but organized under threat or after some persuading.* After the Soviet military campaign began and the remnants of the Polish state organization quickly atrophied, the inhabitants of soon to be conquered areas were somehow apprised that they must stage receptions for the Red Army. The request for a friendly greeting traveled ahead of the incoming troops, and local residents generally obliged or on occasion were forced to do so.

---

* Sometimes the impetus came from the Germans. Myszczyce (Kobryń county), for example, was originally occupied by the Wehrmacht. According to Janina Zawiasa, "When they were about to leave, they told everybody that the Bolsheviks would come and that triumphal arches would have to be built to meet them, or else everybody in the hamlet would be killed. All went to work right away" (HI, Poland. Ambasada USSR, Box 47, Janina Zawiàsa; see also PGC, 2978; lida, 7).

EXPLAINING THE MOTIVES

The overwhelming majority of the Ukrainians were sincerely glad to see the collapse of the Polish state, and this is what they were celebrating when they cheered the Red Army, as was obvious whenever the blue-and-yellow colors were unfurled on those occasions. Local activists of the Organization of Ukrainian Nationalists immediately seized the opportunity to strike at Poles and Jews whom they wanted to chase out of the area as soon as possible. Indeed, for nationalistically minded Ukrainians there was one other perceptible advantage in the Soviet military advance: unification of the Ukraine. Lev Shankovsky, a teacher from a distinguished family of churchmen, visited Metropolitan Andrei Sheptyckii shortly after the Soviets arrived and heard the head of the Greek Catholic church say, "We occupied only a few rooms on the ground floor until recently and now we have it all to ourselves. There is still a tenant on the first floor, but when we push him out the entire house will finally be ours."[44]

Great excitement circulated among Ukrainians because an intolerable situation of ethnic discrimination had finally come to an end. To be sure, Ukrainians would have preferred German occupation, as is clear from the pattern of immediate population shifts throughout the border area. Whenever the Wehrmacht gave up some territory that belonged in the Soviet zone of occupation, Ukrainians moved out with the Germans. Jews, on the other hand, followed the Soviets. In Przemyśl, where the frontier established along the river San cut the city in half, two columns of refugees were soon marching in opposite directions—Jews to the east bank, Ukrainians and a few Poles to the west. By the end of 1939, 30,000 Ukrainian refugees had fled from Soviet occupation to the Generalgouvernement. In addition, with the help of the German-Soviet Repatriation Commission, some 10,000 Ukrainians, mostly from the intelligentsia, were "returned" to Germany with the assistance of sympathetic Abwehr functionaries who disguised the Ukrainians' true ethnicity.[45]

The Belorussian countryside had also been alienated during Polish rule, but here national aspirations had not yet been awakened. There were welcoming celebrations wherever the Communist Party of Western Belorussia had throughout the 1930s maintained its strongholds. But, being generally lukewarm toward any outsiders, Belorussian peasants took the opportunity created by the momentary power vacuum primarily to settle neighborhood grudges or to assault the nearest towns or passing refugees. They maintained, as one observer put it, "a rather passive and reserved attitude toward the Soviet army."[46] This does not mean that the Red Army was not publicly welcomed throughout Western Belorussia. Indeed, the reception here differed little from that in the Western Ukraine, because in both lands the Jews, settled all over in towns and shtetls, had come out in substantial numbers to receive the occupiers.

What Poles and Ukrainians report, often with biting irony, the Jews do not deny: "Jews greeted the Soviet army with joy. The youth was spending days and evenings with the soldiers." "Jews received incoming Russians enthusiastically, they [the Russians] also trusted them [the Jews]." "The first days of the Bolsheviks' presence were very nice. People went out into the streets, kept looking over tanks, children walked after the soldiers."[47] Jews welcomed the Red Army in 1939, and it is not very difficult to explain their initial reaction. For one thing, there were proportionately more communist sympathizers among Jews than among any other nationality in the local population, though in absolute numbers they were not many, even after the influx of refugees from western and central Poland brought communists freed from Polish jails. Thus the welcoming crowds were most certainly a mixture of marxist converts and ordinary God-fearing Jews who also happened to fear the Germans. And here is the principal clue to the joyous atmosphere surrounding the entry of Soviet troops: where they came, the Germans did not.

Rumors and tales travel before invading armies; then refugees follow with more stories to tell. In the Western Ukraine and Western Belorussia local inhabitants had in addition the direct experience of German occupation; several counties of Lwów and Białystok voivodeships in particular had been overwhelmed by the Wehrmacht before they yielded quickly to the Red Army. Scores of local Jews were murdered and brutalized throughout the German-held territory during this brief period. In one episode the Germans rounded up 600–700 prominent Jewish citizens—doctors, lawyers, rabbis—and executed them in Przemyśl. At times local Ukrainian inhabitants assisted the Germans in drafting lists of Jews and Poles to be shot. Indeed, their vulnerability to pogroms during the power vacuum that followed the disintegration of the Polish state gave Jewish communities a reason to wish fervently for the quick arrival of the Soviet army. There were lootings, robberies, and assaults on Jews and their property by their neighbors.[48] In the village of Aleksandria, near Równe, a crowd of Ukrainians armed themselves for an anti-Jewish pogrom after the Polish army and administration left town. Luckily, the commander of the police precinct, issued weapons to panicked Jews, who quickly organized a militia. "A front line was established—Ukrainians on one side and

Jews on the other. But nothing really happened, as on the first day of the offensive Soviet tanks had entered the village."[49] I should think that they were indeed given an enthusiastic welcome by the Jewish community.

In the power vacuum created for a day or two, or even a few hours prior to the occupation of a given area by the Red Army, Poles and Jews were vulnerable to the vengeful wrath of their neighbors. They were a minority in these lands, religiously and ethnically distinct and disliked. Small craftsmen, tradesmen, and middlemen by profession, Jews were the first link between the peasant and the broader, urban-based market economy. Thus, unavoidably, they were also resented as exploiters and provided a choice target for any peasant *jacquerie*. Peasant crowds converging on towns of the Western Ukraine and Western Belorussia had innumerable shtetls to choose from. As always in the Jewish diaspora, only a central authority could protect it from the surrounding population. And so, having no tears to shed for the now defunct Polish state, Jews welcomed the Soviets—not without reservations, one should add, but with visible relief mixed with a sense of satisfaction at seeing the Poles, who had patronized them contemptuously, now humbled. "You wanted Poland without Jews, so now you have Jews without Poland," they teased the Poles, turning around a Polish nationalistic slogan from before the war.[50]

Poles, another vulnerable local minority, despondent and crushed by the defeat of their country, came around to a similar view in the course of a few days. It was safer, and they could come out of hiding and return to their households, only *after* Soviet authority established itself in a given area.* As the sense of loss faded, and as the Soviets were perceived more as filling a void than as displacing something treasured (i.e., Polish authority), their appearance was more appreciated. When it became a question of choosing not between a Polish or a Soviet administration but between a Soviet administration or none at all, the preference was clear. An intuitively grasped truth is obvious here: the weak are better off when some authority regulates their relationships with others.

---

* When "anarchy" began in Drohiczyn county, "everybody hoped that some pacification detachments would come—it didn't matter whether ours or foreign—and restore order." Józef Użar-Śliwiński, a military settler who wrote these words, fled to Drohiczyn, where "the Soviet authorities and the military had already arrived." Only after three weeks did he dare to return to his village (HI, Poland. Ambasada USSR, Box 47). A forester, Władysław Wilk from Dolina county, recalls that he "had to leave the house and all their possessions and hide with the whole family in the forest until the Soviets came" (HI, Poland. Ambasada USSR, Box 47; see also HI, PGC, 2432, 8764; AC, 1078).

Yet, I think, this overt enthusiasm was a thin veneer with which a tiny, though vocal, minority covered the general mood of gloom and foreboding. The Soviets were appreciated mostly as the lesser evil. The older generation, for instance, generally knew the Bolsheviks from twenty years before and was genuinely scared. A teacher from Myszki village (Postawy county) tells us that "when news that the Red Army had crossed the frontier reached us, many people started to run away, even though there was nowhere to escape to; they left everything, including children and wives. It was a horrible moment when standing by the road I was observing the fleeing, myself barely conscious."[51] He goes on to say that some people committed suicide, and others join him in this observation. Many fled their houses to hide in nearby forests or anywhere they could.[52] Others, especially in the larger towns, stayed at home, afraid to appear in the streets.* Fear of the Soviets was widespread.[53] A chimney sweep from Rohatyn county sums up: "When the Bolshevik army was coming into Polish territory, total depression and panic prevailed; the weaker ones took their lives, others hid in the woods, and the strongest were nervously observing."[54]

This reaction was true not only for ethnic Poles. When they learned that the Soviet military was approaching Wsielub (a village in Nowogródek county), the local Jews proceeded to lock up their stores and hide all the goods. A Belorussian woman from Słonim county also recalled panic in her village after the Soviets came into Poland: "People started to dig in the ground and bury their things and grain." In at least two instances, in the town of Chodorów and in Lwów, Ukrainian nationalists put up armed resistance against the entering Red Army detachments. Among the older generation of Jews and Ukrainians and among the Ukrainian intelligentsia, apprehension was felt by those who owned any property, including impoverished masses of Jewish small traders and artisans.[55] It was primarily minority youth who were seen cheering in the street, but they were quite numerous.[56] In addition, those who had communist sympathies went wild with excitement and joy. Celina Konińska was caught up in the eager anticipation:

* "The days following the Red Army's entry to Szczuczyn were so frightening and sad that I didn't leave the house during that time. People were grabbed in the streets and hauled to prison, or had red bow ties attached to their garment and nobody could say anything in protest" (HI, Poland. Ambasada USSR, Box 46, Czesława Maliszewska; see also PGC, 11303). The general sense seems to be that terror arrived in the towns later than in the countryside. It took a few days for the initial wave of arrests to begin in towns—I suppose the Soviets had to check records and assemble adequate manpower to carry out the task—and hard times began a few days *after* the Red Army arrived. People in the countryside recall the terror or, in its absence, the sheer insecurity of the days *preceding* the arrival of the Red Army as the worst (see, for example, HI, PGC, 4282).

I think the Jews awaiting the Messiah will feel, when he finally comes, the way we felt then. It is hard to find words to describe the feeling—this waiting and this happiness. We wondered how to express ourselves—to throw flowers? to sing? to organize a demonstration? How to show our great joy?[57]

Certainly such enthusiasm must have been plainly visible, even though in any one community only a few may have been overwhelmed by those feelings.

VIOLENCE

Killings, beatings, and destruction of property went on throughout eastern Poland for days before the Red Army actually occupied any given area and continued for several days afterward. Ethnic hatred ran deep in the Ukrainian and Belorussian countryside, and it filled the power vacuum created by the collapse of the Polish administration with blood. Poles, a numerical minority in the area who usually settled in cities and were only thinly dispersed throughout the countryside, were cruelly victimized.[58] Thousands were killed, often with primitive and premeditated brutality.

We already know a little about the context in which these killings took place or were occasionally averted. Much of the outcome hinged on local circumstances or even sheer coincidence, such as whether a lost Polish army detachment had passed through the area recently and how it had behaved. But there was something else that substantially influenced the course of events: slogans disseminated by the entering Soviets encouraged the local population to rectify the wrongs it had suffered during twenty years of Polish rule. Leaflets urged soldiers to turn their weapons against their true (i.e., class) enemies—capitalists, landowners, and officers.[59] Other leaflets called for assaults on Polish landlords and their stooges with whatever was at hand—scythes, axes, or pitchforks.[60] "Poliakam, panam, sobakam—sobachaia smert' [For Poles, Pans, and dogs—a dog's death]," allegedly read the text of one such tract disseminated in Mołodeczno.[61] Leaflets signed by the commander of the Ukrainian front called Ukrainians to arms.[62] And although we may not be sure of the exact content of any specific leaflet without seeing a specimen, the message sent throughout the conquered land was deeply imprinted on the memories of those who experienced the Soviet invasion:

After the Red Army entered the village [Maszów, in Luboml county of the Wołyń voivodeship], Lieutenant Minkov, battery commander Velov, and the commander of the 234th regiment of heavy artillery from Kiev ordered everybody to assemble and delivered a fiery speech saying that they brought freedom and equalization to all classes. They said that they authorize people to go and take away what rightfully belongs to them and to avenge the pains of twenty years of exploitation—kill and take the property of those who filled their pockets and barns with your blood. If you do not succeed on your own, the Red Army will assist you.[63]

Similarly, a Soviet officer addressed the inhabitants of Świsłocz village (Wołkowysk county, Białystok voivodeship): "For twenty years you lived under the yoke of the masters who drank your blood, and now we have liberated you and we give you freedom to do with them as you please."[64] In the village Horodziej (Nieśwież county, Nowogród voivodeship), "Commissar" Danilov climbed onto a makeshift platform and addressed the population that was brought to the marketplace: "If someone has a grudge against somebody else, he can do with him what he wants—take his property or even life."[65] Michał Garus from Łososin hamlet (Kosów Poleski county, Polesie voivodeship) remembers that "as soon as the Red Army entered into the nearest village, Różana Grodzieńska, immediately their so-called politruks started visiting neighboring hamlets and began their so-called agitation against the entire Polish state, against the government; they kept saying who was murdering you during the Polish times you can now go to him and do to him whatever you want."[66]

Though the reporters of these first encounters with the Red Army lived in several different voivodeships of eastern Poland, one is struck by the similarity of their experiences. Throughout the occupied territory the conquering army decreed a period of lawlessness. "What's the matter with you? Let them play a little," answered a local Red Army commander to a forester who complained about robberies and killings in Kalnica (Wilno voivodeship).[67] Indeed, the phrases used by speechmakers were clichés very common in Soviet rhetoric, which suggests that they were recurrent and recognized norms of conduct rather than slips of the tongue or the momentary aberrations of individual propagandists.[68] For several days a general dispensation was granted to do as one pleased: "After the Red Army came, the Soviet authorities permitted the local communists to avenge themselves on the local Polish population. I was informed about this by a local communist, Dimitri Gavriluk, a Ukrainian, from Korsynie village in Kowel county."[69] People were told that they could "square accounts" with their enemies.[70] Not that they weren't doing it anyway, but they were certainly not discouraged by Soviet propagandists.

This, then, was the kind of thing being said when the local population encountered the soldiers of the entering Soviet army in meetings described in the Soviet press and made vivid in the now standard photographs showing a Red Army soldier encircled by a group of men, women, and children.[71] The encouragement to "get even" for past miseries and exploitation fell on eager ears. Wherever resentments existed and circumstances were especially conducive, peasants have taken justice into their own hands. A brutal, nightmarish bloodbath ensued.

"Ukrainian villages assaulted Polish settlements, such as our hamlet Łęczówka [Podhajce county, Tarnopol voivodeship], for example. The landowner was tied to a pole, two strips of skin peeled off and the wound covered with salt, and he was left alive to watch the execution of his family."[72]

In Kamień Szlachecki (Kobryń county, Polesie voivodeship), "they took my sixty-eight-year-old father and a cousin, all neighbors who didn't escape in time, and a few officers caught on the road. All were brought to the schoolhouse. A Soviet commissar came by and shot one lawyer who admitted that he had prosecuted in some communist trials; the rest he left for the hoodlums to do with as they pleased. They were taken into the fields, ordered to undress, and were shot one after another. They threw them into pits, still alive. My father was alive when they threw him into a pit, and when he stood up and shouted at them 'even if you murder us, Poland will still be here,' they smashed his skull with spades. They broke the legs of an acquaintance, a teacher, and then buried him alive. Such killings were taking place all over the area."[73]

In gmina Szczorse (Nowogródek county, Nowogród voivodeship), its voyt, some policemen, and several settlers—twelve people altogether, it seems—were brought to the gmina seat, condemned to death, and then killed with axes. Scores of nameless others died there. A. Sobczak spent three days at the gmina office, standing all the time, so crowded were the some 300 prisoners. Every night a group was led to execution. Later, he says, they killed people with hammer blows. In Karczówka (Łuck county, Wołyń voivodeship), twenty-four settlers were tied with barbed wire and then shot or drowned by Ukrainian peasants. In Prużana, Belorussian peasants stoned to death a captain of the Polish army and a policeman. Antoni Szelingowski's nose and ears were cut off and his eyes gouged out as he was killed in Kościuszków (Łuck county). Michał Czyżewski's genitals were cut off. Bodnar, Smyszniuk, Kot, Kaczaraj, Hnałyszyn, and Orejda were among the Ukrainians who terrorized Poles in Brzeżany county. In settlement Żydomla (Grodno county, Białystok voivodeship), a number of settlers were taken away by an armed mob and disappeared. Despairing women kept looking for them throughout neighboring villages until, four days later, "a woman found a freshly covered pit. When we dug them out we couldn't recognize them. Their heads were busted and covered with blood."[74] In gmina Gorlice (Stryj county, Stanisławów voivodeship), a Polish soldier was tied to a horse and dragged along stony banks of the river Stryj until dead.

"Daddy was killed when the Soviets arrived [in Dubno county, Wołyń voivodeship]. A lot of people came, my daddy came into the courtyard, and there Wacław Iwanowski hit him in the head with an ax. Daddy lived two more weeks and died." "I luckily escaped death," wrote the man's son, "I was only hit with a pitchfork."[75]

In gmina Pulmo (Luboml county, Wołyń voivodeship), according to farmer Jan Kisiel, some 500 people were killed during three days of rampage in Wólka Chrupska, Piszcz, Pulemiec, Grabowa, Huta, and Olszanka. "With my own eyes I saw rows of corpses lining up the Włodawa-Kowel road." Makar Zeluk, Kuźma Zeluk, Mikołaj Horuń, Maksymiuk, and Zendel Nestior were among the perpetrators. (The latter was elected as a deputy to the National Assembly of the Western Ukraine in October 1939.) Eight settlers were killed in Ostrów (Kowel county, Wołyń voivodeship); the entire family of Antoni Bulak, seven people in all, died in Józefówka (Tarnopol county, Tarnopol voivodeship); seven settlers from Kazimierzowo (Prużana county, Polesie voivodeship) were murdered, "and Stefan Kozewski lost his mind after a beating." Beatings in general were massive and vicious.[76] Dyoniza Grodzik's father, along with a dozen others, was killed somewhere in Wołyń, as was Zofia Urban's father, together with Józef Piotrowski, Stefan Jabłoński, Stanisław Kajkowski, Maria Kucharska, Józef Machowski, Józef Nowak, Ignacy Kowalczyk, and Witold Kradzik in Ściurzyn (Łuck county). The village, away from major roads, was quiet until Soviet agitators came by and invited the local population to assault the Polish settlers. The list of victims, if we could ever hope to complete it, would be very long indeed.[77]

The sense of helplessness felt by the victims derived not only from the absence of any established authority but also from the dreaded fact that the perpetrators of violence were frequently the very agents of the nascent new authority in the area. Peasant groups on the rampage, which usually started as no more than vigilante squads, were frequently recognized as militias by a passing Soviet commander or a political commissar and empowered to become the official enforcers for the new regime. This meant, in practice, that their behavior received official sanction. Indeed, the circumstances of some of the killing episodes—namely, those where people were first detained in some makeshift prison or sentenced in a quick public "trial"—show that militias were involved. By such innocuous relabeling of vigilante groups, spontaneous violence imperceptibly became organized coercion; and although the official complicity may have made little difference in the actual course of events, it certainly further undermined the morale of the victims. With the local militia on a killing spree, there was no one to whom they could turn for protection.[78] Many concluded that only nature could offer a safe sanctuary. To survive the wrath of their neighbors, people took off into the wilderness, braving the discomfort and cold of late autumn nights. Three brothers hid in the forest for a month and a half, living on food brought daily by their younger sister. Youth from Borawskie (Łomża county) every evening set out for the woods, afraid to spend the night in the village. For a few weeks, writes a forester from Dolina county, "we hid in the forest like wild animals."[79]

The encouragement offered by Soviet propagandists was not simply a mechanical repetition of revolutionary rhetoric, a speech mannerism not meant to be taken seriously. Only too often the victims who appealed for protection to representatives of the Soviet army or the barely established administration met with indifference or a rebuke.* There is evidence from all over the occupied territory that the Soviets routinely ignored appeals to restrain the excesses being perpetrated by Ukrainian and Belorussian peasants.[80] "The Bolsheviks," a cooperatist from Równe concluded, "didn't want to take over administration from our civil servants, but they frantically kept organizing and looking for a 'revolution' that would conquer this power."[81]** Nachalnik (boss)

---

* Two colonists from Kosy Dwór (Nowogródek county) went to complain to the Soviet authorities on behalf of several Polish families from the area who had been robbed and beaten. They were detained by a "commissar" who then asked assembled peasants whether they should be shot. Three peasants said yes, while the rest begged to let the colonists go because they were "good people." Nevertheless the commissar ordered them shot next to the Catholic church in Niechniewicze. Their names, it appears, were Stanisław Majek and Konstanty Żurek (HI, PGC, 2575, 7546; see also HI, PGC, 2335).

** "They constantly tried to 'revolutionize the masses.' The Bolsheviks were really disappointed that the people did not take over the land and power, that they did not square accounts with their oppressors. They started to inspire such revolts. Examples: in Ukrainian villages surrounding some Polish military colonies near Tuczyn rumors were spread that colonists had picked up weapons from the Polish army and that they planned to attack Ukrainians. Some peasants believed this. Apparently a frightened Ukrainian woman came to Równe's town commandant begging him for help and protection. He,

Sirotko, in charge of Nieśwież, publicly chided an audience that it had not yet made a revolution because it had not yet killed any landlords or taken away their property.[82] In garrison towns, soldiers' families (i.e., women and children conveniently quartered in distinct compounds) fell prey to angry mobs and were left to fend for themselves by the Soviets. A half-naked woman, a captain's wife, ran into the office of Mołodeczno's stationmaster calling for help. An NKVD operative present on the scene dismissed her, saying "nichevo tam ne budet, poguliaiut rebiata i uidut [nothing will really happen there, kids will just play a little and they will go]." In Kobryń a Soviet soldier encouraged an excited crowd to "go and play" in the barracks where only families of the military lived at the time, but a Red Army lieutenant cut him short. In Postawy and in Dzisna county, military families were not as lucky.[83]

One ought to note here what seems to have been a pattern of Red Army behavior in some cities: wild, random, or unnecessary shooting sprees. In Buczacz, for example, people were confined to their houses for two days following the occupation of the town by the Soviets; tanks moved up and down the streets, machine-gun fire was heard all around, and numerous arrests and house searches were simultaneously carried out. In Tarnopol, Soviet artillery pounded on one or two of the town's churches, and there was random shooting in the streets. In Nowogródek during the night of September 19–20 the Red Army shot wildly in the streets, allegedly against some Polish resistance. In Dubno, on the second day of the Soviet occupation, the military mounted machine guns at street intersections and sprayed neighboring houses with volleys of bullets, killing scores of civilians. In Pińsk, as the new occupiers entered the town, they bombarded the church of the Jesuits; and two days later the artillery was brought out again, this time against the town's Orthodox cathedral. Whether these were measures of intimidation, accidental circumstances, or overreaction from some trigger-happy or nervous Soviet commanders, we cannot tell anymore.[84]

As with so many other aspects of the utter confusion of these early days, we can observe in Red Army attitudes a contradictory disposition. In several instances the Soviets actually used force to stop vio-

---

acting surprised at the small size of the delegation, told her to go back home and tell peasants to arm themselves and to destroy these Pans' dogs. In another case a peasant delegation came with the request that authorities divide land among them. And again a characteristic answer: we will not divide land among you. Take it in a revolutionary manner—do with the landlord whatever you want and take the land yourselves" (HI, PGC, 3162).

lence on the part of peasant militias. Many witnesses will readily testify to the Red Army's peaceful, disciplined, and calm behavior at the time of entry into Poland.[85] But as we have also seen, the soldiers were usually restrained to the point of ignoring excesses taking place in their presence. They seemed hesitant, one observer noted, to spread all over the countryside. And for several days, while county seats and major roads were bulging with Red Army personnel, the outlying territory was left to its own devices, ruled in effect by committees formed by the local population. "My impression was that Soviet authorities on purpose stayed away to give local people an opportunity to do as they pleased for a while."[86]

Undoubtedly, instructions for Soviet personnel despatched into the Western Ukraine and Western Belorussia were packaged in the rhetorical language of ideological slogans. They were therefore useful in support of all, even contradictory, courses of action. Surely the Red Army was to assist in the national and class liberation of the people from under the rule of the Polish Pans. But the comparative well-being of the countryside—an ironic impression, I may add, for this was generally the poorest area in a relatively backward European country—made the soldiers wonder where "the people" were. With some obvious exceptions, they could not immediately distinguish "people" from "Pans." Even the Polish military settlers—truly the bêtes noires of ideologically sophisticated Soviets because the majority of them were veterans of the Polish-Bolshevik war of 1920—lived and looked like any other peasant in the vicinity. "When the first Bolshevik tank came to our village [Girewicze], a Bolshevik said 'zdrastvuite tovarishchi, gde vashy pany [hello, comrades, where are your Pans?].' Nobody said anything and peasants surrounding the tank silently went back to their houses."[87] What this friendly Soviet tank commander did next, we are not told, but he was certainly put on the spot. Another encounter in Mołodeczno county with a similar beginning had a benign denouement, which, we are assured, was routine in the area. "When a Red Army soldier came into a house, he would ask 'are there Pans here?' and his second utterance was 'mamasha davai kushat' [mother, give something to eat]."[88] These were lost souls, and quite hungry on the top of it.

It is also possible that political officers had instructions different from and possibly even unknown to military commanders. This was the situation on the German front, for example, where the content of SS-Einsatzgruppen orders were kept secret from the Wehrmacht.[89] The general ideological framework of the Red Army's assignment—class and national liberation—was certainly known to all. But the visible display of ideological zeal and revolutionary temperament may have been a strictly rationed commodity, with some specially designated propagandists, for instance, authorized to be more inflammatory than others. Also, along with fear, professional soldiers must have harbored resentment over the recent devastating purge of the officers corps. Given a safe opportunity, some of them might have wished to thwart or countermand the political commissars' initiatives. Indeed, local people report numerous conversations with sympathetic Red Army soldiers and officers who warned them about the future and in general commiserated that they were all now in the same boat.[90] While the nachalnik Sirotko eagerly encouraged revolution in Nieśwież, the military commander in Kowel, for example, scolded local zealots for establishing a *revkom* (revolutionary committee) when they had no revolution there. But he was in no hurry to remedy this lack. He told the committee that it was now the town's provisional administration, taking away along with the old name much of the glamour, and he appointed himself to be in charge.[91]

I have already noted that Soviet presence in an area might have had a restraining influence. Even many Poles felt safer with Soviets in the vicinity. But because sustained Red Army presence existed only in the towns at first, we may once again be talking about a difference between distinct social environments. In a rural milieu the security breakdown was more profound, and violence more likely to occur if only because the choice victims at the time, Poles, were fewer there and thus easily overcome. In these easternmost hinterlands of interwar Europe each hamlet or village was to a large degree an isolated universe. As often happens in such an environment, intense personal hatreds were harbored, and an ethnic and religious component gave them the potential to engulf entire communities. Yet, much as the violence represented an explosion of combined ethnic, religious, and nationalist conflict, I am nevertheless struck by its intimacy. More often than not, victims and executioners knew each other personally. Even after several years, survivors could still name names.[92] Definitely, people took this opportunity to get even for personal injuries in the past.

But the Red Army, though generally quiet and withdrawn or neutral, engaged in more than occasional propaganda. Indeed, it joined in the violence both directly and by sponsoring a provisional executive instrument of administration, the militia, and condoning its violent behavior. In part, I think, the general population was not struck by the Red Army's violence partly because its actions were selective rather than random, directed mostly against Polish officers, policemen, and landowners. These killings were simply not very visible; they occurred mostly on the roads or on rural estates, rather than in towns or villages where there would be many witnesses who would themselves feel threatened. "There were two Polish officers on the road going home to their wives and children," recalled a twelve-year-old boy from Radziechów county. "Some Ukrainians and Bolsheviks grabbed them. After three days of real murder they were shot, and the Ukrainians took their shoes and clothing. Before he died, one said to tell his wife he was alive no more."[93] In the end, however, enough witnesses survived, many of them soldiers who had been taken into captivity and spared while their colleagues were killed. Again, several brief episodes will give a feeling for the scope and style of the Soviet army's behavior.

When the rear guard of KOP's Polesie brigade was captured on September 28, officers and NCOs were separated from the rest of the prisoners. In the officer group there was Captain Mokuliński from KOP's regiment Dawidgródek, a retired navy officer named Brodowski, and the nameless informant who left this testimony. A Soviet captain asked Mokuliński to identify himself and then, saying in Russian "this will teach you to be a professional [officer]," shot him in the head with a pistol. Brodowski in vain tried to explain that he had put on his old uniform only to travel more easily with the army to Gdynia on the Baltic coast, where he lived with his family. The Soviet officer shot him in exactly the same way. Our witness survived because a higher Soviet commander ordered him to be taken to headquarters for interrogation.[94]

"I was taken prisoner by the Soviets," writes Maksymilian Mendakiewicz, "between Hrubieszów and Zamość near Grabowiec on September 27, 1939, at nine, during a military engagement. After the Soviets took us we were brought to one spot. When some 5,000 soldiers were assembled, militia men together with the Bolsheviks went around looking for officers, NCOs, and policemen. On this spot, in front of our own eyes, six Polish officers, eight NCOs, and 150 policemen were shot."[95]

The commander of the police precinct in Podhorce (Złoczów county) waited as ordered for the Soviets' arrival. He was then taken into custody and on September 18th brought to the town hall in Sassów. By the next day about 500 policemen and officers captured in the vicinity were already locked up there. Suddenly, in the evening, as they were looking out the windows, machine-gun fire was opened against them. They were under fire for about half an hour; grenades were thrown into the building as well. Then, after a brief pause, they were fired upon again. Several dozen people died in this massacre.

Regular soldiers were sometimes mistaken for officers and executed as well.[96] Personal identity, as a matter of fact, was often established rather carelessly. "They ordered us to line up and they checked everybody's hands. And they ordered to step forward those whose hands were not worn out from physical labor and beat them with rifle butts, and one policemen was shot with a revolver."[97] In another instance, four KOP soldiers were taken from a homebound train near Augustów on September 20. Jan Gowora and Stanisław Staniszewski had their military ID cards with pictures, possibly in parade uniforms with epaulets resembling those worn by officers. It did not matter that their IDs identified them as privates. The Soviets paid no attention (probably they could not read Latin script) and shot them. Zygmunt Markowski, whose testimony I am relating, had no ID card and was let go.[98]

Many dramatic episodes marked the path of the Red Army through the Western Ukraine and Western Belorussia. Soldiers, officers, and policemen often lost their lives in casual and quick encounters.[99] In Tarnopol and in Grodno small groups of soldiers and officers who fought entering Red Army units were summarily executed. Several KOP guardposts, captured after a brief fight, were demolished and their defenders, now in Soviet custody, shot to death. Chivalrous conduct of the defeated sometimes cost them dearly.[100]

But the Soviet military was not after men in uniform exclusively. Rather, "the Pans," the so-called *beloruchki* (those with white hands) of all kinds, were the enemy. Thus certain categories of civilians were vulnerable as well—landowners, local officials, and priests in particular. A shot was fired when a Red Army detachment passed through Mirosław Łabuńka's village in Brzeżany county. Amidst nervous inquiries about the identity of the perpetrator, someone volunteered that it was "a Polish priest." This is just what inhabitants of the village used to say, sententiously, whenever something occurred and no one claimed responsibility for it. "Who did it?" "A Polish priest" would be the answer. But this time the priest was actually grabbed by a Red Army soldier and shot. But not killed. He was left wounded by the roadside, and every passing soldier who so fancied used him for target practice. A dozen bullets must have hit him before he died at the end of the day.[101] S. Kowalski, a gmina voyt from Lida county, was taken amidst his neighbors' lamentations and pleas for mercy to the edge of a nearby forest by a squad of Soviet soldiers.

There they searched him, undressed him down to his underwear in front of the crying people, they still beat him with butts at the end until he had bruises, mistreated him, kicking him, threatened that he shouldn't expect that Poland will ever rise again. They shot him, powerless, in the chest with a revolver. They asked that someone knock out his golden teeth, because it's a pity to leave them behind. After everything they threw him into a hole under a fir tree and there they buried him.[102]

Scores of civilians lost their lives in incidents of this kind.[103]

LOOKS AND MANNERS

Not all was so gruesome about the Red Army's coming. There was the stealing and requisitioning to be expected from any conqueror, but also a rather shocking, and in a way even amusing, realization of the deprivation suffered by Soviet soldiers. They were ill-fed, ill-clad, smelly (they used malodorous tar to impregnate footwear), and unacquainted with a variety of material objects that were commonplace to Western Ukrainian and Western Belorussian peasants.

The sheer, overwhelming volume of the Soviet armada—the tanks and trucks they brought along—made an impression on the local population. Not so the soldiers' outward appearance. Some Soviet cavalry rode with saddles and some without; some soldiers had shoes, others only cloth wrapped around their feet; some wore long coats, others short ones; some had belts while others had only strings attached to their rifles. "Torn uniforms, dirty coats, hands, and faces, they washed their boots in puddles, they picked papers off the streets and rolled cigarettes, they were pitiful," recalled a ten-year-old boy from Lwów.[104] The visual contrast between the Wehrmacht and the Red Army underscored this overall impression for those who saw both armies in these days, as many did.* The horses looked no better than the men, which is perhaps why many peasants, on the occasion of their first meeting with the Red Army, had their horses stolen or requisitioned (the boundary was often unclear) or exchanged for the nags the Soviets rode. A Soviet soldier might jump on a grazing horse or simply take the animal from a peasant working in the field.[105]

The Red Army also gave the impression of being rather shy. It earned the nickname "silent army," so withdrawn and restrained were its soldiers on the whole.[106] They were under orders, of course, not to

---

* HI, PGC, 3319, 7182. The following counties were first occupied by the Wehrmacht in September 1939 and then yielded to the Soviets: Białystok voivodeship (Łomża, Ostrów Mazowiecki, Wysokie Mazowieckie, Ostrołęka, Białostocki, Białystok counties); Polesie voivodeship (Brześć and Kobryń); Lwów voivodeship (Lubaczów, Jarosław, Dobromil, Sambor, Przemyśl, Gródek Jagielloński, Jaworów, Drohobycz, Turka, Sanok, Brzozów, Lesko, Rudki, Lwowski).

interact with the local population—not to engage in conversations, to buy anything, or to accept handouts. Years later in a labor camp Karol Bartosz met a group of Soviet youths who had been in Grodno in September 1939 as Red Army conscripts. They had been confined to the Grodno barracks under the pretext that the local population was out to stab solitary Soviet soldiers; but they frequently slipped into town and bought whatever they could, watches in particular. They went home for furlough and only there, when showing off their acquisitions, were arrested by the NKVD and sentenced to twenty years in labor camps for "counterrevolution and praise of capitalism." In another instance, a Soviet nurse was immediately sent back to Moscow from a military hospital in Brześć after she proudly wore on the ward a fur she had bought in town.[107]

What Red Army conscripts saw in this backwater of provincial Poland, in small villages and towns, not to speak of cities like Lwów and Wilno, were unknown marvels and undreamed-of abundance. No one could stop them from seizing a taste of these goods. A veritable invasion of shops, restaurants, and markets took place. This must not have come as a total surprise to the Soviet authorities, as they were clearly hesitant to enforce their own orders prohibiting such behavior.[108] In the first issue of stern occupation ordinances announced to the local people immediately upon the Soviets' arrival in a town, there was one seemingly concerned with the inhabitants' welfare: all shops must remain open and offer all merchandise at prewar prices. Judging from the Red Army's behavior, I think that the real motivation behind this ordinance was to prevent widespread looting by offering Soviet soldiers an opportunity to buy goods, even against explicit orders. It was wiser to give them this liberty than to contend with what might otherwise have become a total breach of discipline.

The soldiers could not resist what was clearly a once-in-a-lifetime opportunity. A Soviet lieutenant sentenced to three years for drunkenness in Lwów told Captain Marian Siekierski later in a camp that he would gladly take another chance to "live like this" for a while and then be sentenced again to three years in labor camps.[109] The wild buying spree immediately relaxed the tension between occupiers and occupied, so self-absorbed did the soldiers become and, in a way, oblivious to the local people. Indeed, the locals themselves thoroughly enjoyed the spectacle, until after a few days a scarcity of foodstuffs and other necessities began and prices shot up in response to this unexpected, unlimited, and indiscriminate demand.

A school composition entitled "My Experiences in Russia," by a twelve-year-old witness of the Soviet invasion of Łuniniec county, begins:

In September 1939, when the Soviet army crossed the Polish border, a great uneasiness settled over the Polish people at the sight of the things that were going on. And what went on I will tell you. The soldiers ran in town from shop to shop, bought up whatever they could, mostly watches, rolls, sausages, dress fabrics, and bicycles. Two Soviets went into a shop and asked the shopkeeper how much this watch cost—one hundred złotys—I have no złotys—well then in rubles all right, he asks the prices of other watches—until finally he says to the other soldier "znaesh, Kolia, vezmiom vse ruchnye chasy [you know, Kola, we'll take all the watches]." They took twenty watches, paid, and went to the next shop, where they took dress material in whole rolls; they could barely carry it, but they saw sausage—"Kola, let's go and buy the sausage now," and "surely there is no sausage, there is only a wooden one on display in the window like at home in Moscow." "All the same let's go and look." They go into the store and ask if it is possible to get 100 grams of sausage: "why not," and "can we get half a kilo," "you can even get five kilograms." "So give us 10 kilograms each of sausage," and they put it around their necks because they were already loaded with bread rolls, even their hats. Because they bought rolls by the hundreds and then when he got tired and they became heavy he threw out a few.[110]

Though rather passionate and somewhat fictionalized (i.e., the dialogue), this description by the young Pole is undoubtedly grounded in the everyday experiences of many. "I saw in the marketplace in Zdołbunów how these Soviet people ate eggs, shell and all, horseradish, beets, and other produce. Country women rolled with laughter." In a restaurant a Red Army soldier might order several courses or a dozen pastries and eat them all on the spot. As a teacher from Braszewice (Drohiczyn county) put it, with the Soviet invasion of Poland "a hungry world and a satiated world came in contact."[111]

The sheer variety of material objects overwhelmed the newcomers. After the families of those assigned to administer the newly conquered provinces had arrived, it became proverbial how Soviet women wore nightgowns and slips to the opera and various gala performances as if they were the most elegant dresses. A soldier was seen outside a hosiery shop wearing women's bras over his ears for earmuffs; another, standing in the middle of the street, tried to blow one up, looking it over with incredulity. They rushed all the stores, cutting ahead of people standing in line, and bought up everything—while at the same time denying that they lacked anything in their own country.[112] "Do you have oranges?" "We produce them in factories," a Soviet soldier would answer. "Do you have Amsterdam, or Greta Garbo?" "We have plenty"—*u nas vsio est*—was the standard reply. Young pranksters in Lwów and other towns entertained audiences by engaging Soviet soldiers in such conversations.[113] But the Soviets had the last word in these discussions. When pressed and ridiculed about why they were buying everything so voraciously if there was such abundance in the Soviet Union, they snapped back angrily that they had tanks, guns, and airplanes while Poles had silk stockings and perfumes. "Frankly, it was a shrewd point, which often cut the discussion short."[114]

Still, for a long time, and in spite of the exploitative economic policy to which the territory was subjected, the Western Ukraine and Western Belorussia remained a land of plenty to the Soviet citizens who slowly filled the newly occupied territory on job assignments.

> Long trains with Soviet functionaries and their families, mostly from Kiev and Kharkov, began pulling into the station. Streets filled with crowds of shabbily dressed and dirty people frantically eyeing already modest-looking store windows. They bought almost everything available to them, especially watches—the most sought-after commodity.[115]

A Ukrainian journalist who came to Lwów on assignment from Kiev recalled that, about two weeks after the Red Army occupied the Western Ukraine and the first foreign-made cars and elegant pieces of clothing made their appearance in the streets, excitement swept over the republic's capital. Everyone wanted to go to Lwów or Tarnopol to buy things, and *komandirovka* (travel authorization) to some town in the newly occupied territory became the most sought-after document.[116] For individual citizens, it was safest to consume these newly found riches on the spot. Any transfer of wealth into the Soviet Union proper was risky. It is even possible that parcels sent by ordinary Soviet citizens to their families in the Soviet Union were confiscated on the old Polish-Soviet border, where strict documents and customs controls were kept long after the incorporation of the Western Ukraine and Western Belorussia into the USSR.

The invaders' enjoyment of food and material objects humanized this strange war, which could be otherwise very brutal. Along with greed, curiosity, and hunger, there could be a yearning for human contact, personal encounter, and face-to-face conversation that occasionally triumphed over fear and suspicion. Then it turned out that, beneath the wooden lingo and stereotyped clichés, Soviet soldiers were generally sad. "Ne raduites', khorosho ne budet [Watch out, bad times are coming]," a young Ukrainian conscript advised in a low voice, anxiously looking around, when asked about life in the Soviet Union.[117] Many expressed disappointment that they had brought communism to Poland instead of being liberated from it at home by the Poles.[118] More enterprising individuals made the most they could from this unexpected opportunity; desertions from the Red Army occurred on a large enough scale to prompt authorities to issue a special ordinance specifically prohibiting the sale of civilian clothing to Soviet military personnel. Yet numerous attempts to cross the border into Rumania or Germany were undoubtedly successful, as attested later by Soviet soldiers who were caught and shared prison cells with civilian inmates all over the Western Ukraine and Western Belorussia. In one instance a group of Red Army soldiers taken prisoner by a Polish detachment after a skirmish chose to stay with their captors and go with them to Rumania, rather than to be released and to return to their outfit.[119]

This, in general, is what the first encounter with the Red Army was like in the Western Ukraine and the Western Belorussia. So, we can only marvel at the unflinching dogmatism of a highbrow literary and political monthly, *Nowe Widnokręgi*, launched in January 1941 by the intellectual elite supporting the new regime. In a long introductory statement in the second issue Stefan Jędrychowski, later to become one of the principal dignitaries in the People's Poland, described the circumstances of the Soviet entry into Poland, "How Did We Get Acquainted With the Red Army?" Completely oblivious to the actual circumstances witnessed by everybody, the article is thus a deliberate insult to all. Characteristically for what was then official journalism, it mixes socialist surrealism with the widely experienced sense of radical rupture in the continuity of society's existence.

> For all categories of inhabitants it was a real novelty to get to know the Red Army from up close when in September of 1939 it crossed the border of the already non-existent bourgeois Poland.
> . . . One could not notice even a shade of estrangement between the army and the people . . . already during the first days of its presence fraternization between the Red Army and the local population took place. . . . How pronounced was the difference between the high culture of the Red Army's commanders and ordinary soldiers and that of an army of a capitalist country. . . . The high level of intelligence and political knowledge which the

49

Soviet soldiers demonstrated gave an indication of success achieved under socialism in education and popular enlightenment. Conversations with Red Army soldiers awoke among the working people of Wilno a desire to become just like them, and moved the youth to seek to join the Red Army as soon as possible. . . . Their marvelous attitude and unsurpassed discipline moved people and filled them with admiration. . . . The inhabitants of the liberated Ukrainian and Belorussian territory, as well as of the Wilno area, were inspired with the feeling of unusual security by the whir of strong bombers' engines and those of agile fighter planes, by the clatter of countless heavy and light tanks. The population, which was until recently threatened with the horror of bombs and the danger of being drawn into the heat of an imperialist war, could now breathe slower and freer. An armed hand of a socialist country extended forward in their defense.[120]

Yet even a young, ardently committed Jewish Communist recalls a moment of pause after the initially breathtaking enthusiasm that overtook her and her friends.

First contacts with the Russians—I mean with the Soviet soldiers—struck us with something strange and unpleasant. We thought that every soldier was a Communist and therefore it was also obvious to us that each must be happy. So their comportment, their behavior, struck us as queer. First of all their looking after things, after material objects—watches, clothing—with so much interest and so much rapacity. We waited for them to ask how was life under capitalism and to tell us what it was like in Russia. But all they wanted was to buy a watch. I noticed that they were preoccupied with worldly goods, and we were waiting for ideals.[121]

MILITIAS AND VILLAGE COMMITTEES

Shortly after the Soviets arrived in a village or town, they moved to establish instruments of a new administration. Among the first ordinances issued by the military authorities in each occupied locality was an instruction for everyone to return to work and in general to continue routine daily life as if nothing had happened. People were told that they would not be punished for whatever they had done while carrying out their jobs prior to the Soviets' arrival.

Even at the time, these assurances sounded hollow and were in a matter of days contradicted by a wave of systematic arrests carried out with great precision and at first primarily affecting the functionaries of the local administration, members of the judiciary, policemen, political and social activists, and other prominent citizens. All the department heads from the Wołyń voivodeship office, for example, were taken into custody at a conference to which they had been politely invited in order "to discuss the new organization of work."[122] This was only one among many efficient police operations carried out in those days in the Western Ukraine and Western Belorussia. Captured records as well as local collaborators provided all the information necessary to remove the leadership stratum quickly from every community. Celina Konińska, a young activist from Żółkiew, recalls how shortly after their arrival the Soviets were busily employed sorting the county archives and learning who in this office had been responsible for what policies.[123]

For efficiency in this police action, local support was necessary. After a brief period of encouraging violence against various segments of local society, especially in the countryside, the Soviets proceeded to organize the instruments of local authority—not necessarily to contain the terror but rather to harness it for more specific tasks that had to be carried out almost immediately, such as supplying the Red Army, or making arrests of the leadership stratum, or preparing the October elections. In establishing the framework of the Provisional Administration (as it was called in the cities and at the county and voivodeship level), the difference between cities and the countryside came into prominence once again. In the most general terms, that difference resided in the policy of keeping on a significant segment of middle- and lower-level city administrations (especially in the larger cities) and weeding them out slowly as replacements from the Soviet Union could be brought in and trained for these jobs by working alongside their Polish predecessors.[124] In the countryside, on the village and gmina level, personnel changes were immediate and radical. Committees were established—from volunteers mostly, or via an electoral process of sorts—and, simultaneously, the militias. Indeed, militias appeared all over, in larger cities as well. Nowhere, I believe, did the Soviets simply take over and entrust the Polish police with enforcement of the new order. On the other hand, a Citizens' Guard could have its life extended as a militia well into the Soviet occupation—and then be slowly purged.

How were militias and village committees constituted? The answer is that they did not so much *get* established as they established themselves. An episode from a Russian novel describing the Red Army's victorious march through this territory twenty years earlier offers a perfect rendition of the circumstances.

"Where are you from, Comrade?" "I'm from this town, I've been waiting for you to come." Sergei was soon surrounded by Red Army men. "I know him," the Chinese said in broken Russian. "He yelled 'Long live comrades.' He Bolshevik, he with us, a good fellow!" he added with a broad smile, slapping Sergei on the shoulder approvingly. Sergei's heart leaped with joy. He had been accepted at once, accepted as one of them.[125]

As in this fictionalized account of the Ukrainian civil war, whoever greeted the entering Soviets and cared to step forward in September 1939 was accepted and put in charge—as a militiamen or a committee member—in his village or town or gmina. The armed groups that had formed during the period of anarchy to protect their communities or harass refugees or assault neighbors were obvious candidates to receive the mandate from Soviet military authorities to police their domains. And, indeed, this happened frequently.[126] Initially, whoever was already mobilized in a vigilante group had an edge over other members of the community; the rest of the local inhabitants were in general disoriented, suspicious, and therefore passive. Also, the tasks visibly assigned to the newly forming administrative skeleton were not so different from those the vigilante groups had undertaken on their own. They could in fact continue those activities, now with official approval.

But soon, when more constructive tasks were imposed on the new administration—in addition to merely terrorizing the population and dismantling the remnants of the old structure of authority and influence—its usefulness often proved questionable. Hence, a rapid rotation of personnel occurred at the local level during the initial weeks.[127] In one way or another local committees proved unsatisfactory throughout the early phase. Or perhaps, as an insurance policy and an exercise in intimidation, the Soviets on principle purged a quota of early supporters. Whatever the reasons, numerous respondents to Polish questionnaries pointed out that people who had persecuted them at the beginning of Soviet rule (as committee members and militiamen) were now in the Polish army in Iran.[128] This is because many who had initially opted to take an active role in the new order were later arrested and deported.

As we shall see in the case of many other initiatives as well, the Soviets were in general not concerned with screening for reliability those who were placed in lower-level executive positions. They depended mostly on self-recruitment; or, when no volunteers were forthcoming, they simply assigned tasks to people chosen at random. An episode from Kowel, to which I have already briefly alluded, illustrates the style of these personnel decisions. One is tempted to say that it reflects the arrogance of power, except that the people who exercised power were themselves vulnerable. A two-man delegation visited the newly arrived Soviet military town commander in Kowel to tell him about the local *revkom* (revolutionary committee). The commander told them to forget about *revkom*, because there had been no revolution in Kowel, then appointed himself head of the provisional city administration and designated his two interlocutors as deputies. They then went to the city hall to interview the terrified employees of the local administration who were assembled there. When they finished, the Soviet officer turned to one of his two deputies (who left this testimony) and said: "I am leaving now. I'll be back in two hours. You—*sadis' i upravliai* [sit down and rule]."[129] What a phrase—sit down and rule! Like all great literature, it defies commentary.

Somehow, the Soviets must have believed in the infallibility of the institutions of "the system" they were about to set up; apparently, it could function regardless of the individual qualifications of the people staffing it, partly because people could be discarded without much ado at a moment's notice. But there is a deeper reason than mere convenience for this purely instrumental attitude toward human beings. Time and again, when candidates' poor qualifications for office were pointed out by those assembled at a public forum (which, I hasten to add, could take place only for election or appointment to the lowest-level positions), the presiding Soviet official would answer: "It does not matter; we will teach them all there is to know. They will learn on the job."[130] I take this attitude of Soviet officialdom—obviously derived from twenty years of experience in their own country—to reveal much about the nature of Soviet communism. Indeed, it unwittingly discloses that the system rested neither on the professional qualifications nor on the ideological reliability of the individuals who were part of it, but on something else that human beings have been found to possess in abundance. I shall return to this point when offering a reinterpretation of the nature of Soviet totalitarianism.

VILLAGE MEETINGS AND THE NEW ADMINISTRATION

"We ... burst into Berestechko to the sounds of thundering march. The inhabitants had put iron bars across their shutters, and silence, almighty silence, had ascended its small-town throne. . . . Notices were ... posted up announcing that Divisional Commander Vinogradov would lecture that evening on the second congress of the Komintern. Right under my window some Cossacks were trying to shoot an old silver-bearded Jew for spying. . . . The stilly dusk turned to blue the green around the castle. . . . A meeting was being held in the square below. Peasants, Jews, and tanners from the outskirts had assembled there, with Vinogradov's voice above them, fired with enthusiasm, and the ringing of his spurs. . . . He is passionately persuading the bewildered townsfolk and the plundered Jews. 'You are in power. Everything here is yours. No more Pans. I now proceed to the election of the Revolutionary Committee. . . .' "[131]

Berestechko and the myriad of other shtetls and villages throughout the Western Ukraine and Belorussia had not changed much in the two decades since 1920, when Isaac Babel rode through with Budenny's cavalry army. In 1939 it was Valentin Kataev's turn to write an artistic glossary to the Red Army's exploits (in September and October 1939 issues of *Pravda*). The literary canons and the caliber of the talent still permitted to "sing the song" had changed more than anything else, for even the actors—the local inhabitants and the conquerors—were often the same. Indeed, in selected localities witnesses reported the return of individuals who had been active there as Bolshevik organizers in 1919–1920.[132]

And in 1939, just as in the episode described by Babel, countless village meetings were called to elect local councils, the village committees. The Soviets offered little intimidation or even interference during these meetings. Unless a given locality was on the itinerary of the invasion force, only a few Soviet representatives would arrive in a village to organize an election meeting. The scenario was more or less fixed. After announcing that the assembled "are in power" and that "everything is theirs," a presiding Soviet might stipulate certain limitations on the choice of committee members. Those who had held office under the Polish administration, or even peasants who owned larger farms, might be a priori excluded. In the majority of elections the Soviets explicitly favored or encouraged selection of the poor (*bedniaki*). Sometimes they came prepared with a list of those to be elected.[133]

In most villages elections were no trouble at all; there were, as I said before, volunteers anxious to take the job. The OUN, for instance, directed its members to infiltrate the nascent Soviet administration in much of the Ukrainian countryside.[134] Leftists and Communist sympathizers, many of them Jewish, stepped forward, especially in the towns and cities. But perhaps just as often the assembled villagers proceeded to elect candidates of their choice. When they failed, it was not primarily because they lacked the freedom to choose but rather because the winners repeatedly declined to accept the honor.[135] In many communities, however, the new representatives did not decline, or were not allowed to; so they began to exercise their power, hopelessly caught between the impossible demands of the occupiers and their sense of loyalty to the community. A Ukrainian forester from gmina Zahatyń was threatened with arrest if he did not accept election as head of the village committee. He gave in.

> After I accepted, they told those assembled to disperse and took me alone for a confidential conversation, where they told me that they would pay me well and that I would be fine so long as I would no longer think about Poland, because there would be no more Poland, and they would deport and arrest all Polish nationalists, not even a trace of them would remain, and the same would happen to me if I would not do what they told me to do. . . . I was given the following orders: to parcel the priest's land, to report to them everybody who is against the USSR, to indicate immediately who engaged in politics during Polish times, to tell people that they would not have to pay any taxes, to forbid the priest from going to the village school, to remove all official portraits and Polish national emblems, to keep the priest under observation, to confiscate all weapons, to inform about everybody—who goes to meet whom.[136]

A number of village heads are reported to have been helpful and to have assisted their communities by warning people who were immediately endangered and by cushioning in various ways the impact of Soviet policies.[137]

Here and there the old village head (*sołtys*) might be re-elected to preside over the new committee, even though the Soviet organizers present during election could exercise their veto power on the spot or might order new elections and appoint a new committee a few days or weeks later.[138] Needless to say, there were no clearly revealed procedures for interfering with the electoral process. But from early October one could read in the official media calls to "unmask" enemies who had managed to "sneak into" the executive organs of the people's power. Thus, for example, during one of the conferences of village committee representatives (gmina- and county-level conferences began immediately after local elections), the head of the Dziatkowo village committee was revealed to be "a Polish civil servant and a Petlurite [Ukrainian nationalist]" (a rather incongruous set) and was, we are told, chased out of the conference and off the committee.[139] *Czerwony Sztandar* (March 12, 1940) praised a certain Rychwa for unmasking the elected village committee in Sielce-Benków (Kamionka county) and taking it over from the first incumbents.

The sham of the earliest village committee elections is exposed precisely through such episodes, which followed shortly after the voting: elected officials were "chased out," elected offices were "taken over," and people were, on the whole, "unmasked." But deceit did not affect the legitimacy of the new regime: those who already believed in the Soviet system were not shaken by such violations of a bourgeois concept (that popular sovereignty means binding election results); and skeptics were not convinced by the freedom to choose village authorities that they would really be governing themselves under Soviet rule. What happened most frequently during committee elections was that outcasts and radicals (i.e., individuals with prison records or the socially marginal), unskilled, landless farm laborers, and teenagers (the minority youth) were put forward and placed in charge of the village in spite of the open scorn and disrespect of their neighbors.[140] Here and there organized criminal bands deliberately joined the militias in order to plunder with impunity.[141]

This peculiar recruitment pattern to the new administration had an important symbolic consequence. The state in a peasant society has always been a distant and hostile force. Its agents appeared only to collect taxes or to enforce laws that were quite often incomprehensible or contrary to local customs. But even though they were exacting and severe, state representatives customarily carried themselves with a certain dignity, wearing uniforms or city clothes and putting on an air of importance and formality. And so one yielded to this superior force as one yields to fate or to the elements, paying tribute to those higher in the social hierarchy. But bending to the will of social inferiors—youths and ruffians, shabbily dressed and unkempt—added insult to injuries that the peasant community had suffered since the very beginning of Soviet occupation.

CRIMINALS IN THE NEW ADMINISTRATION

A Polish underground report destined for the London government stated, with perhaps some slight exaggeration, that security (i.e., the absence of crime) was very good during the early days of Soviet occupation because criminals were absorbed in the militia and therefore "theft was practiced legally, in the line of duty."[142] The charge about common criminals staffing the Soviet-sponsored administration is repeated frequently, but the witnesses' obvious prejudice against Soviet-imposed rule forces us to investigate it with special care. In general, three kinds of arguments can be brought forth in support of this claim: a doctrinal point; personal information about individual militia- and committeemen; and the record of their behavior, especially during early months of the new rule.

The doctrinal point is straightforward. A bourgeois state, this instrument of repression honed to perpetuate capitalist exploitation of the toiling masses, keeps its class enemies in prison. Even common criminals belong to this category, for why should it be a crime to violate unjust laws or to take something from a well-to-do person who had obtained it by exploiting the proletariat? "Criminals" are no more than victims of class domination; they have been driven to crime by the living conditions created under capitalism. Thus, *a prison record in a bourgeois state indicates that one had been either a class enemy of the bourgeoisie or its victim.* Either is a good enough recommendation for inclusion in the administrative organs of the Soviet state, which, after all, intends to impose a dictatorship of the proletariat over the bourgeoisie.

Also, by the time of the September 1939 Polish campaign, Soviet penological practice included the widespread use of common criminals to police and terrorize political prisoners in labor camps (see Solzhenitsyn's *Gulag*, for example). Even within the Soviet Union itself, authorities apparently found them more trustworthy than the so-called *sotsialno-opastnyi element* (socially harmful people), as the euphemism for political prisoners put it. And from the point of view of Soviet practices as well as Soviet law, *everyone* in the newly occupied territory was potentially "socially harmful" simply by virtue of having lived in a capitalist state for twenty years after the October Revolution.

Thus, neither in doctrine nor in experience were there any impediments to assigning custody of an area to an administration staffed largely by criminals, particularly since these new cadres were readily available. The Red Army liberated prison inmates from many a jail along the route of its victorious march. Even though political prisoners had a distinct status in Polish prisons, the liberators made no effort to discriminate and keep common criminals locked up. Indeed, the latter got wind immediately of what was going on and commonly claimed that they had been sent to prison in prewar Poland primarily for political reasons.[143]

Another kind of evidence that cannot be ignored consists of numerous detailed and intimate identifications of militiamen and village committee members by their neighbors, who also disclosed their criminal past. Some caution is of course necessary here. But provided we remain sensitive to figures of speech in witnesses' statements (which often lump together those who were punished or persecuted for their political activities with the common criminals), we acquire reliable evidence about many an individual's biography. The simple fact is that in small communities people knew each other very well, and one could hardly have kept anything of importance that happened in one's life from being known all around. Hence we have to give credibility to very specific information whenever linguistic misunderstanding can be ruled out, especially since such testimony abounds in all corners of the occupied territories:

> As the gmina voyt [gmina Wołowiczowce, Augustów county] served Józef Proński from village Kadysze, who was imprisoned for six years for the murder of Michał Mieszczański during a robbery. A thief from my village, Bronisław Sadkowski, became militia commander—he was four times imprisoned for stealing with a criminal band and for taking speculators across the border into Lithuania. As deputy commander of the militia they appointed a thief, well-known in this area, named Mieczysław Zaniewski, who was imprisoned several times. In general the Bolsheviks put in office those who had served prison terms in Poland—why they would call to service people of such reputation, I do not know. Maybe they came from such a caste themselves, or perhaps they thought that only such Poles would serve them faithfully and fulfill their orders.[144]

In a list of some thirty names a forester from Sieniawka (Nieśwież county), Szymon Kucharenko, sketches profiles of supporters of the Soviet authorities in his town. Several are identified as communist sympathizers who had been jailed for distributing leaflets or for trying to cross the border illegally into the USSR. But several names on his list belong to thieves and murderers, including "a participant in the killing of a policeman's brother-in-law" and several others whose infringements of the law are described with similar pedantry. "The militia," a former Polish policeman from Trembowla is eager to assure us, "was organized from common criminals personally known to me." In gmina Pańszówka (Czortków county) the following had joined the militia: a thief who had spent four years in prison; two men who had stolen from a farm and were sentenced to two years and to one and a half years, respectively; a robber with a four-year sentence on his record; and a man sentenced to four years for beating a construction worker. A shoemaker from Sokal reveals that the local militia commander had a prison record for theft and cheating in a card game.[145] And so on, including Andrzej Stelmach, Mikołaj Kuziow, and Bazyli Bojczuk in

Jarosławice (Tarnopol voivodeship); August Borowik from Borki and Adam Szeremiet from Śwież (Nowogród voivodeship); Wasyl Pałasiewicz from Złotkowice (Lwów voivodeship); Józef Daciw, Gragon Biernacki, and Mikołaj Zarzycki in Krużyki; Paweł Mocze-lewski in Modzele Stare; Aleksander Sołowiej in Supraśl; and many others, whose names can be safely condemned to oblivion without impoverishing the historical record of these times.[146]

The final point, and perhaps the most significant, is the militiamen's behavior as petty criminals—thieves, to be exact. The importance of this evidence goes far beyond mere proof of the widespread presence of criminals in the Soviet-sponsored administration. One is bound to conclude that thievery, or the appropriation of material objects for personal use while on duty in the militia, was officially sanctioned. A farmer from Kowel county said as much in his testimony: "Agitators went to poorer folks trying to persuade them to sign up for the so-called village militia and they promised good remuneration and that *free of charge they will be able to take grain, meat, as well as other things from neighboring estates and wealthier peasants*" (emphasis mine).[147] Voluminous evidence proves that this advice was imple-mented all over the occupied territory.

What does this evidence reveal about the nature of Soviet authority? Can this behavior be fitted into a comprehensive interpretation of the regime, or is it an accidental quirk deserving no more than fleeting mention? Sanctioned robberies took place on a monumental scale throughout the occupied territories during the first weeks of the new administration. They were committed not only in the context of taking over and dividing larger estates, or church property, or government buildings, but also in hundreds of thousands of face-to-face encounters between militiamen and individual inhabitants of these territories.

Virtually every dwelling, for example, was subjected to search, alleg-edly for weapons, and often more than once. A group of militiamen, sometimes accompanied by a Soviet official or some soldiers, would take over the searched premises for a period of time, usually at night, and wreck the place and intimidate the occupants. The head of the household, or sometimes all in the family, might be ordered to go into one room or to stand facing a wall while the functionaries went around the house carrying away whatever struck their fancy.[148] Many were severely beaten after answering negatively to the initial request to sur-render weapons that they did not have.[149] And then they had to watch helplessly as their house was plundered.

"There were daily searches for weapons and suspect articles. After each search lots of things were missing; they were taking whatever they could lay their hands on, so that after a few visits closets were emptied of clothes, and rooms of furniture."[150] A worker from Kobryń complained that "in my house a search was made every two weeks, which meant that my apartment was looted every two weeks, not to speak of my pride and feelings."[151] Jadwiga Łącka's house in Łuck was searched over twenty times in the period between September 1939 and February 1940, when her entire family was finally deported to the Soviet interior.[152] The spoliation people suffered repeatedly could not even be called thievery, as a peasant from Żelazowszczyzna rightly remarked, "because they took anything they wanted, with their superiors watching, and we couldn't even complain."[153] Victims were frequently humiliated even further by being forced to sign a statement that nothing had been taken from the house during a search.[154] After a fruitless search for weapons in a peasant's house in Staniewicze, a Soviet officer took the man's horse instead. When the peasant requested a receipt, he was laughed at scornfully and told, "I can take *you* without a receipt as well."[155]*

Searched premises were frequently left in a ruined state: floors were ripped up or stoves destroyed in a deliberate mockery of a thorough inspection. Personal possessions and documents (ID cards, for example) were routinely confiscated: "They took everything, beginning with Polish books and ending with tiny photographs, which were later torn to pieces and burned down in the marketplace."[156] Any accumulation of goods fell prey to the militiamen's greed, and the complaining owner could be threatened with arrest on suspicion that he

---

* Józef Naruszewicz from Glinówka (translated Mudhole; gmina Słobódka, Brasław county, Wilno voivodeship) tells a story about a radio. It is very typical, I believe, of a mild form of expropriation practiced at the time. "For illustration I will tell you how a lamp-radio was taken from a wealthier peasant living in a village next to mine. One day a militiamen came to his house and told him to surrender his radio so that foreign broadcasting stations could be blocked on it. When the peasant refused, he said he would give him a receipt so that he could demand its return. The peasant agrees. He keeps waiting and waiting, but he is not getting his radio back. So he finally goes to the militia commander who tells him, 'You should be pleased that nothing else was taken from you, and the radio, comrade, you will see no more.' But the peasant persists and somehow discovers that his radio is now kept by a certain Soviet officer. He goes to him and shows him the receipt proving that the radio is his property. The officer threatens him. But the peasant persists and says that he will denounce him to higher authorities. Then the officer calls the militia commander and together they implore the peasant to sell his radio. So, seeing that he will not win against them, the peasant agrees and sells his 3–lamp radio of the Elektrit brand for 200 rubles. In this way they took from people many precious things for free, because nobody dared to claim them since it was very difficult to get them back and one would only betray oneself as an enemy of the Soviet regime" (HI, PGC, 9926).

was a black marketer. A surplus, militiamen argued, was certainly acquired by exploitation and therefore did not rightfully belong to its owner. A butcher from Hancewicze, for example, was forced to sign a self-incriminating statement while two members of the town militia robbed him of personal possessions. Just as cattle or land were taken away from well-to-do peasants, so in the name of equality might ordinary people be deprived of all but their last pair of trousers.[157] But deep down they considered themselves lucky, for as the Soviet officer's laughing remark showed, their freedom, or even their lives, could have been taken away just as easily.

TASKS OF THE NEW ADMINISTRATION

As soon as the new village committees and militias were in place, they had their hands full. The execution of all the assignments pressed on them required long hours, particularly since many police measures were routinely carried out under NKVD supervision at night. In addition to enforcing the emergency regulations issued by the occupation authorities, the new administration helped to plan urgent, sweeping arrests that in fact aimed to decapitate the local society through detention of all its elites. A forester from gmina Zaostrowicze put it in one sentence: "In the first place they arrested the Roman Catholic priest, the school principal, and the voyt."[158] The list, though short, is highly symbolic and to the point: the soul, the mind, and the conduct of daily affairs in the community were thus stripped of guidance. Although arrests were, so to speak, community-specific, their general direction is shown in this brief quotation. Teachers, particularly school principals, were vulnerable everywhere, as were policemen and top functionaries of the local administration. Judges and public prosecutors, activists and prominent members of political organizations or voluntary associations, landowners and businessmen, leaders of the Ukrainian community, officers (even reservists), sometimes also state pensioners, or scouts—all went to jail.[159] Scores of priests were arrested, though not without occasional (and sometimes effective) opposition from their parishioners.[160]

The bigger the town, the more complete the list of those arrested immediately. In Białystok, for example, all walks of society were swept up, and people were mixed together who surely never expected to meet anywhere, least of all in a prison cell:

On the first day they arrested the town's mayor, Seweryn Nowakowski, the deputy mayor, K. Piotrowski, who died in jail two

61

months later, the chief judge of the district, Ostruszko, the chief prosecutor, as well as all judges and deputy prosecutors, court clerks, employees of the voivodeship office, police functionaries, officers, etc. On the next day the following were arrested: the party leadership of the SN [National Democratic party], the NPR [National Workers' party], the OZN [Camp of National Unity], the Bund [Jewish Socialist party], and other parties. Then it was the turn of politically and socially prominent citizens, teachers, priests, capitalists, merchants, upperclassmen from high schools, etc.[161]

Arrested or not, people lost all privacy. A Soviet soldier might at any time enter anyone's house, ask for something to eat and drink, and then strike up a conversation or sit down to a game of chess or dominoes. Likewise, a militiaman or a politruk could (and did) walk into an apartment, look around, ask a few questions, and stay a while.[162]

Of course, the authorities did not find everyone they might have wanted to arrest. Polish society was in the middle of a calamity, subjected to the swiftest and most devastating military campaign in its history, which sent millions of citizens on the road, fleeing from somewhere or looking for somebody or something. One could easily get lost or, willingly or not, *be* lost in the midst of this confusion.

In order to sort matters out, to supply the steadily increasing contingent of the Red Army, and to set the stage for implementation of the promised social revolution, the new authorities issued a number of regulations. Some of them were simple and familiar enough, characteristic of virtually any emergency legislation—a dusk-to-dawn curfew, for instance, or surrender of civilian-held weapons. More generally, they appealed for calm and urged the population to continue with normal life and activity. It was forbidden to change one's domicile or to travel without official authorization, and everyone was required to return to work. Store owners in particular were obliged to open for business and continue selling their merchandise at prewar prices. Further, it was generally forbidden to give shelter to strangers—"Polish officers" and policemen were specifically singled out as pernicious elements who should be surrendered to the authorities—or to assemble in public places (three people walking together might be considered an assembly). In some localities, variations on these broad general orders confined people to their homes or farms and forbade them to move around the village at all or to meet with neighbors.[163] Or an ordinance prohibiting food sales might be issued, directing that only the village committee could buy from individual farmers.[164]

Then there was a host of additional, locally binding ordinances, some of which, however, were widespread enough to suggest they were part of a preconceived plan. Thus, the appearance, outside and inside, of private and official buildings was regulated by two separate ordinances: one urged the population to take down official portraits and symbols of Polish statehood and the other, to decorate houses with red banners.[165] In several localities radios were confiscated or registered, or residents were warned not to listen to foreign broadcasts.[166] In some villages people were told to get rid of all books and periodicals in the Polish language; school libraries were similarly purged, and heaps of the sequestered printed materials were then burned.[167]

In Łapy (Wysokie-Mazowieckie county), "on the premises of the Railwaymen's Labor Union they [the Soviets] burned banners of the PPS [Polish Socialist party], the TUR [Society of Workers' Universities], and the Women's Club. When asked what was the meaning of all this, they said that when an organization will become deserving it would receive a Soviet banner. And the flags that were burned have served the bourgeoisie."[168] In Wilamów (Łomża county), residents had to surrender all ID cards, while in Jedwabne the head of each household had to report daily to the local militia. In Mołodeczno and Zabłudów, it was forbidden to ring the church bells; in Poniatycze, the surrounding woods were declared off limits to local residents. In Rudki, people had to surrender bicycles and in Nowa Wilejka, typewriters. In Rokitno (Sarny county), "a few days after their arrival, they collected sewing machines, allegedly in order to set up a large factory. When they had already assembled a lot, they shipped them all to Russia."[169] Finally, it ought to be said that all existing organizations were immediately disbanded and their files confiscated.[170]

Altogether these early tasks were imposing, and because the stunned population would not or could not comply with them expeditiously, it had to be disciplined—sometimes shot, more frequently arrested, but most of all "written down." That is, people's names were recorded by the authorities for some future, unspecified retaliation. In addition, the Red Army had to be kept supplied. And, in partial fulfillment of the famous revolutionary slogan "Land and Freedom," land had to be distributed to the people.

ARMY REQUISITIONS AND EARLY LAND DISTRIBUTION

Even before village committees and militias were set up, the Red Army availed itself of all the supplies it could take from the land in the

Western Ukraine and Belorussia. The fate of peasants' horses is already familiar. But other items were requisitioned as well.

> Our estate [Krzeszone] was near the main road so that the "red visitors" were with us virtually all the time. With pointed rifles they sprawled all over the buildings, and took everything. . . . We were plundered around the clock. They took grain, hay, horses, cows, and all the equipment, as well as household items.[171]

Not only was the boundary between plunder and requisition imprecise—passing outfits continuously resupplied without paying or leaving receipts for future payment—but estates were de facto placed outside of the law. Indeed, making them "lawless" seemed to be part of the transition to new rule. But individual peasants did not fare much better. Army trucks would pull into the farm, fill up with goods, and depart without so much as a thank-you. And this went on for days. No property was exempted from supplying the victors, but a volunteer militia in a village could direct the Soviets to a specific address, usually a Polish colonist, and have him plundered before anyone else. Within a few days, much of the village committees' work was to coordinate the Red Army's early requests and to make sure that they were fulfilled by setting quotas among the residents for whatever the Soviets wanted from a village.[172]

There was no reprieve from mandated deliveries. Households that did not have the items demanded had to buy them and send them to the army. "When we went to the authorities complaining that a lieutenant went around and took away our hay and the best horses, we were told that everything belongs to the state and he therefore has a right to take things from us."[173] In Bogdanowo (gmina Głębokie, Dzisna county) Polish colonists were forced to bring food supplies to the Red Army in wagons decorated with a red flag and to sing songs to the accompaniment of an accordion while making deliveries. In Horodyszcze the gmina committee, undoubtedly to systematize the handling of requests for foodstuffs, ordered that all supplies from estates and larger farms be brought to the committee, which then issued rations to individual households.[174]

Along with the transfer of property from the local population to a newly arrived Soviet organization (such as the Red Army) or to individual Soviets (e.g., soldiers), a redistribution of property *within* the local population also took place in these early days of the occupation. We have already discussed one of the procedures applied for this purpose, namely, house searches by village militias. But direct land distribution was practiced as well, although not systematically and in a rather haphazard way, which permits us to view it as a ritual, didactic, and symbolic gesture rather than a step in a long-term policy that the authorities had determined in advance. Indeed, what they had really decided was to eradicate the landowning peasantry and to collectivize agriculture, a policy that any well-informed observer would have recognized at the time from the record in the Soviet Union proper.[175] In the first weeks, or few months at most (by February 1940 the propaganda campaign on behalf of collectivization was in full swing), the Soviets moved ahead with land redistribution not so much to appease the peasantry as to involve it with the new authority and to create havoc in the countryside.

All over the Western Ukraine and Western Belorussia landowners, well-to-do peasants, colonists, and their families were chased out of their properties—lucky to escape alive—and much of the forcibly vacated land was promptly divided among residents of neighboring villages.[176] These expropriations were, in a way, the tail end of the outburst of class and ethnically motivated violence that had spread throughout the countryside. They were perhaps more deliberately managed by the newly arrived Soviet organizers than all the other manifestations of this otherwise spontaneous *jacquerie*, with mock trials of landowners staged in front of their farmhands, for instance.[177]

Yet, despite riding on the crest of deeply felt, freshly released resentments, the new authorities repeatedly failed to win the confidence of the local people. Landownership is perhaps the single most important matter to the peasantry, and the Soviets executed their land redistribution in such a way as to raise people's doubts that it was meant seriously. Someone—a militiaman, or a committeeman from the village, or a Soviet official who came especially for the purpose—would walk a number of steps over the property of the church or of a landowner, mark the limit with a stone or a peg, and assign this patch to a peasant. If the peasant asked for more land, the official would simply add a few paces before measuring another plot for the next person. An estate might be divided by a visiting official "from this tree to that pile of stones" for village A, "up to that hill" for village B, and so on. Then each village would move onto the assigned patch of land to divide it among individual families, and for days the interested candidates would drive in pegs to mark the plots they claimed for themselves and remove those already planted by others.[178] Maksymilian Hubert, the school principal from Ostapie (Skałat county), remembered such a scene:

> In front of the gmina seat hundreds, and probably even thousands, of wooden pegs were being prepared. I wondered what they were for? Soon the matter cleared up—the whole council *in*

corpore walked over to the landed estate and began to divide the property for the "poor ones," using pegs to mark the boundaries between individual plots. But it was Sysyphus' labor because some people apparently decided that they had a better use for these pegs and went into the fields with sacks to take them away. They were excellent firewood.[179]

Many peasants, sometimes entire villages, refused to participate in land distributions. In Suchowce (Zbaraż county) an NKVD man threatened the assembled villagers that those unwilling to take shares of the nearby estate would be prosecuted as counter-revolutionaries. In Zydaczów, after the enthusiasts of agrarian reform had received their share, so much land was still left for distribution that even "town merchants and coachmen" were ordered to take some under threat of deportation if they declined the offer.[180]

One wonders whether the underlying motive for redistribution by coercion was not to have as much acreage as possible under cultivation and thus susceptible to the immediate collection of tax in kind. In any case, individual farming was not meant to last long under Soviet rule in the Western Ukraine and Western Belorussia. Very early, the new gmina and county authorities began registration of the peasantry in three categories according to farm size. Simultaneously, a detailed registration of all material property owned by peasant households was begun, as well as compulsory accounting and restrictions on its use for individual consumption. Within days the items that farmhands and willing peasants had been encouraged to plunder from estates or colonists—livestock, household inventory, lumber, and furniture, for example—were carefully traced to individual peasant households and confiscated by the village or gmina committee. Afraid for their property, many peasants slaughtered livestock and, skeptical about benefiting in the future from the fruits of their labor, refrained from planting winter crops.[181]

There are no reliable data on the scope of these early expropriations. Some statistics were printed in the official press, but I doubt their accuracy. According to *Pravda* (October 21, 1939), 2,654 landowners had their property confiscated in Nowogród voivodeship. At the end of November *Czerwony Sztandar* claims that 67,718 hectares had been distributed in Stanisławów voivodeship (November 24, 1939) and 213,000 hectares in Tarnopol voivodeship (November, 30, 1939). On November 26, *Pravda* reported that 717,000 hectares were distributed in Lwów voivodeship. The reason for such discrepancies between voivodeships is impossible to determine now.

SELF-SUBJUGATION

Notwithstanding the official rhetoric of liberation, the occupiers' plan was to have the population subdued, not enfranchised, as early as possible. But the wisdom of the Soviet regime had been that *the population must subdue itself* and that with a little encouragement it generally would. There were deep enough conflicts within most communities to assure that those who had suffered in the past would gladly take the opportunity for revenge. As we have seen, the Soviet organizers of village elections in fact encouraged such reversals of power, favoring the poorest peasants in the village or candidates of non-Polish nationality. And after the first days of occupation, with killings confined to the basements of militia headquarters and outright robbery replaced by confiscation, expropriation, and stealing in the line of duty, the arbitrariness of power was employed as a preliminary phase of sovietization to bring the fear of fellow human beings into every community, eliminating its leaders, depleting its material base, and undermining its moral cohesion. Upon returning to gmina Pulmo from the Lwów meeting of the National People's Assembly of the Western Ukraine, a representative informed his constituency that all colonists had been placed under the authority of the village committee, "which can do with them whatever it wants."[182] And the former secretary of the village committee from Maczkowce (Łuck county), Józef Popławski, reveals that committee heads and secretaries were instructed during the first gmina conference to shoot anyone who disobeyed or ignored the orders of the village committees.[183]

It is important to understand that this situation of random violence was not the exception but the rule; nor did it result from abuse of authority. It was instead a routine mode of operation condoned, if not encouraged, by the Soviet overseers. "Whoever took up weapons became a militiaman," complained a former Polish policeman from Kołomyja, undoubtedly offended in his professional pride.[184] "The power of the militia was undefined," observed a blacksmith from Michałowo, "they could do whatever they wanted, while a man's life depended on their whims."[185] The range of the militia's arbitrariness stretched from the mere inconvenience they might choose to inflict on their prey, such as denying them the right to buy foodstuffs in local stores, to beating them up during a house search or, for instance, having someone's house dismantled brick by brick and then sold (a certain Dereza's house in Maków was thus sold by the local committee to the village committee in Radziechów for 3,000 rubles).[186]

The new authorities allowed unusually open access to its enforcement apparatus—so open, in fact, that it was soon judged counterproductive. On October 2, 1939, the leadership of the Lwów militia issued an order "to prevent robberies from stores and individuals as well as unauthorized searches, arrests, and requisitions . . . by people who act on their own as if they were representatives of the workers' militia." The order threatened such individuals with the severest of penalties and commanded militiamen to apprehend them. But in the very same sentence it also appealed to the town's population "to track, detain, and deliver to neighborhood precincts of the workers' militia all who disturb revolutionary order and peace in the city."[187] Even as an inadvertent contradiction, the statement shows persuasively that anyone could be an enforcer for the new regime and that in fulfillment of this role one was welcome to rely on hunches.*

The helplessness of local inhabitants was compounded by the drastic shrinking of their world. A student of Lwów University who visited a small village in Tarnopol voivodeship relates:

> There was no appeal from the decisions of the village council. And there were basically no orders from the Soviet authorities either, or in any case they were not announced to the public nor did the administrative organs such as village councils or committees refer to any ordinances presumably issued by a superior Soviet authority. At most, as I remember, the village head would say that a "politruk" told him to do what he was doing.[188]

There was no appeal beyond the village. This was admittedly a voluntaristic system, and it could easily go awry.

Whenever the personal satisfaction of individuals serves as the principal motivation for their behavior, a sort of market is established, and with it opportunities for exchange. The population of the Western Ukraine and Western Belorussia suffered terribly because there were no rules binding on authorities, but it could occasionally, when circumstances permitted, buy preferential treatment. Karp Serwaczyński, militia commander in Wiktorówka (Kowel county), told arrested colonists that they could buy release for 1,000 złoty each. One fortunate man and "a few other colonists who paid the ransom were let go;

---

* Describing the first year following the creation of the Soviet secret police in December 1917 (originally known as the Extraordinary Commission, or Tcheka for short), an American historian of the Russian revolution notes that "there were offices of the Tcheka which established themselves in different regions. People who wanted to persecute former bourgeois, to confiscate their property, etc., constituted themselves into the Tcheka. There was very little direction or surveillance of their activities from the capital" (Malia, *Comprendre la Revolution russe*, p. 147).

others stayed in jail, and I don't know what happened to them in the end."[189] Prices differed, of course. In Lwów militiaman Mikołaj Rusin requested 2,000 American dollars and 15,000 rubles from the Petrykiewicz family for release of the head of the household. It was well known that militiamen in Lwów could be bought. The Radziechów militia ran regular truck transportation to Lwów, hauling passengers as well as merchandise for handsome fees. A Łuck physician noted that criminals in the local militia acted so brazenly that much of the original personnel soon had to be dismissed.[190]

I suspect that corruption of the new state employees was frowned upon by their Soviet superiors not because it undermined bureaucratic fairness and the objectivity of the apparatus but rather because it introduced a marketlike reciprocity into the relationship of subordinates to state authority, which was meant to be arbitrary and capricious. Corruption represented, in fact, an unwanted improvement rather than a deterioration in the new administration's performance, since it allowed for calculation and predictability and therefore diluted terror.

Thus a small-town teacher's simple comment about this situation— that "chaos and bribery" ensued when people without proper qualifications were put in charge[191]—may be adequate as a description but not as an explanation. If one looks upon chaos and bribery simply as inadvertent and unanticipated consequences of some attempt to institute social justice, then one is bound to dismiss the Soviet experiment in rapid social engineering as a demonstration of incompetence. But seen instead as a stage in the subjugation of the local people to a new, distant, and absolute authority, this is a perfectly sensible and functional strategy that very shortly results in a weakening of the community bonds around which resistance would be likely to crystallize against impending measures. The complaint of a policeman's wife from Łodziszki (Wilejka county) expresses the heart of the matter quite well:

> An especially difficult situation was that of a common man, accus
> tomed to legal order and state-imposed hierarchy, since there was
> no organized administration or even clear instructions as to what
> to do. Nobody knew whom to obey, since different, often contra
> dictory orders were being issued by word of mouth by different
> commissars, NKVD men, the militia.[192]

"No ordinances were communicated to the general public," remembers a woman from Grodno, "nobody knew what was allowed, life was completely changed."[193]

CHAPTER ONE

DURING those beautiful autumn days of 1939 the role of the state was instantly revolutionized in the Western Ukraine and Western Belorussia: from a routine, dull, and predictable bureaucratic instrument, it became arbitrary and capricious. Worse still, it no longer attempted to shield its subjects from violence; on the contrary, it now meted out violence against them. Whenever influence was for sale, arbitrariness could be mitigated by the law of supply and demand; but in any case it was always a spotty "market," subject to frequent intervention from the outside.

Rendering people incapable of knowing what is allowed and making them experience their lives as "completely changed" was precisely the Soviet administration's aim, and it invented a remarkably simple and economical device to this end: each community was to undermine its own cohesiveness, being therefore overpowered not from without but from within. This enabled the regime to ignore, or at least postpone, resolution of the critical shortage of qualified manpower, while the community was simultaneously deprived of the opportunity to consolidate against an external threat. If there is a meaning to the concept of revolution, at least as practiced by Soviet communists, it certainly must include this awesome characteristic: the induced self-destruction of a community.

TWO

Elections

THE TURMOIL of the first weeks following the invasion had not yet begun to recede when another completely novel experience was introduced into the Western Ukraine and Western Belorussia: elections. Indeed, during the twenty months following the establishment of Soviet authority, the inhabitants of what was soon to become the westernmost part of the Soviet Union got a heavy dose of electoral politics. They had three opportunities to elect representatives during that brief interlude, including two elections crammed into the first six months of occupation (October 1939 and March 1940).[1] The most significant and the best remembered took place on Sunday, October 22, 1939, and produced the National (People's) Assemblies of the Western Ukraine and of Western Belorussia.

Officially, preparations for the October 22 elections began on October 4, when the Military Councils of the Ukrainian and Belorussian Fronts issued appeals to carry out elections for the two National Assemblies. But secret clauses in the 1939 Soviet-German treaties leave no doubt that full incorporation of the Soviets' partition of Poland had been decided well in advance. Thus, just in case the Western powers hastily sued for peace and another *Pax Germanica* on Hitler's terms was established in Europe, it was important for the Soviet leaders to cast their territorial conquest in the respectable guise of a plebiscitarian change of sovereignty. They did not want either to be drawn into war or to be taken for Hitler's allies.[2] There was also an internal reason to move ahead quickly with incorporation: the coming anniversary of the October Revolution. It was customary for Soviet Communists to celebrate great accomplishments on this festive occasion, and in 1939 they did not have to search for one. For they had already accomplished a *tour de force* of diplomacy: having set their enemies at each other's throats, they were handsomely rewarded for the trouble.

But apart from this background to the elections, the official history of how they took place, as it can be reconstructed from newspaper accounts, is somewhat mysterious. The date of the elections was communicated to the public for the first time in local newspapers of the Western Ukraine and Western Belorussia on October 6.[3] Strangely, though, despite daily detailed reports from the area, one looks in vain for any mention of the elections in *Pravda* or *Izvestia* until October 11, when a TASS dispatch in *Pravda* began vaguely, "A few days ago." The event that for a number of days would be the main preoccupation of officials in the Western Ukraine and Western Belorussia, and the most important subject dealt with in the local newspapers, escaped the attention of correspondents and editors of the main Soviet newspapers.

Without doubt, it had not yet been cleared for widespread public knowledge, and the apparent reason is uncertainty relating to events so important that they might conceivably have forced a change in the timing or overall geography of the elections. On October 10 *Pravda* carried a lead article about the conclusion of negotiations with the government of Lithuania that resulted, among other things, in the Soviets returning the city of Wilno and the neighboring area to Lithuanian sovereignty. A dispute over how to absorb the Wilno area—whether immediately with the Western Ukraine and Western Belorussia or, in the future, with Lithuania and other Baltic states—may have prevented the nationwide release of news about the forthcoming elections simultaneously with the launching of the campaign.[4] In any case, the personnel of the main electoral committees had been selected, the laws governing the elections (eight chapters and forty-seven articles) published, and local preparations and propaganda well started by the time the Soviet public was apprised of these facts.

Officially published announcements calling for elections and setting the date were signed by the Ukrainian and Belorussian front commanders, Syemyon Timoshenko and Michail Kovalov, as well as by members of their Military Councils. But according to newspaper accounts, the electoral initiative was carried by the Lwów Provisional Administration and the Białystok Provisional Administration. Each established a Committee to Organize the Elections, and, independently, each turned to the provisional administrations of other cities in their regions (Lwów in the Western Ukraine and Białystok in Western Belorussia) to ask support for their initiative. In the meantime, the organizing committees turned for help to the praesidia of the Supreme Soviets of the Ukrainian and Belorussian SSR (*Pravda*, October 11 and 12, 1939). In both cases their requests were granted and the chairman of each presidium, as well as some other members (M. S. Grechukha and Alexander Korneichuk from Kiev and N. Ia. Natalevich, N. G. Grekova, and L. P. Paikov from Minsk), were assigned to join the committees.[5] The process moved quickly. When on October 6 *Czerwony Sztandar* published a story about the Ukrainian Committee to Organize the Elections, both Grechukha and Korneichuk were already listed among its seventeen members, along with some local people who became prominent in the provisional administration and some Soviet military and security officers. The official framework of the elections conformed to the electoral law promulgated in the Stalin constitution of 1936:[6] in principle, elections were to be universal, equal, direct, and secret. Much was written in the pre-election period about the great benefits that these principles bestowed upon the population, and the enthusiasm of official propagandists should not be entirely dismissed, for the Soviet people themselves had only recently acquired these rights formally in the Stalin constitution.[7]

Much was made of the projected size of the national assemblies. As the article "About Rotten and True Democracy" in *Czerwony Sztandar* (October 8) put it, "democracy's ideal is for a nation to have as numerous a representation as possible. The more representatives there are, the better." Beyond this evocation of the virtues of direct democracy, no other theory of representative government was furnished to justify the October elections.

The organizers made certain technical arrangements for the October elections. There would be one deputy elected for every 5,000 people, and only one list of candidates would be presented to the voters in each district. Electoral districts drawn accordingly were then divided into precincts, more or less three per district (90 electoral districts in the city and county of Lwów, for example, were subdivided into 292 electoral precincts). An election commission was established in each precinct, theoretically consisting of five to seven persons (a chairman, a deputy, a secretary, and two to four members).[8] For the purposes of the pre-election campaign, however, the entire territory of the Western Ukraine and Belorussia was divided into yet smaller units, each assigned to an "agitator" responsible for the organization of propaganda.[9] The agitators' territories were deliberately small—an apartment building in a big city, or a block, or a street (as the size of the city went down), or ten peasant houses in a rural hamlet (they were therefore often called *desiatniks*, a person in charge of ten).

In theory, candidates for representative could be nominated by various collectives, such as meetings of workers, the working intelligentsia, village soviets, or the workers' militia. The only requirement for proper registration by the district electoral commissions was to show the protocol of the meeting where the candidate's name was suggested and he accepted. Yet only one name, or at most a few, appeared on each district's electoral list. As evidence from pre-election meetings shows, neither in the selection of electoral commissions nor in the designation of candidates was any local initiative tolerated. Although local people were among the organizers of the elections and partici-

CHAPTER TWO

pated in many important roles and ways, their *spontaneous* input was not welcome at this stage. They were presented with electoral commissions and with the candidates. Indeed, many were drafted to serve in one capacity or another to their surprise or against their will.[10]*

In the many districts where electoral lists carried more than one candidate, it is unclear whether only one or more than one deputy was elected to the assembly and whether, as a rule, the same candidates were presented in several districts. We shall see also that many different voting procedures were adopted in different districts, or even precincts. I am not sure how to explain this variety where one would expect uniformity. It is likely that a number of approaches to the election process were being tested and that local organizers were given considerable leeway in the fulfillment of their assignments, since they, after all, were being tested as well as the voters. Eventually, it seems, all but an unlucky thirteen candidates were elected to the national assemblies.

The Pre-Election Campaign

In a territory of about 200,000 square kilometers, mostly rural, forested, part of it covered by impassable marshes, with a sparse railroad network and roads unfit to support automobile traffic for most of the year, with a premodern peasant population uninterested in politics beyond local issues and mistrustful of outsiders, with the larger cities crowded with refugees and much of the indigenous population on the move due to mobilization and then military defeat in the September campaign—in short, in a backward country plunged in chaos, the Soviet conquerors undertook to elicit from every person eighteen years of age and older the simultaneous performance of a specific series of acts on demand. It was as if someone had planned coordinated calisthenics for a whole nation.

Before cooperating, people would at least have to be convinced that the exercise would benefit their health. The pre-election campaign was designed to suggest this, or to make it plain that abstention would be injurious. It is a wonder, but the organizers managed. On October 22, 1939, the authorities knew and monitored the whereabouts of just

* Adam Polewka, a writer who later fled to the Generalgouvernement, was visited one morning by three grim-looking Soviet officers. He was convinced that they had come to arrest him. They proceeded to interview him, checking answers against a file they had brought along. When they finished, the senior Soviet inquisitor shook Polewka's hand and announced proudly to him: "You will be a deputy to the National Assembly!" (Borwicz, "Inżynierowie dusz," p. 141).

about every adult citizen in the Western Ukraine and Western Belorussia, even provisional residents. The overwhelming majority of the population actually performed as expected, and most of those who failed to do so were identified, which means that their behavior was monitored as well.

As noted above, October 4 marks the beginning of the election campaign in the Western Ukraine and Western Belorussia. Simultaneous with the appeals of the Military Councils of the Ukrainian and Belorussian Fronts, a big rally was held in Lwów. In the spacious Atlantic cinema a dense crowd assembled to hear speeches by, among others, Nikita Khrushchev, first secretary of the Ukrainian Communist party, and Commander of the First Rank Timoshenko. The latter minced no words about the future of the occupied territories: "One of the speakers said that the concept of Western and Eastern Ukraine ought to be united into one—the Soviet Ukraine. If this is what the workers, the working people, want, then I think we don't need to bother with diplomacy—this will certainly take place."[11] And diplomacy was indeed put aside. Instead, a period of mass mobilization followed. For the two weeks before they were given the unique opportunity to express their "authentic and sovereign" will (as Andrei Vyshinskii put it),[12] residents of the Western Ukraine and Western Belorussia were ensnarled in a web of intimidation, coercion, abuse, and, more familiar, electoral palm-greasing and corruption.

The propaganda campaign started immediately in high gear. Local reporting in *Czerwony Sztandar* reveals that, besides the big event in the Atlantic, rallies were also held in factories and in the countryside, thus giving the population of every stratum an opportunity to express its ardent wish for unification with the Soviet Ukraine. "We want to lead the same life as our brothers—nations of the great Soviet Union. We want to join the friendly, brotherly family of Soviet nations," workers from Lwów's Kontakt factory concluded, as certified by the signatories of their declaration. A speaker at a meeting in the rural hamlet of Zaszkowice (Gródek county) said more or less the same: "I think that I am expressing the feelings of our entire nation when stating that we are striving to blend into one family with the great Soviet nation."[13]

This beginning of the campaign was perhaps less equivocal than its conduct in the days to come. Later the population would hear more about the Soviet constitution and less about the Soviet nation (*sic*); but the multipronged offensive, so well illustrated by the simultaneous invasion of a workplace and of a residential area and the staging of a public occasion in a movie theater, suggests the atmosphere of those days. "The pre-election mobilization was carried out by means of posters, meetings, propaganda movies, marches, and demonstrations." The speaker might have added that it was taking place in the streets, in people's dwellings, in their workplaces, at lunchtime, after they got home in the evening, and in the queues in front of ill-supplied stores. "Propaganda was so developed that, literally, not one step could be made without stumbling onto it." It pursued everyone around the clock and assaulted all the senses. Posters and slogans were displayed all over towns and, in one recorded incident, were dropped from an airplane; movie teams were dispatched around the country and staged shows even in isolated hamlets, while sketches and live tableaux added spice to pre-election meetings.[14] Audio messages followed visual displays: loudspeakers mounted in the streets of newly occupied towns broadcasted propaganda bulletins daily at full blast.[15] From a *Pravda* dispatch of October 15 we learn of a "propaganda train" (*agitpoezd*) that left Kiev the day before for Sarny, Zdołbunów, and Lwów. It carried a museum, a movie, a staff of journalists, some musicians, and a dance ensemble. By far, however, the several hundred thousand Red Army soldiers already stationed in the Western Ukraine and Western Belorussia formed the bulwark of the pre-election campaign. They, primarily, supplied the propagandists for the main event of pre-election mobilization, which was "a meeting," a gathering of usually a few dozen, but at times a few thousand local inhabitants,[16] called to hear a speech. Everyone, or almost everyone, living in the area attended a number of such meetings, and the atmosphere, frequency, and circumstances under which they were held mainly set the tone of these two weeks for the local inhabitants.

"Suddenly cities and the countryside swarmed with throngs of propagandists—mostly Red Army or NKVD lieutenants. All in leather coats or jackets."[17] "At the end of October 1939 our country was deluged with a new human wave—people we didn't know, military and civilians, who spoke Belorussian and, as it turned out, came as 'political workers' [politrabotniki] from Minsk"; "not a day passed without a rally or a meeting."[18] "Red Army agitators are doing great work," according to *Pravda* (October 19, 1939).

How many propagandists were set loose on the population of the Western Ukraine and Western Belorussia, we do not know exactly.[19] But according to witnesses, they were everywhere in abundance. This is less surprising once we realize that no special qualifications were necessary for the role. Illiteracy might be a hindrance, given that the most important task was to read aloud from a prepared text (a newspaper or the Soviet constitution). But even those wanting in reading skills might be useful to mingle with the crowd, to fake spontaneous responses following cues from the main speaker, or even simply to be visible at a gathering and thus to intimidate.

Nor were the organizers shy about "inviting" the collaboration of virtually anyone in the local population. Ideological reliability made no difference. Enough terror had been dispensed in the two weeks since the occupation to make everyone understand that refusal to contribute services suggested by the authorities would invite severe sanctions. To reinforce the message, physical intimidation and verbal threats were constantly used, though accompanied by lofty declarations and promises of a happy future. Thus, as stated above, people were drafted to serve on electoral commissions or even as candidates for deputy.

Scores of teachers were sent around to compile electoral lists (literacy was necessary to accomplish this task successfully).[20] Dependent on the state for their jobs, quite often outsiders in the community (especially in rural areas), and tainted on account of their association with awkwardly implemented Polonization, teachers were now vulnerable. In addition, they had skills that could be put to use: reading, writing, and the ability to speak in public. When they appeared at people's doors with pencil and pad to take down names and personal data and sometimes to fill out long and complicated questionnaires,[21] they seemed to be hostile intruders, agents of the occupier, poking into people's lives and exposing them to unknown dangers. Even though most were coerced to work against their will—"a teacher from the primary school in Krewo, Bondarowicz, came to write my name on the electoral list, and she cried that they force her to do it"[22]—and were undoubtedly recognized, especially by acquaintances, as acting under duress, they could not show this to everyone, partly from fear of denunciation. And so, to strangers in particular, they must have seemed like just another cog in a machine that was slowly grinding everyone into submission—which, in fact, they were. In addition, they were often called on to work as propagandists.[23]

As a rule, propagandists did not have to be creative to disseminate the message. Their function was usually to meet with the assigned group of people, check attendance to make sure everybody obliged to come was present, and then read some propaganda literature that had been distributed in advance. How alienating this role was can be realized only when we see clearly the population's resentment over compulsory attendance at these meetings and its fear of sanctions. The conscripted propagandist—in effect a hostage now pushed, now blackmailed by local Soviet- or even NKVD-affiliated organizers—

would get upset over his fellow citizens' reluctance to play along and gradually become more energetic in the fulfillment of his imposed task. He felt less and less patience and understanding for people who seemed so little concerned about *his* predicament and vulnerability. For, in the context of general terror and intimidation, such conscripted collaborators were, unlike the rest of the general populace, individually targeted and conspicuous.

There were also genuine volunteers who truly believed in the ideals the Soviet regime promised to implement in the Western Ukraine and Western Belorussia. Former members of Communist parties in Poland, the Western Ukraine, and Western Belorussia (even though past membership was a dubious credential under the Soviet administration, since the parties had been disbanded by the Komintern in 1938) and radical left sympathizers, especially among the young—thousands, if not tens of thousands of idealists were accepted by the organizers of the elections simply because every volunteer was welcome. Anyone who felt moved to speak at a public gathering could do so, even though a few days later the NKVD might find his or her leftist credentials reason enough for arrest.[24]

But as a matter of routine, rather than wait for volunteers to come forward, the Soviet authorities appointed supporters in all settings. In an apartment block in Sambor the Russian organizer distributed propaganda brochures among the local residents and assigned to each a date when he or she was to report to the group on its content.[25] In a neutral or even hostile crowd forcibly brought together, a crowd that wanted to remain anonymous and uninvolved, the organizers called on people at random to speak on the Soviets' behalf. From lists of attendance, someone might be called by name to step forward and address the meeting.[26] Forced to attend a meeting in a factory, office, or school, an unsuspecting individual might be invited to join a presidium that faced the gathering, and he might receive a few pages of text or none at all, along with information about when it was his turn to speak.[27] Thus one was suddenly brought, alone, face to face with Soviet authority and denied the opportunity to display sympathy and support autonomously. People who refused the invitation were forced by this method to declare themselves openly as enemies of the new regime. And it is very difficult, we know, to give self-incriminating evidence.

In the beginning of October a lieutenant with some civilian came along. It turned out this was an engineer from Moscow, sent here as a political worker. They told me that they wanted to organize a meeting and that because I had influence with the local people I should give a speech, in Russian. To my question why in Russian and not in Polish, they said not everybody would understand me—that is, they wouldn't, though they were in control. First I tried to talk them out of it by claiming that I did not know Russian well enough, but they had an answer—the speech was already prepared and written, all I had to do was read it. I didn't really understand at the time the consequences of my refusal to participate in the meeting, but I declined nevertheless. In the speech one had to contradict everything which for many years of my career as a teacher I was conveying to the young—well, one really had to spit into one's heart. I didn't lose anything in the end, for as it turned out later, also arrested were those who acted against their conscience in the first moment of weakness.[28]

Franciszek Syzdal, a country schoolteacher from Mołodeczno county, stood his ground and survived to tell about this experience. But many—given a very restricted choice of going to jail or serving as spokesmen—chose not to identify themselves immediately as opponents of the regime.*

To monitor everyone's behavior before and during the October elections, organizers had to inventory the population of Western Belorussia and the Western Ukraine. This they did by compiling voter lists during the first days of the electoral campaign on the basis of existing registers of inhabitants or taxpayers, which included the names of many who had died in the past year or who had been conscripted into the army.[29] These names might have passed unnoticed except that in the general campaign to overcome the resistance of the local population to the elections, the Soviets rightly suspected people of using any kind of ploy to avoid pre-election meetings or the voting itself. Thus families were constantly queried as to the whereabouts of missing relatives, for once a name appeared on the voter list, it was unlikely ever to be stricken from it. In the end, after the fashion of Soviet elections, all but a fraction of a percent of eligible voters fulfilled their duty as citizens, meaning that "also those had to vote who had died over the past year."[30]

* People were not aware yet that, as *Pravda* put it on March 25, 1930, "the Bolshevik voluntary principle" differs from the "Social Revolutionary–kulak voluntary principle" in that "pressure from the proletarian party and the advanced collective farmers . . . is a constituent element of the Leninist voluntary principle" (Davies, *The Socialist Offensive*, p. 276). Indeed, during collectivization ("voluntary" in principle), "those who did not wish to join were required [in some areas at least] to opt out in writing, and were being treated as members while their statements were being considered" (ibid., p. 222).

But written records had another, much more serious drawback: they were incomplete and lacked the names of many who had just arrived as refugees from central and western Poland, for example. To make sure that no one was missing from the rosters, swarms of "activists" were sent door to door to write down the names and addresses of all local dwellers. Refugees were added to the rosters, as well as Soviet citizens residing in any part of the area[31] and very often minors from age sixteen.[32] In Łuck, Wołyń's capital of 36,000, 62 people worked four days to complete the job (*Pravda*, October 17, 1939). Teachers, as I said before, were customarily detailed for this assignment. House superintendents or recently established house committees were sometimes entrusted with the task.[33] In a few instances voter lists were compiled under some pretext sufficiently attractive to lure people into giving their names and addresses. Some residents of Białystok were notified to sign up for winter rations of firewood, and in Przemyśl and Horochów refugees were told to apply for exit visas to return home.[34] Finally, everyone had to check in person to be sure that his or her name had indeed been put on a list.[35]

This complicated procedure of repeated cross-checking and verification was just one in a series of registrations taking place all the time for a myriad of alleged purposes. Combined, the lists provided constantly updated records for the Soviet authorities. Thus the personal information taken for voting lists was certainly collected with broader goals of population control in mind. In Terawa Solna, it seems, voter registration was undistinguishable from a routine NKVD interrogation.

> For the compilation of voter lists I walked at night, at eleven, for about two miles, and they would take down all my biography. Everybody had to go for those lists and usually at night, for a specified hour. When one went to be registered, one bid farewell to the whole family, because one didn't always come back home.[36]

In addition to organizing individuals through this massive collection of personal data, the new regime also harnessed existing social networks for purposes of mobilization. Indeed, the pre-election campaign focused on the two basic components in the life of any community—the residential neighborhood and the workplace—thereby using already constituted *groups*, which, with their self-policing potential, could effectively discipline every individual. "Landlords were ordered to march their tenants to meetings in compact groups. The whole street marched together." "Entire hamlets were marched to these meetings and rallies in compact groups, with slogans, music, and singing." "They ordered one person from every third house to conduct pre-election propaganda." "In factories they locked gates after work and didn't let anybody home, and began to organize meetings."[37]

An apartment house of ten or fewer families or a section of a village (again usually ten families) constituted the basic forum for pre-election propaganda. A house or an apartment would be selected as the site for the meeting and an announcement made of the time (usually in the evening after people got home from work.[38] The landlord or the super-intendent, or even the tenant of the selected apartment or the farmer in whose house the meeting was scheduled, might be charged with ensuring that everybody attended as ordered. There were also, though less frequently, larger public meetings in squares, theater halls, or schools.[39] But the most common propaganda unit was the neighbor-hood group and the group of workmates. In every place of work, irre-spective of meetings held later in the evening at people's residences, employees were forced to assemble during lunchtime or after work and listen to pre-election speeches.[40]

At home or at work, the names of all who belonged to the propa-ganda unit were easily available. Local enforcers or even outside prop-agandists quickly found out who was supposed to be present at every meeting, and before the program started, attendance was checked against a roster or a list had to be signed by everyone.[41] How much choice voters would have on election day still remained to be seen, but for the duration of the pre-election campaign they had practically no choice about attending the meetings.

Initially we were lured to pre-election meetings under the pretext that shoes or some other foodstuffs would be sold, but when people discovered their lies and didn't want to go anymore, they were forced to come by the local militia.*

* People were offered all kinds of inducements as a reward for participation in a meeting. In Boruny, Nowosiady (oszmiana), Zieniewicze (lida, 20), Bobrowicze (kosów poleski, 20), Horodno (luboml†, 8), and undoubtedly in many more villages, land and cattle were given to peasants on the occasion of a pre-electoral meeting. A factory store might open after a meeting (Białystok, 35) or a cooperative in a village (mościska, 18; dubno†, 19; kołomyja, 39; krzemieniec†, 20a). Candy, in great demand because of the sugar shortage, could be bought after a meeting in Włodzimierz Wołyński (HI, PGC, 6612). In Sokółka county, and also in Suraż (białostocki, 33), Łukawiec (lubaczów, 27), Wolcza-Dolna (dobromil, 22), and Wesołówka (krzemieniec, 61), people were allowed to take lumber and firewood from the state forest—but they were ordered to deliver everything to a lumber mill in Wality immediately after the elections (HI, PGC, 2982). As a high school student from Dubno wrote: "Meetings and pre-election rallies were not only obligatory but also with a trick—when a meeting went well the cooperative store was opened and people could buy matches, cologne water, shoelaces, and toys" (dubno†, 19).

Participation in pre-election meetings was compulsory; they pointed out that those not coming would be excluded from the village and the Soviet authority would take care of them. It was known that the care of Soviet authority meant prison or deportation to Siberia.

The population was called to the meetings almost every day. The electoral committee and the militia, mounted on horses, rode from house to house and every grown up had to go, or at least one per family.

A bolder one, who skipped a meeting, was written down, and on the next day a Communist visited him with questions: pochemu ty tovarishch ne biv na mitingu? Chto, tiebie nie nravitsia soviet-skaya vlast? Pomini, kto nie s nami, ten protiv nas. My takikh vrogov sovietskovo soyuza unichtozhayem. [Why haven't you been at the meeting, comrade? Maybe you don't like the Soviet authority? Remember, who isn't with us is against us. We destroy such enemies of the Soviet Union.] After these threats, willing or not, one went to the meeting because everybody was afraid of being taken to jail during the night. The Communist instructor knew well every Pole by his last and first name and his patronymic.

On the day when such a pre-election meeting was scheduled the NKVD sent a dozen of its collaborators as "catchers." Each "catcher" had to bring at least ten people to the meeting. They would hunt for voters at dinnertime, to catch as many people as possible at the dinner table, and they were quite successful.[42]

These few episodes illustrate the variety of methods used to ensure attendance at pre-election meetings. It was implied that only enemies of the Soviet state would abstain from these meetings,[43] and many people were indeed arrested.[44] Some were brought to meetings under armed escort;[45] others had to justify each absence. For example, in Taboryszki and Dywin only a doctor's certificate would do as an excuse.[46] In a Drohobycz factory, absence from a meeting had to be justified to the job supervisor, and sanctions for unauthorized absence might include dismissal from work.[47] At times the recalcitrant ones had to sign the written notices that had informed them of a meeting, in effect openly declaring themselves to be in opposition.[48] And all were constantly threatened with being put on a blacklist—an awesome, fear-inducing sanction.[49]*

* "They organized meetings very often, and who didn't go they wrote down in a black

Yet the most accurate one-word characterization of pre-election meetings that comes to mind is "nuisance." In themselves, the meetings were rather inoffensive occasions.

> Pre-election propaganda began with teaching the constitution. After office hours, employees were assembled in one room, a Soviet soldier stood up and read successive paragraphs of the constitution in Ukrainian, asking from time to time *poniali* [understood]? Those present nodded their heads.[50]

In one village, "two politruks taught paragraphs of Stalin's constitution and all the benefits that it brings. During these meetings 60 percent of the peasant listeners slept, tired after a whole day of work and bored with a speech they didn't understand."[51] Indeed, very often speeches and readings were delivered in Russian or Ukrainian, which the audience did not understand.[52]

Along with the predictable readings from the constitution, one might be treated as well to improvisations on one of the propaganda meetings' other main themes: the dreadful life that Polish citizens, along with the present audience, had been living for the past twenty years, and the wonderful conditions of life and work in the Soviet Union. The latter theme offered much room for flights of imagination. But the other was a point well taken, for a substantial majority of the local inhabitants had many justified complaints of material deprivation and political discrimination suffered under the Polish administration. Yet even while recounting these matters of common agreement, Soviet propagandists managed to astonish their audiences time and again by their choice of arguments. Beata Obertyńska recalled a meeting in Lwów, her hometown, where a young man "was talking

---

book and said this is an enemy; they kept an eye on him and arrested him after a few more times" (HI, Poland. Ambasada USSR, Box 47, Helena Kitajewska; see also krzemieniec†, 19; dubno†, 20; łuck, 57). There is something highly symbolic in this seemingly marginal practice of blacklisting. It reveals, more than many central features, the kinship of twentieth-century totalitarianisms. In the heart of the Eurasian landmass in the 1930s and 1940s one's fate might be decided by a policeman, a doctor, a political worker, a member of some committee—anybody. Criteria, moreover, could be equally vague—a tired look, wounded pride, a crooked nose, or a crying child. One man singled out another, pointing at him to step left or right, writing down his name or his number. Thus ration cards for life were distributed. We might call it an extralegal procedure if one could speak meaningfully of any legality in Stalin's or Hitler's empire. But the flagrant arbitrariness in the disposition of a person's most prized possession—his life—stands out conspicuously in the spectacle of someone's name being scribbled on a piece of paper, thereby sealing his fate. One never knew for sure in the Western Ukraine or Western Belorussia of 1939 whether this meant deportation in a few months or arrest the next evening.

complete nonsense. He claimed, for example, that every count, officer, and landowner could cast six to ten votes in elections in Poland, while a peasant or a worker had no right to vote at all."[53] Similarly a speaker from the Białystok's Planning Office stated that whoever had had dollars in Poland could, proportionate to his fortune, cast more votes in elections while the poor had been disfranchised completely. Usually people paid little attention to speakers' pronouncements; but this time another sympathizer of the new regime, indignant at such nonsense, stood up from the audience and denounced the scandalous appearance of so stupid a propagandist before a group where everybody had at least a high school education (an intervention for which he later had some explaining to do).[54] Nor was this an isolated episode.[55] On the whole, however, propaganda speeches seemed to be either boring or laughable, and most listeners responded to them accordingly at first.

What made propaganda meetings so bothersome in October 1939 was primarily their duration and frequency and the sanctions for non-attendance. Every person's life was in chaos at that time. People were looking for missing relatives and friends, ways to make a living, places to hide. Preoccupied with these serious problems, they were forced every day or every other day to spend several wasted hours listening to what was basically nonsense.[56] So they stalled initially, tried to sneak away, disappear, and were subjected in retaliation to a variety of repressive measures. One might be arrested or thrown out of work for not appearing at pre-election meetings. Szereszów village in Prużana county was burned down because its inhabitants were particularly obstinate in their refusal to attend meetings. One could also be thrown out of school or forbidden to buy anything at a local store; one's cow might be taken away, or one might be ordered to deliver a quota of potatoes, meat, or hay as a penalty or to do some physical chores without reimbursement.[57] A fine was frequently imposed with, on occasion, an imaginative procedure for payment: a peasant from Orzechowiec had to pay a one-ruble fine in five-kopeck daily installments, but he had to make the payments at the county seat seven kilometers away from his village.[58] Tomasz Włodarski had an additional tax assessed against his store because he failed to appear at a meeting, and a vocational school principal from Horochów was confined to his apartment for two weeks. In Raków two unenthusiastic participants of a meeting were locked up for fifteen days because they failed to applaud after a propaganda speech. In Różki (Wołkowysk county) people were routinely clubbed for non-appearance, while in Zofiówka (Trembowla county) the windows of nonparticipants' houses were broken in reprisal.[59] *Clearly, just as they could say whatever they pleased, organizers of October elections could also do to their audiences whatever they saw fit.*

"WHAT the voting was for . . . I don't know."[60] The disarming sincerity of this peasant from Suszyca-Wielka could not be justified by pleading lack of information. The unwelcome knowledge was easily available in almost any written material, whether local newspaper, poster, or a leaflet with slogans, where the theme of unification was repeated at every opportunity. Among the thirty-five official slogans that appeared in *Czerwony Sztandar* three days before the elections were: "Chosen ones of the working people—vote for the entry of the Western Ukraine into the Soviet Ukraine, for the only free and blossoming Ukrainian Soviet Socialist Republic"; and "We will abolish forever the border between the Soviet and Western Ukraine; long live the Ukrainian Soviet Socialist Republic." "Our frontiers are inviolable," read a prominently displayed headline in the October 15 issue of *Czerwony Sztandar*. The same paper sent out a firm message along with an appeal one week before the elections.

> Mendacious and provocative rumors are being disseminated by enemies of the working masses, according to which the Red Army intends to abandon the taken-over territory of the Western Ukraine. [Presumably, the transfer of Wilno to Lithuania gave birth to these rumors.] Propagandists and agitators should explain to the local population that these and similarly slanderous rumors are completely wrong . . . the USSR's frontiers, *established in the West by a treaty with Germany*, are stable and immovable. . . . Rumors about the withdrawal of the Red Army are pure invention, provocatively designed to foment panic among the local population. [Emphasis mine]

The same issue carried a brief note about the October 13th meeting of a group of Polish writers, where Aleksander Korneichuk, a writer-politician sent from the Soviet Ukraine to supervise the Sovietization of intellectuals in the Western Ukraine, gave a speech: "After elections to the Ukrainian National Assembly, after nationalization of land and banks, after incorporation of the Western Ukraine into the USSR, we can start reorganization of the Writers' Union." No "ifs," no conditional, all in the affirmative.

But people failed to recognize the issue, and the organizers did not seem to care to draw attention to this particular point. Perhaps it was not psychologically possible for the recently conquered population to quite realize that it was being forced to *commit itself*, seemingly forever, to the custody of Soviet sovereignty. Rather, people remember a hodge-podge of propaganda catchwords that presented little but an image of chaos and confusion. There will be no more Poland, people were told repeatedly,[61] and neither France nor England ("old prostitutes") nor America ("young prostitute") will help; anyway, all of them, and Germany as well, will be conquered eventually by the Soviet Union.[62] Everything will return to what it used to be, only under Soviet protection. Today's Bolsheviks are different, unlike the ones of Revolutionary times; nowadays there are laws, and everything goes according to plan. There will be no taxes, everybody will be equal, all will be able to go to school without paying, and everyone will get land. Life will be good; sowing will be done from airplanes.[63] There are all kinds of machines in the USSR that help ordinary people:

> There are millions of factories, cars, field guns, tractors, tanks, and 665,000 combine harvesters. Soviet workers are masters, they go every year for vacation to health spas. . . . they retire at 65 and it is not true that when aged they are used for soap.[64]

They danced the tango in Poland, and in Soviet Union they made tanks.[65] Everything will be available in abundance—"sugar, salt, candies, kerosene, leather, vodka, clothes. When people asked why they hadn't brought all of this yet they said that they had to widen the railroad tracks first."[66] And before a predominantly Jewish gathering in Równe an agitator threatened that pogroms woud start again in the Ukraine unless they voted for Stalin.[67]

In the countryside people believed that they were simply voting for a deputy to the National Assembly, not for any particular issue or agenda. Many thought this was only a provisional assembly, perhaps because the word "provisional" frequently appeared in the names of official administrative organs that had been set up since September 17. A few thought they were actually voting for a "free" Belorussia or a "free" Ukraine.[68]

Consequently, the overwhelming majority of the electorate apparently did not know what was at stake during this election. Asked whether they voted on October 22 for the incorporation of the Western Ukraine and Western Belorussia into the USSR, all but a few answered an emphatic *No*. The goal, the purpose of the elections was universally unknown.[69] Somehow, despite all the exposure to pre-election propaganda, its most important message got lost. Or perhaps this was not its most important message at all? But then, what was?

The answer to this query, to anticipate somewhat, is McLuhanian: the medium was the message. People of the Western Ukraine and

Western Belorussia were being drilled into obedience. There was an external benefit in having them processed through a voting booth, allegedly expressing the will to secede. But it really did not matter what they were doing so long as they performed some coordinated action according to instructions. Indeed, what we observe from October 4 to October 22 throughout this territory is not the transfer of sovereignty from one state to another but the transfer of individual sovereignty from each person separately to a state. And this was a process that took place in installments, every time people visibly yielded to coercion and surrendered some control over their lives.

CANDIDATES

At some point during the pre-election campaign the focus shifted from general issues to a concrete task: the designation of candidates for deputy to the National Assemblies of the Western Ukraine and Western Belorussia. Usually after a few preliminary meetings, the day would come when a candidate, or sometimes only his picture, was introduced to a gathering in a given district. Since virtually any collective could sponsor a candidate, it was very often unclear whether a candidacy was actually being initiated or merely presented for approval in a particular instance. The audience itself was often confused and tried at times to exercise what it presumed was its right, only to be rebuked politely or with an admonition:

> On October 15th to my village, Pronki, Prosecutor Minkova came and ordered a meeting. During this meeting she introduced . . . I don't remember the name of the candidate and I don't know where he was from. Then one of the inhabitants of our village, Piotr Kuczyński, asked Prosecutor Minkova (she was a Soviet citizen and Jewish), whether because the candidate for deputy was unknown to us she would allow us to put forward as candidate someone we knew and respected. To this Minkova answered that the candidate had been appointed by the head of Postawy county, Captain Brykov, and that he could not be changed.[70]

Since the obscurity of candidates was their most prominent characteristic, it is easy to imagine that such conversations between propagandists and their audiences took place all over the Western Ukraine and Western Belorussia.[71]

The reluctance of the electorate to embrace the unknown was handled in a variety of ways. A certain Wicik, against whom peasants in Szczuczyn county objected because they did not know him, was ordered by the presiding politruk to climb on a table so that everybody could see him. A similar objection against another candidate in Szczuczyn county, Davidson Mikhal Abramovich from the USSR, was answered simply: "You don't know him; well, you will get to know him."[72] The people at a meeting in Łuck county asked specifically if they could name their own candidate; the Red Army lieutenant presiding pulled out a notebook and without a word read the name "Paraska Maryszczuk."[73] When the peasants of a Ukrainian village in Wołyń insisted on selecting their own candidate, both he and those who sponsored him were arrested.[74]

An episode that occurred at the Lwów Polytechnical School clearly illustrates the confusion and clash of mentalities between the Soviet organizers—unable to comprehend that anything but proper sponsorship from above could matter in assessing a candidate's credentials—and their local audience, puzzled by so brazen an insistence on an obviously fraudulent procedure. A student recalls:

> I stood up and said that I was not going to vote for this candidate and that I would like to propose another. The chairman of the meeting asked me whether I could accuse his candidate of being dishonest, of having killed somebody or stolen from anyone? I said I couldn't because I didn't know the man at all. So he told the candidate to read his biography, which he had himself written. And that is how the candidate was "elected." I didn't participate in the elections proper because I was arrested on October 18th.[75]

In hindsight we must appreciate the candor with which the election organizers approached their audiences. They did not hesitate to name the authority who had the real power to select candidates embodying the will of the people—some Captain Brykov from Postawy county, for example—or to reveal the qualities that were really sought in a nominee. The rhetorical questions asked in defense of a challenged candidate—was he a thief or a murderer?—suggest that it was relatively unimportant whether he had ability. Rather, candidates were chosen for what they had *not*, for the deprivations they had suffered. As Józef Naruszewicz from gmina Słobódka rightly noticed, there was a standard candidate biography, repeated with only minor variations: from a poor family, went to work early, worked hard, was always exploited, lacked everything.[76] In the cities, worker candidates usually had been unemployed and had a prison record to their credit.

Perhaps from a Marxist perspective one could hardly reproach such candidates. But class consciousness was as yet undeveloped among the masses of the Western Ukraine and Western Belorussia. So they were disturbed just as much, if not more, when they knew the candidates and their qualifications as when they knew them not at all.

Teofila Dorożka from Kapczany village was the candidate. She was around forty, semiliterate; she worked as a maid and had no parents since the first World War. During this propaganda, when she was introduced publicly as candidate during a meeting in Racicze village [Augustów county, Białystok voivodeship], she admitted that they had taken her from a farm where she was a cow herder and that she didn't know and wouldn't know what to say. Soviet propagandists stopped her talk then and said it's all right that she is ignorant, precisely such people are elected in the Soviet Union and they learn on the job, because they are ashamed in front of their co-workers. Teofila Dorożka was elected as deputy to Minsk.[77]

Apparently there was not enough time to choose appropriate candidates and coach them sufficiently so that they would not publicly embarrass their sponsors. In Drohobycz (Lwów voivodeship) another poor girl stood for a while in front of a crowd, bewildered and blushing, then ran off stage in tears crying, "ta shcho si one mene chepyly, shcho one vid mene khochut [why do they bother me, what do they want from me]."[78] When a candidate in Horodziej (Nowogród voivodeship) got so frightened on stage that she could not utter a word, an NKVD man filled in with a speech claiming that she had a sore throat.[79] These were local women, known to the audiences all their lives, and many such instances occurred all over the Western Ukraine and Western Belorussia.

The organizers had a standard answer to audiences' objections that the candidate was an ignoramus: "We will teach her all she needs to know."[80] At a meeting in Brasław county (Wilno voivodeship) a Mr. Kowalewski spoke everyone's mind: "You are on purpose selecting idiots for candidates so that they will merely appear as names on a list." He was arrested.[81] Scores of candidates were thus known and held in contempt for their low status and lack of respectability.[82]

But the electorate of the Western Ukraine and Western Belorussia was even more daringly challenged. Along with the unknown (many of whom could only be identified as recently arrived Soviet citizens)[83] and the unqualified, individuals with criminal records were presented as candidates and defended in a patronizing way when challenged.[84] This is not at all surprising, given what we already know about the composition of the village committees and the militias. Also among the candidates were scores of prewar Communists who had served time in

CHAPTER TWO

Polish jails during the interwar period.[85] But at the beginning of the Soviet occupation many people claimed to have been jailed by Polish authorities as proof of political persecution under capitalism. The resulting confusion makes it difficult now to distinguish common criminals from former political prisoners. Nor does it help that local inhabitants frequently spoke of Communists who had spent time in jail before the war simply as criminals with prison records. Still, in the midst of these linguistic confusions and deliberate misrepresentations, one can find enough unambiguous evidence about people's identities. When they did not speak in slogans, neighbors could describe what had been going on in their communities, and they knew very well who was who. During a meeting in Włodzimierz Wołyński, for example, "a local thief, released from prison during the war, was one of the candidates. When some bolder person said so . . . the Soviet in charge said that he had to steal because there was hunger in Poland. Everybody laughed because they knew that he was stealing chickens."[86] During a meeting in another part of the country, near Świr (Wilno voivodeship), "one of the peasants, Michnowicz, stood up and said that [the candidate] Kuźma Sobolew stole from his cart a bagful of oats on a market day in Świr and, on some other occasion, a cover from his horse, and that other peasants had similar complaints. To this the politruk replied kindheartedly that this will not repeat itself and that Kuźma will steal no more."[87]

Whether Kuźma, or Kalitka in Kiwerce (Łuck county), Tararuk and Gajda in Dubno county, Wiktor Bajda in Hołoby (Kowel county), Andrzej Szubka also from Kowel county, Józef Pałacki from Mołodeczno county, or Proskurniak from Kołomyja county—people knew them and could not be fooled about their abilities.[88] To be fair, the organizers did not even attempt to do so. They simply invoked *diamat*—the rule of class exploitation—and dismissed objections as invalid on the grounds that the candidates were only victims of an unjust society. But this explanation literally added insult to injury, because most members of these audiences were poor peasants themselves, who also eked out a miserable living, but without stealing or robbing anyone. They knew that a thief is a thief, and anybody who told them otherwise was either ridiculous or insolent. They laughed at the Soviet organizers, but deep down they knew that they were being insulted.

In a few instances, we are told, a proposed candidate did enjoy an audience's respect. Such was the case of a woman from Brześć, a rich peasant from Szczuczyn county, and a Ukrainian doctor from Brasław county.[89] But like all the other candidates, they had been appointed by

90

the organizers and were kept under close watch during appearances at pre-election meetings.

It is difficult to avoid the conclusion that considerable freedom of action was delegated to low-level supervisors from the rudimentary administrative apparatus set up during the first weeks of Soviet rule. In the larger cities, big factories, and important industrial centers, personnel matters were handled directly by some high-level authority that kept close watch over day-to-day activities to detect snags and resolve them promptly.[90] But in rural districts, heads of gminas or, certainly, county soviets, who were also frequently in charge of district electoral commissions, could choose delegates as they pleased. Some of them may have followed common sense rather than class instinct and opted for persons acceptable to their audiences,[91] especially since they knew that delegates were expendable just like anybody else. Indeed, some deputies were soon arrested.[92] But it was more or less up to Captain Brykovs to decide who would appear in Lwów's and Białystok's theaters on the 26th and 28th of October to express the will of the Ukrainian and Belorussian people.

The electoral procedure used at the nominating stage of the process was very simple and quite consistent with all the other measures of intimidation used. When the name of a candidate for deputy to the National Assembly was finally introduced during a meeting, the presiding chairman would ask only one question: "Who is against?" Typically there would be silence, and the candidate's name would be entered into the protocol as having been unanimously endorsed.[93]* This procedural detail was one of many ways in which the regime forced those who wanted to remain aside and uninvolved to step forward and identify themselves. Consequently, by being passive and anonymous, one was placed in the position of appearing to be the regime's supporter.

VOTING

As October 22 approached, people became uneasy. Mobilization for election day overshadowed all other preoccupations, not so much in the cities, perhaps, but certainly in villages with substantial contingents of Soviet activists and militia detachments.

---

* In Trembowla county a zealous propagandist decided to coach his audience in advance. He would scream the name of the candidate, then "Who is for?" or "Who is against?" and shout, dictating tempo with a hand motion "vsye" (everybody) or "nikto" (nobody). The crowd, always amused by such a spectacle, joined him in shouting "vsye" or "nikto" (HI, PGC, 3098).

Arrests, which the population interpreted as preventive measures to ensure compliance during elections, were carried out with renewed intensity all over the Western Ukraine and Western Belorussia.[94] In Skałat prison Stanisław Widomski, who was there from the beginning of October, saw scores of young Ukrainian boys brought in around the 20th as hostages to make sure their parents behaved themselves on election day. A number of socially prominent Jews, Poles, and Ukrainians, arrested one day before the elections in Międzyrzec, were ostentatiously marched through town under escort. In Andrzejewo (Ostrów county), for about two weeks preceding the elections one could not visit a neighbor's house in the evening without risking arrest for allegedly anti-electoral propaganda.[95]

Occasionally people report some let-up in tension just before the elections—fewer arrests, the re-introduction of religious instruction in schools, or an improved supply of selected consumer goods.[96] But the Soviet organizers did not really try to endear themselves to the local population. They could fake popular enthusiasm by themselves, at least in writing, as in these rhymes printed in *Czerwony Sztandar* a day before the elections: "So tomorrow, my dear Charlotte, / Meet me, honey, at the ballot," and "Every house and every hut, / Goes to choose a delegate."[97]

Voters in the Western Ukraine and Western Belorussia got up early on the morning of October 22. Voting stations opened at 6 A.M. Moscow time (i.e., at 4 A.M. locally), and there was pressure to go to the polls as early as possible. Superintendents began pounding on apartment doors at 4:00 or 4:30, urging sleepy residents to get it over with, and returned about every hour until midday, when they were replaced by militiamen who then began to check on the inhabitants.[98] In a small town in Białystok voivodeship people were ordered out of their apartments at 4 A.M. and told that the church would not open (it was Sunday) until they finished voting.[99] When a man in Równe complained at 5 A.M. that it was too early for him to vote, he was beaten with rifle butts by two militiamen who had come to remind him of his duty.[100] There is some truth, therefore, in the dispatches printed in *Pravda* that describe crowds of voters milling in the streets of Równe, Stanisławów, Białystok, Brześć Litewski, and Lwów from the early morning hours.*

* "Everybody wants to vote as early as possible," concluded chairmen of several electoral commissions observing the large gatherings of voters in front of their stations (*Pravda*, Oct. 23, 1939). They were not entirely wrong. In one of the precincts of gmina Druja the first person to vote received a 100–ruble bonus (brasław, 10); in one of Pińsk's precincts the first voter to appear was promised a choice job afterward (pińsk, 51). In

But the atmosphere of the day was not necessarily gloomy. Banners and decorations were on display, bands played in front of polling stations, and columns of people marched as on a festive day. In Równe free bread was distributed in the streets. The local priest in Janów, a familiar figure who no doubt inspired confidence, stood in front of the polling station calling his parishioners in. In Śnieżyce village a militia detachment rounded up voters to the accompaniment of a small musical band. In every other precinct there was accordion music or some such simple but pleasant entertainment, perhaps a place to dance, and certainly a good buffet.[101]

No method was rejected out of hand that might deliver the voter to the appropriate precinct. The only limitations were finite supplies of manpower and means of transportation. But somehow, enough militiamen, activists, and soldiers were found to check on virtually everyone, more than once if need be. Often people were brought by armed escort to an election precinct.[102] Transportation was available for those who could not walk. And for those who were too sick, too old, or too busy, or too forgetful and who had not shown up by late evening, the ballot box was conveniently brought to their homes, to the hospital, or wherever they might be.[103] In Wojtówka (Białystok county), about twenty horse-drawn carts with militiamen went back and forth, bringing reluctant voters to the polls.[104] "When threats were of no avail they bound people up, put them on carts, and took them to voting stations."[105] The truly recalcitrant were often arrested,[106] though even this condition did not necessarily save them from casting a ballot.*

Zambrów village, near Łomża, people were promised sausage if they voted early: "In the beginning they were giving half a pound of sausage and a handful of candies, later less, and in the afternoon nothing at all" (łomża, 63; see also jaworów, 28). Virtually all voting stations offered buffets, which had been stocked before election day so the population knew about this opportunity in advance. But it was not prudent, as the Zambrów example shows, to count on supplies lasting forever. In Lwów, in the 18th precinct of the 8th electoral district, "two men arrived together and neither wanted to let the other be the first to vote. They dropped their ballots into the box simultaneously" (*Pravda*, Oct. 23, 1939).

* Antoni Rokicki, a peasant from Ściurzyn (Łuck county), was brought by the NKVD to the basement of the building where the voting station was set up, lost a tooth in the solid beating he got there, and was then told: " 'dumaesh polskaia sobaka chto budet Polsha i ne khochesh podchiniatsia sovetskomu soiuzu iak se ne podchinish tak padokhnesh' [you think, Polish dog, that there will be Poland and you don't want to obey the Soviet Union; if you will not obey, you will croak]. With these words one of my oppressors gave me a ballot that he had filled in himself and told me to go to the room where voting was taking place and give it to the man standing next to the ballot box. This one took the ballot from me, smiled ironically, dropped it into the box, gave me a receipt

In many areas, rather than policing individuals, the authorities went after entire segments of the local population, whether at the place of employment or the residence. "We were told that we would march together in a column from the railroad station, with a band, and that all employees must be present." Those who were working on that day in Równe and Lwów were brought to voting stations in supervised groups from their places of employment. "In order to give a festive appearance to the elections voters from each electoral district were told to appear at the appropriate voting station with a band and singing." Landlords were made responsible for their tenants' collective appearance at the voting booth. In Lwów, for example, residents of sections of a street or of an apartment building were marched together to vote. Whole villages were first assembled, or surrounded by militia, and then delivered to a voting booth in orderly procession.[107]

Voters approaching their polling places were struck by the ubiquitous presence of the military and armed civilians. On the access road to the Różanka polling station people were allowed to walk only by themselves; even a small group of two or three marching together was ordered to disperse. The Soviets had only barely wrested this territory from another state, it is true; but the saturation of voting stations with armed soldiers, militiamen, and NKVD operatives, both uniformed and in civilian attire, could be justified only if the authorities expected a prolonged siege[108] or if they had something other than security in mind—such as intimidation. A peasant from Teklówka remembered a row of militiamen posted "from the entrance to the exit" of the polling place.[109] The scene there may have been more intimidating than at other polling stations; but it was generally true that, in addition to the military men in Soviet uniforms seated in electoral commissions,[110] an armed soldier was usually posted near the ballot box and scores more, uniformed or not, covered the premises, sometimes advising voters on a procedural matter, sometimes just standing there. "Vote as the law

---

showing that I had voted, and told me to return it to the man who was guarding me in the cellar. He took it from me and said, 'teper stupai damoi, a kak ne budesh podchiniatsia sovetskomu soiuzu ub'iom' [now go home, and if you will not obey the Soviet Union we'll kill you]" (HI, PGC, 2611). Testimonies from jails in Nieśwież (nieśwież, 50), in Nowosiółka in Przemyślany county (HI, PGC, 9822), in gmina Jasienic (ostrów, 18), and in gminas in Pińsk (p. 43), Kosów Poleski (p. 27), and Równe (p. 29†) show that inmates were made to vote in the October elections. One can hardly blame the Soviet authorities involved in these episodes, except for their overzealousness. Without a specific court order suspending their voting rights, everybody over 18 was enfranchised according to Soviet law, "except the scarlet fever and diphtheria wards and hospitals for lepers, whose inmates take no part in elections" (Vyshinskii, ed., *Law of the Soviet State*, p. 695).

says, not according to your wishes, or there will be regrettable consequences," the head of local NKVD kept saying as he prowled around
one of the voting stations in Wilejka county.[111] In Dzisna, people were
advised that anyone who crossed off a name on the ballot would be
registered and arrested.[112] But even motionless silence could be highly
suggestive on these premises: "There was a booth covered with red
cloth in the second room, presumably to choose a candidate freely, but
at the entrance to this room a uniformed NKVD man was standing, so
nobody dared to use it."[113]

In the voting station one usually followed a simple procedure: one's
name was checked against the list of eligible voters; one got a ballot,
received instructions about how to proceed, and dropped the ballot
into the ballot box; finally, one sought the promised entertainment.
There were variations, of course, in the way each stage of this familiar
and generally accepted procedure was actually carried out. But everywhere an effort was made to keep the voter always under the guidance
of some official or in the commission's field of vision. Indeed, although
people may have been brought to the voting stations in large groups,
they were frequently admitted inside only individually so that they
were surrounded by officials or their helpers throughout these fateful
moments.[114] "I was guarded all the time," a railwayman from Łuniniec
county later said, "as if I were a prisoner."[115]

Voters received all kinds of advice from the electoral commission.
Some of it was needed when unusual voting procedures were used
locally. Otherwise, it might just be a general admonition to do as one
was told, or else. But one also encountered more general hints that it
made no difference if names were crossed off the ballot or left on: those
who were appointed as deputies would become deputies anyway, so
what was the point of a negative vote? It would be ignored in order to
foil counterrevolutionary plans that would prevent the election of a
"true" National Assembly.[116] It was clearly futile to vote "no."

The officials of a police state are not famous for sincerity, but why
this open flouting of an election process that had been glorified by such
a dazzling pre-election campaign? Perhaps by such frankness they
completed the subjugation of the voters, for if a "no" vote does not
count, by implication neither does a "yes." Consequently, there is no
reward even for those who succumb to coercion, no positive recognition. But what was the purpose of those elections if the authorities
showed contempt even for their supporters?

Leaving aside such complex questions for the moment, we can perhaps better appreciate now the arrogance that confronted the people
of the Western Ukraine and Western Belorussia on October 22. They

had not expected a fair election, not least because most of them had never in their lives witnessed one. Yet, the few moments spent in the polling stations on this Sunday were grafted in great detail on people's memories.

> After entering the building one was given a sheet in an envelope. This sheet had to be taken to the room with the ballot box and deposited there. We were instructed how to carry the envelope. One had to hold it between two fingers in a hand extended forward.[117]

This recollection of a carpenter from Koźlakiewicze is by no means the most bizarre. But it evokes a visual image pregnant with symbolism. As in a religious procession, but holding envelopes instead of votive candles, peasants of this obscure village went to appease the new, mysterious forces that ruled their destiny. Mysterious, because envelopes that seemed to be the focus of the ritual were sealed. Presumably a ballot was inside. But what did it matter if one was not even allowed to look at it? And this was no aberration of some contemptuous gendarme in charge of a local election. All over the Western Ukraine and Western Belorussia the population, especially in rural hamlets, was frequently ordered to deposit unopened envelopes into the ballot box.[118]

So much for choice during the October elections. As to secrecy, which had been pledged in the pre-election campaigns and had a "structural" underpinning in the design of voting stations (each one had booths or a special area set aside where voters could withdraw alone to mark the ballot), it was handled most awkwardly in those precincts where people were actually instructed to *sign* their ballots.[119] In Leszczowa Dolna there were three candidates on the ballot, and one had to put one's signature next to the name one chose.[120] In Touste signatures were collected in advance on a list supporting the designated candidate, and no one was called to vote on election day.[121]

But the methods of control did not have to be so obvious. In any case, what did they yield? Certainly not a differentiation between docile and defiant citizens. Sealed envelopes all look the same. Signed ballots rarely bore any marking other than the signature. Either procedure amounted only to a record of attendance, which had been noted anyway as people first identified themselves and their names were checked against the list of the precinct's eligible voters. So other methods were also used to monitor voters' behavior. Though not as blunt perhaps, they were sometimes even more pernicious because they induced in the less observant a false sense of anonymity.

It was an old trick, but it worked: ballots were numbered. Most frequently they were assigned the number under which a voter's name appeared on the electoral list, or they were consecutively numbered and were then recorded next to voters' names on the list as they were handed out.[122] Many did not notice, or perhaps they decided to ignore it. As they then crossed these ballots or marked them with obscenities or patriotic slogans, they were leaving their signatures, only coded in numbers. Arrests followed soon after the elections, and the authorities were not at all shy about revealing the reason.[123] In Nowosiółki, for example, it took no time at all to correct a straying voter's behavior: "If someone didn't deposit his ballot in the box, or if he wrote something on it, or crossed something off, then after leaving the room with the ballot box he was brought back before the election commission, got another ballot, and had to drop it in under supervision, and a few days later he was arrested."[124] In some villages where monitoring had somehow failed, people were called to the gmina office after the elections to give samples of their writing. In any event, the experience of a sergeant from Broszniów was certainly not unique: the authorities quoted to him verbatim the inscription he had made on the ballot.[125]

It would seem from the evidence that the roughly 15,000 local organizers responsible for setting up polling stations throughout the Western Ukraine and Western Belorussia were given a free hand to sequester for election day whatever they pleased—an office building, a school, or a private dwelling.* But they must have received one explicit instruction: on each premise there must be a voting booth or its equivalent. Yet they must also have had orders to monitor the voters closely. One solution to this problem, as we have seen, was to mark the ballots or to have them identified by the voters' signatures. Another was to inspect the ballots before they were deposited in the box: each voter would pass the ballot to a commission member stationed by the box who would read it and then drop it inside. "When I left the partition, I came to the box where I had to drop the envelope, and then Sokół Miron grabbed me by the hand and wanted to see whether I had crossed off, but I managed to switch hands and I dropped it into the box myself." It was a pyrrhic victory, for this shrewd peasant voter was later arrested and deported.[126]

The other general method of monitoring ballots was never to lose sight of the voters while they were in the polling station. The most elegant and commonly employed means of discouraging privacy was

* There were 6,109 voting stations in Western Belorussia, according to *Pravda* (Oct. 25). Because the Western Ukraine had a population half again as large, there must have been some 9,000 there, which gives us a grand total of 15,000.

the spatial arrangement of the booths or partitions. They were set up in such a way that people had to make a special, highly visible effort to use them. In a polling station set up in a three-room Dzisna apartment (whose tenants were ordered out for the day), one room was set aside for use as a voting booth, but it was awkward to get to and therefore "difficult, especially for a Pole, to go there and cross off." In Królewszczyzna, a few partitions were in the far corner of a big room. One did not have to go there to get to the ballot box, so "with only one candidate on the ballot, it was obvious why people went there."[127] In an elementary school on Kordecki Street in Lwów one large room was divided down the middle by a row of tables stretching from the entrance to the opposite window. All business was conducted on one side of the room, while in the other half stood a few numbered and decorated booths. One had to squeeze through a narrow opening between tables and cross over an empty space to reach them.[128] In Kostopol voters were advised either to drop their ballots into the box immediately or, if they did not support the candidate, to go to a separate room where they would be instructed how to register their negative vote. There were booths in this room and an NKVD man to tell people what to do. Somehow no one wanted to find out.[129] How does one chose a course of action in such circumstances, especially if the name of each person using the booth is ostentatiously recorded by the commission?[130] Or what does one do when faced with the kind of choice presented to villagers in Uzłomy: a blank piece of paper and instructions to deposit it in one of the two boxes placed on the table in front of the seated commission, depending on whether one is for or against the candidate.[131]

Sometimes, to observe the proceedings in the booth or behind the partition, a helpful assistant escorted the voter there (in direct violation of a specific prescription of electoral law).[132] But most often the voters who entered the booths alone were spied on.[133] Behind each of the eight partitions set up in a movie theater in the Pińsk seventh precinct, one or two civilians were comfortably seated, peeping out through narrow slits.[134] A voter in Marysin suddenly realized he was being watched through a crack in the ceiling over the partition where he was standing. In other places, a mirror suspended high on the wall offered an unobstructed view to commission members seated at a distance.[135] In Rumejki, in Pomorzanka, and in gmina Krasne an assistant went into the booth after each voter's exit to check on the position of the pencil to see whether it had been used.[136] In Lwów, "a very large ballot box was put against the wall and it was generally believed that an NKVD man was inside to check each envelope."[137]

An especially baffling procedure was adopted in Podhorki (Kałusz county). According to a local baker,

A voter, after identifying himself, was given a piece of paper where it was forbidden to write anything, and gave it in turn to a functionary hidden behind a suspended bed sheet who, after a brief moment, returned it to the voter folded in two. The voter then dropped it into the ballot box. It was forbidden to look at this piece of paper in the meantime so that one didn't know what was done behind this mysterious bed sheet—was anything written or stamped on this paper or was it just an abracadabra?[138]

There, it seems, roles were reversed and the electoral commission voted in lieu of the entire district. In a way, this was probably the fairest procedural rendering of what had been happening all over the Western Ukraine and Western Belorussia.[139]

Yet these unusual forms of coercion in the polling station caused less surprise than the offer of a genuine choice, or even the semblance of one. In a number of precincts throughout the Western Ukraine and Western Belorussia, more than one candidate's name appeared on the ballot, and voters were told to communicate their preference somehow. In many instances it was just another sham, as in Rypne (Dolina county), where voters were brought before the commission, given a piece of paper, pen, and ink, and then told to write two names and drop the ballot into the box nearby.[140] In the Kobryń precinct two of three names were already crossed off when voters received their ballots, and the candidate whose name remained was sitting in the flesh with the electoral commission.[141] In Trzcianiec, voters had to underline one name out of three on the ballot in full view of the commission, and in gmina Holszany they were instructed not to write anything at all on ballots listing the names of three candidates.[142]

But in many precincts voters could actually withdraw behind partitions to cross off or underline some names or to write them in (according to instructions).[143] Needless to say, they engaged in mischief. Electoral procedures that involved extensive manipulation with a pen or a pencil created opportunities, even though ballots may have been marked or partitions under observation, and people made ample use of them.[144] Moreover, the voters, at least those who had not been sufficiently terrorized, were angry.

There had been enough disruption of pre-election meetings for the organizers to anticipate hostility at election time as well. In one precinct, "there was a big outcry during elections because the majority of citizens crossed off both candidates and did not vote for either one."

In another, "because there was no control at the ballot box, people put in different pieces of paper with inscriptions that they wanted neither the Soviet authorities nor any elections at all." In both precincts, as soon as the results were discovered, another vote was held, this time closely monitored.[145] The Soviet authorities admitted officially to thirteen instances of second elections: eleven in the Western Ukraine and two in Western Belorussia.[146] But neither of the two just mentioned was included in the official communiqué listing eight precincts in Łuck county, three in Lwów county, and two in Wysokie Mazowieckie county where candidates failed to obtain the necessary absolute majority. New elections were scheduled, but I cannot tell whether they were actually held before the National Assemblies were convened in Lwów and in Białystok.*

Why these precincts were selected for a public admission of failure rather than others where the results most certainly did not warrant the election of the candidates, we shall probably never find out. But the turnout, especially in ethnically homogeneous rural areas, whether Polish as in Białystok voivodeship or Ukrainian as in Wołyń, might often have been abysmally low.[147] Entire villages were known to have fled into the woods on election day. Even after the army was sent to discipline them, some balked, but not everywhere.[148] Later, inhabitants of many such villages were subjected to arrests, forced food contributions, cutoffs in supplies, and, in the end, deportation.[149] But in many rural areas in the third week of October 1939, people were still oblivious to the full range of repressive measures that this new regime was capable of unleashing. So, if they thought they could get away with it, if there was coordination and mutual support in the community—"I know for sure that my vote and votes of inhabitants of Drukowszczyzna, Henrykowo, Kurjany, and partly Sobolewo were invalid because we so agreed among ourselves"[150]—if they were fed up or desperate—"on election day I fled with friends to the forest [where] we met hundreds of the Polish Nation who wanted to avoid coercion"[151]—they kept crossing off candidates' names or writing statements on the ballots expressing their true feelings.[152] "Everybody was overjoyed by the thought," one person later said, "that when they

---

* For the second vote, organizers in Western Belorussia no longer bothered with any semblance of secrecy—no booths or partitions were provided. People had to deposit their ballots immediately, in full view of the commission. As Franciszek Dworakowski, a peasant from Gąsowka-Skwarki (Wysokie-Mazowieckie county), put it: "During meetings preceding the rescheduled elections they didn't propagandize anymore, they threatened" (HI, PGC, 3001; see also PGC, 10128; Poland. Ambasada USSR, Box 46, Bronisław Markowski).

read what was written on these ballots, maybe they would finally understand and stop praising this regime of theirs."[153] Naiveté about the workings of the Soviet regime is obvious, but how could they know otherwise?

And so they continued prankish protests, substituting ballots with pieces of paper brought from home, appropriately inscribed, rubbing their fingers with a dark pencil before they went to vote and then surreptitiously smudging ballots (Sulejów in Rohatyn county), reproducing the Polish eagle from a coin on scraps of paper ("it came out beautifully") and dropping these into the ballot box as their votes (Wielkie Sioło in Mołodeczno county). In some mountain villages where there were no pencils and peasants were illiterate anyway, people brought tiny bits of cow or horse manure, slipped them into the ballots, and then stuffed them into the box.[154]

COUNTING VOTES

It is quite a testimonial to the resilience and obstinacy of the local population that, although a majority had no regrets that Polish administration over this territory had ended, that in spite of all the intimidation preceding the October elections, and irrespective of the discipline and coercion exercised on election day, the organizers still had to falsify the results. We have reliable reports from all over the occupied territory that vote tallies were rigged. In some precincts, such as Kolońsk and Bircza, the Soviet in charge of the electoral commission removed the ballot box and, except for the official communiqué, we have no way of knowing what was in it. In other places only trusted members of the electoral commission were allowed to stay for the count.[155] But we have testimony from many who witnessed the count or who heard from reliable witnesses about widespread fraud committed at this very final stage of the procedure.[156] "I was present when the votes were counted and even though there were tampered-with [i.e., crossed-off] ballots in the box, they were counted as valid." "Unfortunately all crossed-off ballots were counted as good votes. I know this for a fact because I was present at the tally" (in Busko). In Karolówka (Rohatyn county) only twenty "good" votes were found in the box after it was opened. The frightened chairman of the commission suggested that they substitute new ballots for the crossed-out ones. Other members agreed.[157]

Some members of electoral commissions who had been unwillingly drafted for the job left particularly illuminating accounts of the vote tally. Feliks Zarzecki, who later fled his native village to avoid arrest after the elections (only to be deported later from Białystok in an unrelated matter), tells the following story:

> When the box was opened it turned out there were eighteen good, clean ballots; the rest were crossed over and peppered with inscriptions: "down with Stalin, down with communism, we want Poland, long live Poland"; cartoons of Stalin were drawn and many derogatory words for him. I thought the Bolsheviks would explode from anger when they read some of the words against Stalin and that so few votes were good for them, so they started to fuss around and pick ballots where the first name was crossed off but the last name intact, or the other way around, and they said to include them in the good votes, so the Bolshevik chairman of the commission made it so that there were 50 percent good votes and 50 percent not so good; then I and another member of the commission, a certain Jackiewicz Adolf, didn't agree and we didn't want to sign a protocol; we bargained for two hours but in the end we signed only for 25 percent of good votes. After this quarrel and the vote, he [the chairman] said to us "you are Polish henchmen and I will remember you."[158]

The lives of those responsible for a commission's work were at stake during the election, and they fought hard to keep them. They had to rely on local help, which in many instances proved unreliable, or cunning, or unafraid. They had to improvise, and many who were inexperienced in the management of terror were vulnerable. Frequently, I am sure, they did not know how to handle a group of non-Soviet people whose instinctive reactions vis-à-vis the state power were totally unfamiliar. Sometimes they were overwhelmed, as in the eleven precincts where electoral defeat was officially admitted. At other times they were able to recover in the face of adverse circumstances and impose their will:

> After twenty-five votes were checked out, only two were valid. The Komsomol girl got into a fit, she took all the ballots and threw them into the burning stove, then put the necessary number of new ballots into the box. Then she ordered the commission to sign blank forms of protocols and left.[159]

An episode from Michnicze (Święciany county, Wilno voivodeship) gives a comprehensive view of the troubles that accompanied the delegation of authority during this revolutionary stage of transition to the Soviet regime. Whoever appointed the electoral commission in this village made a blunder. There was a conspiracy there to begin with, for the people eventually appointed to the commission pretended to have much smaller plots of land than they in fact owned. On election day, when a Soviet agent was sent to supervise the commission's work, he could not figure out the conspiracy. The inhabitants of the village, including the commission members, had agreed to cross off the name of the official candidate and write in that of a person they had chosen together. When people showed up to vote, commission members told them how to go about it. After the votes were counted (220 for the local candidate, 5 for the official one), the Soviet supervisor was beside himself but could not intimidate the rest of the commission. So they took protocols along with the ballots to the gmina seat in Świr.

> We went there by horse at three in the morning. As soon as we enter, the head [nachalnik] asks us did all go well? We say yes, he screams in anger, how well? Did everybody give good votes? We tell him the tally and he immediately grabs a pistol and goes to us and says he will shoot us for allowing the population to spoil so many ballots and put their own people up for deputies, for breaking the laws of the Soviet Union, for having organized elections against their orders, and that it does not count, you don't want the Soviet power, we liberated you, we gave you land, forests, water, all of this is yours, there are no masters who beat you, humiliate you, plow with you, we didn't let Hitler get you, we brought you Freedom, opened jails, and you don't want power of the Soviet Union, you are counterrevolutionaries, and he kept us under the wall as long as he didn't get all the votes from all the precincts where they went 100 percent according to their principles and all valid, and in the end, after several hours, after votes were counted, their candidate won, and then he let us go home, only scolded us more, called us names—dogs, thieves, bandits, threatened us with death, prison, etc.[160]

The man who uttered these threats seems to have been a nervous wreck himself, just as were his superiors or their counterparts from another county, about whom we also chance to have an intimate report.

> On election day we were sitting in Dziuba's office [head of the Zbaraż Provisional Administration] in the building of the old county administration, together with a number of Soviet functionaries sent from Kiev. Dziuba's secretary, F. J. Retz, was receiving telephone messages from the area. More or less hourly each district called with information on how many people had already voted, and Retz transmitted these numbers to voivodeship head-

quarters. If a percentage in some district was small, Dziuba turned to one of the Soviets and told him to go there personally and make sure that all worked out as it should. He was getting nervous because of reports from Stary Zbaraż. By 11 in the morning the result there was only 3 percent. And it remained that way until 1 P.M. Tarnopol was already specifically asking about the situation there. Then Dziuba turned to me and said: "Stary Zbaraż will compromise us. What a number—3 percent! Take an automobile or a buggy, I give you Wajrych (a cooperatist from Kiev) and Suk-hanov (a military man) for assistance, and make sure that 80 per-cent vote. I count on your energy. You must press and scare local leaders of the Polish population, but quietly, only face to face. . . .[161]

This unusual firsthand account of the seamy side of elections by Dziu-ba's assistant, Wiktor Jerzy Brandes, shows the complicated mecha-nism of what to people in the street appeared in a relatively simple guise. But in fact, an entire infrastructure was involved in the appear-ance of an armed squad at a voter's door, a system of multiple layers of control and command linking the man in charge of a precinct with First Secretary Ponomarenko in Western Belorussia or Khrushchev in the Western Ukraine.

We have seen in these vivid recollections the anger and fear of offi-cials at the precinct, gmina, and county levels, who seemed all-pow-erful to their subjects but who were only on the ladder of Soviet power, and were rather low at that. And just as they were subordinates, so too were all their superiors up to the very pinnacle of the hierarchy, for such is the inner structure of every bureaucracy. Yet this bureaucracy had some peculiar features: no citizen or task was beyond its domain; it was oriented, in T. H. Rigby's expression, toward "task-achieving" rather than "rule-applying";[162] and the penalty for failure was fre-quently death. Within it, the evaluation of one's performance as a sub-ordinate depended on the performance of one's own subordinates. Again, a familiar enough situation, except that there were no rules one could invoke to justify failure. This introduced an imbalance: one could use any means, including the very real threat of death, to induce good performance; but if one's subordinates failed in spite of all, one was in turn unprotected from the wrath of one's superior (who was, of course, accountable to the wrath of his superior, and so on). What made the Soviet hierarchy all-powerful at every rung on the ladder— its purely instrumental orientation to subordinates—made it also infi-nitely vulnerable. This is what made Ponomarenko and Khrushchev sufficiently interested in the performance of every single voter throughout Western Belorussia and the Western Ukraine to have elections monitored on an hourly basis. Looking at the Soviet bureaucracy from the bottom up, one saw a long line of ruthless, fear-inspiring creatures. From the top down, however, they were all vulnerable and sick with fear. "The ruling serfs," Moshe Lewin has called them,[163] with complete mastery over subordinates' destiny and yet held by them in a potentially murderous embrace. A weird case of reciprocity indeed, and how unsettling, especially if you do not know these subordinates well, if you have not worked with them long, and if you are new at the job yourself.

The many political workers sent to all corners of the Western Ukraine and Western Belorussia had as many qualifications to organize elections in a hostile, foreign country as illiterate deputies had to act as representatives in a National Assembly. They had all received some preparation prior to being dispatched on this assignment, many undoubtedly in the fairly recent assault on the Ukrainian peasantry during the forced collectivization in the Soviet Union. So if a good-sized militia detachment was available locally, or if the community was consummating decades of ethnic rift, they did a fine job. But local conditions varied, just as individual political workers had different ideas and talents (within certain limits, of course). Hence the different solutions produced by matching local resources with imported skills. There was, for example, widespread voting by Red Army soldiers;[164] people were induced to vote for missing relatives or for strangers who had not shown up.[165] Or, to simplify matters even further, commission members openly stuffed ballots into the box for absent voters.[166] At the other extreme, truckloads of enthusiasts went from one precinct to another and voted repeatedly.[167] Children, mostly from sixteen years of age, were brought to voting stations as well.[168] Anything, from coercion to bribery, that could be translated into an unmarked ballot deposited in the box to the credit of election organizers was practiced. "To push through a young criminal, Jan Minic, upon showing him the ballot before depositing it in the box, the village head in Moroczno, Bereźny Adam, authorized the buffet to give the voter a bun, candies, and tea. During Bereźny's absence authorization to feed the loyally voting citizen were issued by militia commander Łukaszczuk Jan, a known drunkard and rowdy."[169] "I don't know about voting because I didn't vote," a schoolboy later said. "I only saw how people were leaving after they voted—they carried small packages of sugar, candies, pastries, a few pieces of each that they got after the vote."[170] Largesse of the workers' and peasants' power toward its own, or revealing testimony about the rapid depletion of consumer goods in the area since the Red Army occupation started?[171] However one answers this question, it was not a clean election.

RESULTS OF THE OCTOBER ELECTIONS

As one may expect, statistics for the October 1939 elections in the Western Ukraine and Western Belorussia are somewhat confusing. Participation was high, though modest by Soviet standards. In the Western Ukraine, 92.83 percent of those eligible to vote took part in the elections, and of those, 90.93 percent voted for the official candidates. In Western Belorussia, 96.71 percent of the eligible voters participated, and 90.67 percent supported candidates on the ballot. The strongest support (98.57 percent of "yes" votes) and the highest voter turnout (99.02 percent) were registered in Polesie,[172] a region famous for its wetlands ("Polesian marshes"), impassable forests, and insular, pre-modern peasantry speaking a dialect of its own and identifying itself overwhelmingly as "locals."

The published election results lack even internal consistency. In the Western Ukraine, 1,484 of 1,495 deputies were elected (second elections were required in eleven precincts). But in a speech by one of the deputies, I. Sydorenko, we find that there were 1,482 delegates altogether to the National Assembly of the Western Ukraine.[173] In Western Belorussia, 911 names appeared on the list of candidates published in the October 19 issue of *Pravda*; yet on October 25 *Pravda* declared that 927 had been elected for 929 vacancies in the assembly. But one day later, *Pravda* gave the ethnic background of 911 *elected deputies* to the National Assembly of Western Belorussia.

Seemingly, the corps of deputies was in a fluid state and underwent constant transformations even after the elections. There were 239 women in the Western Ukrainian Assembly, for example, on the 25th of October, according to *Pravda*; but on November 3, in the speech by Sydorenko, the contingent of women expands to 251, only to shrink two weeks later back to 239 in the speech of another deputy, Peter Franko (the son of a famous Ukrainian poet).[174] Sydorenko and Franko also differ considerably on the social background of the deputies: 415 workers (Sydorenko) vs. 402 (Franko), 766 peasants vs. 819, 270 working intelligentsia vs. 234 (neither breakdown, incidentally, gives the grand total of either 1,482 or 1,484). Of course, attributions to such categories are somewhat arbitrary and may differ depending on who makes them.

It is a bit more troubling, however, that the ethnic background of the parliamentarians also fluctuated from one issue of *Pravda* to another. On October 29, among 911 delegates to the National Assembly of Western Belorussia, there were 659 Belorussians, 105 Poles, 75 Jews, and 38 Russians; five days later the number of Belorussians declined to 621, the number of Poles increased to 127, and the number of Jews changed to 72. There were now 5 more Russians—43 in all—but out of nowhere (or, rather, mostly out of Belorussians) 53 Ukrainians appeared—yielding a new total of 916.[175] Data about the nationality of the Western Ukrainian deputies also present a small puzzle, for 8 Russians, 1,389 Ukrainians, 44 Poles, and 61 Jews make a group 1,592 strong—yet a third grand total for the Western Ukraine.[176] Sydorenko claims that there were 24 illiterates among the deputies to the Western Ukrainian National Assembly, but fluctuations in the size, social background, ethnicity, and sex of this closely scrutinized group make a dose of skepticism justifiable before accepting his word for fact.

The National Assemblies met on the 26th and 28th of October in a Lwów and a Białystok theater respectively and deliberated for two days. Each session was opened by the oldest deputy—Professor Kiriło Studyński in Lwów and Stepan Strug, a peasant, in Białystok. There were four items on their identical agendas: the nature of state authority in each territory, unification with the corresponding Soviet republic, confiscation of large private landholdings, and nationalization of banks and large industry.[177] Following discussion, the predictable conclusions were drawn. In the meeting hall in Lwów a musical band from time to time played the "International"; in Białystok, on the evening of the 29th, deputy Lewczuk read his poems to Stalin from the rostrum.[178]

Apparently the assembly session in Lwów was organized under strict police supervision. Every third seat was occupied by an NKVD agent, and delegations appear to have been dispersed throughout the hall so that people were always seated next to strangers. Two independent sources report that one dissenting vote was cast in the Lwów assembly, but they differ as to the protagonist. Bonatt identifies the Ukrainian lawyer Vinnichenko as the lonely dissenter. The Tchortkiv (Czortków) District memorial book brings forth the young Mikhailo Dovgan, who was arrested and never heard of again once he returned to his village from Lwów.[179]

At the end of their deliberations each assembly empowered a Special Commission—66 delegates from the Western Ukraine and 65 from Western Belorussia—to travel first to Moscow and then to Kiev or Minsk. There they were to appear before the Fifth Extraordinary Session of the Supreme Soviet of the USSR and before the Third Extraordinary Session of the Supreme Soviet of Belorussia and that of the Ukraine. In Moscow, on behalf of the Western Ukrainian delegation, Dr. Panchishin presented the request for incorporation into the Soviet Union and the Ukrainian Soviet Republic. Andrei Vyshinskii delivered the seconding speech on behalf of the Soviet government, and the request was unanimously approved on November 1, 1939. The following day Pritickii spoke on behalf of the Western Belorussian delegation. His request for incorporation was seconded on the Soviet side by Nicolai Bulganin, and it was then unanimously approved by the Supreme Soviet.

Both delegations spent twelve happy days in Moscow. In a farewell letter to Stalin written just before they left the Soviet capital, the Western Ukrainian delegation expressed heartfelt thanks: "From the kingdom of darkness and boundless suffering which the nation of the Western Ukraine bore for six hundred long years, we found ourselves in the fairy land of true happiness of the people, and of true freedom."[180] Then they set out for Minsk and Kiev, where the Belorussian and Ukrainian Supreme Soviets approved their respective requests for incorporation. The laws that finally settled the matter were published on the 14th of November in Minsk and on the 15th in Kiev.[181]

In the meantime a wave of post-election arrests swept the Western Ukraine and Western Belorussia.[182] Returning assembly delegates who on occasion met with their constituents were booed and shouted down, or met with dead silence after cuing the audience to respond with a "long live" or a "hurrah." Delegate Powajbo apparently was killed by the underground a few weeks after the elections.[183] Two delegates from Kostopol county are reported to have been brought back dead from the session in Lwów. They were buried with honors, as victims of Polish terrorists. But the authorities, as well as other delegates from the area, said little about the circumstances of their deaths, and the Ukrainian population believed that they had been killed by the NKVD for refusing to vote approval of the incorporation.

THE MARCH ELECTIONS

The population of the territories conquered by the Red Army in September 1939 was given four more opportunities to choose representatives, and the blueprint laid out in October, with minor variations, was followed faithfully on each occasion. On Easter Sunday, March 24, 1940, the Western Ukraine and Western Belorussia chose delegates to the Soviet of the Union and the Soviet of Nationalities as well as to the

Republican Supreme Soviets. On the 14th and 15th of July 1940 Wilno and its vicinity (occupied by the Soviets for the second time since the beginning of the war) elected their respective National Assemblies (together with the rest of Lithuania, Latvia, and Estonia, which the USSR had invaded that summer).[184] On December 15, 1940, local soviets were chosen in the Western Ukraine and Western Belorussia. Finally, on January 12, 1941, together with other Baltic states and Bessarabia, which had been swallowed during the summer of 1940, the Lithuanian electorate sent its representatives to the Soviet of the Union and the Soviet of Nationalities. One ought perhaps to mention also the December 1939 elections in the labor union organization. Since membership in a union was virtually required for employment, the entire working population was involved in them. This election also provided an opportunity for mass mobilization, indoctrination, and screening as people were forced to participate in a closely monitored public ritual.

In accordance with electoral law, the March 24 elections were preceded by a two-month preparatory campaign that began on January 24.[185] The membership of the electoral commissions was soon made public, and it turned out that several deputies elected six months earlier to the provisional assemblies were now prominent among the personnel.[186] The propaganda campaign was carried out just as energetically as the autumn campaign of 1939.[187] As we read in *Czerwony Sztandar* (February 9), for example, each Lwów school decided to delegate five or six propagandists "from among its best teachers." Special portable libraries of election literature were issued in "hundreds of thousands of copies" at affordable prices (from 75 kopecks to 2 rubles, 50 kopecks), and plans were made to send high school seniors and labor union activists peddling them from door to door.[188] As was done in many other places, the propagandists in the village of Łatoszyce challenged their counterparts in Ładańce to a "socialist competition": "There are 15 propagandists in Łatoszyce, and even though there are 23 in Ładańce, Comrade Musiyezdov, in charge of the Łatoszyce propaganda column, is confident of his victory. Dymitro Solishyn is best on the team—he had 18 meetings with his group of 22 voters." The story was filed by *Czerwony Sztandar* on February 14, not even halfway through the pre-election campaign period; since the pace of agitation would quicken as the election date drew near, we can only sympathize with the people subjected to Dymitro Solishyn's zeal. (He was reading Ostrovskii's *How the Steel Was Tempered* to his group; and, as anyone who has ever made it through the entire novel can tell, the second volume is much more tedious than the beginning.) Prospective voters were also treated to occasional entertainment, such as a motorcycle ride through Lwów in a snow blizzard exactly one week before the elections. And a new theme "wove like a golden thread" through propaganda speeches during this campaign: collectivization.[189]

There were well over 100,000 propagandists in the occupied territories at the time.[190] Although in Dawidów only 40 propagandists attended to more than 3,000 voters, in Malechów 45 covered the population of 1,163.[191] In Lwów's twelfth electoral district 1,400 voters were supervised by 57 propagandists who took special care to decorate individual apartments with "slogans, Soviet state emblems, and portraits of the Politbureau members."[192] The ratio of propagandists to voters seems to have varied between 1:20 and 1:30.[193]

But the number of propagandists, though large, was not decisive. As *Czerwony Sztandar* noted on March 4, 1940, unintentionally speaking the truth, "the best propagandist was the surrounding reality." Preeminent in people's minds was the first mass deportation organized all over the occupied territory during the night of February 10. "Those who remained in their homes [afterwards] were in a state of panic fearing deportation, so that they were prepared to do anything the Soviets might order them to do."[194] Many were arrested on the eve of the elections, and it seems that in general the population was more carefully supervised in March than it had been five months before.[195]

The methods used in October to round up the voters and supervise the balloting were implemented once again in March. Terror and subjugation prevailed. Somewhere in Wilno-Troki county a desperate but still defiant population apparently destroyed a few voting stations.[196] But on the whole, after numerous arrests and a mass deportation, people were already cowed into submission. "I shall never forget this sad, gray Easter eve with pale-faced crowds standing quietly, sometimes showing anger, but on the whole resigned," wrote Emilia Karwowska of the pre-dawn spectacle in front of the voting station in Bieniakonie in Lida county.[197] Voters were herded there promptly by *desiatniks*, themselves threatened with imprisonment unless everyone in their custody showed up to vote. Parishioners leaving churches on this holy day were escorted by armed militia to vote. A peasant from Macieszyn (Brasław county) who went to church *before* fulfilling his "sacred duty at the voting station" (as *Czerwony Sztandar* put it in its March 22 issue) was severely reprimanded by the village head and ordered as punishment to bring his own horse and wagon and ride for the rest of the day with the portable ballot box. In yet another village people were told in advance that tobacco could be purchased by those showing up early to vote.[198]

One week before the elections voters had been notified of the decision by the Supreme Soviets of the Union and of the Republics that envelopes would no longer be used in these elections.[199] Open ballots were to be deposited directly into ballot boxes. It hardly matters whether the decision was due to a sudden paper shortage or, more likely, unconcern about maintaining even the pretense of secret balloting after the territory had been incorporated into the Soviet Union. As a locksmith from Lwów put it, voters "were strictly forbidden to write or cross anything on the ballot."[200]

According to the official propaganda, the atmosphere of the March elections was joyous and playful.

> A thick, beautiful rug is spread on the floor of a spacious room. How good it feels, how pleasant it is to play on such a rug. Two boys with Red Pioneers' ties are tinkering with a tank. Four girls, holding hands in ballet fashion, are practicing three steps forward and a right turn to the tune of a melody. Happy, smiling faces of workers' children. . . . How long have you been playing here—I ask. From early morning. . . .[201]

One wonders how long it takes before the dream world of a propagandist begins to impinge on people's everyday lives, blurring distinctions between the real and the imaginary? Journalists were not accountable to the public for what they wrote. The will of the new authorities, not surrounding reality, was the referent of their stories. "We did not abandon our propagandists," stated *Czerwony Sztandar* reassuringly on May 30, 1940. "We tried, and we still keep trying to educate them further." To a few readers in the Western Ukraine this news item might have offered some bitter consolation after all.

In March all candidates scored electoral victories. No seats were left vacant for lack of sufficiently strong support from the electorate. Indeed, according to electoral statistics, support for the designated candidates was almost unanimous.[202] The 2.9 million voters in Western Belorussia elected sixteen representatives to the Soviet of the Union (including Kovalev, the officer who commanded the Red Army's Belorussian front in September 1939, and Ponomarenko, the first secretary of the Belorussian Communist Party) and six representatives to the Soviet of Nationalities. The Western Ukrainian electorate sent twenty-seven deputies to the Soviet of the Union and another six to the Soviet of Nationalities.

The December 1940 elections had the same scope as the two previous ones and harnessed equal organizational efforts, but the novelty of a mass mobilization campaign had already worn off and the election is barely mentioned in the archival sources at our disposal. Of course, since three of four major deportations had been completed by June 1940, many of our earlier witnesses were by this time resettled in the

Soviet interior. Yet a significant number of people whose testimonies have survived were in the Western Ukraine and Western Belorussia in the winter of 1940. Apparently, they barely noticed their third opportunity in slightly over a year to delegate power. And yet in December 1940 the number of people actively involved in the elections in some official capacity was higher than ever before; every eighth or ninth grown-up was an election organizer. According to official sources, 90,000 electoral commissions were set up in the Western Ukraine alone, and more or less 116,000 deputies to village, raion, city, and oblast soviets were elected in the Western Ukraine and Western Belorussia.[203] One-tenth of 1 percent of the candidates failed to receive an absolute majority of the votes in their districts and were not elected: 69 for village soviet slots in the Western Ukraine, and 71 in Western Belorussia. Among the successful candidates there were many old hands who had already served in the National Assemblies.[204] According to the secretary of the Presidium of the Ukrainian SSR, O. S. Mezsherin, this had been the broadest and the most complicated electoral campaign ever in the Western Ukraine and Western Belorussia. In his words, "elections to the local soviets of deputies mark the end of the reconstruction of all organs of the Soviet power in western oblasts of the Ukraine [and Belorussia] on the basis of the most democratic constitution in the world, Stalin's."[205]

INTERPRETATION

In his thoughtful book devoted to the early years of World War II, John Scott confesses his inability "to write about Soviet elections. They are essentially not elections at all but processions."[206] Undoubtedly with a similar reservation in mind, Władysław Broniewski, a man of the left who was already a famous poet (after the war he became the Mayakovskii of the Polish People's Republic), summed up the experience of the October 22, 1939, elections in a brief answer to the questionnaire distributed among soldiers of the Polish Army in the East: "Voting [in Lwów] took place calmly, in an atmosphere of irony by the Poles about the form and content of these elections."[207] Szymon Kimmel, a lawyer from Sambor, commented similarly: "No one attributed any importance or meaning to these elections."[208] But they were wrong, I think. The essence of the October vote was captured more perceptively by a Mr. Kwiatkowski, a fiscal employee from Zaleszczyki:

> Among more intelligent Poles and Ukrainians one can observe a little shame and discomfort. Everybody knows that he is doing something wrong, but is also aware that by skipping the elections

he may get in trouble. This is why everybody goes as if to a funeral, to drop a handful of dirt on the casket of a dead friend.[209]

Indeed, there were many good reasons why, to quote a *Pravda* dispatch from Lwów, the voters unanimously agreed that "elections like these have never been seen here before."[210]

For the local inhabitants, these elections were unprecedented in more than one sense. It was their first exposure to modern political mass mobilization; the first infusion of Soviet reality into their daily lives; the first experience of coercion-induced compliance in full view of their fellow citizens—and of the loss of dignity that accompanies such exposure. It was a practical lesson in intimidation and collaboration, superb conditioning for both the subjects of the new order and its enforcers. During the October elections voters of the Western Ukraine and Western Belorussia were subjected to the exercise of naked power: talked to senselessly, they had to listen; pushed around capriciously, they had no one to complain to.

On this occasion the Soviet authorities, even though barely installed, proved capable of reaching and processing individually almost all inhabitants of the Western Ukraine and Western Belorussia, who by and large gave in, even though many wore ironic smiles on their faces, or dismissed their gesture as insignificant, or registered protest in the dubious privacy of voting booths. But the importance of symbolism in collective life weighs heavier than such protests; public humiliation severs bonds between victims. No irony exchanged in private can repair this damage entirely. Neither can one completely cleanse oneself of a residual feeling of shame in the aftermath (and thus fear that others no longer hold one in respect), or overcome in the future the suspiciousness of others whose compliant behavior one witnessed. In such a spectacle all are shown to each other in an act of betrayal of their beliefs for fear of sanction. What expectations of loyalty can one hold from prospective associates who behaved so? And then, in the end, no one can ever know for sure who acted in earnest.

From the October elections on, the overwhelming majority of the inhabitants of the Western Ukraine and Western Belorussia were tainted. By submitting to the authorities and casting a ballot, they had lost their innocence. They had made a contribution; they were implicated. For the only interpretation that makes sense of the otherwise absurd herding of the people into pre-election meetings and then voting booths lies in the recognition that Soviet authorities have never sought *engagement* from the population in their custody,[211] only complicity.

113

THREE

The Paradigm of
Social Control

ALTHOUGH the specifics of the initial arrangements established by the Soviet authorities in the Western Ukraine and Western Belorussia varied according to the local context, there emerged a consistent framework and certain regularities in the way Soviet activists managed, or at least supervised, the transition to the new rule. Admittedly, the evidence accumulated so far came from the earliest, hence the most chaotic, period. But the Soviets knew what general direction they wanted to impose on the area. They had just completed in their own country a replay of their original civil war and revolution—that is, the collectivization of the peasantry—and the occupation authorities in the Western Ukraine and Western Belorussia came with a tight and well-defined schedule to implement their agenda. By October 22, 1939, they had organized a political campaign and elections that required the supervision and monitoring of virtually every inhabitant of the Western Ukraine and Western Belorussia. Whatever happened during the establishment of village committees and temporary administrations in the cities was meant to happen.

I have already called attention to the most striking feature of this early period: the Soviets did not interfere with, and even encouraged, the spontaneous outburst of violence and internecine struggle that engulfed the area after the Polish state authority collapsed. One could of course point out that violence in a poor, peasant, and ethnically split society is endemic, that a breakdown in state authority is likely only to make it worse, and that a foreign invader should allow these conflicts to exhaust the local society, leaving no emotional energy or material resources that could be mobilized for resistance to the occupation. But the Soviet attitude went far beyond such a clearly prudent course of action. The Soviets harnessed these intimate personal animosities to serve their own cause in ways that ought to make us rethink the nature of the Soviet regime. A look at Soviet actions in their own country a decade before the events described here will give us a firmer hold on the argument.

On January 30, 1930, at the close of the All-Union Conference of

Marxist Agrarians convened in Moscow, Iosif Vissarionovitch Stalin mounted the rostrum and pronounced these fateful words: "We have gone over from a policy of limiting the exploiting tendencies of the kulak [prosperous peasant] to a policy of eliminating the kulak as a class."[1] Within one month, guidelines for the implementation of this policy were drafted. Kulak households were divided into three categories: "the counter-revolutionary aktiv" (Category I), "the remaining elements of the kulak aktiv" (II), and the remainder of the kulaks (III). The January resolution of the Politbureau established an all-USSR limit of 63,000 households for the first category, 150,000 for the second, and at least 396,000 or possibly (the numbers, for some reason, cannot be established with precision) as many as 852,000 for the third.[2] Quotas were then divided among regions, which in turn divided them among oblasts, and oblasts among raions and villages. Lists of counterrevolutionaries were drawn up by the local secret police, but village meetings of poor and collectivized peasants decided who would be included in the other two categories of kulaks. Punitive measures varied—immediate execution was reserved only for the first category—but all kulaks were subject to confiscation of property and exile (the destination and the list of personal items that could be kept differed somewhat from one category to another).

How were the quotas for exile established? Where did the numbers come from? The answer is that, just like the designation of the social category itself, they were arbitrary. To ingratiate themselves with the higher authorities, "enthusiastic regional party committees sometimes increased the quota set by the Central Committee: in the Moscow region, the quota for those to be exiled (presumably those in Category II) was increased from 7,000 to 13–16,000 and in the Ivanovo-Voznesensk region from 4,000 to 7–8,000."[3] And all over the Soviet Union, as the official press readily admitted, " 'ideological' kulaks, i.e., middle and poor peasants who resisted collectivization," were also expropriated.[4] What was the sense of this mélange of arbitrary figures and meaningless categories? Who, after all, *could not* be exiled as a kulak of one kind or another?

A quota—like any other quota, except that this one counted humans—was imposed on every community from above, and the community was then charged with redistributing it among its members. The sacrifice was not of another cow or of a quintal of grain but of one's life—sometimes literally—as one knew it. A community was thus condemned to be all powerful and powerless at the same time. It could ruin a life or grant a stay of execution in any *individual case*, but it could not lift the sentence: a certain number of its members had to be destroyed. Thus a structural framework was provided for the self-destruction of peasant communities. The rest is an already familiar tale:

> The confiscation of the personal property and dwellings of the victims was a prominent feature of dekulakization. Some poor peasants and batraks [landless peasants], as well as being motivated by the desire to pay off scores against their former exploiters, were also attracted by the possibility of benefiting from a share in the spoils, and this also corrupted some plenipotentiaries. And as it was inherently difficult to distinguish between a kulak and a well-to-do middle peasant, the race for personal gain often resulted in the arbitrary expropriation of middle peasants and the theft of their belongings, and in the theft of kulak property which should have been transferred to the kolkhoz or to the state.[5]

A secret police report from Smolensk oblast, dated February 23, 1930, for once confirmed the images drawn from the official press:

> Middle and even poor peasants were being arrested by "anybody"—by raion emissaries, village Soviet members, kolkhoz chairmen, and anyone in any way connected with collectivization. People were being transported to militia prisons without the slightest grounds or evidence. . . . Some poor peasants and "activists" were blackmailing the richer peasants, taking bribes for removing them from the confiscation or deportation lists.[6]

The point in retrieving these images from Soviet history is to show that the conquest of the Western Ukraine and Western Belorussia in September 1939 in many ways followed a well-established pattern. But in the midst of such disruption, what happens to the state's monopoly on the use of coercion—this most jealously guarded, exclusive prerogative, the feature that differentiates the state from any other organization in society? In other words, in the light of the evidence here discussed, what is the nature of the Soviet state?

Theories of totalitarianism have pointed out how the state envelops individuals by eliminating all forms of collective life but those it sponsors itself. It thus eradicates peer pressure and the constraint of group norms except as they are state sponsored; it monopolizes not only coercion but also the mechanisms for social conformity. A direct, unmediated relationship between each individual and the state results (known as *Gleichschaltung* in its German Nazi version). Nothing, not even the most private family life, can be legitimately shielded from state interference and regulation.

Yet this theory offers only a description. This is how Stalinism must have felt to Soviet citizens, especially during the periodic intensive drives to eradicate some new enemy and overcome some new obstacle. But the mechanism of bringing together individuals and the state remains a mystery; no mere decree replacing voluntary associations with a network of state-sponsored ones could have produced such results. Theories of totalitarianism solve this mystery by positing an activist state. Through mobilization and the energetic promotion of ideology, as well as terror, the totalitarian state *reaches out* for everybody. It fills the vacuum created in the process of the destruction of all voluntary associations and institutionalized forms of group life by establishing new, state-controlled organizations and forcing people to join them. *It thus appears that the totalitarian state confiscates the private realm.* My point is, however, that this is only an appearance and a deceptive one. Although the distinction between private and public realms is indeed obliterated under totalitarianism, this occurs not because of the confiscation of the private realm by the state* but primarily because of the *privatization of the public realm.*

We are already familiar with much of the evidence from the Western Ukraine and Western Belorussia leading to this conclusion. We have noted how Soviet speakers at first inflamed personal hatreds and encouraged the inhabitants of occupied villages and hamlets to square personal accounts. During this earliest stage of sovietization the victims and their tormentors knew one another personally.[7] When local militias and village committees soon took over the enforcement of law and order in this territory, personal vendettas were relabeled revolutionary justice. The volunteers who flocked into local committees and militias were often the same people who had responded enthusiastically to the Soviet invitation to take justice into their own hands, so the personal mode of exercising coercion continued as the main feature of the newly established regime. Thus, for the local inhabitants the establishment of Soviet rule was characterized by *privatization* of the instruments of coercion.

"The so-called temporary authorities began their functioning from squaring personal accounts," wrote a student from Kosów Huculski in Stanisławów voivodeship. Soon after the setting up of temporary com-

---

* Confiscation of the private realm may be the institutional or formal appearance of this process. But we should not forget that many regimes that we would not call totalitarian have also banned independently established institutions and promoted their own. Thus, if totalitarianism is unique—that is, if we do not, as I think we should not, want to describe all nondemocratic regimes as merely more or less totalitarian—its essential feature must be embedded in something other than a proscription order.

mittees, "arrests and searches began, often motivated by personal enmities," recalled a painter from Kiwerce in Wołyń. Similarly, in Łuck a high school teacher reports that arrests very often resulted from local militiamen's actions motivated by personal hatred.[8] Indeed, a number of people from different localities confirm a pattern of behavior whereby law enforcement agents and other representatives of the state settled private disputes while carrying out their official duties.[9] More precisely, *the pursuit of private interests appeared to be the principal mode of carrying out official duties and establishing authority.*

In principle, then, the new apparatus in the Western Ukraine and Western Belorussia was motivated by *particular* interests, like avenging personal wrongs, assuaging hunger, or satisfying greed.[10] Local militias and temporary committee personnel appropriated material objects for their personal use while carrying out apartment or house searches or while preparing inventories of confiscated real estate or commercial property. The spread of this practice and its duration beyond the initial few days of anarchy preclude an interpretation of this phenomenon as incidental behavior or the abuse of and departure from officially sanctioned procedures.

That privatization of the state was an official policy finds striking confirmation in yet another kind of evidence. The personnel records of the local authorities who were sponsored by the Soviet Union in occupied Poland show conclusively that *throughout the occupied territory the newly introduced Soviet authority was vested in a network of families** that held executive power—the power of life and death—over

---

* A sample list, with villages drawn from several different voivodeships: three Furman brothers and their sister were nominated to the red militia and to the village council, also the Samosenko couple (Dederkały, Krzemieniec county in Wołyń; HI, PGC, 3356); in Żurawica (Łuck county in Wołyń), Jakub and Dymitr Maksimczuk ran the village committee (HI, PGC, 3107); in Swisłocz (Wołkowysk county of the Białystok voivodeship), the gmina committee was headed by Piotr Kordosz, assisted by his daughter Luba and his brother Aleksander (HI, PGC, 8791); in Chołojów (Radziechów county of Tarnopol voivodeship) a Ukrainian named Szulba and his two sons "took the power" (HI, PGC, 5285); in Wolica Derewlańska (Kamionka Strumiłowa county of the Tarnopol voivodeship) Jan and Bazyli Baka, Jan and Teodor Szczur, and Stefan and Łać Bohonos were on the village committee (HI, PGC, 2827); in Bratkowce (Stanisławów voivodeship), among the "activists" of the local committee were Iwan Żyrdak and his brother Jarosław and Teodor Chiczyj and Irena Kaczor, Teodor's daughter (HI, PGC, 4032); in Więckowice (Sambor county of the Lwów voivodeship), Michał, Grzegorz, and Jan Hołowa were in the village militia (HI, PGC, 2837); in Złotkowice (Mościska county of the Lwów voivodeship), Mikołaj and Józef Sydorowicz ran the local committee (HI, PGC, 10273); in Kirżana village (Wilejka county of the Wilno voivodeship), the Hryszkiewicz family—Jan, Onufry, Tymoteusz, and Eustachy—were in charge (HI, PGC, 704); in another village of the Wilno voivodeship (in Szaniowce in Dzisna county), Jan and Józef Izojtko presided over the village committee (HI, PGC, 10264).

communities in their jurisdiction.[11] The state had been franchised, as it were, to these individuals, for strictly speaking they *were* the state. They were allowed to carry weapons and to use them with impunity; or, in a Weberian phrase, they were given the monopoly of legitimate use of coercion in this territory. From time to time they were ordered to deliver a quota of foodstuffs, to parcel a landowner's property, or to mobilize local inhabitants on election day. But how they managed these tasks was left to their own discretion. They could use for their own benefit whatever had not been claimed by the hierarchically superior organs of the state. They could redistribute the burdens in the community so as to punish personal enemies and benefit friends.[12]

This pattern of drafting entire families into state service and of giving them authority to pursue private interests in the name of law and order conforms to the characterization of the nature of the Soviet regime that I have described as *privatization of the state or the public realm*. Thus, nepotism appears not merely as a distortion of socialist development that one might find decades *after* the takeover and *after* institutionalization of a Communist ruling class and its privileges; rather, privatization starts *during* the revolution itself as a principal instrument to destroy the existing authority structure and to implement coercion.

Furthermore, in accordance with my interpretation of totalitarianism, it is possible to demonstrate that ordinary members of Soviet society have a relationship to the state similar to that of its functionaries; that is, they can and do use the state freely for the settlement of private disputes. This phenomenon is also grounded in the nonmediated, direct character of the relationship between individual and state under totalitarianism, as recognized by traditional theories. But once again we must reverse the direction in the relationship: on close inspection it turns out that under totalitarianism everyone has immediate access to the apparatus of the state and is encouraged to use it against other members of society. Consider the following personal accounts:

Soviet authorities conducted searches and arrests ... directly in response to denunciations by neighbors who had personal accounts to square.

Accusations, denunciations, and personal animosities could lead to arrest at any moment. People were officially encouraged to bring accusations and denunciations.

Whoever had a grudge against somebody else, an old feud, who had another as a grain of salt in his eye—he had a stage to show

119

his skills, there was a cocked ear, willing to listen. Posters encouraged people to bring denunciations.

There is no person in the world who can please everybody, and so one person's enmity caused another person's arrest.

Personal grudges, intrigues, denunciations, suspicions, and suppositions—this was the fertile ground which allowed NKVD men greedy for victims to penetrate into people's most intimate affairs, drawing from them monumental or trivial conclusions. A friend of mine by the name of Bolesław Szlamp had a personal enemy from his school days who accused him of preparing to escape across the frontier. Soviet authorities had no other proofs and sentenced and deported him for ten years to the USSR for forced labor.[13]

This is merely a sample of recollections from several voivodeships. The behavior they evoke is familiar to students of Soviet totalitarianism: motivated by personal enmities, people denounce one another to the secret police.[14] Even under the stabilized Soviet regime, the practice acquired a gruesome urgency, as in the famous Leninist phrase *kto kovo?*—but in this case it had become "your life or mine" since the introduction of article 58 into the penal code. As a result, people who failed to denounce others about whose alleged antistate activities they had, or could have had, prior knowledge were themselves subject to punishment for antistate activity.[15]

Thus we see that the principal mechanism for the penetration of the state into the private realm is the practice of denunciation. But an act of effective denunciation (i.e., one resulting in state reprisals against the denounced) can be seen paradoxically both as a service rendered to the state (providing it with wanted information) and as a service rendered by the state (the favorable settlement of a private dispute). Yet, since private enmity, or the instinct for self-preservation, was the primary motivation for bringing denunciations to the authorities, we cannot understand totalitarianism's all-pervasiveness and awesome power in terms of its being well informed and efficient; on the contrary, the evidence suggests, and students of totalitarianism readily concur, that a totalitarian state is "structurally" ill-informed and mismanaged. Thus, in accordance with the evidence presented here, I propose that *the real power of a totalitarian state results from its being at the disposal of every inhabitant, available for hire at a moment's notice.* The absence of the rule of law in a totalitarian regime finds its concrete and most characteristic expression in the fact that every citizen has direct access to the coercive apparatus of the state, unmediated by lengthy and complicated judicial procedures. Everybody can use the political police against everybody else—quickly, without delays or undue formalities.

The ubiquity of terror, as well as terror's random quality, has its roots in the privatization of the state that I have described. There was little a Soviet citizen could do to protect his innocence once the state was let loose on him.* One could write letters to higher authorities, not infrequently to Stalin himself, laying out one's sorrows and grievances in the hope that the abuse one suffered would be brought to an end by intervention from above. And it sometimes was. The all-powerful distant ruler would occasionally accept the case of a little man and destroy a local clique that made the little man's life miserable. The point is, however, that, even though activated to uphold some general sense of right or justice, the mechanism at work was no different from a case of denunciation. Whether through denunciation or through petition, an individual directly mobilized the state, in a highly personal fashion, to settle his problem.** Thus, the mechanism that re-established momentarily a sense of justice in the experience of Soviet citizens was also predicated on the principle of privatization of the public realm.

A peculiar variation of the right of petition was used in the Western Ukraine and Western Belorussia. Local people in good standing with the regime—outspoken sympathizers, collaborators, or those who were as poor or poorer than anybody else around—could certify that an arrested or about to be arrested person had done no harm and was no exploiter. Very often such a voucher was as good as a "not guilty" pronouncement in a court of law, though the procedure was used

---

* "A young writer, who in 1938 was five years old, said to me recently, 'May I ask you something? How was it that you survived?' What could I say? . . . I shall never know." This is the famous writer Ilya Ehrenburg reminiscing (*Memoirs*, p. 429), certainly not an enemy of the Soviet regime. The vulnerability of Soviet citizens did not originate in the fact that everybody was engaged in anti-Soviet activity and that the state knew all about it. Although the overwhelming majority of Soviet citizens practiced obedience to the party line, they felt no sense of security. And *they had reasons to be afraid, because the decision about their freedom or incarceration was left, more or less, to the discretion of anyone at all from among their fellow citizens.* One could be arrested because a neighbor took a liking to one's apartment or one's wife or husband, because of envy on the job or the desire to get even for some personal injury that one had caused long ago.

** "Now, Ivan Petrovich," wrote a desperate petitioner to the Smolensk Obkom secretary, "there is only one hope—you," or as in another personal plea to the Obkom secretary, "I trust you implicitly, and whatever your opinion will be on this problem, it will be law for me" (Fainsod, *Smolensk under Soviet Rule*, pp. 399, 229).

exclusively in agricultural villages and relatively small communities and was not without risks for the sponsors themselves.[16] But it was simply "reverse denunciation." A person whose word could pluck someone out of jail could just as easily put someone else there. And, the latter happened much more frequently.

Good and evil were meted out in the Soviet system in the same fashion, without slow procedures of institutional mediation, in response to individuals who pulled in the state whenever they felt driven by greed, maliciousness, jealousy, or despair. That justice was occasionally dispensed only reinforced the very mechanism that exposed Soviet people to the whims of their fellow citizens; such deliverance offered occasional proof that the system works, and, as we know from social psychology, an intermittent reinforcement schedule perpetuates behavioral patterns more than any other.

Strange as it may seem, in Stalinist Russia decision about *who* would go to jail was left largely to the discretion of ordinary Soviet citizens. Because anyone could cause anyone else's arrest, Soviet terror acquired the awesomely random quality that rendered it so effective; there were as many reasons for being sent to jail as there were different motivations inspiring individual denunciations. Despite the built-in stratification of the Soviet society, in which even access to commonplace goods depended on one's position in the bureaucratic hierarchy, the famous *uravnilovka* (equalization) of Soviet citizens was real: everyone shared the power to bring down and destroy any individual. It was an unusual power, however, capable of destroying but not of protecting. And no one was able to provide for the security of one's own person; hence, we see the well-known process of social atomization under totalitarianism. For in the end, what brings social atomization is less the outlawing of voluntary associations than the fear and distrust inspired by a system of social control that allows individuals only to cause harm to one another and at the same time renders each defenseless against such attempts by others.

122

PART TWO

CONFINEMENTS

FOUR

Socialization

As WE MOVE beyond the period immediately following the Red Army's invasion, our primary interest remains unchanged: to study the mechanisms responsible for the imposition of a specifically Soviet institutional order. Although no data exist to give a fully comprehensive description of daily administrative routines in the Western Ukraine and Western Belorussia, we can discuss in detail what the Soviet authorities removed from the mainstream of society and declared unacceptable. An investigation of penological practices and population transfers by the Soviet authorities allows us to observe the implementation of social control mechanisms throughout the period of Soviet rule.

As a convenient steppingstone in the analysis of social control, let us begin with a discussion of the socialization of youth. The forging of a new man has always been a pet project of the Soviet regime, and, for best results, the process should begin early in life. Thus, not surprisingly, upon entering the Western Ukraine and Western Belorussia, Soviet authorities were well disposed toward youth. Here was a group with few stakes in the old regime—even, if properly encouraged, with many claims against it. Not yet fully socialized into the old ways, youth was malleable into conformity with the new ones.

And if any segment of the local society fell for the new regime it was the youth. The sheer activism, the spirit of adventure, the promise of change embodied in a social revolution attracted youth. One Polish boy, ten years old at the time, sheepishly admitted to experiencing a sense of excitement when he was dispatched with his family in a cattle car for deportation to Russia.[1] This attraction had nothing to do with Soviet policies or anything clearly associated with Marxist ideology. Rather, it was a vague welcome to the unknown, to the shakeup of old institutions, to the opening up of new opportunities, to the breakdown of discipline.

The sudden role reversal and normative ambiguity introduced by the Soviets—so threatening to older, established citizens—intrigued and tantalized the young. Every time grownups, especially those who had held authority under the old regime, were scolded or humiliated in their presence, the young were somewhat liberated from their culturally prescribed subordination. Each time youngsters were treated as grownups, as when they were asked to evaluate their teachers' behavior in class or to inform about their families' private affairs, they were liberated a little more. In the end they were often placed in grownup roles.

We are familiar with the general pattern underlying this situation: the imposition of a new order involves the destruction of the old. But in the midst of ongoing disorganization, it takes time and wisdom to recognize that one framework of authority is simply being replaced by another. In the meantime one may say that youth's developmental needs—its rebelliousness against authority in general—attuned it well to the strategic needs of the occupiers. Both were anxious, for their own good reasons, to be rid of the old regime, whether at school, in the family, or in the city hall. But the commonality of their outlooks mostly ended there.

Schools and Language

The school system sponsored by the Soviet authorities in the Western Ukraine and Western Belorussia was put in place with dispatch. By January 1, 1940, the reformed system was already installed: all private schools were abolished, and a uniform pattern of public education was introduced, with coeducational four-year elementary schools, seven-year "incomplete" secondary schools in the countryside, and ten-year secondary schools in the cities. In addition, the language of instruction, the program of instruction, and the instructors were changed. Not everything was new, of course, but there was enough innovation to disrupt the educational process radically for most children.

Although many teachers had fallen victim to the early violence and chaos (as I already mentioned, school principals were particularly vulnerable to persecution and arrest at the time), on the whole they seemed to fare better than other civil servants. Unlike policemen, members of the judiciary, or administrative officials, they were not systematically imprisoned. More like postal workers or skilled employees of the local administration, they seemed to be valued for their expertise. They had to undergo rapid re-education themselves, but their pedagogical skills apparently were not immediately dispensable, so initially they were pressured to resume their careers in the new school system.[2]

Structurally, the four-, seven-, and ten-grade system was a replica of the Soviet paradigm, but the new number of grades was less of a shock than the new educational policies. Among these, two were most visible: the school system was secularized and depolonized. Religion, previously taught as a separate subject, was banned from the schools along with history,* the Polish language (generally limited to two hours per week), Latin (wherever it was taught), and geography. Crucifixes were pulled down from classroom walls along with the Polish eagle (the national emblem) and the portraits of Polish statesmen.**

The most conspicuous aspect of depolonization was the introduction of a new language of instruction. In theory, parents were to decide on the language in the school attended by their children. Thus, given the ethnic composition of the majority of the non-Polish population in the area, parents were likely to choose Ukrainian, Belorussian, or Yiddish. As it turned out, however, the new administration was interested in promoting Russian as well.[3] Parents' assemblies in urban areas were not infrequently pressured into accepting solutions not of their making. In Szczuczyn, for example, a postal worker remembered:

> A meeting of all the parents was called to decide whether Polish or Russian would be the language of instruction. During the meeting, in the presence of the NKVD, the parents found out that they had to vote for either Russian or Belorussian. Because of this scheme some women stood up and tried to leave the meeting, but under the threat of drawn guns had to return to their seats. The chairman of the meeting, a Communist, turned to the assembly and said that he would consider all discontent as sabotage and that people must forget about the Polish language.[4]

In somewhat similar circumstances parents in a Śniatyń high school allegedly chose Ukrainian over Polish, and so on.[5] On those infrequent occasions when Polish was kept as the language of instruction, the schools were either moved to new, inferior facilities to make room for Ukrainian, Belorussian, or Russian schools, or they were forced to accept a deliberately awkward afternoon schedule, rotating occupancy of the premises with a non–Polish-language school that met at the normal morning time.[6]

Of course in the majority of schools, especially throughout the countryside, the transition to Ukrainian or Belorussian was in accord with

---

* As Wanda Węgrzynowna put it: "They stopped teaching Polish history and religion, they even denied that God exists. They argued that men come from monkeys, and other similar nonsense" (HI, AC, 14264).

** According to an anonymous memorandum prepared in Bucharest on August 24, 1940, crucifixes were sometimes left on classroom walls, presumably to accommodate a more intransigent community. Still, portraits of Lenin and Stalin would be hung alongside, resulting in a triptych reminding the local people of Calvary and prompting comments that once again Christ was spread on a cross between two criminals (GSHI, Collection 82, File 29, "Bilans 10-o miesięcznych rządów sowieckich w Polsce").

the strongly felt preferences of the local population. In fact, if there was one aspect of the new order that had the unreserved support of the so-called national minorities, it was precisely the introduction of the majority language of the locality into the public sphere of schools, offices, and geography (e.g., when street names were changed). The minorities benefited from this policy promoting their national culture and sense of national identity, and they derived a symbolic sense of satisfaction as well.

Teachers had to improve their linguistic skills promptly. Special courses were organized to familiarize them with Marxism-Leninism and to teach them Ukrainian or Belorussian. On October 12, *Czerwony Sztandar* printed a story from Western Belorussia about how 7,000 teachers were already participating in such remedial courses in the county towns of the province. The timing of this report is telling: it appeared less than one month after the Red Army's invasion of Poland. I can hardly picture 7,000 teachers studying Belorussian in mid-October 1939 surrounded by the chaos of administrative reorganization and mobilization for the pre-election campaign. But even if the report is indicative of wishful thinking rather than actual accomplishments, the intentions of the new authorities were unambiguously revealed. Indeed, in due time they would be systematically implemented. During the Christmas break, from late December 1939 through January 1940, special courses for teachers were organized throughout the Western Ukraine and Western Belorussia, and as of January 1 the Soviet organization of the school system was officially adopted.[7] All of these new requirements hardly alleviated the teachers' burdens, compounded as they were by political supervision, curriculum changes, and the breakdown of classroom discipline. As a teacher from Brasław put it: "It was hard to teach in Belorussian, a language I didn't know even though I went to a course."[8]

Officially, the policy of introducing a variety of national languages into the school system was governed by a doctrine of ethnic equality and nondiscrimination. Yet the policy was implemented somewhat selectively from the beginning. First, far fewer Yiddish-language schools were allowed than should have been if the principle were adhered to faithfully.[9] Second, the Polish language was not simply returned to its status of one among many; instead, it was systematically purged from the school system (frequently against the wishes of the parents). In numerous instances pupils were forbidden to speak it at all.[10] "Even on the way home from school," complained a child from Wołostków in Mościska county, "we were forbidden to speak Polish."[11] The Hebrew language was also targeted for extinction. It stood for Jewish nationalism (i.e., for Zionism) as well as for the piety of the Jewish people, and it was banned outright from the school system.[12]

It was doubtless most difficult to make Polish literature fit the propaganda needs of the new regime (even though brilliant writers were involved in the preparation of new compilations, including Mieczysław Jastrun and Julian Przyboś),* but the Soviet authorities were so sensitive that they were able to find Polish textbooks on such seemingly innocuous subjects as mathematics, biology, chemistry, and physics unacceptable as well. As a teacher from a provincial town of Choroszcz said later, "They banned textbooks on arithmetic because they disliked the content of problems and prices mentioned there."[13] In the context of pervasive shortages of goods and runaway inflation, a simple mention of scarce commodities or prewar prices read as an indictment of Soviet-induced misery. Only with translated Soviet textbooks could such suggestions be avoided.[14]

But control over the curriculum was calibrated to reach beyond the selection of subjects and books. The aim was to police the content of each encounter between teachers and students, to program each lesson in accordance with new requirements. One powerful mechanism ensuring that teachers would not speak against the Soviet regime but would follow its educational policies was, of course, the fear of denunciation. Students were openly invited to report on their teachers—and were given credence and credit whenever they availed themselves of the opportunity. Outside inspectors passed through schools continuously,[15] in principle to check on the quality of school work and educational progress but in fact to ascertain the political suitability of the teaching staff and of the school environment. Usually this meant finding out whether crosses and eagles had been pulled from classroom walls and old portraits replaced by new ones, what the teachers were telling their students, and whether children were wearing religious

---

* A review of a new Polish literature reader, printed in the January 14, 1941, issue of *Czerwony Sztandar* and naturally full of praise, mentioned a few shortcomings as well, such as omissions of works that should be studied or factual mistakes in biographical sketches of writers. There may have been some problems of interpretation also. At a writers' union meeting in October 1940, the general editor of the readers, Jerzy Borejsza, pointed to a pernicious tendency to overestimate some writers: "The incorrect theory of 'talentism' still prevails, which bases evaluation of authors on talent alone, without taking into consideration their efforts to improve literary skills and political understanding" (*Czerwony Sztandar*, Oct. 27, 1940). Janina Broniewska, "Brakujące ogniwo," *Nowe Widnokręgi*, no. 4 (1941); Władysław Bieńkowski, "O wypisach z literatury polskiej," *Nowe Widnokręgi*, no. 1 (1940). See also the section "Kronika" in the first number of *Nowe Widnokręgi*.

medallions to school. Needless to say, supervision and intimidation of teachers never stopped; everywhere there were new local administrators openly engaged in policing the staff. To stress the point, they might occasionally come to work with casually tucked sidearms.[16]

As in any other domain of collective life, a procedure for self-policing had been introduced into the schools. It was predicated on a very simple idea: everyone was put under obligation to keep a record on oneself. "Every school and every individual teacher must prepare detailed plans of their work" according to *Czerwony Sztandar* (January 4, 1940), which are necessary to conduct methodological evaluations and analyses during teachers' conferences. This meticulous planning even had to take into account extracurricular activities, such as afterschool programs or "enlightenment work" with students' parents. In a word, teachers were obliged to prepare an advance script of all their public encounters, whether with students or parents. Lew Wasyl, who taught at the time in Kowel, recalls that the teacher's plan for each lesson, no matter what the subject, was supposed to include an example or argument proving that God does not exist.[17]

Not that all teachers necessarily obliged and followed the script every day, but frequently they had to speak against their conscience (at least those who did not espouse the new ideals). Janina Hobler, a teacher from Gródek Jagielloński, remembers with relief the moment of her arrest: it brought an end to the increasingly burdensome daily hypocrisy of scolding students for expressing views that she shared herself.[18] Nor was her experience unique. "It was an awful job," wrote a teacher from Dworzec. "Children screamed continuously, 'We want to study from our books.' They didn't want to use unfamiliar Belorussian textbooks, which they loathed. So after a month I took a leave of absence from school and left."[19] But only a lucky few could afford to pack up and go away. And besides, teachers were sometimes pressured by the community or their own sense of responsibility to stay on the job to protect and screen the local children from the zeal of the educators who would be appointed in their stead and, presumably, mercilessly implement Russification.[20] Not only Polish teachers, but also Ukrainians, who otherwise heartily applauded depolonization of the school system, found their new jobs to be burdensome because they were forced to speak against God.[21]

MILITANT ATHEISM

The other most characteristic feature of the new educational policies was secularization. Not only were religion and religious symbols

130

banned from classrooms, but forceful atheist propaganda was aimed at schoolchildren as well. Indeed, the assault on the youths' religious upbringing was comprehensive and, in a way, rather imaginative. The school calendar, for example, was changed so that every sixth day rather than every seventh was free; most children were required to attend school rather than go to church on Sundays, and Jewish youths remained in their Yiddish-language schools on the Sabbath as a result.[22] The policy was ultimately abandoned after only haphazard implementation because of the opposition it encountered.[23]

Another clever device in the campaign against religion among the young involved mini-spectacles staged to demonstrate the omnipotence of Stalin or Soviet power and God's inability to deliver earthly goods. In effect, they suggested to the young that the new authorities had a "better" religion on their side and that it would be advantageous to change allegiance. The proof was offered in a very simple experiment repeated throughout the occupied territory with such faithful adherence to an unchanging script that one can only conclude it was written and distributed from some high echelon in the Soviet educational establishment. Pupils were told to say prayers in the classroom and ask God for candy. Predictably, nothing happened. Then, it was suggested that they pray to Stalin, or the teacher did so on their behalf. And, also predictably, a miracle followed: classroom doors would open and a basketful of candies or white rolls would be delivered.[24] The younger the children, the better it worked; and when staged with a certain finesse, it made a powerful impression indeed. In a Siberian classroom where a ten-year-old boy from Baranowicze county was continuing his education after deportation from Poland, two holes were drilled in the ceiling: "To one hole the Commandant said, 'Boh, Boh dai perokh' [God, God give dumpling], and nothing happened. To the second he said, 'Sovet, Sovet dai kanfet' [Soviet, Soviet give candy], and candy came pouring down. He laughed that God gave nothing. Polish children ran away."[25]

On other occasions "they took medallions with images of saints off children's necks and gave them ones with Stalin's picture instead. For children who didn't protest the exchange they also had sweets."[26] In the ongoing antireligious campaign this was an example of the "carrot" strategy, appropriate for a county town like Sambor. But in the backwoods a stick was more likely to be used. Thus Bolesław Nobis, a teacher from the small Wołyń village of Suchowce in whose classroom two children were caught wearing religious medallions, was taken to the local jail for six days; and "how many blows I was struck

131

only God, the neighbors, and my wife can tell since I was black as soot from the beatings."[27]

A more concerted effort to purge religion from young people's spiritual life came around the first Christmas–New Year season in the already socialist Western Ukraine and Western Belorussia. The point was to shift the emphasis and timing of the holiday season and, by conflating the celebrations, to overcome centuries of backwardness and superstition. Simply, New Year's Day was supposed to become the equivalent and replacement of the Christmas holiday, with everything (i.e., decorating a coniferous tree and gift giving) preserved except the religious content of the occasion. In schools, factories, and offices, gatherings were organized for children around a decorated tree, where gifts were handed out in celebration of the New Year.[28] Organizers aggressively emphasized the polemical point of these festivities. An article in *Czerwony Sztandar* (December 25, 1939) entitled " 'Christmas' and Winter 'Holidays' "—with both "Christmas" and "Holidays" in quotation marks to convey the ironic distance of the author—went to the heart of the matter without equivocation: "Science established a long time ago," wrote a certain F. Oleszczuk, "that Christ was a thought up, a mythical figure. He never existed and therefore he could never have been born. . . ." In case someone was not convinced by the force of this logic, other arguments could be mustered as well. For example, when a group of visiting Red Army officers and local officials brought gifts to the New Year Tree celebration in a Nowosielce school, they asked the children where the gifts came from. Those who said they were God's gifts were told to put them down. But the village children had not tasted sweets for some time by then; most turned around and awkwardly, half-smilingly said what was expected—that the gifts came from Stalin—and got to keep them after all.[29]

But it was not so much in such events as in a relentless, stubborn, everyday drive that the determination to root religion out of youngsters' lives manifested itself. Special recreational areas were set up in schools, so-called red corners, and children were encouraged to join "circles of atheists," an ecumenical alternative, one is tempted to say, for those who had not yet reached the maturity in socialist outlook required of a prospective Komsomol member.[30] Teaching materials were combed for suitability, with the result that many a school library was torched or confiscated—"deported," as it were.[31] Polish textbooks were kept in use only briefly, and after they were withdrawn there were no school manuals of any kind until translations of Soviet textbooks were made available. These were soon introduced as replacements for subversive Polish textbooks on the grounds that they offered a "materialistic interpretation of nature."[32]

Whether this strenuous campaign of secularization weakened the religious spirit of the indigenous population is very much in doubt. But it must have further undermined their sense of social responsibility by promoting duplicity and mendaciousness, as it forced many people to speak and behave publicly in ways incompatible with their privately held convictions. By ridiculing the ethical foundations of most people's beliefs, the organizers of the new order, perhaps not altogether unwittingly, were inviting license.

THE ESTABLISHMENT OF DISORDER

To all the difficulties piled on the teaching profession that I have already enumerated, another must be added: the breakdown of discipline. Among the questions put to schoolchildren by inspectors was: "Does the teacher allow children to address him with 'Pan'?"[33] The Soviets, as we already know, made a hostile symbol of this commonplace Polish form of address.[34] Disregarding the dual meaning of the word "Pan" (one of which is to denote impersonal courtesy, much as in the word "mister"), they seized upon its more archaic meaning of "master" and virtually banned it from the vocabulary as a symbol of class-ridden, bourgeois, if not aristocratic, Poland. Schoolchildren were told to use "comrade" or the common Russian form (first name and patronymic) instead. As this would be a totally artificial construct in the Polish language, children were in effect required to address teachers by their first names.[35] Given the traditionalism of the countryside, the inculcated respect for persons older than oneself and of a higher status (typically bestowed on a country teacher), this was, mildly put, an invitation to license or, worse, a blow to the school's authority. The breakdown was emphasized when the teacher was saddled with the responsibility of enforcing this odd, even demeaning form of address.

Yet, on the whole, this was a relatively innocent item in the general overhaul of the educational system, which was itself only a fragment in the general design to re-educate the entire society. It was essential to change people's perception of the source of authority. Thus, along with infusing new content into the courses taught at school, the new regime was concerned to capture for its own purposes the more general, the broadest learning that youngsters acquire in school, namely, the capacity for and habit of obedience, the recognition of authority beyond the family circle, and domestication, as it were, into membership in society. Since in school these social requirements are inculcated along with respect for learning and discipline, so both had to be compromised in order to wrest children away from the old ways.

"Students took to smoking cigarettes in class, they insulted the teachers, and the like. Delegations of children went to the commission to lodge complaints against parents and teachers," a teacher from Rożniatów complained as soon as she got the chance.[36] This loosening in school discipline was not merely the side effect of an incompletely thought through educational reform but rather its core, at least in the reform's initial stages. Before installing a socialist mentality in their new fellow citizens, Soviet educators had to undermine the prevailing framework of authority, and for the moment it did not matter that the ensuing void was filled with the secret yearnings of malcontents. Clearly, the early stages of Soviet rule would captivate a diverse constituency: ethnic minorities, youth, landless peasants, and even the urban poor responded to the process of liberation that unfolded before their eyes. In the broadest possible sense, the Soviet regime lifted, temporarily, the full panoply of social controls, not only the old governmental authority and enforcement apparatus but also customs, tradition, and even plain common sense.

In every public forum—the school being only one of many—the same spectacle unfolded: society was stood on its head. Władysław Matczyk from Sokal county captured the spirit of the times in a brief passage of his recollections: "They decided during this meeting that the rich people would take the place of the poor, and the poor ones would take the place of the rich."[37] And the same applied to a variety of other polarities: national minorities and Poles; children and parents; youth and grownups; secular and sacred; incompetence and expertise; social marginality and social respectability. To an extraordinary degree, this process was content-blind and structure-sensitive: any social hierarchy was a likely target.

School principals who were not arrested were demoted. Sometimes jobs were swapped, as Matczyk described: "I was let go as a school principal and demoted to be a subordinate teacher and my once-subordinate teacher, a Ukrainian, was appointed school principal."[38] Frequently, outsiders were brought in to take over schools or as additional teachers. Many came from the Soviet Union. These new appointees usually lacked qualifications, and even though the subjects they taught may have been the Soviet constitution or the history of the Bolshevik Communist Party, they still left an impression of ignorance and of being ill at ease as educators.[39] That the curriculum was simultaneously being revised did nothing to promote quality in education. As a result, there was little learning going on at school during the period of transition to the Soviet system of organization. Janusz Eichler recalls the atmosphere in his Wilno high school:

> Classes began, but without a fixed curriculum, which was constantly being changed. For example, the history professor retracted his lectures and started teaching something else. . . . Our behavior at school was appalling. . . . Nobody thought about learning. . . . Eating carrots in class, throwing apple cores at the blackboard was a natural thing to do. . . . I must admit that the teacher's job in those circumstances was probably rather unpleasant.[40]

Not only were children not learning much in school, but they balked at attending classes at all, and as a result parents were threatened with arrest, deportation, and fines.[41] This resistance was certainly widespread among Polish families, but I expect that the aggressive atheist propaganda also produced doubts in the minds of Ukrainian, Belorussian, and Jewish parents as to the benefits their children would derive from such education even if it were conducted in the national language.

But even as the chaos of the early transitional period subsided, it was not learning above all that the schools found themselves promoting. "Socialist competition," introduced in the spring of 1940, subverted the educational process once again. Schools competed in terms of student attendance and grades. Different classrooms within schools challenged one another on the same issues, setting, as it were, production goals for themselves. On March 12, 1940, for example, schools Number 57 and Number 42 in Lwów committed themselves to raising the percentage of honors grades for students aged nine to fourteen and to entirely eliminating unsatisfactory grades, about 19 percent of the total. Their target date for accomplishing these goals was April 1— barely two weeks hence!

The results of such competitions were monitored closely, and the stakes were high enough to motivate the chief of the oblast's People's Department of Education to give close, public scrutiny to Lwów pupils' school grades.[42] We can easily imagine the impact of this political campaign on grade inflation and the quality of education.[43] Michał Mirski, who was in charge of Kowel's People's Department of Education and monitored the competition in his school district, left an insider's account that is informed rather than bitter (he remained a communist for the rest of his life):

The competition was voluntary, but no teacher had the courage to exercise his right of free choice. The competition between different classrooms, teachers, or schools was about educational results measured in terms of grades that teachers gave their students. . . . The total number of good grades accumulated by students determined the location of a school vis-à-vis other schools in the competition. No teacher wanted to come in last in the competition among teachers of a given school, and his performance was judged by his students' placement. Nor did the school principal want his school to come in last, as this would reflect less on the performance of his teachers than on his own.[44]

To be sure, students took advantage of the situation, stopped working, and resorted to blackmailing their teachers on occasion.

Of course, as noted earlier, enticing children to report on their teachers and parents was quite common. Thus, "they would ask children about anything, believing that kids don't understand what's going on and would tell them, and they offered candy and toys as rewards."[45] In this way the young were drawn away from the tutelage of their elders. Szymon Ważyński, a Wilno high school student, believed "they were demoralizing school children by inciting them against their parents. A child who wanted to avoid some well-deserved punishment would run to them and return home with an NKVD man who forced father or mother to beg forgiveness from the child, or else threatened parents with a prison term."[46] Ważyński was perhaps especially sensitive, but other witnesses also noted this particular bent of Soviet educational philosophy.*

As another way of separating youth and elders, young people were kept busy away from home, which must have been very attractive to many. In addition to the frequent meetings where participation was required, numerous new opportunities for participation in public life were offered to youth, including sports events, afterschool activity circles, and evening dances.[47] A former student in a Ukrainian high school near Stanisławów recalled with great fondness numerous school choir competitions in which she participated,[48] and *Czerwony Sztandar* carried stories about "olympiads of indigenous artistic creativity." The first such district-level olympiad in Lwów involved "608

---

* On this issue the most compelling evidence is provided by the cult of Pavlik Morozov, a lad who denounced his father during the collectivization campaign and was promptly killed by his grandfather. Hero worship of him was shamelessly nurtured by the Soviet authorities. See, for example, E. Smirnov, *Pavlik Morozov*, and V. Gubarov, *Syn*.

theatrical circles, 450 choirs, 143 orchestras, and 97 ballet collectives established in the district since January [1940]. . . ."[49] This report is about the situation in *one* district only, and there is reason to believe that, unlike information about other kinds of exercise in Stalin's Russia, this report was reliable and perhaps even underestimated the actual achievements.[50]

For purposes of socialization, an extensive apparatus of propaganda was fielded in the attempt to frame each person's life in such a way that one would be constantly in the presence of some paraphernalia of the new order. For example, various anniversaries and celebrations were introduced to the calendar with such frequency that there was little respite from public occasions one might be compelled to attend. Electoral campaigns alone occupied some five months altogether. There were, in addition, anniversaries of the October Revolution and of the recently accomplished liberation of the Western Ukraine and Western Belorussia, the First of May celebrations, an extravagant commemoration of the eighty-fifth anniversary of Adam Mickiewicz's death in November 1940, another for the Ukrainian writer Ivan Franko, and one for the Jewish actress Estera Rachela Kamińska. The XXVI International Day of Youth was remembered on September 1st (but not a word appeared in *Czerwony Sztandar* on this date about the first anniversary of the outbreak of the war).[51] These, and many more, must have provided an abundance of happy occasions to join together in cheerful celebrations.

But one was really in the constant company of official propaganda every day of the week. The displays put together for the October elections were never dismantled. Loudspeakers in the streets continued to broadcast songs, news bulletins, special programs, and transmissions of official celebrations. Everywhere posters mocked Poland, Polish statesmen, and the ruling classes, as well as war-mongering England and France. Quite a few monuments were put to new uses. During a meeting near Głębokie, Danuta Dziewucka witnessed how an agitator knocked off the head from Marshal Piłsudski's monument with a hammer blow. The rest of the monument was left intact, and in a few days Lenin's head was propped up on the marshal's shoulders. In Białowieża the Soviet authorities simply covered President Mościcki's monument with red paint.[52] Oblast- and raion-based newspapers, as well as wall-newspapers in factories, schools, and offices, flourished.[53] Artists and intellectuals were sent out *en masse* to meet with the common people.[54]

All this attention, directed predominantly at young people, must have been to their liking. It certainly undermined the traditional authority of school, church, and family, because only the new authority had exclusive command of the resources to entertain or the benefits to bestow on its young clients. Furthermore, the process of undermining traditional authority and turning society upside down was accompanied by a tacitly encouraged revolution in sexual mores. Reverend Bolesław Dudzewicz, who taught in the Drohiczyn high school, believed that "they kept youth in a state of sensual excitement to make it easily susceptible to their tendencies and the slogan of free love."[55] Although a priest may have been rather more sensitive in this area than the average person, I am confident that most witnesses of the epoch would agree with the assessment of a postal employee from Stanisławów: "They tried most of all to win over youth, starting with young children."[56]

RESISTANCE

Not surprisingly, the susceptibility of young people to the new order was matched only by their resilience. Perhaps no other group in society was so restless and outspoken in its rebelliousness against the Soviet regime. Most of the existing evidence sheds light on the critical attitudes of Polish youth, but one can infer from the heightened intensity of OUN activities and the persecution of Ukrainian patriotic youth that there must have been widespread internal opposition to the Soviet regime among the minorities as well.[57] Although we lack the evidence to judge the numbers, we know that Jewish youth participated in the Zionist conspiratorial network devoted to smuggling young Halutzim to Palestine through Wilno.[58] Throughout the Soviet occupation, masses of Jewish youth also attended religious classes in private homes in defiance of the official ban on Hebrew instruction.[59]

Indeed, scores of illegal networks were established all over the occupied territory immediately after the invasion. Conspiracies proliferated in cities, villages, and hamlets, and their breadth, dynamism, and resilience are important indicators of society's reluctance to espouse the new order. Thousands of officers and NCOs who escaped captivity were involved, but also numerous civilians, who organized around skeletons of various prewar political parties, for example.[60] Peasants joined in, along with workers, civil servants, priests, and teachers, as well as youth of school age and in their early twenties.

The military set up the underground on the very day of the Soviet invasion, September 17, 1939.[61] In besieged Lwów, about to be surrendered to the Red Army, General Marian Żegota-Januszajtis began putting together a military conspiracy, drawing on the youth scouting organization. Januszajtis's initiative was very popular and well known around town.[62] In the trenches with the 3rd Company, 1st Batallion of the Lwów's Brigade of National Defense (staffed entirely by recently called-up reservists who lived in the city and its vicinity) platoon commander Jan Jaworski ordered his soldiers on the day of the surrender to hide weapons near their positions, to go home, and to maintain contact with one another.[63] The mushrooming of conspiratorial organizations all over the Soviet-occupied territory was truly astounding. As Marian Ruczkowski-Słomski from Bitków in Nadworna county concluded, after describing the patriotism that moved him to launch one such independent initiative:

> A lot of Poles thought along the same lines I did. Before establishing the first cell I prayed to God for help and blessing of my undertaking, I apologized to my fiancée, and having assembled all my cash and other valuables totaling about 12,000 złotys, inspired by a visionary dream, I began to organize military units that would later receive the name ZWZ.[64]

Even though the Polish authorities failed to establish a successful underground leadership structure in the Soviet-occupied territories (several designated commanders of the military network, as well as many other top officers, had been arrested and from January 1940 Colonel Emil Macieliński, in charge of the Lwów district of the Home Army had been turned into an NKVD informer[65]), citizens' underground initiatives proliferated. Those assembled in the independently established networks busily gathered and conserved weapons, recruited new members, sometimes put out leaflets or distributed underground newspapers, and spread rumors. Occasionally groups engaged in sabotage and terrorist attacks against the occupier.[66] Unlike under the German occupation, however, this rather typical repertoire of activities never coalesced into a coordinated effort because both a central authority and financial assistance were lacking.[67] In the end, these spontaneous citizens' initiatives became directionless, their members grew careless (in many instances membership lists had been kept and were apprehended by the NKVD), and the groups proved easy targets for penetration by the NKVD.[68]

Left to themselves, the citizens' groups were prone to act on provocation or the restlessness of their local commanders. The bloodiest tragedy occurred probably in Czortków, in Tarnopol voivodeship, where a premature uprising in which many high school students participated broke out on or around January 21, 1940.[69] Four groups staged attacks on two separately located military barracks (hoping to find weapons there), the prison compound, and the train station. They took over the barracks, the post office, and the hospital. But the armories turned out to be empty—and a trainload of Soviet troops, unbeknownst to the Polish fighters, was waiting in the station. This more or less orderly, though unsuccessful, scenario has been provided by Tadeusz Bańkowski, apparently one of the leading participants. A more skeptical observer who filed a report that reached General Sosnkowski in London put it differently: "After two hours of senseless shooting, in which a lot of people not knowing what was going on participated as well, 'the Uprising' was over."[70]

Massive arrests continued for several days afterward. Many of the arrested were high school students. Perhaps as many as 600 people were rounded up (in a town of about 20,000); many were taken away immediately and, apparently, shot. Those placed in the Czortków jail were most brutally beaten during interrogation. Eventually some of the participants were put on trial. A group of twenty-eight was brought before a court on September 25, 1940, in Tarnopol. Thirteen received death sentences; the rest were given ten years of prison each. Tadeusz Bańkowski, one of the thirteen, had his death sentence commuted, apparently because he was under eighteen years of age. The fate of the others is unknown.[71]

Youth conspiracies flourished everywhere—in the large cities of Lwów, Wilno, and Białystok, and also in smaller provincial towns, such as Horochów, Słonim, Augustów, Czortków, Gródek Jagielloński, and many others.[72] But perhaps more significant were the repeated public demonstrations of youth's defiance of Soviet ritualism. The youth somehow recognized that to lie in the presence of one's peers is corrupting, rather than an unimportant token gesture, which is how its elders probably justified their actions, judging by their behavior during the October elections.

The show of defiance at public meetings was a widespread phenomenon. Several Lwów theaters in early October 1939 witnessed incidents of massive protests by schoolchildren. Young people were not intimidated by the shrewd and usually effective stratagem of Soviet meeting organizers. When asked who was against the incorporation of the Ukraine into the USSR, all the children, with very few exceptions, raised their hands. One such meeting ended with the audience bursting into the patriotic religious hymn "We Want God" ("My chcemy Boga"). Danuta Polniaszek Kossakowska remembered in addition that, while the audience sang "My chcemy Boga," the meeting's organizers stood on the stage facing the huge crowd of young people with clenched fists thrust forward, singing the "International."[73] Children were often enticed at the conclusion of meetings to shout in unison "Khai zhive batko Stalin," or some such slogan, but they might scream some Polish patriotic slogans instead or, more likely, be silent—a very eloquent form of protest at the time.[74] To overcome such stifling silence during a school gathering in Złoczów, where several appeals to the audience for shouts to honor leaders of the Soviet Union went unheeded, one of the high school teachers took the floor with a conciliatory speech. It would take time, he stated, before young people could begin to appreciate the opportunities that had now been opened to them as a result of the Red Army's arrival. As for now, he concluded, " 'let us shout together to honor all hardworking Poles on the entire globe,' and only then the shout 'long live' resounded thrice in the hall."[75] In many instances, however, no peaceful resolution of tension was found, and young people were assaulted, beaten up, while the meeting disintegrated into a cacophony of voices. Needless to say, arrests of schoolchildren were commonplace.[76]

IN some strange way, the occupation produced a bifurcated reality. There were more schools, more opportunities for higher and professional training, free education,[77] instruction in the native language, encouragement of physical and artistic development—as if most of the bottlenecks traditionally impeding upward mobility had been removed. There was also a drastic inflation of employment; some factories and offices needed twice as many workers and administrative personnel as before the war. As Marian Śmietanko put it, "Anybody who asked for an office job, got one."[78] And there were indeed those few tens of thousands—a small and an enormous number simultaneously—mostly young, predominantly of Jewish or Ukrainian stock, for whom Poland's defeat was no loss to mourn but rather an exhilarating opening, an undreamed-of opportunity to become immersed in visible political activity, not in the confines of their ethnic ghettos but before the larger general public. Consequently, they assumed roles that were never meant to be theirs with an energy and zeal commensurate with the uniqueness of the occasion. And to the extent that these changes equalized opportunities, they were favorably received by the majority of the population.

But the genuine excitement stemming from being treated just like everyone else petered out quickly; the previously discriminated against minorities soon found out that sameness was imposed upon them under the guise of equality. It was a reversal of the classical pattern of discrimination (and therefore so confusing) with which the Jews in particular were familiar from their long experience of persecution in

Europe. So long as they kept to themselves, minorities were tolerated. But whenever the process of social change brought them out of self-imposed isolation, or when they actively sought assimilation, they provoked maximum anger, contempt, and violence from their neighbors. The opposite was true under the Soviet regime: here their insularity, their willful separation from the rest of society could not be tolerated. Jews could acquire Soviet citizenship, with all the rights and entitlements that went with the honor, but they could not sustain their community life anymore. Once again they could not be Jews *and* citizens of the state that claimed jurisdiction over them; whether before or after the revolution, it was always an either/or.

So, as the limitations and absurdities inherent in the new society became apparent, enthusiasm slowly receded. If one wanted a career as a nurse or an engineer or a physician, one could realistically expect to achieve that goal in the future. And this was of course important. But what if one wanted *also* to be a Jew, or a Ukrainian, or a Pole, or well off, or independent? Freedom was being curtailed, economic conditions were deteriorating, a sense of national identity made one precariously close to being a nationalist—a criminal category. As a result, discrepancies between the alleged goals and everyday practices of real socialism could be unsettling for those whose opportunities in prewar Poland had been nil. A short *Czerwony Sztandar* article about health-care services for babies said it all. The pitch of the piece, combined with its concluding paragraph, strikes me as conveying a deeply accurate portrait of Soviet reality:

> The opening of the Central Milk Kitchen for infants was received joyfully not only by mothers but also by the population of Lwów. Only the Soviet authority, for which the welfare of the citizen is the supreme concern, can spend so much effort and devote such attention in order to spare its youngest citizens, denied the benefit of maternal milk, billions of germs which cause illness and sometimes even death.

But the city health department did not budget any transportation via which infant formulas could be delivered to the needy. "What use is there," Magda Treblińska asked despairingly, "for good, sterile formulas if they cannot be delivered to those for whom they were meant?"[79]

It is easier, of course, to perceive contradictions in hindsight than to see through the confusion of events as they unfold. Nor did Soviet propaganda help its audience to think clearly about their predicaments. On September 17, 1940, the first anniversary of the liberation of the Western Ukraine and Western Belorussia, Wanda Wasilewska mounted the rostrum in Lwów to speak before the assembled Soviet leaders and a huge audience. "In strong masculine words she called on listeners to look honestly into their souls after this first year of freedom in work."[80] Everything is mendacious in this statement: a woman materialist speaking with a male voice invokes a religious metaphor and calls enslavement freedom. Even for well-wishers who readily absorbed all the "good sterile formulas," it was a helplessly confusing situation, and they could make no good sense out of it.

FIVE

Prisons

AMONG THE MANY ITEMS that were brought from the USSR to the Western Ukraine and Belorussia in September 1939, one of the most appreciated was a maxim: "In the Soviet Union there are only three categories of people—those who were in prison, those who are in prison, and those who will be in prison."[1] Dropped by some society wit as a clever joke, it caught the fancy of the Soviet people and was spread by the conquering army to the periphery of the new empire like a bylaw of Stalin's constitution. And although the conquered people retained little from repeated group readings of that "most democratic constitution in the whole world," the one-sentence summary of a Soviet citizen's destiny was well remembered. Indeed, from the evidence of daily life, one had to conclude that what lay in store for all Soviet citizens was this rather peculiar rite of passage: "Many people were arrested soon after the Red Army came. We thought, so many, that this will be it, but it was only the beginning."[2] Waves of arrests intensified with periodic campaigns against particular categories of people, but the constant flow of indiscriminate arrests instilled fear in all but the most outspoken enthusiasts of the new order. "I knew I couldn't avoid it forever because I am not worse than anybody else. I also felt like a Pole, and so I had to be arrested sooner or later."[3]

Anticipation of impending personal disaster brought psychological tension that many could not bear. When the arrest finally came, they felt a sense of relief, as if the threat, being realized, was removed. One could call this good conditioning: in the new circumstances, the well-adjusted personality was the one that *welcomed* the anticipated imprisonment. Only then was one rid of the fear of arrest and able to reach some peace of mind (for example, by gaining freedom from the guilt of being unable to provide for the material well-being and security of one's family).* The widespread attitude was one of fatalistic anticipation of the unavoidable. Ironically, deliverance from the

---

* HI, AC, 5908. A top-secret document of the state secret police (March 27, 1931) reported on popular attitudes in connection with deportations. "The report cited a 'characteristic' case where one citizen came to the raion procuracy and begged to be deported together with the kulaks, reasoning that he would at least have a chance to start a less hectic life" (Fainsod, *Smolensk under Soviet Rule*, 249–250).

144

attendant mental and emotional anguish came only via a gratuitous act by the very same state responsible for it.

ARREST

Denunciations were common throughout the period of Soviet rule. The NKVD recruited confidential collaborators from all social milieus without necessarily confining themselves to the regime's supporters. Families of the arrested, susceptible to blackmail, were approached quite often. A number of arrested officers' wives later testified that they had been called to assist the NKVD. Many were simply offered monetary incentives. Some jobs, like house superintendents, were unavailable except to those who cooperated with the police.[4] Spontaneous in the early stages and direct in its exploitation of personal animosities, the whole system of denunciation became institutionalized. Whoever felt like it would simply send a denunciation by mail.[5] But, of course, the new authorities would not accept a merely auxiliary role in the matter of arrests. While the communities in the newly incorporated territories were gripped by terror, produced mostly by unexpectedly zealous self-policing,* the NKVD had its own priorities and procedures distinct from, though comfortably blended with, the "initiatives" of the local people.

Initially, the elite in all walks of life was removed—skimmed off the top of society, as it were.[6] Then, the intensity of arrests fluctuated: a sudden increase was followed by a temporary lull and then another peak, which subsided after a while. The induced spontaneity of denunciations alone does not seem to account for this rhythm. If one were to postulate a "denunciations curve," the number should multiply early, when the opportunity to settle scores was fresh, personal enemies were still at large, and the yearning for revenge burned hot. But the number of arrests did not decline steadily over time. Moreover, they swept from one social group to another, taking people away sequentially, in

---

* A characteristic vignette from the city of Wilno: "My mother, at the time in the NKVD building to find out about my father who was already arrested, told me that at some point an employee came out from his office and announced to the waiting crowd: go home, comrades, today we will accept no more denunciations" (HI, AC, 13975). Or take this reminiscence from Nadworna, a small town of 12,000 in Stanisławów voivodeship: "In the early days of the occupation the NKVD found many people who were devoted to them as confidential collaborators. They were of all ages, both men and women. Everyday from 10 P.M. until 1 or 2 in the morning they gave reports from their daily work to the chief of the local NKVD" (nadworna, 40). The two stories illustrate quite persuasively the breakdown of social solidarity both in an urban setting and in a relatively small community, with the image of people *queuing up to denounce* their fellow citizens.

orderly procession, which would not follow were spontaneous denunciations the only road to imprisonment.

Mass arrests by social category resulted typically in immediate deportation, and I shall describe that phenomenon in detail in Chapter 6. Their timing depended on the availability of material resources, primarily the means of transportation to carry out the assignment. It took about two months to complete the round trip between the newly incorporated territories and places of forced settlement all over the USSR. In mid-February, mid-April, and late June of 1940, long freight trains carried hundreds of thousands of Polish citizens eastward. Then there was a one-year respite: it took that long to digest the Baltic states that were swallowed in the summer of 1940. Deportations resumed in June 1941, to be stopped only by the outbreak of the Russo-German war. To the four deportations one should add the mass arrests that followed immediately after the Red Army entered the Western Ukraine and Western Belorussia and those following the October 22, 1939, elections, as well as the imprisonment in mid-December 1939 of large numbers of officers and reserve officers of the Polish Army who had previously registered with the Soviet authorities.[7] During the twenty-one months of Soviet rule, mass arrests swept over the territory seven times, each pass affecting from a few thousand to about a hundred thousand people. Together with POWs and those arrested in the intervals, about 1.25 million Polish citizens (of a total of roughly 13.5 million)[8] found themselves in the summer of 1941 residing in labor camps, in prisons, and in forced settlements all over the Soviet Union.

Police methods and arrest procedures varied greatly and kept the population in suspense, for one might be detained at any moment under the most unexpected circumstances. The sign of an impending arrest, both under Hitler's and Stalin's regime, was the screech of car brakes in the night.[9] Indeed, night visits and interrogations were routine events. It is certain, however, that the NKVD was working around the clock.[10] In the hubbub of daily life the secret police were perhaps less conspicuous, but they were nevertheless busy meeting their quotas, like everyone else.

Thus, there were two systems of mass arrests: by broad social category, and by what I have called induced spontaneity. The latter was institutionalized through a wide network of secret freelance collaborators (so-called seksots) who practiced denunciations as a sideline. The two systems, however, were not incompatible. Indeed, in a rare exception in this centrally planned and administered society, they allowed for a comfortable blending of general policy guidelines emanating from top leadership and grass-roots initiative.

The numbers to be arrested and the broad social categories from which they should be taken came from the administrative hierarchy, while the actual choice of victims was left to the local enforcers and their friends. Even when the target was a specific occupation (e.g., foresters) or a social class (e.g., landowners), any individual could be exempted by the locals.[11] Once a prisoner fell under the jurisdiction of higher-level NKVD officers, however, few dared to intervene on his behalf, and even fewer were successful when they did. Wanda Wasilewska, a representative to the Supreme Soviet and the grande dame of the regime in the incorporated territories, derived her stature precisely from her unmatched ability to use her personal connections with Stalin to get people released from jail in Lwów or from forced settlement or labor camps in the USSR.[12]

Spontaneous, random arrests of people not selected in advance by the security police took the form of street roundups (though less frequently than under the German occupation) and individual arrests on the street. Even in largely urban settings, the relative safety of *anonymity* on a crowded street was progressively stripped away under the Soviet regime.[13] One's pace or facial expression or an article of clothing might catch a prowling militiaman's eye. A housewife from Baranowicze wrote, exaggerating somewhat, that "every passerby who was better dressed—and all of us Poles like to dress up—was taken in for interrogation." In Równe "the local militia pointed out people in the street and the NKVD arrested them on the spot."[14]

In the country one might be arrested in equally capricious circumstances. A peasant on the way to a mill in Skałat county was accompanied by his son. "Two militiamen were coming from the opposite direction. Stop. Come with us. They put father on their cart and took him away. I was allowed to go home. Where they took father I don't know even today."[15]

Not everybody accosted in the street by the militia was immediately arrested, but one could never tell what was intended.

> On October 21, I was walking down Zyblikiewicz Street [in Lwów] with Mrs. Wanda Stamirowska. We were talking about some family matters. Suddenly two men separated us brutally and proceeded to question us about the subject of our conversation. Since our answers were identical, we were released. But I know of people who were arrested in this manner.[16]

The Soviet security apparatus adopted two complementary strategies in its police work: in addition to acting as a vacuum cleaner, deporting broad categories of people without inquiry into the details of their individual biographies, it simultaneously monitored carefully and removed selectively individuals whom it identified as the regime's enemies. The NKVD was a professional organization and had the manpower to do routine police work. Many deportees and former labor camp inmates tell of the virtually identical circumstances under which they were captured. Forewarned that they might be arrested, they fled their homes and hid, sometimes for months, in faraway places. But if they returned home just for one night or even a few hours, to bid farewell before crossing the frontier or to get something they needed, like winter clothing, or to rest while ill, the police would come to arrest them within hours.

The NKVD could pinpoint individuals and track them down quite efficiently. The Polish military underground organization, the ZWZ, which thrived under the German occupation in spite of persistent Gestapo efforts to destroy it, never had a chance under the NKVD. Indeed, from the spring of 1940 a Polish officer turned NKVD informer was in charge of the ZWZ in the Soviet-occupied territories. The NKVD was equally persistent in settling long overdue scores that may seem rather petty: a man in Buczacz was arrested and sentenced for having given testimony in a 1934 trial of some Communists who distributed leaflets around town.[17]

It became quickly evident that the NKVD was exceedingly well acquainted with the biographies of residents of the newly incorporated territories, and not surprisingly. As we already know, most of the archives, files, and official documents of political organizations, voluntary associations of all sorts, and the local government fell into the hands of the Soviets, who immediately set out to establish personal records on every inhabitant of this territory. The numerous registrations that were ordered immediately following the Red Army's entry into the area, as well as captured documents, provided the necessary information. Time and again during interrogations people were confronted with specific questions about their lives stretching back two decades to the 1920 Polish-Bolshevik war. Scores were sentenced for having simply lived their lives as active citizens of an independent, sovereign country in the 1920s and 1930s.

Along with the past, people's present way of life also exposed them to the danger of arrest. Those who showed up late for work, did not pay taxes on time, sold some of their belongings on the free market—in a word, the overwhelming majority who tried to cope somehow with the rapidly deteriorating economic situation[18]—went en masse to jail. "There were 120 inhabitants in my village [Sokółka county of Białystok voivodeship] and by the time I was arrested twenty of them had appeared before the courts."[19] As if to further simplify the processing of those arrested, accusations of past and present crimes were conveniently stereotyped according to nationality. Poles were typically sentenced as counterrevolutionaries in the service of the bourgeoisie, Ukrainians were sent to labor camps as nationalists, and Jews were imprisoned as speculators.[20]

The Soviet security police were also, without doubt, quite cunning. Among their most successful and economical techniques to yield a particularly good crop of prisoners was deception. A scenario would be arranged so that the NKVD had simply to wait for victims to appear at a prearranged place and time suitable to its own schedule and resources. Thus, in April 1940 a group of students from the Lwów Polytechnic got in touch with an organization that promised to take them across the frontier to Hungary. On the first leg of the trip they were to travel by car from the town of Stanisławów. It was a strictly business transaction. They met with their guide, who collected the agreed sum of 300 rubles from each and instructed them to go in twos to the corner of Kopernik Street. And so they went, a pair every five minutes. Indeed, a car was waiting, but with NKVD men inside. Conveniently, two by two, the students were driven to prison.[21]

All along the border the NKVD sponsored individual guides who offered to take people across the frontier. "After my arrest I saw at the outpost of the Frontier Guard a Polish peasant who was being paid by a Soviet lieutenant while arguing that he wasn't getting enough for the number of people that he had delivered."[22] Apparently, there was a per head fee,[23] and the outpost commander was probably trying to pocket some of the money himself. Even the official press was not shy to write about this practice.

> In the last couple of days peasant Dymitro Shvernik noticed a stranger in his hamlet. Comrade Shvernik came up to him and asked: "Whom are you looking for?" "I am hungry, where could I get something to eat around here?"—answered the stranger, unable to hold on firmly on his feet. This aroused suspicion in Comrade Shvernik. He invited the guest to his house, gave him food, and himself immediately alerted the border guards. The stranger was detained. He turned out to be a spy for one of the foreign intelligence networks. Comrade Shvernik already has caught four individuals illegally crossing the frontier. The command of the border guard stated its gratitude and gave him a monetary reward for his vigilance.[24]

The NKVD also established organizations to recruit people for the Polish Army in France and, later, in England, only to arrest them at the frontier.

Periodically, people slated for arrest could be assembled under some credible pretext—a registration, for example.[25] The largest number of arrests resulting from a deception came following just such a registration on the occasion of a visit by the German repatriation commission in the spring of 1940. According to the provisions of the Soviet-Nazi Boundary and Friendship Treaty, some transfers of ethnic Germans and of Ukrainians, Belorussians, and ethnic Russians were to be allowed across the new Soviet-German frontier. When the German commission arrived in the Western Ukraine, tens of thousands of recent refugees, mostly Jews, queued up for days to put their names on lists of volunteers to leave the area of Soviet occupation. The NKVD did not interfere with this spontaneous inventory of the disillusioned and even facilitated it in many ways, only to use the lists thus compiled for sweeping arrests that provided the bulk of the victims for the June 1940 deportation.

Deceptions facilitated the work of the security apparatus: not only were the circumstances of arrest conveniently prearranged, but those caught "deserved" it more—they usually had shown more initiative and less willingness to accept their fate as subjects of the Soviet authority than the rest of the population. They must have *done* something to have fallen into the trap. From the NKVD's point of view, they composed a self-selected group of potential antiregime activists.

To give a complete picture of how arrests were made under the new regime, one ought to note that the NKVD was merely one of many institutions of the Soviet state. Sometimes these institutions worked at cross purposes, but in the end they were all part of a grand design to envelop each citizen in a web responsive to the will of those who at any given time embodied the state's interests. Thus, not surprisingly, various institutions eagerly cooperated with the NKVD in making arrests. One could be called for a business conference or be invited by an obliging superior for an inspection tour of the workplace and end up delivered to a waiting squad of NKVD men. Virtually the entire managerial-supervisory staff of the Polish State Railroad in Wilno was arrested in this way just before the Soviets handed the town over to Lithuania in October 1939.[26] On rare occasions the NKVD reciprocated and adjusted its schedule to fit the needs of some other Soviet institution where its prospective victim was currently badly needed. Thus in Żydaczów (Stanisławów voivodeship) the county agronomist was busily putting together statistics for the recent autumn crops and figuring out how much could be apportioned for various uses.

Around December 10, 1939, two NKVD functionaries visited the office where I was working and spoke at length to the man in charge of my department. Then, while they were still present, my supervisor, Semionov, asked me when I would be able to finish the current assignment and suggested that I be ready in three days as he needed the computations for a conference in Stanisławów. I completed my assignment in the allotted time and on the fourth day, shortly after I came to the office, the said NKVD men also arrived and arrested me.[27]

Under the new regime anyone, at any time, in any place, and for any reason was vulnerable to arrest. Thus the recollection of Julian Sowa of Stanisławów stands out, so unusual is it among the thousands of accounts reminiscing about the circumstances of arrest: "I was arrested on July 11, 1940, for having caused an automobile accident."[28]

OVERCROWDING OF PRISONS

Arrest and imprisonment stunned everyone, even the best adjusted, even those who expected in prison a kind of relief from the eerie atmosphere of life outside. No matter how routine the circumstances of arrest or the formalities of admission, entry into a prison cell introduced one to a new environment where one could find life supports only after adaptive modification of one's organism. The entire experience is suggested in one brief sentence: "The crowd was so thick that when they closed the cell doors behind me I could not move an inch."[29] Inmates lived in such conditions for months, even though many additional buildings all over the occupied territory were turned into prisons by the Soviet authorities. Overcrowded prisons are perhaps the best indicator of the scale of the arrests that swept through the area. As a high school student from Stolin observed: "A temporarily empty prison filled first with the Poles, then with the Ruthenians. But it proved too small, so new construction was undertaken to add to it, even though into each cell they put four times as many people as the cells were designed for."[30]

Additional prison space was requisitioned at breakneck speed, usually without making any physical changes or administrative arrangements for the new institutions. In Szczuczyn, for example, where there had been no prison before the war, Soviet authorities created four: in the Piaris cloister, in an elementary school in the center of town, in the courthouse, and in the basement of a nearby police station in Żołudek.[31] Apparently, they could not improvise even barely adequate toilet facilities in the cloister; so all prisoners had to be paraded outside daily in shifts to relieve themselves in the adjacent meadow. Crowds of relatives stayed on constant vigil there, undeterred by hostile guards, to see their dear ones even under these rather embarrassing circumstances.[32]

In Żołudek, inmates were not fed. Relatives and friends supplied food for the prisoners as well as their jailers.[33] This, incidentally, was not an exception. In the Przemyślany jail prisoners were left to the care or mercy of the neighboring population, which was never told, however, how many there were, so that for days they might have nothing to eat. The same happened in Szumsk (Wilno-Troki county), where the NKVD kept its hungry prisoners in a pigsty.[34]

I shall not discuss the diet, or lack thereof, in Soviet jails, but merely point out *some* of the problems accompanying the rapid, chaotic proliferation of prisons. Armed men can round up and detain almost limitless swarms of civilians. But to keep them locked up requires a logistical support system to meet their bodily needs. Biology imposes limits on what can be accomplished through coercion. Though the threshold of resistance to deprivation differs from one person to another and is generally difficult to gauge, the Soviet prison system functioned at the outermost limits of human endurance, as witnessed by the many who died in jails not from a bullet but from neglect.

As a rule, conditions in makeshift jails were worse than in regular prisons. There were dozens of these jails along the entire border, near the outposts of NKVD frontier guard detachments. They were called "pigsties"—as some of them literally were—by the population, which undoubtedly thought about them frequently in contemplating plans to escape abroad. A lot of people, I suspect, were thinking about fleeing the Soviet occupation, and many must have tried it, since thousands were caught in the act. The unsuccessful ones—men, women, and children together—might be herded into some rickety farm building that qualified as a place of detention only because it could be securely locked. And the detainees in these frontier jails were not only those caught trying to escape but also people seeking entry into Soviet-occupied territory—Jews in flight from the Germans, Communist sympathizers, and thousands of Carpatho-Ruthenian peasants who believed Soviet promises of national liberation and land redistribution. After crossing the border, they trustingly checked into the nearest outpost of the Soviet authority, only to be passed over to the NKVD.[35] For the most part, they ended up in frontier jails and lingered there, sometimes for weeks.

Away from the border areas, better buildings were available for prison use—for example, the architecturally suitable cloisters in Szczuczyn (Nowogród voivodeship), Berezwecz (Dzisna county of

Wilno voivodeship), Zaręby Kościelne (Ostrów county of Białystok voivodeship), and Czerniehów (Tarnopol county of Tarnopol voivodeship). Warehouses were also popular, like the two in Mołodeczno and the one in Włodzimierz Wołyński. Schools served the new purpose as well in Szczuczyn and Borysław. In larger towns, office buildings were frequently taken over: the financial office of Nowogródek and, in Lwów, the insurance company on Zielona Street, where the NKVD moved in and the building of the railroad office on Sądowa Street, which was turned into a jail. Similarly, in Wilno the NKVD prison at Słowacki Street was set up in the former headquarters of the Wilno railroad administration. Prisoners were frequently detained in the basements of government buildings in gmina seats, notably in Łuniniec (Polesie voivodeship), Nadworna (Stanisławów voivodeship), and Wormiany (Wilno voivodeship), to name a few with especially bad reputations. The railroad NKVD set up shop in detached railroad cars (in Zdołbunów and Białystok, for example). In Augustów a Turkish bakery served as a detention center; and in Worochta (Nadworna county of Stanisławów voivodeship), an oddity on the frontier, two boardinghouses, the "Black Sea House," and the "Edelweiss" became jails.[36]

Although we do not hear from most of the villages and hamlets of the Western Ukraine and Western Belorussia, such improvised jails must have existed there as well. Yet even this partial list suggests the astounding increase in the volume of arrests and incarcerations that occurred under Soviet rule, far beyond the capacity of the available prison space. We can appreciate the literalness of the statement by the witness quoted above that not one more body could be pushed into the cell at the Stanisławów prison when he had been squeezed in. And no wonder: it was a disciplinary cell originally designed to accommodate one prisoner in solitary confinement but, under Soviet rule, forced to hold twenty-six people.

I assume here the accuracy of the quantitative data concerning the prisons provided by former inmates. Counting all sorts of things is, after all, a favorite pastime in jail, and there was little else to occupy prisoners in September 1939. How many others were arrested and deported or tortured, and who were they? Measuring the cell or the food ration, counting prisoners, learning about inmates in other cells whenever anyone was transferred, comparing present conditions to those under the Polish administration (with information from former inmates and Polish prison officials who were now incarcerated)—all of these statistics and more were pursued obsessively by the prisoners in order to get a hold on their present condition, if only intellectually.

153

They hoped to find some intelligibility in what gave them a profound sense of unreality. In the words of one prisoner, "while in jail, I frequently asked myself whether my entire life was not merely a dream, whereas in reality we dwelt in the Middle Ages except with modern techniques of torture."[37]*

What were the numbers, then? Here is a sample list of prisons and their populations in the Soviet-occupied half of Poland, in alphabetical order. *Baranowicze* (Nowogród voivodeship): 220 prisoners in a 36 square meter cell. *Białystok*: about 8,000 prisoners in the main prison compound designed for 1,500. In a cell for 20, 110 inmates were kept. In the railroad jail there were 20–42 people in a 15 sq. m cell. *Drohobycz* (Lwów voivodeship): in cells for solitary confinement, 15–20 people were kept. *Dzisna* (Wilno voivodeship): in a two-room basement under the old Polish frontier guard outpost, 180 prisoners were held. *Kowel* (Wołyń voivodeship): cell 24, 5 m by 5.5 m, housed 86 prisoners; cell 31, 4 m by 12 m, was filled by about 200. *Lida* (Nowogród voivodeship): in a 12-person cell, number 10, there were 96 prisoners. *Lwów* (Brygidki prison): in four cells designed for 17 persons each there were 56 prisoners (cell 41), 42 (cell 42), 60 (cell 53), and 57 (cell 56); on the average there were 50 people in a 30 sq. m cell. *Lwów* (Zamarstynów prison): Aleksander Wat shared an 11.5 sq. m cell with another 28 prisoners; in a cell designed for 30–40 people, 142 prisoners were put. *Nadworna* (Stanisławów voivodeship): in a two-room apartment used as a prison, 180 people were kept, in addition to another 200 in the basement. *Nowa Wilejka* (Wilno voivodeship): in 6 m by 7 m cells, about 85 prisoners were held on the average, and on one occasion 112 were locked together; in an 8-person cell, 44 people were kept. *Oszmiana* (Wilno voivodeship): in the old Polish prison consisting of three one-story buildings, which was designed for about 100 inmates, 700 were kept in 1940; in a cell 6 m by 9 m, 90–120 prisoners were crammed. *Przemyśl* (Lwów voivodeship): in a cell for 9 persons, 54–70 were housed. *Przemyślany* (Tarnopol voivodeship): in the courthouse jail designed to hold up to 14 prisoners, 40–70 were held. *Skole* (Stanisławów voivodeship): in 4 m by 3 m cells, over 30 prisoners were kept in each. *Stanisławów*: in a 120 sq. m prison chapel, from 120 to 300 prisoners were locked up. *Stryj* (Stanisławów voivodeship): 60 prisoners lived in a 14 sq. m cell. *Zaręby Kościelne*

* There must have been something compelling about this image, for a strikingly similar one was evoked over twenty years later in the reminiscences of Aleksander Wat: "In this prison [Zamarstynów prison in Lwów] we always had a feeling of a return to the Middle Ages: the way we were treated, the prison itself. This is how medieval prisons, mental asylums, or leprosoria must have looked" (*Mój Wiek*, 1: 341).

(Białystok voivodeship): in an adapted cloister, 86 people were locked in one monk's cell; the cell's dimensions are not given, but we are assured by the witness that conditions there were "horrible."[38]

In spite of all the available details, we can only approximate the total number of prisoners in this period. An estimate compiled in the research unit (Biuro Dokumentów) of the Polish Army in the East strikes me as somewhat overly cautious (indeed, the compilers state that they would rather underestimate than inflate their numbers).* But let us say, as they do, that during the Soviet administration prisons were filled to about five times their original capacity. Given that there were about 25,000 prisoners in the area before the war, we obtain roughly 125,000 as the number of inmates housed in the 104 existing Polish jails. But, according to Biuro Dokumentów, 73 new prisons were established by the Soviet authorities. If we estimate that another one-fifth of the prison population was housed in these makeshift detention centers, then we arrive at 150,000 as the total number of prisoners held in confinement *at any one time*. If in addition we consider seven months as the average period of detention prior to deportation eastward to a labor camp or a prison in the Soviet interior (Biuro Dokumentów estimates the average period of detention at six to eight months), we reach an approximate total of half a million imprisonments in the Western Ukraine and Western Belorussia during the twenty-one months of Soviet rule there in 1939–1941. It is a staggering number for a population of 13.5–14 million (including refugees from western and central Poland). Since men constituted over 90 percent of those arrested, these numbers reveal that about 10 percent of all adult males in this territory were imprisoned.[39]

Prisons and prison life, normally separated from the mainstream of society, mostly affect those on its margins. When arrest does touch others, it carries shame and odium rather than inspiring resignation.

---

* Even when giving the number of prisoners in the area under Polish prison administration on January 1, 1938, the compilers offer approximations substantially lower than the numbers provided in the statistical yearbook for 1938 (GUS, *Mały Rocznik Statystyczny*, p. 354). For the Wilno court district (*apelacja*) the compilers give 7,600, while the statistical yearbook says that there were 7,854 prisoners there at the time; for the Lwów court district the corresponding numbers are 10,700 and 10,828. Neither the Warsaw nor the Lublin court district statistics, quoted in the table compiled by the Biuro Dokumentów, can be directly compared with the statistical yearbook data because only part of these districts were included within the boundaries of the Soviet occupation. For ease of computation and in view of consistent underestimation by the Biuro Dokumentów, I shall consider 25,000, rather than the 23,300 they suggest, to be the total number of prisoners in this area before the war (HI, AC, Archiwum Wewnętrzne Biura Dokumentów [AWBD], doc. 62c, table 25).

For if the boundaries of legality are clearly drawn and are accepted, then to transgress is largely a matter of choice, and such a choice calls for censure. Not so in the Soviet state. There, prison was in the mainstream of society, and imprisonment was merely a part of the life cycle, often cutting it short. So many were arrested that virtually everyone, because of friendships or kinship, devoted a share of time, resources, and thought to life in prison. Everybody knew at least one person who was either deported or imprisoned.

How was this abstraction concretized in the daily life of the cities, towns, and villages of the incorporated territories? As a mass phenomenon, it found fitting expression in the crowds assembled in front of prisons. "The sight of a dense crowd made up of wives, children, and mothers waiting for hours in front of the Kołomyja prison for permission to hand in a meager food package or a pot of already cold soup to the loved one was so moving and tragic that I will probably keep it forever in my memory and in my heart."[40] In all kinds of weather, from the early morning hours, mostly women and children gathered, sometimes in the very center of town—in front of the school and court building in Szczuczyn or the town hall in Kałusz, which were used as prisons—to learn the whereabouts of their loved ones, or perhaps to see them in the street when they were led to interrogation, or to bring a parcel of food or a change of clothing.[41] Countless hours were wasted waiting for capricious and uncooperative prison officials, who accepted or rejected parcels as they pleased, stepped out of their offices whenever it suited them, and cursed petitioning families when they felt like it.[42]* To compound the misery, the dirty linen returned to a wife or a mother was often stained with blood, leaving no doubt that the prisoner had been tortured.[43]

Upon arriving at the detention place, individuals were usually strip-searched meticulously (their clothing often ruined in the process), and, after filling out forms and depositing for safekeeping whatever was not allowed in the cell, they were finally locked up. The first eye contact with other prisoners produced an involuntary reaction of shock and disbelief: "I saw a horrifying scene—a crowd of dirty, unshaved, hungry, and emaciated people in rags. I wondered whether I had entered a bandits' den, or a den of wild animals." This impression from

---

* "And it was like this: we came there to hand in a package, a chief came out, looked around, listened to our pleadings, didn't say a word, and left. And we women waited until the chief comes back from dinner in a better mood and it will be possible then to hand in something. We waited from 7 in the morning to 3 P.M. and it was 35 C below zero. And many, many times we didn't manage to hand in anything because the chief was in a bad mood" (HI, AC, 1613 [Złoczów]).

cell 56 in the Białystok prison, registered on May 12, 1940, is not at all different from that of a new arrival in cell 12 in the Nowa Wilejka prison in December 1939: "My hair stood on end when I entered the cell and I could not overcome the impression this made on me for quite a while. There were 43 people in this cell (I was 44th), old and young, but all pale, emaciated, and unshaved with long beards." The president of Wilno University and some lawyers and doctors were among them, and except for a loincloth they wore no garment. Especially with the advent of warmer weather, prisoners undressed in their cells, which made the misery of prison life even more striking and immediately visible to newcomers. "I was frightened by the prisoners' faces and by their looks," wrote Aleksander Wat. "I thought these were bandits who had been here for years." But it was January 1940: no one among this motley crowd of students, officers, civil servants, lawyers, and merchants had been in the Zamarstynów jail in Lwów longer than three months. "During the first few days of incarceration," Wat remembered, "I couldn't tell the difference between 40-year-old and 70-year-old men."[44]

CONDITIONS OF DETENTION

Wat's last remark is very much to the point. In Soviet prisons people were subject to an accelerated process of aging, similar to that which affects a terminally ill patient. Deprived of adequate food and oxygen, exposed to extreme temperatures (in the Postawy prison inmates' hair froze to the cell walls at night and had to be cut off in the morning with a piece of glass), prolonged mental stress and anxiety, as well as to infectious diseases (through deplorable hygienic conditions and lack of medical care), people suffered as if they were seriously ill. Their organisms were exhausted and vulnerable. Indeed, most of the people were actually sick. As many as half of the inmates, according to some estimates, required immediate medical attention.[45]

It gets very hot and stuffy in an overcrowded cell, especially when the windows are usually kept closed or boarded up. In Oszmiana prison on especially hot days inmates used to scream "air" in unison, but all the warden would say in response was that he would send them tanks. Perhaps he was replaced or he mellowed, for at some point eau de Cologne was sprayed in the cells, but it only added to the stench.[46] Lungs starved for oxygen and already accustomed to extracting it from a very special mixture of gases could not breathe normal air after a while, and many prisoners fainted when taken to the courtyard for an infrequent walk.[47] People smell when they don't wash; sickness and

lack of proper food give them foul breath and make them break wind.*
In addition, they smoked tobacco and, most important, had to relieve
themselves into a slop bucket that was never properly covered and was
emptied only once or twice a day.[48] The warden of Kowel prison teased
his prisoners—such cultured people, he used to say, and you stink so
badly.

There was never even enough drinking water. The daily ration in
Kowel prison was two buckets for 86 people; in Oszmiana, three
buckets for 90–120 prisoners. In Lwów inmates fainted from thirst.[49]
And there was virtually no water to spare for washing or laundry.
Once a week at best, usually more rarely, prisoners might be permitted
a bath and their clothes would be disinfected. Together with daily trips
to the lavatory, these events were an important break in the oppressive
routine of confinement, occasions to recover a sense of the surrounding
space, to walk, maybe to catch a glimpse of the outside world through
an unboarded window, and to take care, even though in rather rudimentary fashion, of one's hygienic and physiological needs.[50]

It is no surprise that the prisons were infested with lice, which cause
constant, severe discomfort and, especially when typhoid epidemics
broke out, literally bled prisoners to death. The misfortunes brought
by lice were hardly compensated by the small sport they provided to
brighten the deadly routine of prison life. Inmates killed them with
improving skill and compared their daily harvests; in Mołodeczno
prison they even raced them along a prison bunk, each inmate poking
his favorite with a match. Whoever managed to steer his louse first
across the finish line got a cigarette from the other entrants in the
race.[51] But as people tired of dirt and lice and stench, they called for
more frequent baths, just as they kept asking to have windows open or
slop buckets taken out of their cells. In most cases their calls went
unheeded. Sometimes they produced unwelcome results.** Only after
typhoid epidemics broke out did the hygienic conditions in prisons
seem to improve as the authorities tried to protect themselves.[52]

When prisoners were allowed to bathe, they were rarely issued any

* In the Stryj prison Ukrainians from the OUN and the educational association Prosvita
used to mock their Polish fellow prisoners by saying "teper krayem polskij hymn" (we
are now playing the Polish anthem) when farting. This incensed one witness more than
any other indignity suffered in Soviet prisons (HI, AC, 3678).

** When an NKVD inspection commission visited the Tarnopol prison in November
1940, inmates complained about lice infestation due to infrequent baths. So, during the
night of November 29–30, in bitter cold, prisoners were ordered to undress, were taken
out into the corridor and courtyard, and were then very slowly processed through the
prison bathhouse. They froze stiff that night. Never again were any demands made for
more baths (HI, AC, 9476).

soap, or they got only a tiny bit that could not wash off the layers of dirt covering their bodies. Also, the facilities were inadequate. All cell-mates were routinely ushered into the shower room together, but the old fixtures had not been expanded to provide for the exploding prison population. There might be a dozen or more prisoners for each shower. Add to these conditions a meager water supply and guards rushing the prisoners through, and the results can be imagined.[53]

While the prisoners bathed, their clothes were usually taken for delousing. The Soviets were very proud of their delousing facilities, and they mocked the Poles when they learned that Polish cities had had none before the war.[54] Somehow, to them delousing stations symbol-ized a higher level of civilization, perhaps marking the difference between the amenities of urban life and the backwardness of the vil-lage. Nonetheless, delousing stations did not seem to work in the prisons of the Western Ukraine and Western Belorussia. Perhaps the volume of clothes needing treatment was too great. As a remedy, the temperature was set higher, which only ruined the articles along the walls of the delousing rooms but had little impact on the rest. Then the garments, most of them barely lukewarm and wet, were taken out and thrown together on a big pile, whereupon a naked crowd of prisoners, often shivering in cold weather, rushed to retrieve each his own.[55] It was altogether very unpleasant, with guards barking orders to move on quickly and everybody angrily eyeing everybody else, pushing and shoving, and always losing something in the process. But worst of all, the lice remained as vigorous as ever. Aleksander Wat theorized that incompetent delousing only aroused them sexually, so that they bit furiously. In any case, the obvious failure of the entire procedure made no impression on the prison administration, which continued to operate in the same manner.

The other venture beyond the cell walls, the daily walk or two to the lavatory, was also marred by inadequate facilities. Sometimes this worked to the prisoners' advantage, as in the cloister in Szczuczyn, where they had to be walked outside and could see their families and friends along the way. But mostly the inmates suffered discomfort and humiliation. In Białystok they had only two or three toilets, and pris-oners were taken there in groups of twenty to thirty for a period of ten minutes at most; in Oszmiana, with six to eight toilets, shifts of thirty were brought for a few minutes; in Włodzimierz Wołyński groups of twenty to twenty-five were marched into a lavatory with six toilets, and in five minutes they had to be out. Many relieved themselves where they stood, directly on the floor. The lavatory was disinfected with lime, which slaked, emitting a dense vapor that hurt the inmates' eyes:

"then the guards laughed, and kept us longer in the lavatory." Trips to the lavatory were organized twice daily in most jails. In Białystok, prisoners went to the lavatory three times; in Orsza, more frequently still, and when there was no warden in the vicinity they were sometimes escorted there individually—unheard of in any other jail under the Soviet administration.[56]

Behind these numbers hides a world of human misery. Stinking slop buckets in prison cells, inmates anxiously awaiting their daily trips to the lavatory and often, unable to wait, relieving themselves in the cell and drawing the anger of other prisoners who were still trying to control themselves. The body became a shameful burden to everyone—dirty, sore from tortures and lice, wanting to burst with excrement, and yet hungry.* And when night fell, there was no rest, not only because of the interrogation sessions but mostly because there was not enough space for everyone to stretch out. All had to cooperate in working out sleeping arrangements. A rudimentary social organization formed in the process of space allocation, varying from the use of sheer coercion to reliance on expertise and the recognition of seniority or personal charisma.

In most prisons the inmates simply slept on the floor, since bunks, if there were any, could not accommodate everyone. But even the floor had more and less desirable spots, so the cell needed a procedure for dividing the available surface into individual "plots" and for assigning them. The task was usually given to the *starosta* (elder) of the cell, who was chosen by the prisoners or imposed himself with the help of a few personal allies.[57] Depending on the source of his authority (election or

---

* Prisoners were always hungry. The mainstay of their food supply was a daily portion of about 500 grams of bread. In addition, there was a thin "soup" twice a day, or sometimes a plate of buckwheat or barley, and tea (HI, AC, 96, 615, 1311, 1545; *Dark Side of the Moon*, p. 93). Some prisons had commissaries, and inmates who had money in the prison deposit could buy some provisions there—typically cigarettes and tobacco, onions, or bread. In Tarnopol there was also butter (HI, AC, 9476), and in Mołodeczno, occasionally, sausage (HI, AC, 1325). But prisoners could not count on supplementing their diet by purchases. In Nowa Wilejka for a long time nothing could be bought (HI, AC, 549). Then, in March 1941, the rules changed: those who had money at the time of their arrest could spend it in the commissary, but no one could receive money for this purpose from relatives outside (HI, AC, 1551). In the Białystok prison the commissary was opened only in September 1940 (HI, AC, 1311). Of course, an individual's buying privileges could always be revoked as a punishment. Nor were there general rules about receiving parcels from relatives. In some prisons people depended on daily food deliveries from relatives and friends. In others, Lida for example, no parcels were allowed at all (HI, AC, 96). In Lwów, at Brygidki prison, one parcel a month was allowed, but without food (HI, AC, 1545). In Szczuczyn one could get a delivery every ten days, but no bread, meat, or fat was allowed (Poland. Ambasada USSR, Box 46, Maliszewski).

usurpation), he might allocate space either by force and arbitrariness or, much more frequently, by some unambiguous rule sufficiently common-sensical to be accepted by a group of prisoners from very different backgrounds who had little respect or sympathy for each other. Seniority was one such rule. In the Oszmiana jail, for example, where there were two rows of bunks in addition to the floor, people moved up during winter months literally and figuratively, in accord with the length of their stay in the cell, and in the opposite direction with the advent of hot summer weather. In Lwów, twenty-eight people living in a 11.5 sq. m cell relied on the geometrical skills of a gifted high school student who fitted them most ingeniously by size into an intricate pattern.

Space was very precious indeed: 30 cm in width per person in Oszmiana; one foot per person in Kowel, laboriously measured out every evening by the cell elder.[58] People lay on their sides in rows, and when anybody wanted to turn over, all in the row had to follow. Conditions could deteriorate even further. In Drohobycz prison the inmates slept sitting up; in Białystok and Wilejka they slept in shifts, half the prisoners standing through half the night.[59] And there were constant disruptions. Anyone who needed the slop bucket or was called out for night interrogation had to step over other people to get there. But few complained of sleeplessness: all were so exhausted that they dozed off even when denied elementary comforts.

In addition to the density of the prison population, its social composition made for a special dynamic of relationships within each cell. Suddenly squeezed together were people who had never mixed socially and who knew each other mostly via stereotyped clichés or ritualized encounters that carefully preserved distance. The oddness of the mixture was due partly to the quasi-feudal structure of prewar Polish society and partly to the rapid pace of sovietization, which telescoped into a year and a half the process that had taken decades in the Soviet Union itself. For example, the assault on the peasantry in the USSR did not begin in earnest until the late twenties and early thirties, but in the Western Ukraine "peasants were being arrested en masse" already in the summer of 1940.[60] Thus they were brought into prisons long before those taken in the earlier waves of arrest were moved eastward. Consequently, any group of prisoners might include the local upper class (mostly Polish), civil servants, professionals, political activists of various ethnic backgrounds, swarms of Jewish refugees arrested for economic crimes (i.e., eking out a living from the black market), and recalcitrant peasants of Ukrainian, Belorussian, and "local" stock, plus a sizable contingent of ordinary criminals. Their mutual relationships varied, and although no simple rule could be invoked to describe them, we can make one general observation: with time, the intensity of ethnic and class conflicts subsided.

During the early phase of the Soviet occupation local people were motivated primarily by resentments and injuries accumulated during the period of Polish administration. The breakdown of ethnic and class domination of the Poles released powerful and hitherto repressed social energies. As a railroad engineer imprisoned in Lwów put it: "Poles were the most miserable prison caste, for both the Soviet authorities and the prisoners of other nationalities held us blameful, and for this reason they made us suffer a lot."[61] In the early period, when people were still overwhelmed by the unprecedented spectacle of the German *Blitzkrieg*, ethnic Poles were even at odds with each other, blaming mostly the prewar Sanacja regime for the national disaster. Only after the still quicker collapse of France did the shock of the September 1939 defeat finally subside.[62] But until then, political and class antagonisms within the ethnic Polish community undermined whatever solidarity one might have expected in response to the strong hostility of other ethnic groups. Thus, in prison Polish "civilians cursed civil servants; policemen, to make up for their past bureaucratic subordination, cursed county prefects; there were even fist fights between rank-and-file policemen and officers."[63]

But by and large, prisoners clustered together in ethnic groups, however stratified they were internally. In time the edge of class differentiation blunted, and personal attributes became increasingly important. There was no private space to withdraw into, no paraphernalia of rank to hide behind. The general composure, calm, and wisdom of some prisoners were readily apparent, and their authority was recognized. Special skills—storytelling or the ability to lead communal prayers or to organize group entertainment—set apart the prisoners who possessed them.[64]

It was nonetheless a very fragile society, in perpetual change, always vulnerable to outside intervention as inmates were moved in and out. Under prison conditions the entry or departure of one individual could change the entire chemistry of a cell's prevailing social relations.[65] The numerical size of each ethnic group and, most of all, the number of criminals in the cell were decisive influences. A few criminals might benefit their cellmates, for they were experienced in prison life and part of a network that extended over the entire prison complex. In greater numbers, however, they were a menace, just as to an even greater degree were convicted Red Army soldiers.[66]

Relationships between different ethnic groups slowly improved. In time all recognized that they shared an equally grim destiny under Soviet rule, irrespective of nationality and regardless of Soviet assurances of national liberation. Though reconciliation was by no means a general rule, we have scattered testimonies from all over the occupied territories indicating that relationships among imprisoned Ukrainians, Belorussians, Poles, and Jews were often good.[67] As one Polish prisoner put it: "The necessity to live together through some very difficult experiences had a positive aspect too, for it allowed a better understanding between different strata of the Polish society and also made possible a certain rapprochement with the Ukrainians and a broad discussion of problems mutually important to both nations."[68] The veracity of this testimony is guaranteed in part by its language, which is akin to that of diplomatic communiqué and shows that the author was aware of the social distance separating the two groups.

But life in a prison cell was mere prelude, an introduction. Detention prior to sentencing was, after all, only a means to an altogether different end. And imprisonment following arrest was only for investigation, not punishment. Hardly anyone served a sentence in the newly incorporated territories; instead, prisoners were only in temporary storage while the investigation lasted or, after sentencing, until transportation was found to take a load of convicts to their destination inside the USSR. A prison cell was, in a sense, a waiting room where one was temporarily left to one's own devices. It was there, curiously enough, that spontaneous social interaction thrived, more so than on the outside, where people were paralyzed by fear of the state's ubiquitous presence. Those who were still free *could* withdraw, or so they thought, into solitude or into a circle of intimates, and they could move about physically. In the embryonic society of the prison cell, on the other hand, many fundamental problems of coexistence were tackled. The consensus of inmates bestowed authority on some because of their natural leadership qualities. Scarce resources, such as space or fresh air, were frequently allocated according to equity or merit. Learning and sharing of knowledge took place in the cell, and also games and entertainment. There was functional differentiation, and individuals with special skills used them to benefit the community. People worshipped together and reached out to one another. Close friendships flourished in prison, as suggested by the fond reminiscences of many former prisoners about their fellow inmates.

But, of course, life in prison was hell, though (and this is a point worth remembering) it was so due to sins of omission rather than of commission: the lack of proper facilities, rather than some purposeful action of the new regime, was to blame. One might reproach the Soviet authorities at most for neglecting to meet the needs of its citizens. Confined to a prison cell, individuals were for a moment—unlike any other moment in their lives under the Soviet regime—ignored by the authorities. But not for long—only until they were called for interrogation.

INTERROGATION

I want to make a firm distinction between life in a prison cell and the interrogation. When the cell door opened at night and the prison guard shouted the fateful words "na bookvoo . . ." ([beginning] with the letter . . .), and those whose names began with that letter came forward, and the guard identified the one whose last name, first name, and patronymic matched those of the written order in his hand—this person was about to cross over into another world. One was left a few seconds to get ready, enough for cellmates to bid farewell and perhaps to offer some additional garment and prayers, for one was embarking on a long and perilous journey.[69]

Interrogation quite often literally involved a journey—not a long one perhaps, but still memorable. In many towns the secret police established headquarters in some suitable office building separate from the prison and not infrequently quite distant from it. People had to be walked or driven there, and, particularly in small towns, this offered an opportunity to see or to be seen by family and friends.* Because prisoners were never told ahead of time where they were being taken, there was some faint hope that the destination was something other than a tête-à-tête with the NKVD. Leaving the cell block in the Wilejka prison, one might be marched straight ahead and then to the right, into the courthouse, where public prosecutors had their offices. But a turn to the left meant an altogether different destination—the former residence of the prison warden, where the NKVD conducted interrogations. One could delude oneself until the order to turn left was barked by the guard on the prison path.[70] Then one could only brace oneself mentally and prepare as best one could for the encounter with the "four-letter word" organization.**

* "After my husband's arrest I stood everyday in front of the prison, waiting for him to be taken to interrogation. I was looking at men being led for interrogation. Until recently full of health and strength, they were thin, with tormented eyes, barely walking. Pushed by their torturers to walk faster. I was looking at the despair of wives and mothers when such a ghost of a husband or of a son was walked by" (HI, PGC, 6771).

** Laughter, a spontaneous burst of emotional energy, is incompatible with drab totalitarian uniformity. Totalitarianism—to add to the list of shortages it creates—is humorless. As an expression of popular defiance, political humor is a ubiquitous phe-

Irony, a symbolic distance, was all that people could use to separate themselves from the torturers into whose presence they were about to be ushered. Thus some of the dreaded interrogation quarters bore innocuous nicknames, as if words could somehow transform an unbearable experience through association with a banal or even a pleasing image. The room in Wilno's district court where the NKVD interrogated its prisoners was called "mimosa," while a small building in the compound of the main Łukiszki prison, also in Wilno, where interrogations were conducted went by the endearing diminutive, "little white house" (*biały domek*).[71]

In a way, Soviet police interrogators had an easy job. The infamous article 58 of the Russian penal code (article 54 in the Ukrainian penal code), as Solzhenitsyn pointed out in *Gulag*, was so encompassing that anyone could be charged with crimes against the state. "Dokazhi chto ty ne verbliud" (prove that you are not a camel) was a popular saying that described the status of law and order in the Soviet Union better than the most learned dissertations on the subject. But still, there had to be fact-finding during the investigation, if only to satisfy the requirements of the article 58. Indeed, I think there were two purposes for gathering evidence from the prisoners, one clearly stated and another, though perhaps intuitive, of great importance to the regime. In the course of its investigations the NKVD was tracking down antistate organizations,[72] and also constantly drawing and updating associational maps of Soviet society. An individual arrested at random and made to recount his autobiography a number of times, as prisoners were, would necessarily place himself in the context of other people and institutions. And this was all that mattered. The rest was largely nonsense—a trumped-up accusation or a beaten-out confession to some crime, deduced according to *diamat* from the circumstances of the accused's life. But in the meantime the Soviet state filed another record of a social network. No matter how innocuous, it was still a record of a *latent organization*. Through millions of such probes, an associational map of Soviet society could be drawn and rearranged at

---

nomenon under totalitarian regimes. In the Soviet Union thousands were sentenced for telling jokes. But the habit could not be eradicated. Perhaps the need to relax and laugh a little is innate to human nature; perhaps the play with words had a cathartic effect on people and gave them, through metaphor, a sense of controlling their environment and destiny, which in reality were overbearing and oppressive. Whatever the reasons, no institution or person was immune to ridicule, not even the NKVD. The acronym was jokingly deciphered as "Nie wiadomo Kiedy Wrócę do Domu" (impossible to tell when will I return home) or simply referred to as a "four-letter word," which in Polish has the same semantic value as in English. HI, AC, 549.

will to find out the character and strength of the ties between any two people in the USSR. The NKVD may never have explored this theoretical possibility, but it strove to attain the capacity to do so out of the correct intuition that power in society derives from association. Absolute power, therefore, could be appropriated by the Soviet state only through a monopoly of association—that is, by denying this opportunity to anyone else—a claim vigorously pursued in the official policy outlawing all but state-sponsored organizations.[73]

This striving, more than anything else, I believe, embodied the utopian character of Soviet communism, for association and the life of people in community are co-terminous. Spontaneous interaction or natural, biologically determined group bonds cannot be eradicated short of the physical annihilation of the parties involved. Even though any specific, concrete association can be destroyed (by murder, for example), kinship loyalties in general are not abolished, nor something even more vague, such as "liking." Wanton killings under the Soviet regime, which seem so gratuitous and paranoid (much more even than under Hitler, who ordered the murder of "others"), or the striking tastelessness of the choice of official hero of Soviet youth (a lad who denounced his parents to the police and was in turn killed by surviving relatives), are revealing, if somewhat extreme, consequences of the utopian character of the Communist project. They are demonstrable proof that the quest for absolute power over society is self-contradictory, for it runs, in the last analysis, against nature. To destroy *all* associations, present and future, one must kill off all potential members— and with them the basis of all power in society, including absolute power. Thus, presumably, the project will never be carried to completion. But this conclusion may console only philosophers. Staggering numbers of people were killed during the Soviet state's accumulation of power.

The mode of interrogation seemed to differ slightly depending on whether the NKVD was investigating an extant antistate organization or a "latent" one. If the latter, questioning sessions were fewer, shorter, and easier to withstand. Prisoners were tortured, but not always, and rather casually, mostly by beating and kicking. More systematic and imaginative tortures were applied against suspects arrested after prior invigilation that established their membership in some clandestine organization, against those denounced by tortured colleagues, or against those whose prewar profession or eminence in the social and political life of Poland were of special interest to their Soviet captors.

There was no way to foretell what might arouse the suspicion of an NKVD interrogator. A confiscated photograph of the arrested person in uniform—any uniform—or the revelation that the person had once traveled abroad might trigger a long and painful interrogation, for such evidence indicated to the NKVD man, by analogy with familiar Soviet practices, that the person had been an activist of the bourgeois state or, worse, a spy sent on a secret mission.[74] Then, too, arrests made in similar circumstances might lead to very different interrogations. The so-called tourists caught trying to cross the frontier illegally were sometimes treated leniently and only threatened, but not beaten, during interrogation, while at other times they were accused of espionage and brutally tortured for months.*

Whenever the NKVD was relatively confident that a prisoner was privy to information it wanted, it tortured him because it found that this method produced the desired results. An event that turned up repeatedly in the reminiscences of those who were in some way connected with clandestine organizations illustrates the point: during some stage of the interrogation, one had a face-to-face confrontation with a member of the organization who had been beaten into submission by the NKVD. This was as true for the youthful, high-school age, scouting type of conspirator as for the professional members of the Polish military underground and the experienced members of the Ukrainian conspiratorial organization OUN.[75] Quite often, members of underground organizations were only briefly interrogated by the local NKVD, if at all, and then transported eastward to Minsk or Kiev, where the proper investigation was carried out.[76]

"Interrogation began. There were 22 of them, all alike. They began with 'confess' and ended with hitting over the face, kicking, and cursing."[77] This is a typical reminiscence. The NKVD routinely obtained confessions by escalating threats and by physical abuse of prisoners. Certain procedures—even minute details, phrases, or gestures—were repeated, but their sequence differed. Thus there was no way to know how the interrogation would unfold. In the case of a man arrested in Dubno, for example (whose participation in a conspiratorial organization had been monitored for some time prior to his arrest), several

---

* In an evocative, though illiterate style, Edward Sobiech remembers his ordeal: "after 4 months of terrible hardships, beatings on the mug and kicking because I didn't want to tell them anything during interrogation they knocked out a few teeth from my snout and a Lot of health they took from me a Soviet woman pinched me on the balls during investigative interrogation to make me tell them about the Germans after all these 4-months long tortures they sentenced me at night from some scrap of paper [a guard would simply come to one's cell and read the sentence passed by a special tribunal in Moscow] for 3 years of prison because I have hurt the frontier, presumably Theirs" (HI, AC, 3560; see also AC, 190).

initial interrogation sessions consisted of a number of NKVD agents beating him without asking any questions. In most cases, however, prisoners were first given an opportunity to confess. Only after they failed to do so did the beating commence.[78]

This delay of torture must have been a severely stressful experience. A prisoner, given an hour or sometimes even a day or two to "think it over," lived in a state of mounting fear, for the determination of his captors to use physical coercion could not be doubted. If one had been in prison for any length of time prior to the first interrogation (and many spent weeks before being called by the NKVD), one had either seen tortured cellmates returning from their interrogation sessions or heard the screams of prisoners being tortured. Investigative prisons were filled with screams and moans at night, which often could be heard throughout the neighborhoods where makeshift provincial police stations and NKVD offices were located. In the offices of the rail-road NKVD in Mołodeczno station the interrogator put on a record to muffle the screams of the prisoners he was beating; in the NKVD prison in Dzisna, Lieutenant Bobrov tortured prisoners to the accompaniment of accordion music provided by a soldier.[79]

What made the prisoners' situation especially hopeless was that they were usually called to confess to crimes they had not committed or to give information they did not have. Those caught illegally crossing the frontier were routinely accused of spying and tortured to tell about their non-existent networks, bosses, and assignments. Almost all of the arrested were quizzed about hidden weapons that they knew nothing about; or they were labeled counterrevolutionaries and asked to name other members of their organization. As a forester from Stryj put it: "They didn't know what they wanted, and the prisoners didn't know what they were arrested for."[80]

Prisoners were confronted with the peculiar reasoning of their custodians, which derived from a Marxist interpretation of historical progress and made no sense to the arrested. Interrogators' argumentation revolved around two especially baffling paragraphs in article 58 of the Russian penal code: paragraph 4 defined as counterrevolutionary crime "aid, under any form whatsoever, provided to that part of the international bourgeoisie that does not recognize the legal equality of communism, which is about to replace the capitalist system," and paragraph 13 defined counterrevolution as "activities against the working class . . . under the tsarist government, or any other counterrevolutionary government during the period of the civil war."[81] Paragraph 4 (corresponding to paragraph 4 of article 54 in the Ukrainian penal code) was broadly applied against anyone who had participated in the political, administrative, and social life of prewar Poland.[82] Paragraph 13 was used mostly against veterans of the 1920 Polish-Bolshevik war. Utter confusion and helplessness overwhelmed the accused. "I was a village head [*sołtys*] in Skórce for eight years prior to the outbreak of the war. And this was the only accusation against me."[83] The man got an eight-year sentence—undoubtedly one year for each year of "counterrevolutionary activity." Józef Dziadul was sentenced because he was "a civil servant in a capitalist state and in this way contributed to the strengthening of a regime hostile to the communist revolution."[84] A veteran of the 1920 war, when he started to argue with his interrogator, learned that he should have deserted at the time to the Bolshevik side.[85]

Suddenly one's whole life history was stood upside down. Virtually all sacrifice, all distinction, and all achievement throughout the preceding twenty years turned into liabilities overnight. Furthermore, the new standards were enforced retroactively. "This formula of accusation is a legal monstrosity," wrote a lawyer accused precisely of having been a lawyer and a reserve officer in the Polish army and thus of having fostered the interests of a bourgeois state. "This runs against the fundamental principles of penal and international law which preclude one state from bringing accusations against citizens of another state who had merely fulfilled the citizens' duties in their own country."[86]

It was indeed a legal monstrosity, but one that could not be resolved by legal reasoning. Instead, one is tempted to say, it was a dialectical contradiction that derived from the very essence of the Communist revolutionary project and could be overcome only within the intellectual framework that went with it: "To my question why do you judge me for having simply fulfilled my duties as a Polish citizen, the interrogator told me that the whole world belongs to them, and that everybody will be judged."[87] This was precisely the answer to the dilemma: once revealed, the logic of history voided all other sovereignty claims but those which embodied it. In other words, regardless of one's place of residence, one had to be subject to Soviet authority. Since October 1917 the struggle on earth was between revolution and counterrevolution, and all individuals sided with one or the other. Old notions of international politics did not apply to the Soviet state and its conduct. Thus the Soviet state by definition could not conquer, it could only liberate; nor could it wage war, it could only carry further "the banner of the revolution." The justification for its actions was no different in Lwów than in Leningrad. Nor would it be different in Paris. Soviet authority was the embodiment of the universal law of history that posited that the contradictions of capitalism can and will be resolved only with the advent of communism. Legal reservations must have seemed rather petty and ridiculous against this historical necessity.

NKVD Personnel and the Use of Torture

To compound their confusion, prisoners were time and again confronted with the ignorance of NKVD operatives. In Kowel prison, for example, Lieutenant Sarkisjan from the NKVD tired to induce a railroad engineer to confess that he was employed by the Polish intelligence service (the so-called Second Department) and supervised a network of confidential collaborators along the railroad line from Kowel to Kiwerce. The man protested his innocence, which only infuriated the interrogator, who then accused him of having been a party activist in Poland because he had a diploma from the engineering school. "Politechnikum, the very name of the school indicates that you were taught party [i.e., political] subjects there," argued Sarkisjan.[88] This would be very amusing but for the fact that Lieutenant Sarkisjan, just as any other NKVD interrogator, had the power to declare who was and was not a political activist in prewar Poland.

The episode illustrates how ignorant the vast majority of NKVD operatives were about the realities of life in prewar Poland. J. W. Russell, a British diplomat who traveled to Lwów on official business in January 1940, came to this very conclusion on the basis of a somewhat humorous encounter:

> The local NKVD and militia (who are also staffed by imported thugs from Russia proper) in all their dealings with Mr. Trant and myself showed a remarkable combination of ignorance, incompetence and unpleasantness. The official with whom we had the misfortune to deal most of the time was a Lieutenant of Militia, by the name of Volkov—nervous, hysterical, illiterate, obtuse and violently ill-mannered, this gentleman on one occasion summoned two militiamen to eject me from his office—I was accordingly compelled to lock the door on the inside and wait until he returned to his senses. This he did after a few minutes of the most violent recriminations and personal abuse which finally left him in a state bordering upon the tearful. He then implored me to leave him alone, saying that he was not used to dealing with foreigners (which was indeed only too painfully evident) and that the flood of refugees had involved him in a mass of work with which, he readily admitted, he was totally incompetent to deal.[89]

This is not to say that the NKVD lacked the relevant information to do their job. The information was available from prewar records and from people who welcomed the Red Army, but the NKVD did not know how to interpret it. Upon reflection, however, one has to conclude that it could not have been otherwise and, strangely, that it was also unimportant. Most of the NKVD cadres sent into the occupied territories— that is, everyone under thirty—had no recollection, or at most a very faint one, of life under any but the Soviet regime.[90] Thus they could use no familiar analogies to make sense of the life histories of people they had in custody. The testimonies stored in the Hoover Archives offer two glimpses into the personal biographies of NKVD field operatives. One of them, very proud of his present high station in life, told a woman prisoner that he used to work as a shoemaker.[91] Another, Aleksander Czaków, a Polish citizen evacuated with the Anders army, had been a jack of all trades before the war, only marginally employed, and was the son of equally marginally employed declassé parents who used to make a few złotys on the side as police informers in prewar Poland.* Why should the rest of the NKVD personnel be radically different in social background from a shoemaker who left his trade or a lumpenproletarian?

We lack evidence to characterize NKVD personnel systematically in terms of social origin beyond occasional individual biographies and the record of officers' use of terror in the service. Granted, each society and social category includes some individuals who pathologically enjoy violence. But I doubt the usefulness of simply dismissing the NKVD as an insane asylum for sadists. People can be trained to dispense violence, even torture, and political police all over the world are familiar with the practice. But it is easier to teach such ways to people who have been socialized to violence early in life. The socially marginal, the lumpenproletariat, presents a better recruitment field for the

---

* Czaków's biography gives a good insight into dizzying prospects of upward social mobility through a career in the NKVD. From unskilled railroad worker at a provincial depot, he moved within one year to an officer's commission and an independent command at the time of German invasion, which gave him power of life and death over the civilian population. (He used that power leisurely, admitting later to killing more than thirty people during the last week of June 1941.) Between January 1, 1940, when he joined as a secret collaborator of the NKVD, and the outbreak of Russo-German war, he moved several times, joined the Komsomol, and held several executive positions in its apparatus, including that of a second secretary in Wilno. He supervised groups of agitators during two elections after the Soviet occupation of Lithuania, developed a network of his own informers, taught at a Komsomol school, traveled widely (even to Moscow on one occasion), and before long had a handsome salary and, in the end, a commission to lieutenant's rank in the NKVD (HI, AC, 13972).

service than any other social category. For the praetorian guard of a tyrannical regime it also suits that they are alienated from and resentful of the rest of society; and with no other loyalty but to their employer, the security apparatus, they can be unleashed against society. They are loyal and brutal, which is what the regime wants them to be, but they are also ignorant.

This ignorance was of little consequence for Soviet security, but it made all the difference for the prisoner being interrogated. Paradoxically, people were driven to despair by the *inability to communicate* with their tormentors, who heaped abuse and blows on them while pressing questions that made no sense. Consequently, the answers made no sense either, and sometimes the interrogating officer did not even listen to them. Lieutenant Gubarov in Wilejka prison pounded on prisoners with the butt of his revolver, repeating after each answer: "You are lying, you sly fox."[92] Silence offered no way out of the immediate predicament either. In Brześć an NKVD interrogator beat his reluctant prisoners, intoning: "ne khochesh govorit', golubchik, to budesh pet' [if you don't want to talk, my little pigeon, you will sing instead]."[93]

The NKVD men were trained to beat prisoners in order to induce their cooperation. A peasant member of the Polish underground organization, arrested in Jedwabne (Łomża county of Białystok voivodeship), was briefly interrogated by two NKVD men. When he failed to "reveal everything," one of the interrogators simply ran out into the courtyard, broke a wooden pole from the courtyard fence, and then "ran back and started to pound on me with this pole."[94] No special instruments of torture were necessary. An NKVD major in Kołomyja used to hit his prisoners with a metal ruler after each unanswered question. Often he beat them unconscious. Prisoners could be grabbed by the hair and have their heads pounded against a wall. In Czortków prison, those arrested after the uprising of January 1940, many of them high school students, were beaten with wooden poles, handguns, bottles, and metal bars, and kicked until their jaws and ribs were broken. In the railroad prison at Białystok, NKVD man Ostapov kicked a prisoner repeatedly in the shin until he lost consciousness. No age or sex was spared.[95]

A trucheon casually waved in front of a prisoner's eyes was called by spiteful NKVD interrogators "the Polish constitution" or, alternatively, "Stalin's constitution." People were thus told in no uncertain terms that it, rather than law, was the foundation of the new order. And it was sometimes applied with great ingenuity. In Nowa Wilejka, prisoners were clubbed over the head through a piece of cardboard or a thin book, leaving them stunned and dizzy for a long time. Upon returning to their cells, they often lost consciousness. Some simple props were used during interrogation in traditional ways—needles forced under fingernails or hands crushed in doors. Many prisoners were ordered to sit on the edge of a chair with legs and hands extended forward. Then suddenly the chair was kicked from under them and they hit the floor on the coccyx bone. In Augustów prison, people were tortured by having vodka, gasoline, or kerosene poured into their noses. An NKVD man by the name of Dzikon (a fitting name, meaning something between a wild boar and a wild man) stood his prisoners next to a burning stove in a spot where water dripped slowly on their heads. "Falling drops," wrote one of his victims, "drove one unconscious and felt like hammer blows."[96]

Prisoners were frequently tortured by exposure to extreme temperatures. Some were ordered to stand at attention, fully dressed, next to a fiercely hot stove; others were thrown naked or in their underwear into cold punishment cells. Water was routinely poured into these cells and it stood there several inches deep, dissuading exhausted prisoners from lying down on the floor.[97] Sometimes, on the other hand, there was nothing else one could do, as in the punishment cell in Oszmiana (Wilno voivodeship):

> It was a hole in the ground where one couldn't either stand or sit, but one had to lie down as in a coffin. It was not aired. I thought I would suffocate. Every day they threw me a slice of bread and half a liter of water. They didn't take prisoners to the toilet. The stench in this hole was unbearable.[98]

In the Pińsk prison (Polesie voivodeship),

> The punishment cell, number 45, was in a tiny space one could enter only by getting down on one's knees. A sewage pipe passed through this space and the electric light was so strong there that it was impossible to open one's eyes. The strongest man couldn't last there longer than fifteen minutes. Unconscious prisoners were hauled back to their cells, splashed with water, and after a short while the treatment was repeated.[99]

In Berezwecz prison people were burned during interrogation. In Wilejka, a prisoner was ordered to stand at attention with head tilted backwards as far as possible; then burning cigarettes were pressed against his chin. In Bukaczowce, a village in Rohatyn county (Stanisławów voivodeship), a prisoner had his penis wrapped in paper and set on fire during questioning.[100]

There were fewer NKVD women among the interrogators, but they were remembered. They beat some of their prisoners and cursed them just as their male counterparts did.* Unlike the NKVD men, however, they reached for the genitals—their own as well as their prisoners'. I have already quoted the reminiscence of a "tourist" who had been "pinched" by a Soviet woman interrogator. A few other former prisoners evoke, strikingly, the same gesture and phrase in their remembrances of interrogation. "We will sentence you to fifteen years and you won't see a cunt anymore," said a pretty NKVD woman to her prisoner. "In the end she lifted her skirt," recalls another victim, "and showing her genitals, she said that I was looking at this for the last time in my life."[101] Marian Płudy was sentenced to one year of prison by a court in Lwów presided over by a woman judge. After the sentence was read:

> Małka, who judged me, stood up and said loudly so that the listening public could hear: *nechevo, zhit' budesh, tol'ko ebat ne zakhochesh i nikogda zhivoi pizdy ne uvidesh* [it's OK, you will live, but you won't want to fuck anymore and you won't see a live cunt], and she gestured accordingly with her hands and lifted her skirt.[102]

A ritual incantation—like "You will see Poland like I will see hair growing in my palm" or "You will see Poland like you will see your own ear"—the mocking phrases and gestures must have been passed around from one Soviet woman interrogator to another. They must have enjoyed the effect, otherwise these would not have become clichés in the repertoire of the NKVD.

Neither skillful manipulators of ideas trained in diamat nor faceless bureaucrats preoccupied with organizational efficiency, the field operatives of the NKVD appear instead as a host of ignorant, brutal, and vulgar individuals.

DEATH IN PRISON

Finally, at the limits of their endurance and their torturers' zeal, prisoners of the Soviet state confronted death. Death came in a variety of

* Verbal abuse, a more or less constant feature of all encounters with the Soviet authorities, left quite an imprint on people's memories. It was definitely a brutalizing experience: "Throughout my interrogation I was addressed exclusively as *polskaia bliat, polskaia prostitutka, polskaia kurva* [all three expressions a variation of 'Polish whore']" (Wilejka, 45; see also, for example, Łuniniec, 43; gródek jagielloński, 25). Marc Raeff points to the practice of "verbal violence" in imperial Russia, where those labeled as state enemies sometimes "ceased to be referred to in legal documents by their ordinary names and were designated instead by diminutives together with insulting epithets" (Raeff, *Understanding Imperial Russia*, p. 14).

guises: as a sentence that might eventually be commuted, as a mock execution staged to break the prisoner's psychological resistance, as the result of tortures and confinement in unsuitable conditions, and as madness and suicide.

Mock executions were widely practiced as a mental torture, so widely that after some time in jail a prisoner would be forewarned by his cellmates and to some degree immunized against it. Usually people were taken at night to a nearby forest and ordered to dig a grave and stand at its edge, while being questioned all along. If one remained silent, the guard fired—and missed.[103] In Wilejka prison, on the other hand, a prisoner was brought to a bloodstained basement cell, undoubtedly used for real executions on other occasions,[104] and stood against a pile of sandbags.

> "Confess who belonged with you to Polish bands, who gave you underground newspapers, where your weapons are hidden, and who else has any, or you will perish here like a dog." I refused to answer and so they called the torturer who was supposed to frighten me by carrying out the execution. He unloaded his gun and gave it to me to check whether it was good, then took it back and gave me some bullets also to check whether they were OK. Then he loaded the gun, aimed at my head and asked for the last time whether I confessed to the accusation. (I knew well by then, from what fellow inmates told me back in the cell, that they do such things just to frighten and that I would not be shot.) Then he shot twice and bullets passed a few centimeters from my ear and got stuck in sandbags. The chief of the NKVD chased him away, saying that he didn't know how to shoot and that he had a woman's heart because his hand trembled. "I will do it myself." Once again he asked for my confession and then he shot a few times, the same way as I was shot at before. . . .[105]

There were such execution cells in other prisons as well, in Łuck for example.[106] The theatricality of the scene may strike us today as a little overdone; but given the circumstances and the reputation of the parties involved, most people were undoubtedly numbed by the experience. The NKVD must have been satisfied with the results, otherwise the little production would not have been so routinely played out.

But real death as well awaited prisoners in Soviet custody. Here follows a random, partial list of victims from all over the Western Ukraine and Western Belorussia. In Łomża (Białystok voivodeship) "in my presence the following have died: Szypulski, Sergeant Czerwiński, Mrugalski, Leszniewski, Goldman, Zajkowski, Chojnacki, and I forgot a lot of names." In Wysoka (Sokółka county, Białystok voivodeship) the wife of Lieutenant Stach died on the way to hospital after a beating with rifle butts during interrogation. In Oszmiana (Wołyń voivodeship) the head (*voyt*) of gmina Soły, Zawadzki, along with Hubieni "and others" died from dysentery. In the railroad station in Białystok, stationmaster Józef Olszewski was tortured to death. In Nowa Wilejka (Wilno-Troki county, Wilno voivodeship) policeman Krawczyk died. In Drohobycz (Lwów voivodeship) the town's mayor, Dr. Piechowicz, along with Dr. Bolechowski and engineer Kilesiński died in prison, as did Colonel Jan Krupa and Lieutenant Stefan Walczak in Przemyśl prison (Lwów voivodeship). In Dubno (Wołyń voivodeship) Sergeant Ćwiklik died from tortures. In Kołomyja (Stanisławów voivodeship) engineer Mastelarz, railwayman Ilnicki, and the voyt of gmina Kołomyja, Captain Błyskal, died in prison. In Kowel (Wołyń voivodeship) the stationmaster from Zdołbunów, Onyszkiewicz, was tortured to death.[107]

These, and perhaps thousands of others, were unplanned deaths, due to neglect, torture, and/or lack of medical attention or proper detention facilities. In the internal accounting of the NKVD they were probably written off as "accidents at work" or something equally inconspicuous. They were different from "liquidations" (to use the Soviet newspeak equivalent of the Nazi "special treatment"), the death sentences or executions (without "legal" justification) carried out on prisoners. But until we acquire the NKVD archives pertaining to these events,[108] we will not be able to estimate even approximately the number of killings that took place.

We do know that scores of death sentences were passed by Soviet courts (though many were subsequently commuted), and we also have evidence concerning mass executions at the time prisons were evacuated before the German advance in June and July 1941. Death sentences were passed by Soviet courts or military tribunals, and the Soviet authorities were not especially shy about it. There were press reports of such convictions from the very first days of the occupation.[109] In the trial of young Ukrainian nationalists (the so-called "Trial of 59"), forty-two of the accused were sentenced to death, though half of them—ten young women and eleven men—eventually had their sentences commuted. Many young people were shot for participation in the Czortków uprising.[110] Death sentences, in short, were given out generously. As to how they were carried out, we can extrapolate from the staging of mock executions.[111]

Finally, there was escape into insanity and suicide. Again, only a few names can be retrieved; but we are assured by witnesses that many

„Наша армия есть армия освобождения трудящихся". И.Сталин.

1. A poster with a quotation from Stalin: "Our army is the army of liberators of the workers." This poster and others reproduced in this book were affixed on public buildings in Lwów shortly after the invasion. Arthur Waldo, who ripped the posters off the walls, felt sure that they were printed well ahead of the outbreak of war.

2. An election campaign poster calling on people to vote for the unification of the Western Ukraine with the Soviet Ukraine.

3. One of many posters ridiculing the Polish eagle—Poland's national symbol—a recurrent theme in Soviet propaganda. Note that the two peasants, as well as the soldier, are the same ones who appear in the poster on the jacket of this book.

4. The inscription on this poster—"They got the long-awaited truth"—is a play on the word *pravda*, the name of the Communist party daily newspaper, which the woman has clasped to her breast.

5. One of the many pictorial representations of the main theme of electoral propaganda: the contrast of "what it was like" with "what is happening now" and "what it will be like" in the future. An inscription at the bottom (not shown) indicates that this poster was sent into production on September 23, 1939—well before the call for elections was announced in the Western Ukraine and Western Belorussia.

6. Frontispiece for the first local Ukrainian-language edition of the main Soviet satirical magazine *Crocodile*, October 15, 1939. A worker, a peasant, and a representative of the intelligentsia hand in their electoral ballots.

7. Frontispiece of the fourth and last issue of the local Polish-language edition of *Crocodile*, dated October 26, 1939. Under the drawing of the façade of Lwów's Grand Theater, the caption reads: "For the first time in the history of this theater the leading role in the show will be played by the people."

8. Comrade Germanyuk, member of the Plenipotentiary Commission of the National Assembly of Western Belorussia, thanking Stalin for the liberation of the people from the Polish yoke.

9. A poster directing Polish citizens born between 1890 and 1921 to register with their draft boards. The poster is in Polish, in Latin script, but the order of the alphabet follows the letter sequence of the Cyrillic alphabet. It illustrates the Soviet attitude toward ethnic groups: "socialist in content and national in form."

10. "Soldiers of the worker-peasant Red Army should always serve as paragons of discipline, organizational ability, and cultured behavior." *Kulturnost'* (cultureness) was a key word in the Soviet lexicon, denoting anything from being properly washed to owning a library.

DO ŻOŁNIERZY ARMII POLSKIEJ

Żołnierze!

Znowu, jak i w roku 1914, wasi krwiożercy—obszarnicy i kapitaliści rzucili was do otworu ogniowego drugiej wojny imperialistycznej. Jak i wtedy, rzeką leje się krew robotników i włościan. Tysiące ludzi tracą swe życie na łanach rzezi krwawej, pozostawiając unieszczęśliwionych żon, dzieci i matek, które utraciły swych chlebodawców. CO ICH CZEKA? Głód, nędza, spustoszenie. Śmierć podniosła już nad nimi swą łapę kościstą.

Winowajcy tej rzezi krwawej są to obszarnicy-kapitaliści!—mościckie, śmigłe-rydze, radziwiłłowie, sapiedzy, sławoj-składkowskie—psy brutalne, które rzuciły naród polski do rzezi krwawej. To oni przez eksploatację niepowstrzymaną, ujarzmienie narodowościowe, wrogość narodowościową doprowadzili naród polski do całkowitego wycieńczenia ekonomicznego i rozgromienia wojskowego.

W jarzmie obszarnika i kapitalisty jęczą robotnicy i włościanie Ukrainy Zachodniej i Białorusi Zachodniej. Oni są pozbawieni swych szkół, literatury, sztuki, prasy. Język ukraiński i białoruski są prześladowane. Ekspedycje karne, sądy polowe, terror biały szaleją po całej Ukrainie Zachodniej i Białorusi Zachodniej.

ŻOŁNIERZE! Niezgoda narodowościowa, wrogość między narodami jest korzysną tylko dla polskich obszarników i burżuazji. Ona dla nich jest niezbędną, żeby ukryć eksploatację robotników i włościan polaków, dla tego, żeby robotnik i włościanin polski nie widzieli łez gorzkich, bezprawnego, nieludzkiego życia ukraińca i białorusina.

ŻOŁNIERZE! Czy można więcej jeszcze cierpieć okropność obszarniczo-kapitalistycznego jarzma? Czy może spokojnie patrzeć naród wyzwolony Białorusi Sowieckiej na bezprawne, ponure życie robotników i włościan Białorusi Zachodniej?

Naród Białorusi Sowieckiej przy pomocy wielkiego narodu rosyjskiego zbudował radosne, bogate i szczęśliwe życie. Przykład jego jako sztandar rewolucyjny pochodnią nieugaszoną oświeca drogę do wyzwolenia ujarzmionego człowieczeństwa od jarzma kapitalistycznego.

Robotnicy i włościanie Białorusi Zachodniej, wznosząc ten wielki sztandar walki wyzwoleńczej, z radością i nadzieją zwracają swe wzroki do wielkiego kraju socjalistycznego.

Wolny naród białoruski przeciąga swą rękę braterską do robotnika i włościanina Białorusi Zachodniej i na pomóc im posyła swą wielką armię wyzwolenia.

ŻOŁNIERZE! Armia Czerwona nie chce ani przywłaszczenia cudzych terytorii, ani cudzego dobra. Armia Czerwona—armia wyzwolenia przygnębionych od jarzma kapitalistycznego. Ona niesie szczęście, spokój, wolność ujarzmionemu człowieczeństwu.

ŻOŁNIERZE!

Obracajcie swą broń przeciwko obszarników i kapitalistów. Nie strzelajcie do swych braci po klasie. Niech z was każdy dopomaga przesunięciu naprzód oddziałów Armii Czerwonej! Walczcie o wyzwolenie od jarzma obszarniczo-kapitalistycznego!

Niech żyje przyjaźń narodów Polski, Białorusi Zachodniej i Ukrainy Zachodniej!

Niech żyje Armia Czerwona—armia wyzwolenia ujarzmionych!

Dowódca Frontu Białoruskiego
Komandarm 2 rangu M. KOWALOW.

---

11. Two leaflets dropped in Western Belorussia under the signature of the commander of the Belorussian front, Kovalev. They incite Polish soldiers to turn their weapons against officers and the well-to-do, and promise a happy future following the victory of the Red Army. Among the many Russicisms, misspellings, and grammatical errors, note that the opening key word "Soldiers" (Zolnierze) is misspelled Rzolnierze in the second leaflet.

Rzołnierze Armii Polskiej!

Pańsko-burżuazjny Rząd Polski, wciągnowszy Was w awanturystyczną wojnę, pozornie przewaliło się. Ono okazało się bezsilnym rządzić krajem i zorganizować obronu. Ministrzy i gienerałowie, schwycili nagrabione imi złoto, tchórzliwie uciekli, pozostawiają armię i cały lud Polski na wolę losu.

Armia Polska pocierpieła surową porażkę, od którego ona nie oprawić wstanie się. Wam, waszym żonom, dzieciam, braciam i siostram ugraża głodna śmierć i zniszczenie.

W te ciężkie dni dla Was potężny Związek Radziecki wyciąga Wam ręce braterskiej pomocy. Nie przeciwcie się Robotniczo-Chłopskiej Armii Czerwonej. Wasze przeciewenie bez kożyści i przerzeczono na całą zgubę. My idziemy do Was nie jako zdobywcy, a jako wasi braci po klasu, jako wasi wyzwoleńcy od ucisku obszarników i kapitalistów.

Wielka i niezwolczona Armia Czerwona niesle na swoich sztandarach procującym, braterstwo i szczęśliwe życie.

Rzołnierze Armii Polskiej! Nie proliwacie doremnie krwi za cudze Wam interesy obszarników i kapitalistów.

Was przymuszają uciskać białorusinów, ukraińców. Rządzące kołe Polskie sieją narodową rużność między polakami, białorusinami i ukraińcami.

Pamiętajcie! Nie może być swobodny naród, uciskające drugie narody. Pracujące białorusini i ukraińcy—Wasi procujące, a nie wrogi. Razem z nimi budujcie szczęśliwe dorobkowe życie.

Rzucajcie broń! Przechodźcie na stronę Armii Czerwonej. Wam zabezpieczona swoboda i szczęśliwe życie.

Naczelny Dowódca Białoruskiego frontu
Komandarm Drugiej Rangi Michuł KOWALOW.

17 września 1939 roku.

12. A few of the many thousands of personal depositions, describing conditions of life under the Soviet regime, that formed the principal source for this book.

more succumbed to despair. In Kołomyja, we are told, policeman Susuł committed suicide; so did Władysław Cyganek, a lawyer, in Przemyśl. In Nowa Wilejka, Lieutenant Stanisław Piórko lost his mind as a result of tortures, as did "many others." In the Łukiszki prison in Wilno there were several suicides and cases of madness. In Stanisławów engineer Bauer cut his wrists and died in the prison cell after a torture session administered by an NKVD man named Morozov, who was feared as one of the most brutal interrogators.[112] And there was the suicide of Eugeniusz Muraszów in the Berezwecz prison near Głębokie:

> In January or February of 1940, after he returned to the cell from interrogation, he told us about brutal tortures he suffered and that he was told that unless he signed a statement submitted to him, his wife and son would be arrested and tortured in his presence. The same night Muraszów, while we were asleep, tried to cut veins on his neck with a piece of broken glass. We noticed what he was doing and we stopped it and held him by the hands. When we let him go he tried to reopen with his bare hands the wounds he managed to inflict upon himself. Then we called guards who came and took him to another cell. There, in the morning of the next day, when other prisoners were out in the corridor, Muraszów put his head into a burning stove. He was pulled away, but the burns were so extensive that he lost sight and was all covered with blisters. He was still conscious though, and gropingly found a wall and rushed against it, head forward, with all his strength. This is how he died. It all happened so fast that the guards didn't have time to remove witnesses from the corridor.[113]

For the record, it should be stated that prisoners resisted their tormentors. Not only did many choose to be silent or evasive under questioning—a heroic enough attitude, given the methods of persuasion used by the NKVD—but some actually fought their captors or filed complaints about their mistreatment. I have three testimonies—from Mołodeczno, from Baranowicze, and from an unidentified prison—of prisoners who actually fought back when NKVD officers began to torture them during interrogation. All three prisoners were quickly subdued and given a solid beating, but all claim that no one ever laid hands on them again during interrogation.[114]

One should not hastily draw conclusions from these three depositions. It may well be that many others resisted and that all were killed; hence, only these three recorded cases have a happy ending. But it is also possible that the handful of desperate prisoners who assaulted their interrogators were treated better as a consequence. The NKVD men, judging by standards derived from their experiences in the Soviet Union, may have viewed them as some weird Polish version of Soviet "criminals," "thieves," or "urkas." These were left alone by the NKVD and could do as they pleased in prisons and especially in labor camps, where they were in fact used by the camp administration to terrorize and police the political prisoners.

Finally, only one complaint of physical abuse during interrogation is reported as having been officially reviewed. A panel composed of two public prosecutors, two high NKVD officials, and a Soviet officer exculpated the NKVD. After an exchange of opinions, the complainant was told that "the prisoners were to blame if the interrogators sometimes resorted to improper measures because they did so, apparently, when the arrested refused to confess to crimes they were accused of."[115]

EVACUATION AND EXECUTIONS

No truth seemed more self-evident during the first twenty months of the war than the conviction that Hitler's and Stalin's marriage of convenience would end. Though their divorce would mean the physical destruction of the Western Ukraine and Western Belorussia, where military hostilities would certainly take place as a result, the overwhelming majority of local residents rejoiced over the prospect and impatiently awaited its realization. The people of the Western Ukraine and Western Belorussia were no different in this respect from the population of Western Europe; only their conviction that the Soviets would suffer defeat in the conflict with Germany set them apart. The rest of Europe yearned to see the former archenemies go to war in order to break out of Hitler's grip, and, in a way, the same psychological motivation was at work in the Western Ukraine and Western Belorussia: they also wanted to break out from under an occupation. The mind-boggling inefficiency, corruption, ignorance, and clumsiness of the Soviet-sponsored administration allowed no doubt about which side would win, especially among those who had not seen Hitler's occupation administration at work.

Nowhere were the prospects for an imminent Soviet-German war debated more vigorously than in the prisons of the Ukraine and Belorussia. And nowhere, I think, were the sounds of that war welcomed more warmly. Little did the prisoners suspect what fate awaited them.

The USSR was unprepared for the Nazi attack on June 22, 1941, and the speed of the German advance was unprecedented. By the first week of July the entire territory of pre-1939 Poland was already under

German occupation. The Soviet administration was routed from the Western Ukraine and Western Belorussia, millions of Red Army soldiers were taken prisoner during the first months of the campaign, and nothing remained of the cumbersome and all-pervasive state machinery recently imposed on the area. In the space of three weeks the Soviet state gave up numerous territories, countless subjects, millions of soldiers, and heaps of secret documents. But it never let go one commodity: its prisoners.

The general orders binding on NKVD personnel in this matter must have been clear: with very few exceptions, all prisoners in the Western Ukraine and Western Belorussia on June 22, 1941 (some 150,000 people by my estimates), were moved east, or killed, or both. But who decided what to do in each case and according to what criteria will probably never be known. It cannot be argued that summary killings were carried out only as a last resort, after attempts to evacuate prisoners had failed. In the Lwów prisons, for example, where many thousands were killed, there is no record that evacuation was ever contemplated.[116] On the other hand, several hundred prisoners from Czortków, were evacuated—only to be killed at their destination, in Umań.[117] Ukrainians, Poles, Germans, Jews, and a Belorussian have identified no less than twenty-five prisons in the Western Ukraine and Lithuania where inmates were summarily executed by the Soviet authorities prior to the Wehrmacht's occupation of the area in the summer of 1941.[118] There is abundant evidence about the evacuation of these prisons and the widespread killings of prisoners there. But mysteriously, no testimony concerning events in Western Belorussian prisons during the summer of 1941 could be found.[119]

Massacre in Lwów

Soon after the first German bombs fell on Lwów on Sunday, June 22, the NKVD began to collect prisoners from different cells in the Brygidki prison, take them to the cellars, and shoot them. "The sound of shooting could clearly be heard in the cells."[120] Executions continued for about twenty-four hours. Then, late Monday evening, a strange silence prevailed. The NKVD guards had left the compound, and upon realizing this, inmates broke down cell doors during the night and ventured into the courtyard in the small hours of Tuesday morning. Some, it seems, ransacked or destroyed records in the prison administration office; but because Soviet troops were moving through the streets, few dared to go beyond the prison gate. In any case, early on Tuesday morning the guards returned, shooting at and killing scores among the crowd assembled in the courtyard. They drove prisoners back into their cells, ordered everybody to lie face down on the floor, shot a few recalcitrant prisoners in their cells, and, having thus restored order, continued with the executions.[121]

Shootings went on for the whole week, through the morning of Saturday, June 28. Truck engines in the prison garage were switched on to muffle the sounds. When the cellars were filled with bodies, a trench was dug in the courtyard and prisoners were executed there. "During that week we did not get any food at all, and many people lost their minds."[122] In a cell housing about one hundred prisoners at the beginning of the week, twelve inmates were alive when everything was over. Bohdan Kolzanivsky, who gave this information, survived because he kept silent when his name was called out; and when guards came for him again, he said that a prisoner by this name had already been led away.

It appears that political prisoners—those accused of crimes against the state under the Russian or Ukrainian penal code—were the first to be eliminated. However, there is no clear evidence that common criminals (*bytoviki*) were spared.* When prisons were evacuated, criminals went along as well, but there was segregation. I even know of one instance when a group of criminals was actually released from Soviet custody.[123] But from smaller prisons, where there was time to dispose of everybody, there seem to have been no survivors, only witnesses who discovered mass graves after Soviet withdrawal from the area. Criminals may have been released from some prisons, of course, but the population living in the vicinity would have remembered.

Clearly, there was bureaucratic supervision of the killings or, at least, of the order in which they were carried out. For one thing, calling prisoners for execution by name rather than taking them cell by cell shows that the treatment was individualized and that, given the paper work this procedure must have entailed, there was some form of accounting. Indeed, several episodes from the Lwów massacre indicate that the NKVD went about this madness in an orderly fashion. Thus, a man arrested in the morning of June 22, 1941, was questioned in prison by a team of prosecutors about the circumstances of his arrest to determine the paragraph under which he would most likely be charged. Using his quick mind and the helpful hints of fellow pris-

---

* There was no formal, clearly spelled out distinction between criminal and political prisoners in Soviet law. Nevertheless the boundaries were sharply drawn: everyone knew to which category he or she belonged, and, especially in Stalin's time, the treatment of each category was markedly different. Political prisoners in the USSR experienced far worse conditions of incarceration than common criminals.

oners, he invented a brawl in which he was allegedly involved, and he was therefore classified as a common criminal.[124] In another cell, after the NKVD returned and apparently found some records destroyed or misplaced, each prisoner was handed paper and pencil and told to write down name, date of birth, and sentence.[125] A group of women prisoners taken out on Friday, June 27 (i.e., after the executions had been going on for several days) were brought back to their cell—to the utter disbelief of the remaining prisoners—because the guards "did not know what to do with them, since there was no information in their files regarding an offense."[126] But I doubt whether anyone was intended to be spared: when the NKVD men finally fled from Brygidki prison, they had killed all but some 600–700 of their approximately 13,000 inmates.[127]

After the Germans entered the city, the grieving population of Lwów went to its prisons to search for relatives and friends. There were heaps of bodies everywhere, many unidentified, many mutilated. Bricked-up cellars full of corpses in the Brygidki and the Zamarstynów prisons were not even opened for fear of epidemics.[128]

Death by Torture

Evidence of torture is especially abundant from smaller towns, whose relatively small and manageable prison populations could be killed leisurely. In Bóbrka, many inmates were scalded with boiling water; in Berezwecz, people's noses, ears, and fingers were cut off, and there were also children's corpses in the prison compound; in Czortków, female prisoners' breasts were cut off; in Drohobycz, prisoners were fastened together with barbed wire; in Łuck, a drum lined with barbed wire stood next to one of three mass graves unearthed in the prison yard; in Przemyślany, victims' noses, ears, and fingers were cut off and their eyes put out; similarly in Sambor, Stanisławów, Stryj, and Złoczów.[129]

The *Ukrainian Daily News*, which began publication after the Soviet withdrawal from the Western Ukraine, carried a story about Dobromil mass graves in its August 3, 1941, issue. We learn that not all the bodies were recovered from the salt mine shaft, but survivors found seventy-seven corpses in the first five meters. More corpses were discovered in the prison compound, as well as in the city hall and in the building of the forestry administration. These victims were mutilated and killed just before the Soviet authorities fled from Dobromil. The executioners, according to the article, were: the head of the city administration, Petrovskii; the secretary of the party committee, Bubnov; and a militiaman, Kremer.[130]

When the Germans entered Borysław (in the Drohobycz county),

> Ukrainians wearing armbands and carrying rifles immediately appeared in the streets. They dragged Jews out of their houses, presumably to work. What kind of work was this? We were brought to the NKVD building—I was taken together with a friend—where there were already about 300 Jews, and we were ordered to bring corpses out of the cellars and to segregate them. Heaps of corpses. We had to wash some of the bodies. I went once into this cellar. Corpses were not really buried. They were covered with five to ten centimeters of dirt. These were fresh corpses. Those were the bodies of people arrested during the past week or ten days. This fellow Kozłowski and his sister were among them. The girl's nipples, she was about sixteen years old, were torn out as if with pliers, her face was burned—people said it was done after the execution so that victims couldn't be recognized but I think not. Kozłowski had only one eye and it was all swollen, his lips were sewn together with barbed wire, his hands were crushed and also burned, the skin was peeling off as if they poured boiling water all over. She was naked, he wasn't. They had no shoes. The impression was horrible. I didn't look at any more corpses, because I simply couldn't. But these were my friends. So I washed their bodies. There were several dozen corpses altogether. I remember a very long row. The majority of these people were not normally killed, with a shot, but badly maimed.[131]

We cannot escape the conclusion: Soviet state security organs tortured their prisoners not only to extract confessions (which we have come to accept as a commonplace and "understandable" procedure in a police state) but also to put them to death. Not that the NKVD had sadists in its ranks who had run amok; rather, this was a widespread and systematic procedure. I am at a loss for an interpretation, especially since the victims did not necessarily speak a foreign tongue, have skin of a different hue, come from a different ethnic group, or even belong to a distinct social class. They were common people, undistinguishable from their fellow citizens who were still enjoying freedom.

Evacuation from Wilejka

Some inmates walked out of prison alive. Their escorts, in good physical shape and fearing for their lives, drove them eastward as fast as possible. Usually, to set the pace, the strongest—common criminals or the recently arrested—were put in the front of the evacuation columns.

"After the war broke out, on June 24, the Nowa Wilejka prison was evacuated. Cells were unlocked and prisoners were ordered to get on the road in front of the prison gate, where they were told to kneel until a certain number of them would be ready to depart."[132] Thus begins the testimony of a survivor of a long march. As late as mid-October 1941 and from as deep inside the country as Artiomovsk in the Donetsk region, prisoners were evacuated on foot ahead of advancing German armies.[133] Here follow details from one such march, not a particularly vicious one, I think. If anything, it may have been relatively benign, since many people lived to tell about it.

On Tuesday, June 24, three columns of prisoners were assembled in front of the Wilejka prison. When they were finally ordered to rise from the kneeling position, many thought they would be walked to the train station.[134] But only the last group, about 450 women, went in this direction. In retrospect, there was no reason to envy them. Perhaps no more trains were available. "In any case," writes Jan Bezdel, who marched in the second column, "none of the women can now be located here."[135] Before the columns were ready to go, several dozen prisoners were called by name, separated from the rest, and led away.[136] These people had been sentenced to death in the trial of an underground organization, and it was somehow clear what would happen to them. Many chose not to respond when their names were called. "Some names were called, mine was read as well to stay in this prison, but I didn't pay attention and I tried to get in among those prisoners I knew who were leaving prison and who helped me in my misery. . . . Some 150 people were ordered to stay in prison."[137]

The column of prisoners, five abreast, marched out of Wilejka at 4 in the afternoon. The several hundred escorts included militiamen from all over the Wilno area, besides the local NKVD personnel. Around 10 in the morning on the next day they rested for the first time. Bread was distributed—some 300 grams per prisoner—a lump of sugar, and cold water. This was the only meal during the entire march. Not until they boarded a train in the village of Borysów five or six days later were the prisoners fed again.

It seems that for the first two days those who fainted or could not continue to march were put on wagons accompanying the column. On the evening of the 25th water was distributed. After the column got on the road again at 3 A.M. on the 26th, the prisoners were not allowed even a sip anymore. "On the third day prisoners started to collapse from exhaustion."[138] Then, around 10 in the morning in the vicinity of the town of Pleshchenitse, German planes attacked the column (some say the attack took place on the 27th rather than 26th).

> During this time, ordered to do so by the escort, everybody was lying in the middle of the road, and whoever tried to crawl into the ditch was shot, with six killed in this way. Bombs fell away from the road where NKVD men were hiding, one was killed and another badly wounded and then he was finished off. . . . After the air raid they ordered us to drop all our bundles and to run to a nearby grove; who could not run was shot on the spot.[139]

Scores were murdered, especially among the sick and elderly trailing at the end of the column. Escort people were in a state of panic and shot indiscriminately. At the end of this wild run some 200–250 people could not be accounted for.[140]

During a brief rest in the grove following the massacre, a high school student, Czesław Siwicki, was shot in front of everybody because he loudly protested against killings of prisoners.[141]

> After a one-hour rest prisoners were ordered to stand up again and get going. When all rose Marczański, a schoolteacher from Święciany county, was very weakened and his son wanted to help him to march, as a son should a father. An NKVD man noticed everything, ran up to Marczański and ordered him to drop his father. The son hesitated, knowing what that meant. The NKVD man shot Marczański in the head without hesitation, killing him instantly, and kicked the son, who, with a heavy heart, had to drop the father and run along.

Several other prisoners were killed in this forest as well.[142]

When the column finally came to a stop on June 29 some fifteen kilometers from Borysów, the escort had to bring trucks from the town to transport the utterly exhausted prisoners to the train station. By then, many people had been killed. While crossing a bridge over Berezyna, a prisoner jumped into the water in a fit of despair. The rest of the column was ordered to lie down while the wretched man was shot. By then the escort had had enough as well. Machine guns were placed on the bridge, and the commander ordered the first three rows of prisoners to stand up in a line for execution. Perhaps all would have been killed on the spot but for a higher officer coming down the road in a car. Unable to get through because the passage was blocked with prostrate prisoners, he ordered that the march be continued. The NKVD men put them all back on their feet and ordered the column to run. Prisoners bent as if in a running position but could not move forward.

Right then prisoner Józef Jaroszewicz, shouting "betrayal," jumped into the river. Once again the column was ordered to lie down, and the would-be escapee was shot. The angry escort, seemingly afraid to kill everyone against explicit orders, trampled over flattened prisoners, beating them with rife butts and sticking them with bayonets.[143]

Finally, in the Borysów train station where the trucks delivered them, and again in Orsza where they changed trains, the weakest, who could not make the transfer on their own, were killed. Fifty-four prisoners from Jan Ciepłucha's cell marched out of Wilejka on June 24, 1941. Fourteen lost their lives during the march to Borysów.[144] Altogether about 2,000 people were evacuated. In a conversation overheard by one of the evacuees, the commander of the escort said that he could not account for 547 prisoners at the end of the march.[145]

Many prisoners were evacuated by train, notably those from Pińsk, Równe, Łuniniec, Nowogródek, and Stanisławów.[146] But the conditions under which prisoners journeyed were appalling, and the loss of life among them was often comparable to that during evacuation on foot. One group of prisoners from Czortków was evacuated by train to Gorki (another group from the same prison was marched to Umań, only to be killed there). The journey lasted seventeen days. People were packed into freight cars with horse manure all over the floor. In a wagon with 135 prisoners, 34 had died by the time the train reached its destination; in a wagon with 89, 5 died; in still another, where 130 began the journey, 41 perished, many strangled by Soviet soldiers (now imprisoned) who terrorized their fellow inmates. And the dead traveled for days with the living in hot July weather.[147]

HUNDREDS of thousands of people, emaciated by incarceration, were tortured to death, shot in the back of the head, sent by train in inhumane conditions, or put on the road and ordered to march for days in the summer heat without food or water. What does it mean for a regime to carry out mass executions of its citizens in the wake of a foreign invasion? Could it be that the NKVD killed the prisoners because of its obsession with security ("obsessed" is the word, for what enhancement of security could possibly be obtained by killing prisoners in the face of a total military collapse?), or because it was anxious to dispose of witnesses to brutalities committed in prisons? These are not plausible answers. Instead, I propose that in this last coordinated action of a nearly defunct Soviet state we can see its own epitaph of sorts, a brief condensed revelation of what it was all about—namely, the mastery and exercise of absolute power. The only body of people that remained in its grip were, literally, those whom it held in custody, and the only institution it still controlled was the penal system. In a word, the power of the Soviet state was at the time confined to the prison population. Rather than give up any of that power, the state gratuitously inflated it to the extreme by wantonly killing off in the final spasm as many prisoners as it could.

SIX

Deportations

THE LAST MODE of confinement I shall discuss has been somewhat neglected in the literature on Soviet practices. In exploring the repressive nature of the Stalinist regime, whether in personal memoirs or in analytical inquiries, observers usually give attention first to labor camp experiences or to the horror of investigative prison. Yet from the October revolution well into the 1950s several successive generations of Soviet citizens—in effect tens of millions of people—were deported. Their confinement has attracted less attention for a number of possible reasons: there were still worse things that might come; the most glamorous of Stalin's victims, the Communist elite, suffered a more conspicuous form of persecution—torture, trials, executions, labor camps; mass deportations affected primarily the illiterate masses (e.g., when removal was the driving force for collectivization in the countryside) or people literate in their own society but incomprehensible to outsiders (e.g., when the periphery of the USSR was Russified through the deportation of national minorities); the majority of the deportees were women, children, and the elderly, whereas the elite, those most conspicuous and active, heads of households, and males of working age were mostly shot or imprisoned.[1] Less articulate or outstanding, the deportees are more easily ignored, though their contribution to this story of suffering was probably no less. In the small Wołyń hamlet of Mickiewicze "the wailing of women and children could be heard all over" on the February morning in 1940 when the first shipment of deportees was collected. In Liczkowce, another Godforsaken hamlet in Tarnopol voivodeship, on the same morning "the screams of mothers were so frightful that one could go mad."[2]

VARIETIES OF RESETTLEMENT

Broadly speaking, I am concerned in this chapter with the forcible resettlement of the civilian population. However, not all instances of resettlement belong to our subject. Before I proceed with a reconstruction of the circumstances under which people were deported to the Soviet interior, I shall discuss a variety of resettlement initiatives carried out more or less within the borders of the Western Ukraine and

187

Western Belorussia. I have in mind here several administrative measures applied to local inhabitants that caused considerable dislocation.

First, a strip of land running along the entire newly established frontier and about one kilometer deep (or 800 meters, according to some sources) was depopulated. People were ordered to abandon their dwellings, and soon thereafter the buildings were razed. In some areas that the military considered more important strategically, such as Augustów county, fortifications were constructed up to 30 kilometers from the border.[3] Moreover, the newly established German-Soviet border ran largely along important rivers that for centuries had supported the community life of the local inhabitants. A frontier zone even one kilometer deep wreaked havoc with the established pattern of settlement in the area. Many hamlets and small towns were abandoned either partly or completely and later destroyed. In one of the largest local cities, Przemyśl, an entire section of town was emptied of residents and put off limits.[4]

Another form of forced resettlement came about as a consequence of the issuing of official Soviet identity cards. Theoretically, the matter of citizenship was settled unambiguously by Soviet law: following the incorporation of the Western Ukraine and Western Belorussia into the USSR, all individuals residing in this territory on November 1 and 2, 1939, acquired Soviet citizenship.[5] It turned out, however, that the actual conferring of citizenship required each person's consent. One could, despite threats, refuse the Soviet passport. It was also revealed that there were different kinds of Soviet citizenship and that each endowed recipients with different rights. Finally, one could be denied identity papers altogether[6] or have them validated for shorter (e.g., three months) or longer periods of time (five years at the most).

The official campaign to distribute identity cards in the spring of 1940 was probably the most important in a series of registrations imposed on the population of the Western Ukraine and Western Belorussia in the early period of Soviet rule.[7] Its immediate use was to establish residency control by issuing or denying permits to settle in the larger cities. Thus the most anxiety-producing experience connected with identity papers—assuming one had decided to accept Soviet citizenship—was whether one would find paragraph 11 written into the newly issued card. If so, one was barred from residence in the principal towns of the area and had to move at least 100 kilometers away from them or the frontier. Transportation facilities at the time made it utterly impractical to commute to work daily from such a distance, and employment opportunities in the countryside were nonexistent. Given the generally prevailing social dislocation, an order of

expulsion from a city was a major catastrophe for almost anyone.*
And tens, if not hundreds, of thousands had to move away from urban
centers (a proud designation indeed for these provincial, backwater,
and recently pauperized towns). In particular, refugees from western
and central Poland were served with such internal resettlement orders
whenever they opted to take a Soviet passport. But we are not concerned here with their lot—at least, not at this stage. Most of them
were later picked up and sent east in April or June 1940 or in June
1941, thus catching up with our narrative after a few months' delay.

A third variety of forced resettlement—displacement by new tenants—affected many people and added a formidable complication to
one's adjustment to the new order of things. An optimistic-sounding
news item from the January 8, 1940, issue of *Czerwony Sztandar*
informs us that the Lwów City Apartment Administration has so far
assigned "5,407 rather spacious apartments" to workers and their
families. And one learns from the same article that the presidium of the
city council established a special commission empowered "to select
seventy large apartment buildings downtown to be put at the disposal
of the City Apartment Administration" in order to continue with the
work of "assigning apartments to workers' families." Here lies the
crux of the matter. Of course there were no new construction projects
that could yield anything approximating the volume of dwellings being
assigned by the apartment administrations of various cities. In fact,
each assignment meant that the current occupants had to be thrown
out of their house or apartment so that new tenants could move in.

Moreover, most recipients of choice living quarters throughout the
Western Ukraine and Western Belorussia were not workers and their
families but the tens of thousands of Soviet administration, police, and
military officials coming to live and work in the newly occupied territories. In every town and village Soviet occupiers took over much of
the available living space by ordering families to abandon their dwell-

---

* A rather benign experience is recounted by Helena Hawrylak, who accepted a Soviet
passport after being pressured to do so following the arrest of her husband (a general
category of new citizens also subject to paragraph 11 consisted of the families of arrested
people). "Finally, having brought a photograph, and my birth and marriage certificates,
I received the passport and I was immediately told to leave the town [Stanisławów]
within a period of ten days. Under threat of arrest they told me to move to a village far
from the town and work there—for one year, they suggested. I found myself in a vicious
circle, since whatever hamlet I went to wouldn't let me in—they were forbidden to
accept Poles. Time went by, but there was no place for us, relatives of arrested Poles.
Finally, I went to Puków village, where they took me in after much hesitation, but every
three days I had to report at the militia headquarters" (HI, AC, 11323). On April 13,
1940, Helena Hawrylak was deported.

189

ings and to leave behind furniture and household utensils for Soviet officers, administrators, and party officials to use, since they came destitute into the area. In the city of Równe, whole streets were emptied of their local inhabitants; in Kałusz, Poles were ordered to vacate apartments in the downtown area and along the Stanisławów-Stryj road; in Rokitno, Soviet officers took over "mostly entire streets"; similarly in Żółkiew and in Wilno, where apartment buildings in the downtown area were ordered emptied within forty-eight hours from the issuance of the eviction notice. "In the small town of Rożniatów," recalls Helena Ćwikła, who taught in the local elementary school,

> there was a constant movement of population for about four months. Every day someone would be ordered to relocate, sometimes three or four times in a row. Apartments, with everything they contained, were taken over by the new arrivals from the USSR. And there were more and more of them coming—the families and children of the military and civilian employees.[8]

In Wilno, the assignment of an apartment to a Soviet official usually triggered a chain of evictions, as the person being displaced would go to the city apartment administration and frequently be given the dwelling of someone lower in the pecking order (an unemployed person, for example), who was evicted in turn. Depending on the good will or corruptibility of the local officials, the entire process might be more or less orderly. But on the whole, as a young girl from the town of Czortków in Tarnopol voivodeship put it, "they threw people out of their homes onto the street and lived there themselves."[9]

One might also be forcibly resettled right within one's own house or apartment. Countless families, many of whom were already sharing their homes with relatives or friends, had additional tenants assigned to their dwellings, who moved in and took over part of the unit. Perhaps, given these times, this imposition has to be considered as no more than a discomfort. But even so, let us admit, it was an awesome one:

> Personal life lost its private character. The living space allotted each person was strictly delimited. The rest of the apartment was given to some newcomer from the east sent by the apartment office. Solitude, personal freedom, the possibility to rest after work—all disappeared. One was constantly under observation and eavesdropped on, as if through a peephole in prison."[10]

Finally, voluntary departure for work in the Soviet Union, especially to the Donbas mining region, cannot be called forced, but it can certainly be counted among the varieties of resettlement. Since many refugees could not support themselves in the Western Ukraine and Western Belorussia, several thousand people (the Polish Foreign Ministry put the total at about 50,000) responded to the Soviet recruitment campaign. Again it is difficult to estimate the actual numbers involved, and official sources are not very helpful. The campaign became a favorite propaganda item and therefore subject to wishful thinking. Thus, for example, on December 21, 1939, *Czerwony Sztandar* reports that 15,000 volunteers had already left the Western Ukraine for Donbas and that every week a new transport of 1,200–1,500 would leave. On March 4, 1940, an enthusiastic dispatch in the Lwów newspaper announced that "close to 16,000 people obtained jobs in Donbas and other areas of the Soviet Union." Obviously, many volunteers had come back since December, or those weekly transports were not dispatched after all. In any case, the topic appeared frequently in the official press. On January 18, 1940, *Czerwony Sztandar* published a letter from a young man who had been living for a month in Traktorówka (Tractorville):

> Let me first describe how we were received and what we do. Well, when we arrived a music band was waiting for us in the station. There were speeches and music, and then we were taken to a party at a dining hall. It was an all-night affair. And so seven days have passed partying with Stakhanovites, going to the movies, theaters, etc. . . .

The rest of the letter is essentially about money—how much one could earn—and it conveys a rather crude materialistic message. How true it was we can try to ascertain by drawing on the experiences of some other people for comparison. Here is a story told by Sara Broder. Her father, a Jewish shoemaker from Pułtusk, had fled from the Germans to Białystok, could not make a living there, and decided to take his family to Russia, where he was promised work in his profession, a good income, and a place to live.

> We got to Homel, where we were greeted with music, speeches, and a good meal served in our honor at the train station. Then they took us to a workers' hotel where we received a small room to live in. It was unfurnished, and we just put our clothes on the floor. The next day father went to the office that was supposed to direct him to work. He was told that there were no jobs and that he had to wait a few days. We had nothing to live on. We could not even boil a cup of water. They kept promising father that he

would get a job, but he wasn't getting any. Finally, they suggested that we should go to a kolkhoz. Exhausted from hunger, we went to the countryside where we were not received very well. We all worked in the fields and in return we got bread rations, some potatoes, and a little soup. Children were given milk once a week. We worked hard, from dawn to dusk, and we were always hungry. . . . The kolkhoz chairman told us after a few days that there was no more work for us and that we had to go back to town. Father kept looking for a job, couldn't find any, and we were about to die from hunger. We decided to return to Białystok. We bought tickets. Mother and two children sat in one railroad car, father with two children in another. We were afraid of the NKVD, but with God's help we made it back.[11]

Inhospitable living conditions, unemployment, hunger—these were common experiences among refugees who had voluntarily gone to Russia to work. Single males (who were quite numerous among the refugees) may have managed somehow, especially if they were of an adventurous disposition. But families could not. They were not allowed to go back without official authorization, but many, like the Broder family, risked the return trip nevertheless. By word of mouth the news about material conditions in Russia spread. After the initial wave, voluntary departures ceased, and soon a mocking rhyme about the experience became part of street folklore: "Hopsa sasa do Donbasa, a z Donbasa na golasa [Hey, ho, cheerfully to Donbas, and from Donbas back—stripped naked]."[12]

Having enumerated various forms of resettlement, we are now ready to address our main topic: the coordinated shipments of civilians from the Western Ukraine and Western Belorussia into the Soviet interior. These civilians, unlike the prisoners sent to labor camps, had not appeared before any sentencing tribunals and were not informed of or, usually, even aware of any administrative procedure having been brought against them. Like most people residing in this territory, they had heard rumors or been threatened with deportation at one time or another; but they were never informed of any rules or conditions they must follow to avoid it or of any authority empowered to enforce those rules. The only ordinance concerning mass deportations that was ever published (i.e., communicated to the public) appeared as item 5 on the official communiqué proclaiming the state of war in the city of Lwów. On June 25, 1941, three days after the Germans launched their eastern offensive, the commander of Lwów's militia was ordered to "resettle out of town all who did not have the Soviet passport."[13] All other deportees from the Western Ukraine and Western Belorussia were subject to a secret administrative procedure implemented by an unidentified body. As a student from Łodziska Górne stated matter-of-factly, "In April I was deported with my mother, brother, and sister to Kazakhstan. We were not given any reasons for deportation. I wasn't put before any court either."[14] Simply, one day an armed escort appeared at the door, and the occupants then had to leave their domicile promptly.

NUMBERS AND DATES

There are no reliable statistics to describe the size and composition of the deported population, only estimates and inferences. Official Soviet data are not available, except for one statistic: 387,932 Polish citizens were held in confinement or resettled into the Soviet interior at the outbreak of the Russo-German war, according to Andrei Vyshinskii, the Soviet deputy commissar of foreign affairs.[15] It is a wild guess, at best, and more likely a deliberate deception.

In my judgment, the most thorough estimate of the scale and composition of the mass deportations was produced by the Polish Ministry of Foreign Affairs in London on March 15, 1944. Its report, "The Computation of the Polish Population Deported to the USSR Between 1939 and 1941," offers a very cautious estimate, not only because the compilers opted in cases of doubt for lower rather than higher numbers, but also because they were aware (and constantly remind readers) that the bases of computation are unreliable. Yet the Polish authorities at the time were probably the best informed about this issue (with the exception of Soviet security officials, who of course kept detailed records). They used numerous lists compiled during the thaw in Polish-Soviet diplomatic relations, when the Polish embassy was not only allowed to function in the USSR like any other diplomatic representative of an allied country but also had been authorized to deploy a vast welfare network to assist Polish citizens then being released from various forms of confinement in the Soviet Union.[16] All sorts of records were accumulated by the Poles during this period for the purposes of organizing and then monitoring the distribution of material aid, issuing documents and establishing the identity of claimants to Polish citizenship, assembling the necessary manpower to build the Polish Army in the East, and assisting Polish citizens and making sure that they were given proper treatment in transactions with local Soviet authorities. The Poles were only partly successful in these endeavors; but, given the chaotic circumstances and the progressive obstructionism of high-level Soviet authorities, they accomplished miracles and accumulated a wealth of knowledge about Soviet society, including numerical data concerning Polish citizens who had been transferred from the Western Ukraine and Western Belorussia to the Soviet interior.

The Foreign Ministry memorandum puts the number of Polish citizens who were moved or went into the USSR's interior during 1939–1941 at 1.25 million. Of this total, some went into the USSR willingly, looking for a job; some were drafted into the Red Army and posted in the interior; some were kept in POW camps after the September 1939 campaign; and about 900,000 were transported east, about half as prisoners (with a labor camp as final destination) and half as "special settlers" (*spetspereselentsy*), that is, deportees. Since the numbers are approximate and the grand total may have been in truth closer to 1.5 million, the experience of civilian deportation that I am about to describe was an episode in the lives of about half a million people.

There were, most sources agree, four mass deportations from the territory of the Western Ukraine and Western Belorussia. The first one took place on the night of February 10, 1940, the second on April 13, 1940, the third in the last week of June 1940, and the last one in the second half of June 1941.[17] In all likelihood the last deportation was not carried out as planned. It seems to have begun on June 20, but the outbreak of the Soviet-German war two days later must have interfered with it.[18] Some of the transportation was probably reassigned for other priorities, such as evacuations of the military, Soviet administrative personnel, and prisons, while quickly spreading chaos, general panic, and heavy German bombardments must have disrupted schedules throughout the Western Ukraine and Western Belorussia, especially those of railroad traffic. I shall assume, then, that more or less equal numbers of deportees were dispatched to the Soviet Union in the first three waves and that half the number sent on any one of these went in the fourth. Each shipment would have consisted of some 125,000 to 150,000 people, and the June contingent anywhere from 60,000 to 80,000.

The numbers are of course tentative, and I introduce them primarily to show the scale of these undertakings rather than to assert a specific size. Likewise, I cannot determine from the data that all deportation waves were roughly equal in volume. In fact, the distribution of authors of the collected depositions indicates that most people were sent to Russia in February 1940; substantially fewer, but still a significant number, were dispatched in April 1940; and only a token number experienced either of the June deportations.*

* I have not counted them all, but this is the overwhelming impression from reading

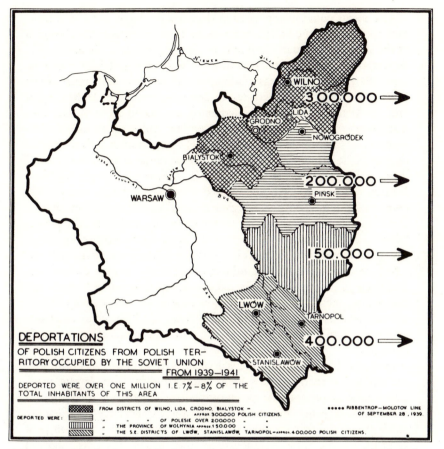

Map prepared by the Cartographic Service of the Polish Army in the East (HI, Poland. Ambasada USSR Collection)

The social composition of each deportation wave and the recruit-ment policies for the Polish Army in the East can explain the direction of the skew in the sample (though not the proportions). The April 1940 deportation consisted predominantly of women and children, and the June 1940 deportation was made up mostly of Jews. Individuals from these groups were not recruited in large numbers into Anders Army and could not have been subsequently evacuated from Russia into Iran, except as members of military families. Although the social com-position of the much smaller June 1941 deportation is less easy to determine, it probably consisted mostly of refugees from central and western Poland—that is, once again a substantial number of Jews. Finally, the peasants who composed the bulk of the February 1940 deportation may have had a higher survival rate in the Soviet interior than later deportees, both because they were used to hard physical labor and because they were better equipped than citizens taken from towns and cities in a spring or a summer wave. How many June or April deportees thought of taking along heavy winter clothes, for example? A description of the circumstances under which they were taken from their homes, which follows soon, will make us appreciate why many must have forgotten them altogether. Their chances of sur-viving the first winter in Russia were on this account alone seriously impeded.

In the end, I suspect that the size of each deportation was primarily determined (if there was any logic behind this decision) by the avail-able logistical support. In two months—from February to April and from April to June—the entire rolling stock could have comfortably made the round-trip journey to the Soviet interior. Deportation pro-cedures, in some respects standardized and uniform, were also tailored to local circumstances. For example, the number of people loaded into freight cars, which after all came in no more than two or three standard sizes, varied widely. The lowest number that I have seen men-tioned is twenty, but no other assessment comes even close to this unu-sually low figure quoted by Jerzy Trylski.[19] The highest number, *not* infrequently mentioned, is seventy;[20] the most often quoted figures, between the low thirties and about sixty.[21] Let us say, then, that forty-five was the average crowd packed into one railroad car. Then about

---

the depositions. Without making any claims as to the validity of my sampling procedure, I take for illustration volume III from the folder marked A in Box 33 of the Poland. Ambasada USSR Collection. It contains 123 documents, filed chronologically, from 88 respondents who were interviewed about the circumstances of their deportation. Sixty-one had been deported in February 1940, 21 in April 1940, 4 in June 1940, and 2 in June 1941.

three thousand freight cars had to be mobilized and outfitted to ferry the deportees into Russia on each occasion—fifty trains of sixty cars each.[22] Given the undeveloped railroad network in the area and the necessity to funnel all the traffic into the few passageways where broad-gauge tracks, compatible with the Soviet system, had been installed, it is not surprising that for several days around each deportation virtually no other freight moved through the Western Ukraine and Western Belorussia, only loads of people.[23]

ECOLOGY OF DEPORTATIONS

Who was deported? Let us go immediately to the heart of the matter, since there is no disagreement as to the broad outlines of the social composition of the successive deportation waves. The "Report on the Relief Accorded to Polish Citizens by the Polish Embassy in the USSR—with Special Reference to Polish Citizens of Jewish Nationality," compiled by the Polish embassy in August 1943 after it was evacuated from the USSR to Teheran, is as good a source as any to draw on for a summary statement. According to the report, the following categories of Polish citizens were affected by the four mass deportations:

(1) February 1940. In towns: civil servants, local government officials, judges, members of the police force. In the country: forest workers, settlers, and small farmers—Polish, Ukrainian, and Belorussian (several villages were thus left entirely bereft of their populations).

(2) April 1940. The families of persons previously arrested, the families of those who had escaped abroad or were missing, tradesmen (mostly Jews), farm laborers from confiscated estates, and more small farmers of the three nationalities.

(3) June 1940. Practically all Polish citizens who in September 1939 had, in thousands, sought refuge in eastern Poland from the ruthless Nazi forces which were then invading Poland from the west; small merchants (a great many of them Jews), doctors, engineers, lawyers, journalists, artists, university professors, teachers, etc.

(4) June 1941. All belonging to the categories enumerated above and who had so far evaded deportation; children from summer camps and orphanages.

It was in the course of the third mass deportation, in June 1940, that the greatest number of Jews was deported to the USSR.[24]

197

It appears that official order to prepare and carry out deportations targeted a different social group on each occasion: in April, families of the arrested; in June 1940, the refugees. In February, the order may have come in the form of a list of professions or organizations, much as the NKVD instructions for "accounting concerning anti-Soviet and socially alien elements" (quoted in Chapter 5). Confusing as such a list may have been, its main impact seems to have been directed at the remnants among the Polish state employees who had implemented Polonization on the community level in this territory throughout the interwar period. I stress "remnants" and "community level" because the top echelons of the civil service, as well as most activists of political organizations and voluntary associations, had been arrested months before the February deportation. Hence, small towns and villages were most affected at the time, giving this deportation a rural character that differentiates it sharply from the urban composition of the April deportation.[25] Most of the February transports were sent toward Archangel.

Why the April deportation was drawn predominantly from urban areas, as many observers have noted, I am not quite sure. At this stage the arrested were undoubtedly mostly urban dwellers, and so were their families. Colonization, even internal colonization, is carried out in stages, and cities are its earliest outposts. The task of dismantling the previous Polish penetration into this periphery must have led the new supervisors at Kiev and Minsk to concentrate arrests in the urban areas first. A still different demographic peculiarity of the April deportation, though quite striking, is easy to explain. On this April day mostly women and children were shipped from the Western Ukraine and Western Belorussia into the Soviet interior—small wonder, since the majority of the arrested were their husbands and fathers. April deportees ended up mostly in Kazakhstan.

The simplicity in the designation of the June 1940 deportation wave—refugees who had fled western and central Poland—is somewhat deceptive because those charged with enforcing these instructions had first to locate the people specified. Refugees who had no record of residency or any employment history in the area were the most difficult to pin down. An ingenious NKVD scheme devised to identify them inadvertently proved revealing about the alienating quality of the Soviet regime in the Western Ukraine and Western Belorussia. The procedure, which I shall describe in more detail below, was to compile lists of people desiring to return to their homes in territories administered by the Germans. The NKVD then used the lists to round up people, mostly Jews, for deportation.

The June 1941 deportation seems to have been the most eclectic. In several instances people report being rounded up in the streets; as soon as some irregularity was found in their documents, they were taken to assembly points and then put on trains to Russia. In all the preceding deportations, name lists of the deportees had been drawn up in advance. Furthermore, also unlike the three preceding waves, the June 1941 transports seem to have been clustered territorially in the northeast (without being exclusively limited to the area). Białystok, Wilno, Nowogród, and Polesie voivodeships seem to have been affected most, perhaps because part of this area had been newly added to Soviet jurisdiction following the incorporation of the Baltic states into the USSR.

I cannot attach any reliable figures to the social composition of the deportees. Statistics compiled by the Polish embassy and its relief apparatus do not differentiate between the deportees and the Polish citizens who were sent to Soviet labor camps under sentence and were released in accord with the Sikorski-Majski pact. But two documents may be particularly relevant for illustration: "The Computation of the Polish Population Deported to the USSR," by the Polish Ministry of Foreign Affairs (quoted earlier), and an elaborate report prepared by the Polish embassy, entitled "Numerical Record and Location of Polish Citizens in the USSR at the Date of the 25th of April 1943."[26] The authors of the Foreign Ministry document consulted 120,000 personal files from the Polish Red Cross records in Teheran to come up with a profile of the occupational background of Polish citizens forcibly sent to Russia (for a summary of the findings, see the note on p. xxi above). One also learns from these data about the ethnic backgrounds of the Polish citizens sent to Russia: 52 percent were ethnic Poles, 30 percent were Jewish, and 18 percent were Ukrainian and Belorussian. The Polish embassy document breaks down the population of Polish citizens known to be in the Soviet Union as late as April 25, 1943, according to area of residence, sex, and age (children under fourteen are listed separately). The embassy had records on about 265,501 people: 35 percent of them men, 36 percent women, and 29 percent children.

People of all ages, races, and social backgrounds had been sent into the Soviet interior. Still the question remains: How were the deportees identified?

DEPORTATION LISTS

Residents of the Western Ukraine and Western Belorussia were subject to registrations from the moment the Red Army arrived. The earlier story of the October elections has shown how some of them were implemented. Yet even before the electoral lists were compiled, a personal record on each citizen had been started. The first task of the occupiers "was to compile a list of people who fought in the 1920 war," recalled a peasant from the village Stymonie. A list of children from seven to eighteen years old who were not attending school was supposed to be finished in Lwów by October 18.[27] In the place of employment one could be subjected to a particularly prying inquiry. In Lwów's hospital number 6 the entire staff was interviewed shortly after the Soviets moved into the city. Each conversation lasted two to three hours and ranged widely from standard biographical data to questions about the various political parties in Poland, how much support the Communist party enjoyed, what working relationships there were between employers and employees, how superiors interacted with subordinates, whether one had ever traveled abroad and at whose expense, how many languages one knew, and the like. The October 1939 registration of army officers—retired, in the reserves, and on active duty—involved an extraordinarily long battery of questions concerning one's service record, as well as personal data, political views, and plans for the future.[28]

People were constantly required to reveal information about themselves—who they were, where they lived, what they knew, what crops they had planted, what material goods or personal qualifications they possessed. Nor were the questions ever meant to be innocuous. Soon after they got a foothold in the countryside, the village committees were ordered to compile detailed registers of livestock and household goods in each resident's possession and to impose severe restrictions on their use: nothing could be sold or transferred without committee authorization, nor could a peasant eat (kill) his own calf, pig, or chicken without it.[29] People immediately recognized and learned to fear the implicit threat of a registration. There was relative safety only in anonymity. Any listing was in effect a blacklisting.

One particularly thorough registration—in fact, a series of registrations—preceded the February deportation, namely, the October elections. People were monitored throughout the pre-election campaign and during the voting itself, and many thought later that they had been put on deportation lists because of their behavior then. But electoral performance was certainly not the only qualifying criterion, though it probably was an important one. Actually, throughout January and early February the frequency of list-compiling and stock-taking in the countryside had quickened. "Frequently they wrote us down, these Soviet authorities, they went to every house and wrote down everybody on a list. When we asked them what does it mean that they keep

writing us down so often, they didn't want to answer anything."
Rumors about impending deportations started to spread. People got
frightened. On occasion local activists, trying to quiet the fears, threatened with deportation those who seemed to give credence to rumors
and were packing and liquidating their households. But there were
even more ominous signals: "From day to day we were awaiting some
kind of a sentence because there were very frequent meetings between
the committees and the Soviet authorities which we were not allowed
to attend."[30]

Helena Wypijewska's experience in Bortnica (Dubno county) was
shared by many a Pole residing in villages and hamlets of the Western
Ukraine and Western Belorussia. Something was afoot. After the meetings between the Soviet authorities and the village committees, the
Ukrainian and Belorussian population of each village was called to
meetings to declare that their Polish neighbors ought to be expelled.
Whether this procedure was followed in every case, I am not sure; after
all, Ukrainians and Belorussians—sometimes entire villages—were
deported as well, though at a later date. Soon enough, of course, the
prospective deportees learned the substance of these meetings, some, I
am sure, from teasing, spiteful neighbors, while others received the
news as a friendly warning.

On occasion the local people demurred. Then the debate, which continued in their midst under pressure of higher-level Soviet authorities,
became more or less public. A Polish military settler from Belmaż has
left a relatively detailed, though somewhat confusing, account of how
the issue was tackled in his village and its surroundings.

> Soviet authorities started to pressure the local committees and
> threaten them so that they would liquidate settlers and Poles and
> so that they would introduce a resolution to deport them from
> Poland as chauvinist and bourgeois enemy elements. But it wasn't
> easy. Conferences were organized with the committees; they were
> called into the raion [county] office; opponents were substituted,
> and they were tricked into accepting a resolution that Poles had
> to be deported because rioting might break out in the area and
> then the committees would be responsible for the Poles. There
> were provocations, that settlers would burn villages and slaughter
> Ukrainians, and then the Bolsheviks presented themselves as
> defenders of Poles before Ukrainians, even though they inspired
> these provocations themselves.

All Polish settlers from the area were deported to Russia on February
10.[31]

The qualifying procedure for the February deportations emerges from these accounts: Ukrainian and Belorussian peasants were induced to expel their Polish neighbors. But not all Polish residents were purged on this occasion, so some priorities must have been established. Lists of residents were put together in each community by village committees and militias, and various information was gathered to establish each person's or family's record. The actual composition of a village deportation list must have been the result of a number of factors: vindictiveness of village committee members, favoritism, stringency of quotas (assuming that each village had to meet one), and the degree of pressure applied by higher-level Soviet officials responsible for organizing deportations in any given area. But without the village committee's authorization, I was told by Mirosław Łabuńka, no one could be deported in February, at least not from his village in Brzeżany county.[32] I think it fair to say, however, that the overwhelming majority of village committees took this assignment in stride, while those that hesitated to carry it through were, in most cases, persuaded to give up their opposition.

The April 1940 deportation lists seem to have been compiled as a straightforward police operation. This wave affected mostly urban residents, and there is no indication of any town meetings where the issue was debated. Families of those previously arrested were sent east—clearly a procedure that could be followed only with police records in hand. But a closer look at the timing of the arrests raises some doubt about the cause and consequence, since a wave of arrests of family heads took place during the Easter holidays and around April 9, barely a few days before the affected families were put in transport.[33] It is much more likely that arrests in those cases resulted from deportation orders rather than the other way around. An important test had taken place shortly before the April deportation: the March 24 elections to the Supreme Soviet and the Soviet of Nationalities. Many people's performance then sealed their fate a month later. Some strongly nationalist Ukrainian villages that shirked their duty suffered the lot.[34]

REGISTRATION OF REFUGEES

Compilation of the June 1940 deportation lists involved more deliberate deception than had been used on previous occasions. The delusive method adopted by its organizers was sustained until the very last moment of the operation, when the roundup was carried out in several cities under the cover of a mock air raid drill.[35] But preparation of the

June deportation lists went on for weeks prior to the dispatch of transports to the Soviet Union.

Two registrations were going on in the spring of 1940 in the Western Ukraine and Western Belorussia: one for identity papers and the other, conducted by the German repatriation commission, for population transfers. The actual decision to deport refugees from western and central Poland may have been taken independently of these two procedures. But only as a result of them were complete name and address lists of the refugees compiled by the Soviet authorities.

Here follows a perceptive and revealing description of how the situation developed in the refugee milieu in Lwów during late spring 1940.

In May 1940 rumors spread throughout the eastern half of Poland occupied by the Soviets that a German commission would soon arrive in Lwów. Its tasks were reputed to be registration and facilitating, in cooperation with the Soviet authorities, return to their prewar domiciles for the refugees from western and central Poland. This rumor, passed around by word of mouth, resulted in the coming into Lwów of refugees who lived in villages, hamlets, and small towns around the city. There was excitement among the refugees over the news of the German commission's arrival. People were aware of how hostile the Germans were vis-à-vis the Poles and that they shouldn't expect to find much to their liking upon returning home, but on the other hand they all lived in permanent fear of a forced deportation into the interior of Soviet Russia, a country about which they heard grim stories [via the mail] from their fellow citizens who had been deported in February and April 1940. Their judgment about Soviet Russia was confirmed by people who went there to work voluntarily and escaped back after a few weeks. Having to choose between these two awesome alternatives, the refugees preferred in the end to reunite with their families and perhaps safeguard their possessions even if only a fraction of them. Besides, they were also reluctant to remain under the Soviet occupation as a burden to their fellow citizens, who themselves were suffering on account of scarce lodging and difficult economic conditions.

Also some of the people who were permanent residents of eastern Poland but who were known for their anticommunism decided to register with the German commission. Passing themselves off as refugees, they wanted to get to the other side of the border. Ukrainians were eagerly awaiting the German commission. In collusion with German colonists from Lwów, Tarnopol, and Stanisławów voivodeships they were to appear as *Volksdeutsche* in order to secure permission to move to the area under the German occupation. . . .[36]

To proceed with the registration in orderly fashion, refugees chose centurions ("hundreders") and "thousanders" who took it upon themselves to carry out a systematic and orderly registration of all who volunteered for the departure. In just a few days boards were put up on all the trees in Orzeszkowa Street, indicating the order in which thousands of prospective returnees had signed up. Every evening the thousanders got together in the presence of NKVD functionaries to put together and keep in order all of their lists. By mid-May 1940, when the German commission arrived in Lwów from Przemyśl, where it had just completed signing up all the refugees wanting to return home, about 8,000 people had signed up.

The German commission opened for business in the villa "Grażyna," on Orzeszkowa Street, just as it was supposed to. As soon as they realized that something was indeed being done about their returning home, refugees started showing up in huge numbers and, strangely, most of them were Jewish. Within a day the number of registered persons jumped to 70,000. . . .

The German commission began its work in the presence of Soviet representatives and proceeded first to compile lists of people who were called for by their families who resided under the German occupation. They weren't very numerous. Then a list of the so-called *Volksdeutsche* was put together by the commission; these were most of all Ukrainians whom German colonists had declared as relatives. There were some Poles on this list as well who had been assigned by the underground to go to the other side of the border and chose to do so even at the cost of assuming German identity, and a few who out of fear pretended to have some relation with Germany. There were several thousand of the so-called *Volksdeutsche*. As to refugees who were put on the lists by hundreders and thousanders, about 1,000 were accepted for departure. The Germans explained that the limit of 30,000 for repatriation had already been exhausted during the registration at Przemyśl. That there was such a limit, people found out for the first time from the German commission itself. After three days the German commission closed its offices and left Lwów.

It was then that the refugees realized that they had fallen into a trap that might have dramatic consequences for them. Suspicion

arose that this entire registration might have been jointly con-
cocted by the German and Soviet authorities. Now the NKVD was
in possession of the exact, true addresses of all the refugees—not
the phony ones that people used to pass around so as to keep
under cover—and now people started to worry.[37]

Statements from other cities confirm in broad outline this testimony
by Helena Antoniewicz. Several witnesses even tell us that after the
commission left, excitement lingered on in the refugee milieu, as people
expected the commission to return momentarily. Lists of refugees
wanting to go home were continually updated. New people were told
to get food and prepare hand luggage for their departure, which might
come at a moment's notice. A committee of refugees sprang up in
Lwów, nobody knew how (in hindsight we can speculate as to its
origins), which instructed people to prepare lists containing one
hundred names each and to designate one person who would be
responsible for every thousand names and who would later be put in
charge of their transport to the Soviet-German border. Jews were lined
up around the clock in front of the NKVD building to register for
return.[38]*

Jewish refugees from Przemyśl, Brześć, and Białystok all repeat the
story of the run on the German repatriation commission wherever it
made its appearance. It arrived in the area shortly after the campaign
to issue identity papers was completed in the Western Ukraine and
Western Belorussia. During that registration, and for the first time so
unambiguously, refugees had been forced to come to grips with their
dilemma: Would they give up their Polish citizenship? Even though
they were seemingly not being asked to give up much (the Polish state,
of which they had not been enamored, no longer existed) and were
expected (and pressured) merely to recognize the status quo guaranteed by the two most powerful dictators on earth, they balked. "My
parents," wrote Tauba Tuchschneider, "didn't want to take Soviet citizenship because they were afraid that they could then never leave
Russia."[39] But the refugees were forced to make a decision: they could
either take Soviet citizenship or opt for return home. The majority of
Jews, after no more than six months' exposure to Soviet rule in the

* "Serov described the following scene to me," writes Khrushchev in his memoirs.
" 'There are long lines standing outside the place where people register for permission
to return to Polish territory. When I took a closer look, I was shocked to see that most
of the people in line were members of the Jewish population. They were bribing the
Gestapo agents to let them leave as soon as possible to return to their original homes' "
(*Khrushchev Remembers*, p. 141).

Western Ukraine and Western Belorussia, chose to return to Nazi occupation.[40]

In truth, as soon as the German commission materialized, it was overrun by Jews vying to be repatriated. And it was not at all easy for a Jewish applicant to be considered, or even allowed to appear before the Germans. When the commission opened up registration in Brześć, Jews from the vicinity were prevented from traveling to the city. Naturally, a black market quickly developed as they offered bribes to Soviet intermediaries who could procure the return authorization from the commission, and many paid staggering amounts of money for the privilege. "During the registration," wrote Chaim Hades from Brześć, "I stood long hours in line and I finally got the authorization card for departure, which was considered at the time a pot of luck. A German officer turned to a crowd of standing Jews and asked: 'Jews, where are you going? Don't you realize that we will kill you?' "[41] Hades changed his mind at the last moment and stepped off the train departing for Łódź. But tens of thousands of his co-religionists were ready to go.

"When German commissions facilitating departure across the river Bug arrived in Lwów, Włodzimierz [Wołyński], and Brześć, it was precisely masses of Jewish 'volunteers' that shouted in hundreds and thousands for Germany and Hitler. Just imagine: Jewish crowds screaming 'long live Hitler.' "[42] Józef Blumenstrauch may have exaggerated what he heard and saw three years before he had the opportunity to write these reminiscences, but I am sure that he remembered well the mood prevailing then among the Jews. A milkman from Łuck, Mendel Srul, summarized in one crafty sentence the general tenor of the Jewish attitude toward the Soviet regime: "I'd rather pass on such a 'liberation,' and I beg of them not to try it on me anymore."[43]

This registration saga shows that from the very beginning, Jewish support for Soviet rule derived to a significant degree from seeing it as the lesser evil, and that in relatively short time this judgment was reevaluated by large masses of Jews.* They could not have expected

---

* A similar change occurred in the attitudes of Ukrainians and Belorussians as well (see, for example, Vakar, *Belorussia*, pp. 164–165, 168–169; Lubachko, *Belorussia under Soviet Rule*, pp. 144–145). Also, a leading Jewish-Communist activist of the period noticed the change. Hersh Smolar, secretary of the writers' union in Białystok and editor of the Yiddish-language daily published there, noted a change for the worse in the attitudes of the Soviet leadership as time went on. The paper allocation for his *Białystok Star* was curtailed in late 1940, and censorship became more rigid. Soon the *Star* was publishing only three days a week, rather than daily. Visiting Yiddish writers from the Soviet Union, the famous poet Markish among them, warned Smolar of an impending crackdown against the Yiddish language and "Jewish nationalism" (inter-

much good on the other side of the border, again only a lesser evil. They were wrong. But that they even considered the Nazi option tells us much about the experience of Stalinism in the lives of common people. An apocryphal story from this period has two trainloads of Jews passing each other in opposite directions at the Soviet-German border; passengers on each train gesticulate wildly to passengers in the other that they must be out of their minds to be going to where they are just coming from.

There are two more small points to remember about the preparatory phase of the June 1940 deportation. For the first time, people were put in transports following street roundups. And second, refugees who had accepted Soviet citizenship were not necessarily spared deportation. They were sent east just like those who had indicated their wish to return home.

There is little to say about the preparatory stage of the June 1941 deportation. It was different from all the others because of the extensive street roundups, which apparently took place on June 14th and 20th to assemble people for deportation.[44] Also, as I have already mentioned, male heads of families were for the first time separated from their relatives as the transports were put together. I doubt that this was a general rule. Nevertheless, males from Zarzecze were separated from their families at the train station and taken to jail in Wilejka. At the train station in Druja, an NKVD squad walked along the entire train calling from each car a few people by name, mostly but not exclusively males, and taking them away.[45]

HOUSE SEARCH

On the night of February 10, 1940, the temperature might well have been minus 40° Centigrade. A group of five or six (sometimes more) burly men armed with guns and rifles (usually with bayonets affixed) burst in on a family still half asleep, forcing the door if it was not opened quickly. "The operation should be commenced at daybreak." Ivan Serov, the people's commissar for internal affairs in the Ukraine, had meticulously crafted his "Instructions Regarding the Manner of Conducting the Deportations" to ensure that victims would be quickly overwhelmed.[46] "The basic premise is that the operations should be conducted without noise and panic," hence the element of surprise figured prominently in the plan of action. "Operative groups," to use

view with Hersh Smolar, Tel Aviv, Autumn 1980; also interview with Sfard, Paris, Autumn 1980).

Serov's terminology, invaded their victims' houses early, while most people were still in bed.

> The hand of the clock was approaching 3 A.M. as it chimed three times at a measured pace, and the sense of fear that was growing in me turned out to be justified—I heard heavy steps, the banging of rifle butts and the word *otkroite* [open up]. And those who were the masters of our lives stepped inside.[47]

The testimony of Genowefa Mąka, a peasant woman from Wiśniowiec who had but four years of schooling, may sound like a bad novel. But the high-pitched, "literary" style of reminiscing about the experience of deportation was not uncommon. Somehow, even after many years, the ordeal was not fully internalized; it still seemed like a fiction rather than an actual experience.

From the moment the armed detachment entered a house, the occupants were surprised indeed. Even though the privacy of their home had been violated often before, this time was different. They were immediately started on a fast-paced routine that gave them no time to regain their bearings. The head of the family and any other adult males were separated from everybody else and ordered to kneel or to stand facing the wall with hands up or to sit in a chair in a corner guarded by one member of the raiding party. The rest announced a search for weapons—again nothing new in the experience of the inhabitants of this territory, except that the timing, the show of force, and, I suspect, the tension were not like before.

The militiamen of the operative groups knew very well that on this occasion their assignment did not end with the search, by then a rather boring, mildly lucrative routine. They had not even come to make an individual arrest. Rather, an extensive operation was under way in which they were to be coordinated with other, similar groups (so that any failure to perform adequately was easily spotted) and in which considerable risks were involved, or so they had been told when instructions were issued. Also, since this was such an extensive undertaking, an enforcement apparatus was put together especially for the occasion, drawing not just on security personnel (perhaps even from other areas) but also on what might be called the activists. Herschel Weinrauch, a Soviet journalist assigned at the time to the Yiddish-language newspaper in Białystok, described his participation in the June 1940 deportation:

> The Soviet police didn't have enough people to make all the arrests, so they called on the civilian Soviet people to help them

with the arrests. The newspaper had to give two persons to help, and I was one of them. They gave us guns and we went together with the police to arrest people and send them to Siberia.[48]

It is unlikely that deportation teams in those circumstances projected the cool detachment of seasoned professionals. And the victims, even before deportation orders were communicated to them, were shocked by the bizarre and threatening circumstances in which the search was taking place.

There were no weapons to be found in these peasant homes, but an unwritten protocol for militiamen's visits required that a search for them be given as an excuse. It was an opportunity to dig out any money or valuables that might still be stashed away or simply to browse around for trinkets. "During the search of my place an NKVD man took from me over 2,000 Soviet rubles, stating that this is Soviet money and that as an enemy I cannot have them."[49] So, operative groups went after the spoils much as they had often done before, except that again this encounter was different: this time people were about to be removed from their belongings, not the other way around.

At this stage of the operation, while the victims were still in their homes, the most difficult point was to communicate the resettlement order. Once it was delivered and accepted or, rather, recognized for what it was, the entire procedure could move forward. The announcement set the timetable—the amount of time people were allowed for packing. It was the psychological threshold of the entire operation. Hear a semiliterate peasant woman recall this moment:

> He tells us to listen what he will read and he read a mortal decree that in half an hour we must be ready to leave, wagon will come. . . . I immediately went blind and I got to laugh terribly, NKVD man screams get dressed, I run around the room and laugh . . . son keeps packing what he can, older Eddie, second Stan, third Freddie, daughter Alice, children are crying and begging me to pack or there will be trouble, and I have lost my mind.[50]

Genowefa Mąka, told to be ready to leave in half an hour, "didn't know what to do first, I thought this is the end, I let my hands down but not for long, since the children's crying woke me up to reality." Even two months later, in April 1940, when the novelty of deportation had worn off, the overpowering impact of this stern communication was not lost on people. Following the house search, the NKVD man read some paragraphs "which I didn't much understand," recalls a youth from Dolina. "But one point got to me—that we were being deported.

Father fainted when he heard those words. We could hardly bring him back."[51]

People were stunned, and the token resistance they put up was primarily in the form of noncooperation.[52] "I refused to get dressed at all, and so thirty minutes later some fifteen soldiers appeared and simply tossed me into a wagon."[53] Only after her children were carried out and put on a sled did a woman from Burłaczek realize that she would be taken from her house no matter what, and only then did she start packing a few things and dressing her children in warmer clothing, "because it was very cold with a blizzard outside."[54] Many precious minutes must have been lost by all who were dumbstruck by the deportation order. Their reaction is most understandable: the decree promised an awesome degree of violence to their way of life and sent them directionless out into a storm that would, before the day was over, take its toll on them.

Some operative groups acted cautiously, even cunningly. Instead of telling people that they were being deported to Russia, they mentioned some other destination—a different voivodeship or county, for example, or Germany. "They were to take us to Germany," wrote fourteen-year-old Maria Wilk, "and they lied that we will have it good there. Poles believed and didn't believe this."[55] When a six-man party came to pick up the Marszałek family in Rohatyn county, "they asked daddy where we want to go—to Russia or to Germany, daddy said to America. Then they became very angry and ordered us to dress because we were going to Germany."[56]

On occasion the exchange may have been more promising or more enigmatic: "they said we will be back right away" ("but it turned out different," Tadeusz Warzybok added with hindsight); "when we asked the NKVD man where they will take us, he said to heaven"; "the NKVD man announced that they take us to another oblast to begin a new life. What life, we asked? No conversation was their answer"; "they told us they will only take us for a talk."[57] One could sometimes bargain a little and get closer to the truth by approximations.

> Before dawn two militiamen appeared and they ordered me to dress. They said I will be taken 100 kilometers away because this is the border [Przemyśl], so we can't stay here. When I told him that he is lying, he said a bit further away than 100 kilometers. Then I told him that they are taking us to Siberia, and he told me that I am going to join my husband, that my husband is waiting there for us.[58]

We should note that these alternative destinations were not revealed just to soothe feelings. They were also used as the rationale for instructing the deportees what household items they should take (or not take) along. Czesław Jezierski's family, for example, was told "not to take anything along, because there will be enough of everything" at their destination in a neighboring county. Similarly, the Warzybok family, which was supposed to be sent back right away, was allowed to take but a few loaves of bread. "We only took bread for breakfast because they told us we would be back for dinner," writes Tadeusz Marków. He adds, "They told us if we put our worst clothes on they would release daddy." Need it be spelled out that the best clothes would thus be left behind in the house? Several other testimonies confirm this linkage between the proximity of the alleged destination and the decreasing volume and variety of luggage that people were allowed or encouraged to take along.[59]

Of course, the operative groups did not need to resort to cunning. They could simply order people to take or leave whatever they pleased, without any semblance of justification. According to the testimonies, people were allowed at most 100 kilograms of luggage per person, but lower figures are quoted more frequently. No one could weigh these loads at the time, of course, so there is little meaning to these limits except that they imposed a more or less severe restriction. A more realistic limit was to allow only what a person could carry out of the house and wear on his body—or nothing at all. Routinely people were told to take food for a few days, up to a month on occasion.[60]

The most severe restriction was the time limit. The shock of the deportation order was accompanied by the startling command that people be ready to leave their homes immediately. The time varied, but only slightly. The longest they were given to pack was two hours; usually half an hour was the allotted time; occasionally they had as little as fifteen minutes.[61] This was yet another impossibility that gave the experience its aura of unreality. How can one get ready to leave one's house forever in thirty minutes? On top of that, husbands, older brothers—any males who presumably could put up physical resistance—remained immobilized under armed guard. The whole burden of coping with the situation, of *doing something*—getting infants, the elderly, or sick family members ready for the road and packing up—was thus left to the women and children. "They ordered us to pack up in half an hour while men had to stand at attention"; "I was not allowed to move, so we took only what the children managed to pack."[62] Irena Kulikowska's mother was not at home, only her sister and the landlady. One of the militiamen stood over them and "kept screaming bystrei, bystrei, poskorei [faster, faster, quickly]. We were packing with the landlady and taking whatever we could, and what they allowed. They sat daddy on a chair and two policemen with drawn handguns didn't let him even move."[63]

The operative groups kept a watchful eye not only on adult male family members but also on women and children, monitoring what was being packed. Edward Dudojc's family was told to put away wool and some good clothes that they intended to take. Kazimierz Zasępa's family had its packing done by the militiamen who came to deport them, "so we didn't take much, because they put aside whatever they wanted for themselves." They "gave one hour to pack, but only to my wife, and she was helped while packing by one of the hoodlums who had been previously sentenced for stealing, Paweł Roman, who took for himself whatever he thought to be valuable during this packing while saying that we will have no need for it." "Mummy," recalled Stanisław Matrejek, "started packing everything, but the Soviet said no and allowed only the more important things."[64]

Serov's instructions directed that the deportees be permitted to take various articles of personal use and food. And those destined for rural districts could also be allowed "a small agricultural inventory." In one episode in Pawłosów a peasant family was ordered out of the house immediately following the search for weapons; they were then forbidden to talk and were simply handed "a saw, an axe, a shovel, and a small pillow for the infant." Throughout the entire procedure people were constantly under guard; no one was allowed to leave the dwelling, even to use the outhouse.[65]

Occasionally, but rarely, some rapport was established between the victims and their victimizers. The journalist Weinrauch, a civilian drafted to serve with an operative group, began to cry just as the woman and her two daughters whom he had been deporting were crying. So did an anonymous militiaman in Pączkowa's house as he helped to load her things. " 'You are crying,' he said, 'but we are crying and suffering for twenty years already . . . my grandma taught me that God exists and that there is a prophecy in the Scriptures that the Polish army will save us from Communism, and we are taking you to Siberia, how is this so,' and he started crying." K. Stepkowski's mother, on the other hand, got the Soviet raiding party drunk. She hauled two gallons of vodka from the basement and invited them to drink it up. They were suspicious, and Stepkowski's father had to take the first drink. But then, promptly, they emptied the whole container. Drunk, they dropped their guns, cursed Stalin, and allowed the family to pack all they wanted. The Stepkowskis even considered running away from the house, but there was nowhere to go, as their village was encircled by an army detachment.[66] Even so, they were lucky to have been spared the trauma that most other deportees suffered.

Despite all appearances of surprise and chaos and the frantic pace that prevailed at the scene, a substantial amount of paperwork accompanied deportations. The operative groups had to familiarize themselves with the personal files of their deportees. They were also given, according to the wording of Serov's instructions, "the supply of necessary forms to be filled out by the deportee." Frequently the raiding party made a rough inventory of the household goods being left behind, which were supposed to be sold later and the proceeds sent to the deportee at his new residence. (Some families in fact received small sums of money allegedly realized in this transaction months after they had been deported.) Sometimes the paperwork was used to humiliate the victim. For example, a shoemaker from Chrynów who had signed a blank form a few weeks earlier was shown it as proof that he had consented to leave his domicile. Or a person's signature on an inventory of household goods left behind was taken as consent to the family's deportation.[67]

Recordkeeping concerning the deportations was meticulous indeed. In many instances children who were in school at the time their families were apprehended at home were detained separately and many hours later, in a scene of panic and collective hysteria, were brought together with their families. Men who had been arrested weeks or months before were let into the very same railroad cars where their wives and children had been locked up in the station. In one recorded episode a high school student who had been put in transport at Postawy was called out when his train reached Woropajewo, and he was ordered to an altogether different train, where he met his family.[68] To the extent that careful recordkeeping and monitoring resulted in families being brought together in transport, the deportees benefited. The other side of the coin was that, once put on a deportation list, no one could beg out. Many a family pleaded to have elderly, sick, or newborn members exempted from deportation, to be left behind with neighbors or in a hospital—to no avail. Records, I suspect, had to be kept in order.

Finally, the time came for people to leave their homes. They were put on wagons, sleds, or trucks, depending on the weather and the transportation available locally. At one glance, they realized that they were not alone in their predicament. Open trucks carrying people and their belongings moved through the otherwise deserted Lwów streets on the night of April 13. Others were parked in front of apartment buildings, waiting to be filled. There was a hopeless traffic jam in the narrow streets leading to the station.[69] Was it comforting to realize that one's misery was shared by others, or did this realization have the opposite effect of sapping all hope that this might be a temporary aberration, soon to be reversed or somehow outwitted? If everyone around was being deported, then there was something final about it. Either way, people were frightened. "Outside one could only hear wailing, the howling of dogs, and occasional shots."

> When we reached the road a very unpleasant sight opened before our eyes. Well, some two hundred sleds with Polish families were already standing there. Children were crying. Along the column, mounted Red Army soldiers kept riding back and forth. It was a moving spectacle.[70]

From their homes to the railroad station, people were moved in columns. Sometimes (probably when they came from scattered small villages or families) deportees were first assembled into a larger group at some school or other suitable building. Then a convoy would be put together at this staging area and from there taken to the embarkation point.

During the February deportation, because of the weather conditions, children and the elderly began to die on this first leg of the journey. "When we were transported by the NKVD on February 10, 1940, from Młynów to the station at Ozierany, five children died, including my son who was one year old. The rest were children of other settlers aged from one to two."[71] Hundreds, maybe thousands of horse-drawn carts with peasant families passed through Przemyśl on the way to the railroad station. "Here and there in the streets," recalled a chauffeur, "on a side-road pile of snow one would find a newborn baby frozen on the way to the station which was discarded by its mother. There were several of them in Przemyśl."[72] From Liczkowce, in Kopyczyńce county, fifty-three families out of fifty-five were deported. They were allowed no luggage at all. Several children froze to death before the column reached the railroad station in Husiatyń, where many other families from neighboring villages were already assembled. "Children frozen to death were taken away from mothers who wanted to board the freight cars with them, and the corpses were thrown away in the snow."[73]

People were frightened, it was very cold, they were not equipped for the journey, some of them were dying. From the moment they stepped out of their houses, deportees were surrounded by wailing, screaming, and crying.

On a few occasions contact was permitted between the deportees and their neighbors or relatives who were left behind. There was enough time for such contacts because typically several days would pass between the deportees' forced removal from home and their final departure from the railroad station. We have an eyewitness statement from one person who visited a family of friends held for a day in a school in gmina Pohost Zahorodzki. She was allowed to see them through the good offices of a village head whom she had known.

> In the evening he [the village head] told me that they were asking for bread and hot water. Mother cooked some kasha with milk, I took a lantern and went. I was allowed in because of P's influence. It was hell. Half-naked people, blue from cold, were packed tightly in a small room. T. looked frightful. Mrs. T. was lying in a corner, moaning. S. out of her wits with a child in arms. Small lamp did not give enough light. Half-naked children, barefoot, covered with rags, were screaming and crying. Women were praying loudly. I left soup and bread and I fled, unable to speak. I couldn't find words or tears in view of this horrible human fate.

And these were but the first hours of a long journey. The next morning people were put on wagons and taken to the Pińsk railroad station. Our witness was at the scene once again.

> Forester J.G. with eight undressed and barefoot children and an old paralyzed father begged permission to leave the old man behind. They refused. The old man died on the way to Pińsk, and one child died already on the train. Mrs. T. was brought out and put on a wagon; they didn't allow us to give them warm clothes.[74]

No wonder that those left at home after the February deportation were numb with fear.[75] They witnessed the destruction of their neighbors, friends, sometimes entire communities. And as far as they could see, it was wanton destruction, not some redistribution, a kind of "new economic policy," however brutally implemented. Except for the resettlement of some Ukrainian families onto the farms of Polish deportees from Tarnopol voivodeship, the property and stock that remained behind were more or less left for the local enforcers to rob.[76] In other words, everything was spoiled, left to rot, wasted—much like the people who had been taken away from those farms.

The population that was left behind had a vague sense that its own future was unfolding before its eyes. Many local inhabitants who came with the raiding parties to deport their neighbors openly expressed satisfaction at witnessing the persecution of Polish settlers and former petty officials. But whenever crowds of local people were allowed to assemble—for example, in front of the temporary staging points—they were visibly saddened and stood in silence or murmured prayers.

We took off for the Luboml railroad station, bid farewell by a silent crowd of Ruthenian peasants who in wide gestures made the Orthodox sign of the cross. A few women were weeping. The Ukrainians did not enjoy our misery. The peasant coachman who drove me to the station shook my hand with a sad smile and said: "Don't worry, mister. Soon we will be taken as well."[77]

AT THE STATION

The train station was usually crowded when the deportees finally got there. I have already mentioned the traffic jam on access roads to the Lwów railroad station during the April deportation. In June 1940 my father, upon learning that his mother had been taken to the station earlier in the day, walked over there, found her in one of the railroad cars, and amidst the prevailing chaos and disorganization escorted her back home. But usually the Soviet organizers had firmer control of the situation. In February in provincial towns there was virtually no access to the deportees, and very little contact was allowed with the people who may have assembled in the hope of helping their friends or relatives. The experience was deeply implanted in people's memories.

There were lots of people here [in the station]; all around one could hear small babies crying as they were freezing because it was very cold.

We waited half a day at the station; it was very cold, and children cried a lot.

When we were at the station one could hear only the screams and moaning of children and the elderly.[78]

It is very important to keep in mind the constant screaming that accompanied this deportation. People were all the time in pain or feeling a horror sufficient to make them scream and wail. This lasted until they were exhausted for the first day or so, but it would pick up with every successive step of the operation—when the train finally pulled out of the station or when it crossed the Polish border.[79]

At some point the victims would be ordered into a freight car. Sometimes they were told to deposit their luggage in a separate one.[80] When the car was packed full (sometimes with up to seventy people), the door was shut and locked from the outside. It would remain locked as long as the train was kept in the station, even up to five days.[81] During all this time the occupants were left to arrange living conditions as best they could, or to die.

Whether in February, April, or June—that is, in cold winter weather as well as in the heat of summer—the tightly packed crowd of mostly women and children got no food or water (some had their own, but not all). The lack of water is reported as the greatest affliction throughout the journey.[82] Nor were they led out to a toilet (there was simply a hole in the floor of the car). They could not even look outside or see well inside the car because all openings were usually boarded up. They were to remain locked up until their transports reached the Polish-Soviet border or the broad-gauged tracks, whichever came first, where they were transferred to another train that would take them to their final destination.

In February, people occasionally found stoves in their cars, with a supply of coal if they were lucky. And in Łomża the deportees benefited from an unusual opportunity to have some supplies delivered from time to time.

> The arrested [i.e., the deportees] stood three days locked up in freight cars in the railroad station. We kept bringing over whatever we could from the village, but we were not always let through by the Bolsheviks. A lot of children died in the station. After three days the train finally departed. I later saw a picture in the Bolshevik newspaper of the train leaving the station and a group of crying people who were running behind it. The caption under the picture read: "Crying families of those who are not going to Russia."[83]

I do not know what paper this man from Konarzyce had been reading. There were numerous county newspapers and wall-journals in factories and gminas where this travesty may have been published, but *Czerwony Sztandar* never mentioned a word about the deportations.[84]

Two details ought to be noted in this eyewitness report: people, again predominantly children, were dying on the still immobilized deportation trains; and, consistent with the image captured in the photograph, the train's departure from the station appears to be the next traumatic experience in the series of steps that severed the deportees' ties to life as they knew it. The February deportation was the most murderous. Whether in Łomża, Wilejka, or Białystok, or Sarny, corpses of young children piled up at the station. "I remember this frosty day when we were brought to the station from our village [in Wołkowyska county]. The Soviets were going from one wagon to the next carrying frozen children under their arms and asking zamersh-chikh rebiat nima [are there any frozen children]?"[85]

When a February transport from Postawy county was readied for departure (though it waited another four days in the station), a coffin was paraded around the motionless train, with musical accompaniment lest anyone fail to notice it. Nor was it an empty threat, for the very young, the old, and the weak were already dying. But the message that was really intended by the event was divulged only upon arrival at the train's destination. "When we got to Russia they said: have you seen there how a corpse was carried around the transport, a man who died and will not return? And likewise you will not return."[86] It is final, forever—your fate is sealed.

On the Road

When the train finally pulled out of the station, the screaming and wailing rose to a higher pitch. Those in transport lamented their fate; those left behind mourned the departing ones. "Loud screaming and crying were heard in the station when the train moved off. Everybody started crying in the wagon, not knowing where they were taking us and for what reason."[87] A teacher from Gródek Jagielloński recalled the night departure of the April transport from her town, with people lying prostrate on the ground, loudly praying for those on the trains, who timidly broke into the Polish national anthem. Screaming, prayers, religious hymns, the national anthem, crying, and, of course, death—the complete repertoire of martyrology.[88]

In February the departing transports left behind a long trail of corpses. "After they left, mostly the corpses of children who died in transport and were thrown away by the convoy were being found along the Równe-Szepietówka line."[89] Children and the elderly kept dying throughout the trip—it was the universal experience in all transports, from every corner of the Western Ukraine and Western Belorussia.[90] And in several instances, though by no means as many as in February, we find mention of death in the April and June transports as well.

During the February transports, at every stop, wagons were emptied of dead bodies, which were then piled up right next to the tracks and sometimes "covered with snow so that it could not be seen that so many had died."[91] So common was death among passengers that people got used to the sight of corpses and usually recorded them in a matter-of-fact style. Treatment of cadavers, however, triggered a more lively response and a sense of shock that they were denied burial, the semblance of a burial, or even respectful handling, that they were cast off, discarded, thrown away. "A lot of small children died from cold. Parents asked for permission to bury them but the NKVD men did not allow, only said to throw them out the window and that they will bury them themselves."[92] It was the treatment of the dead that somehow brought into the sharpest relief for the deportees the value put on human life by their custodians and the impact that attitude was bound to have on their own lives. "My grandpa died in transport and Soviet soldiers threw him out the window."[93] But soon the deportees were forced to do the same; locked for days in the trains, they could not dispose of their decomposing dead in any other way. "The unpleasant and unforgettable impression was for me that from the freight cars in which we traveled the naked bodies of those frozen to death were thrown out the windows because the doors were locked. It was done because there was no room in the cars, and there was no medical attention to speak of."[94]

The deportees stayed in locked cars until the trains arrived at the prewar Polish-Soviet frontier. No food or water was distributed until then.[95] Sometimes the deportees were reloaded into broad-gauged cars earlier, in Lwów, Sarny, Mołodeczno, or Zdołbunów, for example. And at border crossings the deportees broke once again into singing, wailing, and prayers.[96]

Crossing the border was a threshold in more than a symbolic sense. At that point deportees might be allowed to leave the cars from time to time to stretch out for a few minutes, to get some water and food, or to relieve themselves.[97] Food might be delivered to them, though not always; some transports were not fed at all, or the meal that was delivered might cause sickness.[98] But on the whole, material conditions improved somewhat upon reaching Soviet territory. The escort, I presume, must have felt more confident about security and thus no longer compelled to keep the human cargo permanently sealed. Also, unlike the situation in the newly occupied Western Ukraine and Western Belorussia, there was probably an infrastructure available along the railroad lines in the Soviet Union to support trainloads of human beings under detention. They had been commonplace there, after all, for about two decades already.

But death in transport is a matter of a limited moment, so to speak, in a long journey. The substance of the experience was in the struggle for survival. To die of cold, excessive heat, hunger, thirst, lice infestation, foul air, dirt, or diarrhea takes time; people succumb in stages, while putting up a fight. Some suffered more, some less, depending on climate, on what the raiding party allowed them to take from home, how many and what kind of passengers were in the wagon, how long the journey lasted, what and how often they were fed, and many other factors that varied independently and, finally, added up to death for some, torment for a great many, and mere discomfort for a happy few. But too many died on the way for us not to recognize that it did not matter to the organizers whether they survived or perished. The deportees were not meant to be teased, or taught a lesson, or frightened by the conditions prevailing in a transport—they were tortured in earnest. They were truly wasted.

What went on in these trains? We can only glimpse into their dark interiors,[99] for people are surprisingly restrained in what they have to say about the experience. Many indicated that there was not enough water, sometimes in evocative phrases: "we were almost dying without water," or "days were very hot [in June 1940] and people were dying from thirst," or "there were days completely without water; people, especially children, were fainting from thirst."[100] In each case it is just one sentence, rather sparse; we must let our imaginations fill it out into an experience that sometimes extended over two months.[101] Everyone tried to cope with this and other deprivations as best they could. "Children lay down near the door and kept licking frost off the nails, but there wasn't much frost there either." After a week the deportees pulled out bars in the windows of this wagon and lowered a pail on a makeshift rope to harvest snow along the railroad tracks. This procedure was independently adopted in many transports, along with the gathering of icicles or snow from the wagon's roof. In the spring or summer the deportees had to wait for rain in order to collect some water.[102]

It was very crowded on these trains.* Babies and the sick were placed in choice spots, but this did not help much. There was virtually no medical assistance,[103] and nothing could be done about small children's discomforts. "Babies had the roughest time of all," wrote Mieczysław Pytlak, "as they cried for milk but couldn't get any for the

---

* I quoted numbers earlier in this chapter, but again we must use imagination to translate them into real-life situations. What does it mean to have 45–70 people traveling together in a freight car? Mieczysław Ruchlewicz was put on an April transport in Stanisławów: "it was so crowded that the only space I had was to sit with my legs tucked in the legs of another deportee (our spot was on a bunk where we couldn't even stand erect)" (HI, PGC, Box 117). The overcrowding eased somewhat with the transfer to broad-gauge wagons at the border. But it did not necessarily follow that travel on broad-gauge tracks was more comfortable. When Janina Grochocka was deported in April from Białystok, she changed trains in Szepietówka. But there several transports were squeezed into one, and the overcrowding then became really unbearable (Gross and Gross, W czterdziestym, doc. 165).

entire two weeks."[104] In an unusual recollection, Kazimiera Pyrska tells how a small glass of milk was given out for every four babies in her transport as it journeyed two months from Białystok voivode-ship.[105] But such generosity was otherwise unheard-of. Mothers desperately struggled to get some nutritious food for their children, milk in particular. At every stop they offered to trade articles of clothing, a bar of soap, some tea, or sugar (the lucky ones, that is, who had anything to trade) to the local people assembled around the train stations in return for milk or an egg. But to the deportees' dismay and horror, it was the indigenous population that frequently approached the trains first, begging for a piece of bread or lard or for something to wear.[106]

Food, if delivered at all, was scarce, given out irregularly, and of poor quality. Meals of salted fish, the staple of Soviet camp and prison life, are mentioned occasionally, along with the thirst they provoked. Extreme temperatures are commonly cited. February "was so terribly cold that waking up every morning I had to tear away covers that froze to wagon walls."[107] Freight car interiors smelled terrible, lacked air to breathe, and were infested with lice.[108] Colds, high fevers, pneumonia, stomach ailments, and diarrhea were rampant among passengers. "After ten to fifteen days only one wish was on the minds of miserable victims—to get to the place, anywhere, the quicker the better."[109] But even after trains arrived at their terminal, some people had to continue the journey—by sled, by barge, on foot, or in trucks—for several more days. And the trip could still be deadly. When the transport from Białozórka (Krzemieniec county) arrived at the end of the railroad line after traveling for three weeks in February, people were put on trucks. "On the way two children suffocated because it was very crowded"; and on a similar last stretch of a transport from Baranowicze county "a lot of children froze to death."[110]

Yet, finally, the emaciated human cargo would reach its destination. A scrupulously pedantic civil servant from Równe tells what followed then. "From February 23 [when they got to wherever they were going] to March 15 over 50 percent of the deportees were ill, 354 died, which accounted for more than 10 percent of the population of our settlement."[111] When Janina Grocholska got off the train somewhere near Pawłodar with her transport from Białystok, children that were sick and required medical help could not be admitted into the overcrowded local hospital. They died by the dozens every day. People were lying in the open air, under a fence, where scores died.[112]

A nameless respondent from Pałusza (Oszmiana county) summarized the phenomenon of deportation:

I can describe this in a few words: it was murder of babies and children, banditry, theft of other people's property, the death penalty without sentencing or guilt. One lacks words to speak about the horror of this thing, and who has not lived through it could never believe what happened. Having removed from Polish territories to Siberia those whom they found uncomfortable, the Bolshevik Communists announced at meetings: "Vragov sovetskoi vlasti my tak unichtozhaem, budem set' poka ne istrebim vsekh burzhuev i kulakov netolko zdes', no po vsem mire" [This is how we annihilate the enemies of Soviet power. We will use the sieve until we retrieve all bourgeois and kulaks, not only here, but in the entire world]. You will never see again those that we have taken away from you. "Tam propadut kak rudaia mish" [They will disappear over there, as a field mouse].[113]

Around this very time, some two hundred miles to the west of Oszmiana county, in German-occupied Poland, another category of human beings was being likened to lice. There is a common term for the special treatment of rodents and insects that are considered a nuisance: *extermination*. The half million people, most of them women and children, who were deported from the Western Ukraine and Western Belorussia in 1939–1941 were not singled out for resettlement. They were meant to be destroyed.

WHAT must have been most vexing or simply incomprehensible to the Soviet personnel throughout their tenure in the Western Ukraine and Western Belorussia was the fundamental incredulity of the local population that they had come there to stay. To the overwhelming majority of residents the new order seemed but a passing fad, a vicissitude of fate, a strange aberration that must end soon and must consequently be waited out somehow.

This mental disposition alone was a strong impediment against successful Sovietization. Such skepticism, if widespread, would undermine any institutional order, but it was especially jarring to Soviet organizers of public order, for the successful completion of the Communist revolution rests precisely on the sense of historical inevitability. But folk wisdom suggested otherwise: Hitler and Stalin were bound to collide soon, and the outcome of their confrontation was hardly in doubt to anyone who had seen the Red Army in action. And there was also the behavior of the Soviet citizens who had poured into the area and the *spoilation* that had resulted from their presence.

No other word better described the result of Soviet policies. They spoiled things—depleted stocks, destroyed crops, vandalized cities. "Shabbiness . . . the fact that communism makes towns, things, and people's characters shabby" was what Aleksander Wat found most striking and repulsive in communism.[114] But it did not need a refined sensitivity to register the experience: "Within a week our town was completely changed: dirty all around, no one caring to keep it clean, heaps of refuse thrown away by the army disintegrating in the streets," noted a distraught inhabitant of Włodzimierz Wołyński. Kazimiera Studzińska left this account of her home town, Łuck:

> The city, neat and pretty before the war, now assumed an eerie appearance: dirty streets full of mud, lawns walked over and covered with mud, lawn fences and small trees lining the streets all broken down. Display windows, unkempt and covered with dust and cobwebs, were decorated with portraits of Soviet rulers. Store billboards were mostly ripped off, with empty spaces left where they were once attached. All this made an impression of a dying city.

During the Soviet rule of the area, said one Ukrainian interviewed by Milena Rudnycka in 1942, "everyone lived, ate, and dressed worse than before."[115] Would the Soviets have "spoiled" everything for everybody so thoroughly if they really intended to stay?

If anyone doubted the correct reply to this question, it was enough to take note of the widespread, wasteful confiscation and shipment to the USSR of all kinds of material objects—entire factories, loose tiles, door locks and knobs from government buildings—from all over the occupied territories.* As a result of these massive deportations of material objects, which were sometimes recklessly discharged at some railroad station and left to rot, useless and ultimately spoiled, people in the area were led to believe that the Soviets did not intend to stay permanently. Soviet arguments that factory equipment had to be removed to be retooled in the USSR to fit the requirements of a planned economy and that it would then be sent back after rehauling did not seem convincing.[116] The horror of deportations to a large degree

---

* "Through the railroad station at Uściług and at Włodzimierz Wołyński, day and night, freight cars filled with all kinds of objects were going into Russia. From Włodzimierz Wołyński they took a hospital, an electric plant, military barracks, and furniture from officers' and NCOs' apartments. Likewise inventories of landed estates confiscated in the area were sent east. Through Uściług military trucks were carrying things as well" (włodzimierz wołyński, 13, 14). See also, for example, HI, PGC, 1109, 2656, 5004, 8611, 10276; Poland. Ambasada USSR, Box 34, untitled report; Box 51, K. E. Bartosz.

stemmed from the necessity of changing one's idea about the time frame of the Soviet occupation: sucked into the Soviet interior, one's sense of being under Soviet authority as a transient threatened to change overnight, to forever.

Lives were spoiled as well as goods. The evidence presented in Part Two reveals that a staggering loss of life was associated with the establishment and solidification of the Communist rule in the Western Ukraine and Western Belorussia well beyond the initial period of civil war. I submit that the existence of Stalin's regime in the USSR and of Soviet power and all its variations in other countries was predicated on massive extermination of its subjects. For comparable casualty figures, one must look to wars between sovereign states. It may very well be, as Stalin said when declaring war on the Russian peasants, that the state under Communism wages war against society. But rather than a statement of fact, this is a point of departure for reflection about the regime. Can killings go on forever? If once halted, can mass murder resume at any time and under any circumstances? Is the rapid ascendancy over all ladders of social mobility due as much to vacancies that result from the premature deaths of office incumbents as to industrialization, free education, expansion of state bureaucracy, or assimilation of national minorities? If no taboos as to acceptable limits of social engineering have been respected in the past, can they ever be firmly reimposed? Is neglect of ecological crisis under state socialism not rooted, in part, in a similar disregard for the welfare of the state's subjects? No understanding of left-wing totalitarianism is possible, it seems to me, without recognition that in the process of imposing their power and while striving to make it absolute, Communists do not hesitate to tamper with the biological substance of nations.

The Spoiler State

I HAVE PRESENTED in this book the phenomenon of the Soviets' seizure of power and imposition of their regime as it was experienced by ordinary people. Two broad themes guided my description and analysis: Part One showed the mechanisms that were applied to the local population to induce participation; and Part Two detailed the destruction visited upon those people. Although the choice of specific topics was dictated by the quality of the available material, I am satisfied that the result offers a comprehensive insight into the process of installing a Communist regime. After World War II, the Western Ukraine and Western Belorussia still had to go through important stages (like the collectivization of agriculture) before the Soviet regime stabilized, but the data at our disposal allow a wide-ranging view of how Soviet administrators seized power and sapped popular resistance.

If the heavy representation of Polish testimonies suggests the possibility that the victimization of the local elite is unduly stressed here, it should be remembered that a few years before the Red Army crossed into Poland, millions of people were killed or starved to death in the Soviet Ukraine as a consequence of collectivization and the Great Purge. The burden of proof therefore lies with anyone who thinks that the history of the Sovietization of the Western Ukraine during 1939–1941 would sound less harsh if Ukrainians rather than Poles were telling it. Nor can we believe that the Jewish version of the 1939–1941 events would be significantly less gruesome when we recall how the threat to destroy the Jews in the Soviet Union was averted only by Stalin's death. Suffice it to say that all nationalities were victimized during the Sovietization of the Western Ukraine and Western Belorussia. Almost 50 percent of those removed to the Soviet interior, whether into camps or forced settlements, were Jews, Ukrainians, and Belorussians.

To highlight my findings, I shall first complete my assessment of the destruction wrought upon the society of the Western Ukraine and Western Belorussia by putting it in the context of the Nazi occupation of Poland. I shall not present a full-fledged comparative analysis of this important topic here, but the subject naturally suggests itself. After all, the Soviets and the Nazis forced themselves jointly upon Poland in

1939, divided the state into almost perfectly equal halves, and harnessed their conquests to the purposes of their respective imperial domains. How did they go about it? More important, comparison must have been constantly on the minds of people living in Poland. There was continuous traffic across the then Soviet-German border stretching along the rivers Bug and San. Millions, I am sure, kept asking themselves whether they should flee from one occupation to the other, or, having done it, whether they should return home.

But a word of caution is necessary, since the destruction of European Jewry is forever linked to any mention of Nazi behavior during World War II. Especially when it comes to the Nazi record in occupied Poland, the site of most of the concentration camps, an immediate association with this tragedy is evoked and any comparison seems wrong, inappropriate. I wish to stress, therefore, that my comparison is limited to the period that *preceded* the Holocaust.

Where did the people suffer more? Is it possible at all to assess the comparative damage of Nazi and Soviet administrations in Poland from September 1939 to June 1941? I think such a comparison, though awkward, can be made. And if we measure the victimization of Polish citizens in terms of loss of life, of sufferings inflicted by forced resettlement, and of material losses through confiscation and fiscal measures, the Soviet actions, relatively speaking, would prove far more injurious than those of the Nazis.*

Let us consider material hardships. Private property rights were seriously undermined under the German occupation; the Reich took over all state-owned as well as Jewish-owned property. Also, under some vague notion of "public interest," Polish private property could be "confiscated" or "taken over" (two different measures, in fact). The military, the ss, and the police could act with no legal restraint whatever, and in the incorporated areas only signing of the *Volksliste* could save a Polish owned property.[1] Still, the Soviet actions against private property were far more comprehensive: complete expropriation of state, church, and privately owned property when the Western Ukraine and Western Belorussia were incorporated into the corresponding

---

* "I dined with Mr. Ciechanowski last night and we discussed both Sir Stafford Cripps' mission and the conditions in Soviet-occupied Poland," jotted a British diplomat on a copy of Sir Howard Kennard's report to the Foreign Office, dated April 30, 1940. "He told me, incidentally, that conditions in Soviet occupied Poland were now very much worse than in German occupied Poland" (PIA, Weinstein Collection, Box 48, Roll 50). Jan Ciechanowski, later the Polish ambassador in Washington, was serving then as the general director of the Polish Ministry of Foreign Affairs and was privy to most communications reaching the Polish government in Angers from occupied Poland.

Soviet republics; creeping confiscation of personal property through such measures as introducing the ruble as parallel currency on a par with the Polish złoty; withdrawal of the Polish złoty from circulation on December 20, 1939; conversion into rubles limited to 300 złoty maximum; arbitrarily imposed, exorbitant taxation on craftsmen, small store owners, and individual peasants designed to force them to give up their property or to join the cooperatives; and scrupulous inventory of peasants' households in order to monitor and ration individual consumption. As I pointed out in the Introduction to *War Through Children's Eyes*, these actions amounted to an effective suspension of property rights.[2]

A Polish government report assessed the first year of occupation and estimated the material losses sustained by the Polish population. The value of property confiscated in 1939–1940 in the territories incorporated into the Reich amounted to 6,631 million złoty; in the German-occupied Generalgouvernement, 1,921 million; and in the territories occupied by the Soviet Union, 2,176 million.[3] The Germans, then, confiscated almost exactly four times as much as the Soviets. But the total wealth of German-occupied Poland, if one can use such a notion, was certainly more than four times that of the territories under the Soviets, which had less of everything—less productive soil, a smaller share of it suitable for agriculture, and almost no industry except for oil, leather, wood, and timber.[4] Since the area provided less than 20 percent of the country's GNP, the confiscations there were relatively more comprehensive than under the German administration. When we consider in addition the invasion of masses of Soviet administrators, activists, and military personnel—poorer, hungrier, and more numerous than their German counterparts—we can see that their needs contributed to the depletion of economic resources and the ensuing pauperization of the local population. In brief, the inhabitants of the eastern half of Poland started with much less material property than those in the western and central parts of the country and thus suffered proportionally greater losses during the first year and a half of the occupation.

Millions of people in occupied Poland were subject to forced resettlement between 1939 and 1941—roughly 1.25 million under the Soviet occupation and about 2.5 million under the German. With about 13 million people under Soviet jurisdiction and 23 million under German, this form of repression affected exactly the same fraction of the population on each side. But we can appreciate the difference in the resulting hardships only if we also take into account the conditions of deportation and what happened to the deportees at their destination.

Of the 2.5 million victims of German deportations, 1.5 million were sent from western Poland (incorporated into the Reich) to central Poland (the Generalgouvernement). The others were POWs, victims of street roundups, and conscripts sent to work in Germany. (Only a small fraction of this group, 6–7 percent, was confined in concentration camps.[5]) Their trip to either destination was brief—one to three days at most—so that they suffered much less than those deported by the Soviets (assuming they traveled in similar conditions),[6] who faced ten days to three weeks or more of discomfort.

The circumstances awaiting the Nazi victims at the end of the journey were also much less forbidding. Those dumped into the Generalgouvernement were literally abandoned to their own devices upon arrival, to the great annoyance of the local authorities, who would suddenly have a transport of destitute people to provide for. Some, ideally, could be accommodated by relatives or assisted by friends. In any case, they were among compatriots and eligible for some rudimentary form of assistance through the Main Welfare Council (Rada Główna Opiekuńcza). Those sent into Germany for labor were treated shabbily; workers from Poland probably suffered the most among all foreign workers.[7] But they were not dying from exhaustion, hunger, and exposure to the elements, as were scores of their compatriots whom the Soviet authorities forcibly resettled. If nothing else, Germany had a better climate and was much better off materially than the Soviet interior in Stalin's time. That meant the difference between life and death for tens of thousands of people.[8] As for confinement in camps, several hundred thousand people were sent to Soviet concentration camps at the time, while substantially fewer than one hundred thousand met with a similar fate at the hands of the Nazis.

Finally, I must comment on the loss of life among the Polish people under the two occupiers. According to figures compiled by the Central Commission for the Investigation of German Crimes in Poland, 100,000 Polish Jews were killed or died as a direct consequence of German measures during the first two years of the Nazi occupation. From 1939 through 1941, 10,889 Poles were shot by the Germans in mass executions. Perhaps another 10,000 were killed clandestinely, in the backyards of prisons.[9] Thus, during the first two years of occupation the Germans killed a total of about 120,000 victims in Poland. The Soviet security police, on the other hand, matched that figure in just two episodes of mass execution. The NKVD may have killed as many as 100,000 people during the evacuation of prisons in the Western Ukraine and Western Belorussia during June and July 1941 (about two-thirds of the prison population at the time), and in the spring of 1940 the Soviets murdered Polish prisoners of war. (About 5,000 bodies were discovered in mass graves near the Katyń forest, and the remaining 10,000 have never been accounted for.)

But the total list of casualties for which the Soviets are responsible is much longer. Scores of people were killed during the first weeks of the occupation, and executions continued throughout.[10] Further, one-fourth of the deportees and concentration camp inmates must have been dead by the end of summer 1941—another 300,000 victims.* These very conservative estimates show that the Soviets killed or drove to their deaths three or four times as many people as the Nazis from a population half the size of that under German jurisdiction. This comparison, I repeat, holds for the first two years of the Second World War, the period *before* the Nazis began systematic mass annihilation of the Jewish population.**

This somewhat mechanistic comparison may at least serve to counter any possible incredulity at the record of Soviet rule in the Western Ukraine and Western Belorussia. Life was more dangerous in many respects under the Soviets than under the Nazis. And, as I have stated before, people at the time compared the two. Many, including thousands of Jews, came to this very conclusion and voted accordingly "with their feet."

---

* "By the time that the Amnesty was granted in 1941 (for crimes that had not been committed), almost half of the one-and-a-half million Poles deported in the previous years were already dead. The victims included 100,000 Polish Jews, headed by the Chief Rabbi of Warsaw, Moses Shore. The exact numbers will never be known." This is the assessment of Norman Davies in his deservedly acclaimed history of Poland, *God's Playground*, 2: 451. I believe he chose the highest plausible estimates; but, if we accept 1.5 million as the total number of Polish citizens sent to the Soviet interior, then perhaps the staggering 750,000 dead is not far off the mark. Two Polish government reports prepared in London at the end of the war estimated that 800,000 to 850,000 Polish citizens remained in Russia following the breach of Polish-Soviet diplomatic relationships in April 1943. Given that 120,000 were evacuated when the Anders Army left the Soviet Union and that the total number of deportees might have been 1.25 million to begin with, I think an estimated 300,000 deaths in exile is more plausible. See HI, PGC, Box 56, File "Ewakuacja obywateli Polskich z ZSSR 1, 5"; Box 410, File "Uchodźcy w ZSSR."

** The Nazi extermination of Jews began in Poland in late autumn 1941. For more information and documentary sources, consult *Eksterminacja Żydów na ziemiach polskich w okresie okupacji hitlerowskiej*. Comparisons between the Soviet and the Nazi record have been done by other scholars (though not, strictly speaking, with respect to the circumstances I have here described) and a similar conclusion drawn. Stephen Cohen, for example, finds that, "judged only by the number of victims and leaving aside important differences between the two regimes, Stalinism created a holocaust greater than Hitler's" (*Rethinking the Soviet Experience*, p. 95). Cohen repeatedly uses in this essay the term "holocaust" to describe the effects of Stalinism (see ibid., pp. 94, 114).

And yet, despite the overwhelming suffering, the Soviet occupation was somehow less oppressive in its atmosphere and style than that of the Nazis. Although it is a treacherous undertaking to report subjective feelings, especially in the aggregate, I could not compare the two occupations without noting that difference. The welcoming reception the Soviets had enjoyed and the hopes that their presence engendered (even though for a limited period of time and only for certain groups of the population) were very real and conspicuously absent in the experience of Polish citizens subjected to Nazi occupation. It meant something that the new rule kept justifying itself with slogans of social and national liberation, and it did matter that millions of Polish citizens—Jews, Ukrainians, Belorussians—could meet fellow ethnics, so to speak, who came with the Red Army or the Soviet administration.

What was lacking under the Soviet occupation was the sense of pervasive discriminatory contempt, the *Übermensch* airs, so forcefully projected by the Germans. If anything, in the beginning, the Soviets were themselves somewhat awed, insecure, and intimidated. Indeed, what renders this occupation so completely dissimilar to the Nazi or to any other occupation was that the Soviets behaved no differently in occupied Poland than they did in their own country. The Soviet personnel and their families arriving in the Western Ukraine and Western Belorussia had experienced the same hardships (and were likely to experience them again at any time) to which the population of the newly liberated territories was being subjected. "You'll get used to it, or else you'll croak," they used to say, not maliciously, but merely summing up the wisdom life had taught them. "There are three categories of people in the Soviet Union," they tried to explain to the newly adopted Soviet citizens, "those who were in jail, those who are in jail, and those who will be in jail." They did not mean this malevolently; rather, this was the story of their own lives. And I think this attitude was important for preserving a semblance of humanity under these altogether inhuman conditions. For, as a consequence, the Soviets in the occupied territories felt that they were not exploiting; they did not mean their actions as discriminatory; their intentions were not vicious or evil—rather, it was all ordinary behavior. They were simply sharing their own ways. To state briefly what the options were under each occupation: it was easier to collaborate with the Soviets, while the Nazi rule was more hospitable to clandestine conspiracy.[11]

That the policies and practices of the Soviet occupiers were no different from those of the administration at home (unusual as this may be in the history of conquest) is but one more manifestation of a striking structural characteristic of totalitarian regimes. Talcott Parsons described the Nazi *Gleichschaltung* as anomie.[12] With considerably more time and no less enthusiasm, Stalin's Russia went much further in completely blurring institutional articulateness. The Soviet system could boast no clearly defined boundaries of political authority, even though it pervaded *all* institutions; an organization holding all the effective power in the system had no institutionalized rules of succession; its actual governing body, the Politburo, was not even mentioned in the constitution. On the evolutionary tree of social institutions, the Stalinist regime would have to be classified as an amoeba. It was a case of predivision of labor where in principle any person could fulfill any function: an illiterate peasant could be drafted to serve in the National Assembly; a passerby could be given a village to administer; an ignoramus (the case of academician Lysenko is best known) could dictate intellectual fashion that was binding on the scientific community.[13]

One day in 1940 Poles stood on a queue long hours in an Augustów cooperative to buy socks. Suddenly a local Soviet official walked into the store through the back door, looked over a few pairs of socks, and then decided to purchase the whole supply. The salesman, pointing to the waiting crowd, hesitantly objected: "And what about the people, comrade nachalnik?" To which the nachalnik, with arrogance exceeding that of Louis XIV, replied, "narod eto ia"—I am the people—and walked away with all the socks.[14] *Narod, eto ia* (Robespierre said it first)—what a striking expression of the structural anomie pervading this society! Of course it was intended to convey a sense of impunity. But it is precisely arbitrariness, lawlessness that epitomizes the common destiny, rendering everyone vulnerable, indistinguishable. In the words of the poet Aleksander Tvardovski ". . . fate made everybody equal / Outside the limits of the law."[15]

In Stalin's time, the distinction was lost between those responsible for and those subject to public order. No one could count on guaranteed protection, not the secret police, the army, or any echelon of the party. Superiors and subordinates alike contributed to perpetuating the regime, either by acting against someone (as through an anonymous denunciation, which was comparatively mild) or by "breaking themselves in," to use Boris Pasternak's phrase.[16] This novel society required both the participation and the vulnerability of all. Suddenly, under the formula of institutionalized arbitrariness, or lawlessness, or privatization, the paradox of political theory—*quis custodiet ipsos custodes*—was transformed: all were custodians and wards simultaneously. To quote the testimony of another great Russian poet, Joseph Brodsky:

> There isn't a Russian executioner who isn't scared of turning victim one day, nor is there the sorriest victim who would not acknowledge (if only to himself) a mental ability to become an executioner. Our immediate history has provided well for both. There is some wisdom in this. One might even think that this ambivalence *is* wisdom, that life itself is neither good nor bad, but arbitrary.[17]

The image of Stalin's Russia as a gigantic, all-powerful, centralized terror machine is wrong. The fearsome, incapacitating quality of the Stalinist regime came from a myriad of minute, individual, spontaneous contributions. In practice, institutionalized arbitrariness showed itself as a kolkhoz chairman who could terrorize his sixty or so families, a salesperson in a cooperative who could withhold food from a starving citizen he disliked, a nachalnik in a backwater settlement who could work to death any of the local residents, and so on.

As I pointed out in Chapter 3, the structure of opportunities under the Soviet regime was such that people could easily arrange for punitive measures to be taken against others. In other words, the state provided incentives for people to "do in" one another. Some availed themselves of this opportunity from idealistic motives; others acted out of personal resentments or some other kind of selfish justification. But most important, once the process began, it was irresistible. People joined from the instinct of self-preservation, as if the famous question asked by Lenin, *kto kovo?* (who will get whom?), remained relevant even after the Revolution. Indeed, Lenin's immediate successor, Stalin, said this plainly when he proclaimed that the class struggle intensifies during the process of building socialism.

Similarly, the phenomenon of negative selection, widely noted by students of the Soviet regime, has its roots in this peculiarity of the social control mechanism. It presents a formidable challenge to political philosophers; for if there is one common thread in their reflections about society from antiquity to the present day, it is probably the conviction that a stable, robust, or even merely viable system of political institutions must assign talent to positions of power and responsibility. But the history of the Soviet Union runs strikingly counter to this simple wisdom. Or is it, perhaps, that the Soviet regime exemplifies a very different kind of political system and that its historically unprecedented success in concentration of power has not produced an equally unprecedented accumulation of power? There is something strikingly unusual, unique, in the relationship between power and the Soviet regime. I think this is primarily because it conceives of power in a very peculiar sense.

The Soviet regime has perfected a preventive ability, but not a creative or productive one. The creative attribute of power—power as the ability to get things done—has a secondary, derivative place in Soviet politics. Ever since the Bolshevik quest for power in the context of imperial Russia carried over into the postrevolutionary society (where for decades "enemies of the revolution" were pursued), power has been perceived as a relative attribute. Quite simply, the architects of the Soviet state discovered that one could accumulate power best by denying it to others. From the idea of power as a relative attribute follows the idea of the totalitarian monopoly of power, with exclusive state-sponsored institutions amidst an atomized society. Only in this framework does the concept of absolute power make sense. For what is absolute power but that others do not have any? How could it be defined otherwise—as a capability to build pyramids, or the Great China Wall, or carrying out some other exemplary feat? Any such definition would impose a limitation and therefore defeat the enterprise at the outset.

When we look at absolute power as secured by a totalitarian state through the destruction of civic society, we note a striking aspect of the phenomenon, one that is usually overlooked: any monopoly—of power or anything else—simply refers to a mode of distribution, logically and phenomenologically independent from the process of accumulation. It follows, then, that a state organization that monopolizes all power by destroying civil society is not identical with an "all-powerful" state. Have not Communist regimes in east central Europe proved exceedingly fragile? It took only a week for the Hungarian state to collapse in 1956; eight months of popular pressure in Czechoslovakia were enough to prompt Soviet military intervention in 1968; in 1980, in two months, the majority of the Polish working class walked out on the system. Have Pol Pot or Enver Hozha presided over states that could accomplish much for their citizens—feed them, clothe them, succor or shelter them? The history of the Soviet bloc in general is a mine of evidence showing that its countries have consistently failed to meet the criteria of satisfactory performance (in the domains of culture, politics, and the economy) that they set themselves.

I am, then, making a distinction between the state that is all-powerful and the one that has absolute power.* Absolute power is pro-

---

* "[W]hile violence can destroy power, it can never become a substitute for it. From

duced by incapacitating the existing or potential loci of power in society that are independent of the state-sponsored organization. This goal cannot be accomplished by the state through careful grafting or transfer of the existing capacities onto itself. And even if this were possible through some sophisticated merger, the totalitarian state does not avail itself of the opportunity (for lack of institutional means or of time, perhaps, as early stages of monopolization of power take place usually in the context of a real or imaginary civil war). Socialist parties all over Eastern Europe have not been unified with local Communist parties in order to win over their constituencies, accommodate parts of their programs, or transfer their members' allegiance to the new organization. In each case the move was intended as a liquidation and implemented in order to kill hope and real possibility of any other but the Soviet version of left-wing politics.[18] Since power derives from association,[19] it cannot be created, moved around, transferred, or accumulated by decree. It can be destroyed by decree, however, as organizations can be outlawed and people arrested or killed. So the monopoly of power in a society is necessarily destructive of power. It diminishes the overall system's capacity to get things done. Thus, most characteristically, the quest for absolute power renders the institutions of a totalitarian state "freedom sensitive," as they are geared toward detecting and preventing spontaneous association.

The Soviet version of the totalitarian state is not interested in power as the capacity to get things done. It knows about power as a relative attribute, reaching perfection when it is its exclusive repository. As a result, it is a state, unique in history, devoted primarily to making sure that *no one else* can get things done. I propose to call it a spoiler state.

Paulina Preiss has provided the most concise and apt measure of totalitarianism. It is, she wrote, the sum of unwritten books.[20] She meant, of course, the sum of lives unlived to their natural end, of thoughts that remained unthought, of unfelt feelings, of material goods not produced. This is indeed the record of a spoiler state. The sum is doubtless awesome, but one that is bound to remain unknown and

---

this results the by no means infrequent political combination of force and powerlessness, an array of impotent forces that spend themselves, often spectacularly and vehemently but in utter futility, leaving behind neither monuments nor stories, hardly enough memory to enter into history at all. In historical experience and traditional theory, this combination, even if it is not recognized as such, is known as tyranny, and the time-honored fear of this form of government is not exclusively inspired by its cruelty, which—as the long series of benevolent tyrants and enlightened despots attests—is not among its inevitable features, but by the impotence and futility to which it condemns the rulers as well as the ruled" (Arendt, *The Human Condition*, p. 202).

thus of little help in scientific inquiry except as a heuristic device: it points the proper direction for the interpretation of the phenomenon of totalitarianism. Proper, I think, because we cannot be satisfied with any theory of totalitarianism that fails to address its historically unprecedented *waste of human potential*. That there were "distortions" of a basically sound idea or that "mistakes" were made—that, in a word, assorted failures identified as such by Communist power holders themselves were only a byproduct of something else (the *bilan globalement positif* that Georges Marchais termed)—is a rather coarse explanation, deservedly dismissed long ago.

The best writing we have on the subject consists of some well-informed descriptions of the institutions and methods used by totalitarian regimes, such as monopoly of power, control over the economy, apparatus of terror, and ideology. The terminology used is borrowed from political science. These are generally adequate taxonomies and can yield subtle and insightful discussions of historical variations, as demonstrated in Juan Linz's masterful essay on totalitarian and authoritarian regimes.[21] But such analyses define the uniqueness of totalitarianism simply as the outcome of an unprecedented combination of the factors I mentioned, all controlled by the same decision-making nucleus. This does not take us beyond pure description. When we correctly identify the combination as unique, we do not explain its uniqueness, we only state it. A "thick description" is missing from this analysis, and we must continue to grope for the meaning of totalitarianism's uniqueness.[22]

Here we may find helpful the idea of a spoiler state. While states have always exercised their police power to bar or destroy potential or existing groupings, what was new about Soviet totalitarianism was its universal effort to prevent *all* association. But it is in human nature to associate with others. The Soviets found it necessary, therefore, to undermine the very potential for solidarity (see Chapter 3 for a description of the process) or to so modify human nature that people would no longer seek self-realization through association with others. Have the Soviets not always aspired to forge "a new man"?[23] Curiously, even though we associate totalitarianism with Organization writ large, its business is with the individual. It can easily enough destroy organizations, but to prevent association it needs to work throught individuals to eradicate temptation.

Not surprisingly, the theory and the practice of liberation are articulated by totalitarianism's most effective opponents not by advocating some specific form of organization or strategy of collective action to confront and challenge the system of state-sponsored institutions but rather by offering a vision of the individual actor as a moral subject. Do not lie, live in truth. This appeal by Solzhenitsyn in his Nobel Prize acceptance speech resonates throughout the conversations between Valery Chalidze and eleven eminent human-rights activists and self-exiled artists from the Soviet Union.[24] The affirmation of individual dignity has been the backbone of the Solidarity movement in Poland—the most formidable challenge ever made to the state monopoly of power in the countries of "real socialism." The doctrine is wonderfully simple: live as if you were a free person.[25] Precisely because totalitarianism depends for its success on spoiling individuals—on sowing mistrust and demoralization, or by outright killing—the refusal of a single individual to share these ways represents a decisive challenge to the regime.

Here I must turn to the most effective technique that totalitarian states employ to prevent association, the most destructive way the state can come between every two individuals and interfere with the most elementary exchange: language. Why are totalitarian controls still effective, even though terror has abated and ideology has never penetrated beyond a thin layer of the population? The reason is that language has been spoiled under totalitarianism and with it the possibilities not only of communication but even of diagnosis of social ills. Language is the primary tool of social intercourse, and we can imagine neither extensive coordination nor continuity in social action without its benefits. Totalitarianism could afford to spoil language because it is primarily devoted to preventing society rather than promoting its welfare. Here, once again, it has shown great ingenuity.

I want to make clear that the totalitarian style of language is nothing like the ordinary censorship of public utterances by governments in nontotalitarian despotisms or by any country in times of national emergency. Its aim is not simply to prevent the dissemination of information considered adverse to the state's interests. Instead, totalitarianism radically modifies the entire structure of the language. Consequently, the effects it obtains are profound. Ernst Cassirer wrote in 1945, "If nowadays I happen to read a German book published in the last ten years . . . I find to my amazement that I no longer understand the German language."[26] A new language has made an appearance, then, with recognizable features: it is highly rhetorical, saturated with figures of speech, and rigorously structured into slogans (a sequence of slogans is the perfect text). Most important, a fundamental distinction has been erased between what is and what ought to be. It is, in the words of Roland Barthes, "a language expressing value judgements . . . in which definition, that is to say separation between Good and Evil, becomes the sole content of all language, [in which] there are no more words without values attached to them, so that finally . . . there is no more lapse of time between naming and judging."[27]

The ritualization of speech, the imposition of strict ways of using key words and phrases, especially in matters relating to public life, provides a totalitarian regime with a sensitive monitoring device to detect all deviations from orthodoxy. The censor does not have to understand the meaning of a speech or a piece of writing when a mere word sequence or a change in expected adjectives gives away a potential freethinker.[28] Nor does the regime have to explain or justify its own policy changes when it can simply invoke a formula for condemnation and apply it to a policy or a person. Of all possible meanings that adhere to anything—individual, social movement, state, idea, policy— only one bit of information is given in the ritualized language: approval or disapproval. One may recall, for visual illustration, a row of grim faces on the reviewing stand during a national holiday in Stalin's Moscow or Mao's Peking; it was precisely the order of the line-up that mattered, and how it compared with the last time these people had appeared together in public. All it revealed was the degree of approval by the Great Helmsman. Why some were discarded and others promoted, what they argued about, no one knew, was supposed to know, or should want to find out.

Saturation with rhetoric introduces into totalitarian language what some linguists have called "loose semantics."[29] How does one defend oneself against an accusation of being a "running dog of imperialism," for example? When do production difficulties turn into "wrecking"? In China, Khrushchev is an "Elder Brother" one day and "a rotten egg . . . the biggest bad egg on earth" the next.[30] These things are not explained and are quite confusing to ordinary people. Metaphor reigns supreme and displaces simple prosaic discourse. Even the most natural, commonplace activities acquire new meanings. "The descriptive and logical word is transformed into a magic word," and language soon fails to fulfill the function of being "a prerequisite of our representation of empirical objects, of our concept of what we call the 'external world' "[31] This failure, I believe, constitutes the perfect fulfillment of the totalitarian strategy of social control: it is in the "destruction" of language that, literally, the destruction of the public domain takes place, because language *is* the public domain and to take it away from a community is a supreme act of privatization.[32]

Totalitarian language fails miserably as an instrument of persuasion (public messages are received with widespread cynicism and mistrust), nor is it a good instrument for processing information. It is, however, a most effective instrument of social control. There is no paradox when we recognize that the totalitarian state is a spoiler state and that it is geared toward destroying the capacity for human interaction. Thus, totalitarian language functions as an instrument of social control by depriving human beings of the opportunity to check their ideas against the evidence derived from experience. Consequently, those in power can say whatever pleases them and cannot be proved wrong. (Recall the famous watchword of Italian fascism—*Mussolini ha sempre ragione*—Mussolini is always right.) Subjects may spare no effort to play by the rules, but they can never be sure that any correct action will give them well-being and security.

In the midst of forced collectivization, widespread famine, and continuing purges, Stalin uttered a famous phrase, "Life has become better, life has become happier." It was a statement utterly divorced from the evidence of the surrounding reality; but under the rules of totalitarian language usage, Stalin had the copyright on defining reality.[33] The same evidence could as well support a contrary generalization, also proclaimed by Stalin, that the class struggle intensifies as socialism is being built. Very simply, then, even though everyone more or less agreed on the necessity to follow the party line, no one could be sure what that would be from one day to the next. Even the most respected leaders of the revolution, even subtle Marxist theoreticians one after another failed to fathom this party line and perished. People could no longer make judgments about the outside world if they were deprived of their language. It was appropriated by a ruling elite that adopted a peculiar manner of speech, divorced from truth or objective reality. As George Kennan warned in a diplomatic report from Moscow in 1944:

> There is a . . . daring *tour de force* which the American mind must make if it is to try to find Russian life comprehensible. It will have to understand that for Russia, at any rate, there are no objective criteria of right and wrong. There are not even any objective criteria of reality and unreality.
>
> What do we mean by this? We mean that right and wrong, reality and unreality, are determined in Russia not by any God, not by any innate nature of things, but simply by men themselves. Here men determine what is true and what is false.
>
> The reader should not smile. This is a serious fact.[34]

In the ideal totalitarian society, where people can neither make judgments nor draw conclusions about the world around them because their language has been spoiled, they cannot act as independent subjects. They can only obey orders.

THE Soviet regime's special way of involving the populace, as I pointed out in Chapter 2, is best characterized as *complicity*. The regime so structured opportunities and applied coercion that nearly everyone became *implicated* in its doings. Both "implicated" and "complicity" belong to the vocabulary describing involvement with the underworld, with criminal organizations. Since participation in those is punishable, an organization must counter any inhibitions that fear of punishment might inspire by implicating each and every individual so deeply that all lose the alternative of returning to legitimate life. Thus members are separated from the outside world of legal norms and official institutions. This is the logic of complicity. But since the Communist state defines what is legitimate, legal, and official, why need it make that effort? From what is it striving to separate its subjects? What norms is it struggling against? What sanctions does the state think its subjects fear if they consent to participate in its business? What kind of legitimate life does it want to prevent them from being able to resume? Only if there are answers to these questions does the Soviet state's promotion of complicity start making sense.

Since the October Revolution did not take place in a historical vacuum, the new Soviet regime had to contend with the accumulated heritage of every community over which it prevailed. The past was a heavy burden that the new leaders did their best to lift. In particular, they strove to separate their subjects from their own consciences, from their sense of dignity and self-respect. It is the individual conscience, as a carrier of the accumulated cultural heritage, that is the only source of sanctions the state cannot control, so it must be demolished for the successful realization of Soviet society. In the foremost *Bildungsroman* of socialist realism, *Mother*, Maxim Gorki formulates a revealing and ominous prescription: "We are forced to hate people so that the time will come when we can love them all."[35] This pre-eminent engineer of human souls, as writers were called in the Soviet Union, extolled Lenin posthumously for his very ability "to hate in order to sincerely love."[36] Many decades later Georgi Markov recounted a conversation that one of his friends had with an officer of Bulgarian militia: " 'Do you mean to say that you hate nobody and nobody hates you? . . . You are lying, what kind of a man are you not to have any enemies? . . . You clearly do not belong to *our* youth, you cannot be one of *our* citizens [author's emphasis], if you have no enemies! . . . And if you really do not know how to hate, we shall teach you! We shall teach you very quickly!' "[37]

239

Ideally, to pursue to the end the brilliant insight of Maxim Gorki, from the point of view of successful implementation of a Stalinist society, every individual should grow to hate oneself.

And yet, in its skillful effort to exploit the evil in human nature, the Communist revolution paid humankind an unintended compliment. From the beginning, Soviet propaganda refers to the regime's ambitious struggle to forge "a new man." In its own words, it is like the "tempering of steel," it is a *perekovka*. So immune, apparently, is human nature to the design that only fire and hammering can advance the project. But then who, finally, is an ideal *homo sovieticus*? Truly a new man, and therefore unlike any that had been before. Not just *homo sapiens* or *homo faber* or *homo ludens*. Rather, I'm afraid, as in Auden's verse, he is "a ragged urchin, aimless and alone."

HISTORIOGRAPHICAL SUPPLEMENT:
A TANGLED WEB

THE YEARS of the Second World War were among the most consequential in all of Polish history. As a result of war the country suffered a demographic catastrophe without precedent. It lost its minorities—Jews in the Holocaust, and Ukrainians and Germans following border shifts and population movements after the war. A third of its urban residents were missing at the conclusion of the war, either killed or exiled abroad. Poland's elites were wiped out. Fifty-five percent of its lawyers were no more, along with 40 percent of its medical doctors, one third of its university professors and Roman Catholic clergy.[1] The scale of material devastation matched that of population loss. Then the postwar generation was raised on war movies, war-themes-obsessed literature, and official propaganda studded with (West) German/Nazi/fascist villains and Soviet/Russian/communist heroes. Needless to say, everyone had their share of wartime family stories either to tell or to listen to.

For all the impact it made and the coverage it received, as long as the communists held the reins of power in Poland, the Second World War was a deeply politicized subject. And despite a multitude of excellent monographs on a wide range of topics, historiography of the war could not grapple with fundamental subjects—such as the regime of Soviet occupation from 1939 till 1941 in the eastern half of the country, for example, or the makeup and politics of the underground state loyal to the government-in-exile in London, or even the Warsaw Uprising staged by the Home Army (AK) in August and September 1944, when 250,000 civilian casualties were suffered in the city while the Red Army, poised across the Vistula river dividing Warsaw, offered no support to embattled city residents and refused landing rights to Allied planes bringing supplies to the insurgents. Émigré historiography tried to fill the gaps, and over the years scholars established in Western academia wrote important studies on Polish subjects as well. But a free circulation of ideas was impeded, as was, of course, a free circulation of scholars, who would be frequently denied passports, or visas, and access to indispensable sources. As a result, the 1939–1948 decade is a vast open field for historical research, with new fascinating archival collections newly accessible in Poland, Russia, and the Ukraine. Important synthetic studies are yet to be written on the period.

In what follows I will take one thread—the history of Polish-Jewish relations in this fateful decade—in order to confront the stereotyped thinking prevailing on this subject in Polish historiography. Of all the wartime topics involving staggering human suffering and loss of life (Warsaw Uprising, deportations, Katyń, the Home Army—to use a few code words) that were hotly contested among official historiography, émigré authors, and writers who increasingly published in the uncensored samizdat during the 1970s and 1980s, this one has not stimulated in the émigré literature or among the uncensored publications a single piece of writing that could not have appeared in the then government-owned publishing houses in Poland. There was, apparently, a consensus of sorts that the matter had been sorted out and did not need to be revisited. And when in 1987 an eminent literary scholar, Jan Błoński, published a thoughtful essay entitled "The Poor Poles Look at the Ghetto" (in a reference to Czesław Miłosz's poem "The Poor Christians Look at the Ghetto"), the public reaction was loud and clear. The venerable Catholic weekly *Tygodnik Powszechny*, which put it in print, was overwhelmed with letters of protest from its readers and was compelled to publish "A Reply to Jan Błoński," authored by a distinguished attorney, who in the past defended several oppositionists in political trials and had been sentenced himself to death by a Stalinist court in the 1950s.[2] On this occasion he felt compelled to defend the "good name" of his compatriots who were collectively slandered, he believed, by Błoński's suggestion that Poles shared responsibility for the genocide of Jews. "[P]articipation and shared responsibility," wrote Błoński, "are not the same thing. One can share the responsibility for the crime without taking part in it. Our responsibility is for holding back, for insufficient effort to resist."[3] Clearly, the issue could not be revisited without stirring up powerful emotions. And so, it has been left in limbo for most of the time, with predictable consequences. When a random sample of a thousand Poles was asked in 1993, "Do you think that during the war the Jewish nation suffered as much as the Polish nation, or more, or less?" 6 percent of the respondents answered that the Polish nation suffered more, 32 percent that both nations suffered about the same, 12 percent that they could not compare, and 3 percent that they could not tell.[4] Thus, apparently, fifty years after the war, over half of the Polish society does not know that Polish Jews were wiped out during the Holocaust.

Polish-Jewish Relations under the German Occupation

A noted public intellectual, historian of literature, and essayist, Jan Józef Lipski, had written and spoken on the subject of Polish-Jewish relations on many occasions. Indeed one of his essays, entitled "Two Fatherlands, Two Patriotisms—Remarks about Xenophobia and Self-centeredness of the Poles," has been recognized as a masterpiece that boldly confronted various deceptively simplistic and one-sided patriotic stereotypes.[5] In a concise statement delivered in April 1983, at the fortieth Warsaw Ghetto Uprising anniversary celebration, after acknowledging that the Polish underground offered but token, symbolic military assistance to the fighting Jews, Lipski goes on as follows:

The conscience of the Polish nation would be sick and mortally wounded if we did not ask ourselves another question: even if not with weapons in hand did we at least do as much as was possible to help and save the Jews? Paying homage to the ghetto fighters, as well as to its defenseless inhabitants who had been killed, we also have the right and duty to pay homage to those Poles who lost their lives while helping the Jews. There were many Poles who had died a heroic death for their contribution to this most dangerous—aspect of the Polish war. For daring to get involved, they are most deserving of admiration. Extraordinary courage was required at the time in Poland to join in this struggle. Can everyone of millions of ordinary people be expected to behave as a hero?

And yet, there are times, and causes, that demand heroism. We, who remember, let us ask ourselves if there was not too much indifference—even though mixed up with fear, but indifference nonetheless? Did we all do as much as was possible, or less, or nothing at all in those times when dying people and our own moral norms called for doing more than was possible? Yet Poles are often wronged when, in the world, too far reaching generalizations are drawn concerning the collaboration of some Poles in the tracking down of the Jews, or blackmailing them. Criminal and amoral social margins exist in every community, and among their victims at the time in Poland were not only Jews but also general Grot Rowecki [commander of the underground Home Army, AK] and thousands of other soldiers of the anti-Nazi conspiracy. We should reject irresponsible generalizations in this matter, just as we should reject generalizations that

243

wrong other nations. Anti-Polonism is not morally any better than anti-Semitism or anti-Ukrainianism."[6]

What strikes in Lipski's statement—composed of one question and two almost equal in length paragraphs—is his search for balance, for equivalencies. In the first paragraph, he examines, roughly speaking, attitudes. He tells us that while there may have been too much indifference among the Poles vis-à-vis the plight of the Jews, the Poles also demonstrated extraordinary heroism in assisting the Jews. In the second paragraph, he examines, roughly speaking, behavior. Some Poles—a criminal margin—undoubtedly victimized Jews, but these Poles also victimized other Poles. Furthermore, Lipski points to the extraordinary quality of the Polish victims of denunciations. Thus, a further impression of equivalence is conveyed as, on the one hand, we have the overwhelming number of Jewish dead but on the other, a smaller no doubt, yet exclusive, self-selected group of freedom fighters—a general and thousands of soldiers. Then, in the final point, we are taken beyond the wartime period to find out that the Jews have actually victimized the Poles as well. For those "irresponsible generalizations" that one may come upon "in the world" are spread by Jews—Lipski says so explicitly in his speech at Warsaw University in 1981 for example—and, as we learn from the last coda of this paragraph "anti-Polonism is not morally any better than anti-Semitism."

As to the question opening the quote—*the important question* that we must answer in order to confront the subject matter of Polish-Jewish relations during the war—it is left suspended in midair. Lipski identifies the issue—did Poles offer as much assistance and help to the Jews as was possible?—but he does not answer his own question. Neither does he volunteer to prescribe a norm: there are times, he argues, that mandate heroism, and yet, he says, we cannot expect ordinary people to behave heroically; nor does he provide us with an unambiguous description of what had actually happened: Poles, according to him, were too passive, and extraordinarily heroic at the same time.

In spite of the limitations of Lipski's argument, it is appealing that in his statements he does not close off the issue. There is a certain hesitation, and thus an opening of sorts, in his texts as when he says, for example, that "the evaluation of how Poles behaved vis-à-vis the Jews during World War II cannot be, unfortunately, 'simple and unambiguous.'"[7] And he can be quite daring when he states, for example, that "a significant part of [Polish] society was neutral, oblivious, to the extermination of the Jews." "Have we never heard during the occupation," he asks, "the sentence 'after the war, monuments will be built for Hitler'"—presumably to celebrate Hitler's "solution" of the Jewish problem.[8] But, admirable as they are in their sincerity, these observations do not serve as starting points of inquiry: what did it mean to be "oblivious" to the spectacle of the Holocaust in wartime Poland? How large was the "significant part" quoted in his assessment? How did anti-Semitism manifest itself during the occupation? Lipski perpetuates the irrelevant (in the light of the question he had himself posed) framework of the discussion where the socially marginal phenomenon of extortionism from Jews (*szmalcownictwo*)[9] is contrasted with the socially marginal phenomenon of heroism (i.e., active assistance to the hiding Jews), while the investigation concerning attitudes and behavior of the missing in-between—that is, the vast majority of the Polish society—is left undone.

The standard commentary on Polish attitudes toward the Jews includes one very powerful argument that deserves closer scrutiny. It establishes, with compelling force, that Poles did on Jews' behalf as much as could have been expected. Continues Lipski:

> I know people who were caught by the Germans while wielding weapons and who survived concentration camps. But I don't know anybody who survived after being caught when hiding a Jew. There is more to it: a soldier in the Home Army knew that in case of arrest he would be tortured, his wife might be arrested, that he would probably be executed; but he could hope that his children would survive. Those who were hiding Jews could not even hope for this.[10]

The punishment for helping Jews during the German occupation in Poland was death. Entire families were executed if Jews were found hiding in their houses or apartments. Such is the truth about those times. Is it, therefore, surprising that Poles generally obeyed the German injunction? The answer to this question would be relatively easy—no, it is not surprising—but for the fact that there were other kinds of activities prohibited by the Nazis under penalty of death that the Poles massively engaged in. Simply: if we adopt a certain framework for the explanation of people's behavior it must be consistently applicable across the whole range of comparable choices in a given situation. And while we need not match every episode of one kind of behavior with another (which should also be covered by the purported explanation), a wide discrepancy in frequencies would indicate that we did not identify a correct underlying mechanism.

And thus, while helping out the Jews was probably the most difficult and daring of wartime pursuits—because it was so irrevocably
sanctioned with death, and because one's family was inevitably endangered as well—one could argue that the "cost" difference between joining an anti-Nazi conspiracy and helping out the Jews was
frequently marginal. The comparison is spelled out in the just quoted
passage: for a conspirator there is death following torture, arrest of a
wife or a husband, and as he or she would be interrogated as well,
most likely there is a torture session in store for the spouse, maybe
even death or a concentration camp. The child would survive, though
orphaned and traumatized. For helping out a Jew the whole family
died, though without being tortured.

Once again—while remembering that we are merely weighing
merits of an argument, not real motivations of people who actually
had to make these horrifying choices—one could point out that
while undeniably, for individuals with a large family, there was a
difference between the projected costs of the two courses of action,
for childless couples it would have been rather subtle; and for single
men and women, especially those who did not live with their parents,
it would have been altogether negligible. And is it indeed the case
that these Poles, unburdened as yet by family obligations and already
independent, presumably mostly young, engaged in anti-Nazi conspiracy with a zeal commensurate to their efforts on behalf of the
Jews?

Besides, let us not forget that collective responsibility was widely
used by the Germans in their efforts to stamp out conspiratorial activity and, more generally, in order to enforce compliance with numerous regulations. Poland, as stated earlier, suffered proportionally
the largest casualties of all the belligerents. In addition to three million Polish Jews, over two million other citizens died of war-related
causes. Many thousands were shot in public executions throughout
occupied Poland in reprisal for various forms of resistance. How
many among them fell for hiding the Jews? It turns out, that "[o]ne
cannot precisely determine the number of Poles who lost their lives in
the defence of Jews. Sz. Datner in his book *The Forest of the Righteous* (*Las Sprawideliwych*) enumerates over *one hundred* [emphasis
mine] documented cases; information about executions is also provided by W. Bartoszewski, and Z. Lewinówna as well as S. Wroński
and M. Zwolakowa."[11] Even assuming that each known case stands
for a family (i.e., three or four people who were put to death) the
volume of casualties suffered by the Poles as a result of involvement
in anti-German conspiracies would be, roughly speaking, a hundred-

fold greater! Why is it then that so many people pursued conspiratorial activity in Poland and so few were involved in actively helping out the Jews? Why is it that in the memory of witnesses who lived through the war, bringing assistance to Jews appears, in retrospect, as far more risky and daunting than joining the underground network? Clearly, some other factor must have been at play as well for we may not explain the difference solely by reference to the perceived threat of German sanctions.[12]

To my mind the stereotypical diagnosis of Polish-Jewish relations during the war is misleading both in terms of the general image it conveys as well as in terms of the particulars it advocates. Here is the general picture that I read into this position: in the midst of a situation that was utterly unprecedented—namely, a whole nation being put to death by a group of human beings who systematically, deliberately, and over a long period of time applied themselves to this task—in the midst of this scandal of inhuman proportions there exists yet another group of people that keeps its sanity and, on the whole, maintains a balanced judgment. It is on the whole reasonable. It fears sanctions that ought to be feared. Common sense is invoked to explicate the behavior of Polish society when confronted with the extermination of the Jews. The uniqueness of the situation is removed and a straightforward cost-benefit analysis is introduced, plus an observation about the normal distribution of moral character in a population (a "social margin" of heroes who helped the Jews, and a "social margin" of scum who blackmailed them). Thus, there are innocuous causes explaining Poles' behavior vis-à-vis the Jews during the Second World War, a behavior that was also, on the whole, innocuous and easily understandable.

Thankfully the poet rings alarm bells. "Next to the atrocious facts" of the Holocaust, says Czesław Miłosz in his Norton lectures, "the very idea of literature seems indecent."[13] How does the idea of cost-benefit calculation fare in comparison, or of the explanation that there is scum in every society, or the indignation at having a "good name" slandered by "irresponsible generalizations"? None of these purported explanations can help one understand, or can even describe what has happened; none gives a sense of why the surviving Jews are so profoundly and irrevocably scandalized by the Poles' behavior; none brings a better grasp of why public opinion in Poland is so aggressive, or rather defensive, about the subject of wartime Polish-Jewish relations.[14]

In what follows I will suggest a reverse to the mechanism of causation stipulated by the cost-benefit analysis. I will do so by introducing into our discussion the neglected dimension of the attitudes concerning Jews that prevailed in Polish society at the time of the German occupation. And I will argue that it is *because* the Poles were not ready to assist the Jews and by and large refrained from doing so that the death punishment for harboring Jews was meted out by the Germans systematically and without reprieve and the task of helping the Jews was so difficult.

Wartime Anti-Semitism among the Poles

Without beating about the bush let us state clearly that during the Second World War, during the German occupation of Poland, more or less all milieus of Polish society did not sympathize with the Jews. Solid evidence in support of this claim can be retrieved from underground publications. Over two thousand underground periodicals appeared during the occupation, and their editors enjoyed unlimited freedom to print what their wisdom, party line, or personal taste dictated.[15] All political parties and factions, all social groups had their publications, and one could gauge from these writings the state of public opinion on a particular subject. It turns out that with the exception of the communist press and central publications of the Home Army, the underground periodicals were not sympathetic to the Jews. They did not condone Nazi atrocities, though some appreciated the usefulness of the end result, but they all admitted the existence of "a Jewish problem" in Poland, and the need to find for it some solution after the war—such as emigration, for example. Here, for example, is a characteristc passage produced somewhere in the middle of the Polish political spectrum, not by the radical right or even the nationalist press published in the periodical *Poland* (*Polska*) originating in a milieu of *Sanacja* sympathizers.[16] In the 17 December 1942 issue of the magazine, one may read the following article about prostitution, entitled "The Ways of the *Volksdeutsche*":

> Hitlerite periodicals and propaganda publications constantly speak of Jews as criminals against humanity, they put out many well-deserved accusations against them, they condemn the Jews ruthlessly for depravation and demoralization of the young generation as pornographers and pimps. . . . And yet an interesting phenomenon ought to be registered. Jews have been locked behind walls in Polish cities or bestially murdered. One would think then, that this scourge and immoral occupation would disappear from our cities, just as Germans had assured us. But this

248

horrible and debasing occupation was taken over very eagerly in our cities from the Jews by the *Volksdeutsche* . . . who are not different from the Jews at all; they only emulate their ways. It is inconceivable for a decent Pole to have anything to do with these practices. Let us make sure that this horrible activity remains the exclusive domain of the chosen nations—the *Volksdeutsche* and the Jews. It is their privilege.

Much of the published writing referred to such incidentals, only tangentially related to the primary focus of German policies vis-à-vis the Jews during the war. And perhaps because of the gratuitousness of comments about the Jews in such contexts, the prejudice comes out in a sharp relief. But there was, of course, a much more direct and frightening material presented on the right of the political spectrum. Here, for example, is an excerpt from an article published in the milieu of the Socio-Political Committee *Pobudka* (The Wake-Up Call). It was carried by the periodical *Words of Truth*, published on 30 October 1943:

Who are the jews [small letter in original], whom they were for us, and whom they still may become—all should know this. Jews spread among us like pestilence, and Poland was a jewish breeding ground. One fourth of the 14 million jews of the whole world lived and fattened themselves on our Polish misery. Did they feel any gratitude because of this? No! In every war jews were on the side of our enemies, or in the best case—on the side of the stronger. The Polish nation suffered loss after loss, while jews took advantage of every war and every national uprising to enrich themselves and enlarge their influence. . . . Germans did not kill all the jews . . . about 2,275,000 jews were murdered, there are about 550,000 in the ghettos, in camps, and in hiding, and about 525,000 emigrated mostly to the Soviet land. This million of mostly young jews will come out of hiding, from ghettos, from the forests, and will return with the Soviet army when it approaches our borders. Jews will emerge in the critical moment, wreaking vengeance on us and trying to deprive us of the fruit of victory thanks to their influence in the West and possibilities in the East. But we grew wiser in the last quarter-century and we know that a jew is our enemy. . . . If jews would remain neutral we're ready to forgive them a lot and to support their emigration to depopulated territories of southern Russia, or anywhere else. During the peace conference we must insist on recognizing jews as citizens of a nonexistent state, so that they cease to be Polish citizens. The jewish problem in Poland must come to an end.

One may always argue that a few excerpts of journal articles constitute but impressionistic evidence and that they do not prove a general point.[17] But there is persuasive corroborating evidence illustrating the breadth of anti-Semitism among the Polish public, beyond what had been written in the underground press. A number of individuals whose specific task during the war was, among other things, to report on prevailing attitudes among the Poles had their opinions recorded, and we may consult them today. I am referring to people whose responsibility was to be informed, to state objective truth as best they could, and who were certainly not prejudiced against their countrymen, or bent on portraying them as anti-Semites despite evidence to the contrary. Here is what political emissaries, as well as heads of the civilian and military underground in Poland, conveyed in their reports dispatched to the government in exile in London throughout the duration of German occupation.

Jan Karski, who gave such a forceful interview in Claude Lanzmann's *Shoah*, arrived for the first time in Angers (where the Polish government in exile had its official residence at the time) as an emissary from the occupied homeland in the winter of 1940. Later, at the conclusion of his second mission, he would be the first credible witness to personally inform members of allied governments about the Nazi extermination of Jews in Poland. He didn't have such horrible news to report on his first trip but what he had to say was enough for the Polish government in exile to falsify his report, so that allied governments or public opinion in the West would not be informed about the extent of anti-Jewish sentiments in Polish society. "One can feel all over that the [Jews] hoped Poles would recognize that both nations are injustly exploited by the same enemy, and that the Poles' attitude toward them would reflect this awareness. But such an understanding is lacking among the broader masses of the Polish society. Their attitude toward Jews is ruthless, often without pity. A large part avails itself of the prerogatives [vis-à-vis the Jews] that they have in the new situation. They use these prerogatives repeatedly, often even abuse them. To some extent this brings the Poles closer to the Germans. . . . The anti-Semitism of a broad strata of the Polish society did not diminish at all." The Nazis, noted Karski in conclusion, were able to make of the Jewish question "something akin to a narrow bridge upon which the Germans and a large portion of Polish society are finding agreement."[18]

As this was not yet the period of systematic killings of the Jews by the Nazis, what the "large portion of Polish society" apparently agreed to was not murder. Rather, it was the isolation of the Jewish people as well as the economic squeeze to which they were subjected. The government delegate, the head of the civilian underground structure in occupied Poland, was more specific in an autumn 1941 report dispatched to London: "German policies toward the Jewish minority stimulate two kinds of responses. The inhuman terror to which the Jews are subjected is universally condemned and evokes a lot of pity. But the social and particularly the economic isolation are generally approved. A certain fear, especially in merchant circles, goes with it—namely that the Jews might eventually return to their dominant position in the economy."[19] Frankly, there was no dominant position in the economy that the Jews could return to because they had never occupied one. But a Jewish owner could return to his street-corner store, which a Polish plenipotentiary had taken over as a result of German-introduced measures. And this, naturally, was sufficient cause for resentment. On 25 September 1941—three months after the beginning of the Soviet-Nazi war and after the first wave of mass killings of Jews—the commander of the Home Army, Grot-Rowecki, sent the following telegram to London:

> I report that all statements and policies of the government and the National Council concerning the Jews in Poland create the worst possible impression in the country and facilitate propaganda directed against the government. This was the reaction to the "day of the Jewry" (Dzien Żydowstwa), to Szwarcbard's speech, to the nomination of Lieberman, as well as to greetings conveyed on the occasion of the Jewish New Year [in a radio broadcast]. Please accept it as a fact that the overwhelming majority of the country is anti-Semitic. Even socialists are not an exception in this respect. The only differences concern how to deal with the Jews. Almost nobody advocates the adoption of German methods. Even secret organizations remaining under the influence of the prewar activists in the Democratic Club or the Socialist Party adopt the postulate of emigration as a solution of the Jewish problem. This became as much of a truism as, for instance, the necessity to eliminate Germans. . . . Anti-Semitism is widespread now.[20]

Nor would these attitudes change under the impact of the Holocaust. If we move three years forward, to the eve of the Warsaw uprising, when the overwhelming majority of the Polish Jews had been killed, we find the political emissary Celt coming back from his mission to Poland with the following message: "The government delegate asked me to inform you that according to him 'the government exaggerates in its love for Jews.' The delegate understands that such moves may be necessary for the sake of foreign policy, but he advises prudence and restraint. Both under General Sikorski and now the government is too forthcoming in its philo-Semitism, because the country does not like Jews."[21] The government delegate and the commander of the Home Army, to whom information filtered from all over the occupied territory, were in the best position to generalize about the state of mind of the Poles during these years.

Now that we have heard about prevailing attitudes among the Poles from the horses' mouths, it might be possible to consider hypotheses about what had actually happened between Poles and Jews, and why it happened. Take any Polish book on the subject, preferably one with a happy ending, written by or about Jewish survivors who lived through the war assisted by the Poles. One realizes immediately from such a reading that the hiding Jews, as well as the Poles who were helping them, were vulnerable to denunciation. German functionaries, Gestapo agents, or extortionists who blackmailed Jews (the so-called *szmalcownik*), as the literature on the subject tells us, were few and far between in occupied Poland, and therefore the likelihood of a chance encounter with any of them was negligible for a hiding Jew. Why was it so difficult and dangerous, then, to hide a Jew? Reading Bartoszewski and Lewin's volume, *Righteous among Nations*—compiled to show the record of assistance extended to Jews—makes one realize that the precariousness of a Jew's existence among the Poles was due to a generalized, diffuse hostility toward the Jews. Historical record shows, I think, beyond reasonable doubt that a constant danger for a Jew hiding on the Aryan side, *and for the Pole helping him to do so*, came from a casual passerby, a house superintendent, a neighbor, a child playing in the courtyard who might, and frequently did, reveal a Jew's presence outside the ghetto—as in this brief episode from the life of a ten-year-old Jewish boy: "No sooner had I stood by the river when some boys came along, somehow noticed that I was a Jew, and in order to thoroughly convince themselves that I was, three of the rascals jumped me. They pulled down my trousers and started shouting at the top of their voices: 'Jew, Jew, Jew.' Then they grabbed me, twisted my arms behind my back and started deliberating whether to drown me or to hand me over to the German police. I took advantage of a moment when one of them loosened his hold of me, kicked him, and ran away."

There weren't any socially marginal people involved in this encounter, or scum, just children.[22] It was a matter of course that Jews
should be identified when found outside of their designated area of
residence. In a moving volume of little vignettes about his wartime
childhood, Michał Głowiński—nowadays one of the foremost literary scholars in Poland—describes a quarter of an hour spent in a
tiny Warsaw café. He was in transit at the time between safe houses.
His aunt, who thanks to good "Aryan" looks could move around
freely, was making the arrangements. She took the boy along on this
day and brought him to a little café. She sat him at a least visible
corner table, bought him a pastry, and left to make a few telephone
calls after promising to return in a little while (of which she also duly
informed the proprietor).

At the beginning I thought that everything is calm, that I am
sitting quietly as a mouse, eating pastry, nothing is happening
and what the women are talking about (there were no men
around) does not concern me. But after a while . . . it was impossible to doubt that all the attention was focused on me.
Women—either customers, or employees—surrounded the proprietor and were whispering something. They were also looking
at me very intensely. . . . I also heard fragments of the conversation that clearly, I couldn't doubt this, were about me. . . . I
heard: "Jew-boy [Żydek], certainly a Jew-boy . . . she perhaps
not, but he a Jew-boy . . . she dropped him on us."[23] Women
were deliberating what to do with me. . . . I tried not to think
how this will end. . . . I couldn't doubt that my situation was
getting worse by the minute. Women were no longer satisfied
to observe me from a distance, they were no longer satisfied
with figuring my ethnicity from a distance, they wanted to
make sure, perhaps as a final justification for a decision that
they might have already taken. After all, I heard one of them
say: "We must call the police." Agitated and visibly curious
ladies came closer, approached the table where I was sitting. Interrogation began. . . . They tried to ask questions very politely,
sometimes sweetly, but I was not deceived by this manner; one
needn't be very perceptive to feel that it merely covered hostility and aggression. They spoke to me as one addresses a child,
and at the same time a suspect, a criminal in fact. . . . I heard
not only questions addressed to me but also their commentar-
ies and opinions, which they uttered on the side. . . . The
most frequent was the dangerous word "Jew-boy," but I could

also hear the most horrible sentence again: "We must call the police. . . ."

If I knew anything about mythology then, I would have thought that I found myself in the power of Furies, of Erynias, who wanted to claw me into pieces. But would this be a fitting comparison? These ladies, after all, were not obsessed by a hatred that they couldn't control, they did not thirst for vengeance, for they had nothing to avenge on me. These were normal, simple, in their own way decent and honest women, who worked hard and toiled from dawn to dusk to take care of their families in the difficult circumstances of the occupation. I can't preclude that they were good mothers and wives, probably God-fearing, and endowed with a whole plethora of virtues. They just found themselves in a situation that they considered difficult and potentially threatening, and they wanted to deal with it. But they did not think what the cost of the solution might entail. Perhaps it exceeded their imagination, but they had to know what would have happened if they "called the police." Perhaps, this was beyond the scope of the moral reflection they were capable of. . . . When Maria saw my table encircled by the women, she immediately realized what was going on. She took me by the hand and we immediately walked out. I survived.[24]

Let us simply take note that hiding Jews, as well as those who were helping the Jews during the war in Poland, had to be on the lookout not only for extortionists and Gestapo agents; they had to be wary of ordinary folks, casual passersby, and their own neighbors.

Consider, by way of contrast, the difference surrounding the climate of secrecy required for underground work. The folklore of the occupation includes innumerable stories about the incompetence of the underground, how people were sent to a wrong address, mumbled some absurd password only to be patiently directed to an altogether different house or apartment by a neighbor who wasn't involved in this particular conspiracy but knew where the action was nonetheless, *and covered up for it*. One would be hard put to ask to identify such stories *à propos* the hiding of Jews. As if, in a manner of speaking, except for Gestapo agents and rare ideologically motivated supporters of Nazism, everybody in Poland was involved in an anti-German conspiracy.[25] One could say the exact opposite about helping the Jews — except for those who were actively involved, everybody, it seems, was against it.[26] Of course some would more actively and some less actively demonstrate their opposition, just as some would display more active and some less active involvement in the underground. While in casual conversations with acquaintances or even strangers, people would openly discuss their black market transactions (to mention another activity prohibited by the Nazis under penalty of death), and the young in particular would cue (by dressing in a certain way for instance), hint, exaggerate, or even falsely ascribe to themselves connections and credits earned in the underground, yet one would look in vain for a memoir or a piece of literature in which some protagonist boasts in casual company that he or she is hiding Jews. Not only would this be dangerous (as we know, Poles lived dangerously in those days and were proud of it) but, worse, it would be awkward, for it would most likely not meet with social approval.

What differentiated conspiratorial work from helping out the Jews in Poland during the Second World War was not, primarily, the relative severity of sanctions if one were caught but that, by contrast with involvement in the anti-Nazi conspiracy, there were relatively few people involved in assisting the Jews and that they were not supported in these efforts by the surrounding milieu.[27] Jews, by and large, were perceived as an alien element and they were either ignored or else the prevailing attitude toward them was hostile.

It is precisely *because* those assisting the Jews were few and *because* they were engulfed in a social vacuum that it was much more difficult and dangerous to help the Jews than to engage in the anti-German underground, not the other way around. This follows from a simple and well-established sociological principle according to which the enforcement of any norm of behavior depends on the degree of the group's acceptance of the validity of the norm. Had the German-stipulated norm, "Do not help the Jews," been as unacceptable to the Poles as the norm, "Do not engage in patriotic activity," or "Do not engage in market transactions," it would have been enforced more or less as successfully as the other two. If every other Pole "had his Jew," so to speak, just as he had his black market contacts or conspiratorial connections, it would have been much easier to hide among the Poles, and the Germans could not have killed everybody they caught helping out a Jew, just as they didn't kill every conspirator they apprehended. The Nazis did not want the Poles to kill the Jews, or even to help kill the Jews; they only wanted the Poles not to interfere with the Jews' isolation—and to this injunction the Poles by and large consented. The deviant behavior of a few, who were censored for helping the Jews by their own community, was sanctioned severely and very effectively policed.

Let me rephrase the argument one more time: We know three

things about the subject of our inquiry—about the Polish attitudes toward the Jews during the war, we know that there was widespread anti-Semitism; about Polish behavior, we know that relatively few people were involved in helping out the Jews; and about the German-created context, we know that the death penalty was meted out for helping Jews hide. The cost-benefit explanation entirely ignores attitudes, that is, the issue of anti-Semitism, and explains Polish behavior solely by the German-created context. What I have suggested as an alternative explanation links attitudes, behavior, and the situational context.

HOLOCAUST IN SZCZEBRZESZYN

But for a proper grasp of the issue it is imperative to move beyond generalities and immerse ourselves briefly in the wartime life of provincial Poland. Dr. Zygmunt Klukowski, director of the county hospital in Szczebrzeszyn, was an amateur historian and an ardent local patriot of *zamojszczyzna*.[28] Moved by a sense of duty and civic responsibility, he enjoyed the respect of his fellow citizens. Klukowski noted his daily actions and moods, wrote regularly about hospital business and the condition of his patients. But he also collected information from other people and reported the content of innumerable conversations as well as personal observations as he went about town. Since he was competent, courteous, reliable, and he provided indispensable services, he knew pretty much everybody, and people confided in him. On the pages of his diary he is a formidable informant regarding local affairs.

Szczebrzeszyn experienced more than the usual share of turmoil in these troubled times. Germans came there first, then relinquished the area to Soviet occupation for about two weeks and returned in early October. In later phase of war *zamojszczyzna* suffered German colonization experiments with the accompanying terror and breakdown of "public order." Klukowski captures the rapid collapse of norms of civility under the impact of war. "Shops were looted in town yesterday," he writes on 18 September 1939. "Both Jewish and Polish shops were looted. But since Jewish shops are much more numerous, one heard that Jews were being robbed. It happens like this. A few soldiers come in first, take something for themselves, and then they proceed to throw the merchandise into the street. There, crowds of Christian (!) [author's emphasis] population are already waiting, both city people and country folk. They grab whatever they can and quickly take it home. Then others rush into the store and jointly with soldiers rob and destroy everything. If a shop is closed soldiers break the doors open and it gets robbed even faster." Five days later he notes that robberies continued, and since shops had already been emptied, looters were breaking into people's apartments.[29]

Already in this early period of the occupation Jews were beaten up and harassed by the German authorities. Klukowski also records episodes when the Polish population applauded or joined in such brutalities. He further draws attention to symptoms of the breaking down of solidarity within the Polish community. He deplores voluntary sign-ups for work in Germany, female fraternization with German soldiers, and the plague of denunciations. "As a consequence of denunciations gendarmes all the time take away from various people some hidden items. And they don't have to look for them. They come into a house and say up front that in such and such a place, such and such an item is to be found."[30] Cooperation with the German authorities is so routine by the summer of 1940 that we are barely surprised when reading about a manhunt for hiding Jews, of whom only fifty, instead of the requested three hundred, showed up for scheduled departure to a nearby labor camp: "Alongside the police and two militiamen quite a few volunteers from among town inhabitants took part in it, including the mayor Borucki."[31]

Yet, through early 1942, Polish and Jewish populations of Szczebrzeszyn were subjected to a commensurate level of terror by the occupiers. There were more restrictions placed on the Jews, they were more casually beaten up in the streets and humiliated, they were stripped of their possessions (though many managed to give some for safekeeping to their Polish neighbors), but the dangers to which they were exposed were not of a different order of magnitude. "Everybody is anxious that the Germans might come to fetch him at any moment. I am so well prepared that I always keep a packed suitcase ready," writes Klukowski.[32] In Szczebrzeszyn periods of heightened terror alternated with days, sometimes weeks, of relative calm. Then, about March 1942, terror against the Jews intensified abruptly.

Trainloads of Jews from abroad passed through the railroad station. Jewish residents of various little towns in the vicinity were being resettled. Bełżec appeared to be their destination. Horrifying stories about resettlement from Lublin reached Szczebrzeszyn. By early April people already knew that full trainloads arrived daily at Bełżec and then left empty. On April 11 most Jews from Zamość were taken away and the news of unspeakable horrors committed on this occasion paralyzed the little town. The arrival of the gendarmes was expected at any time. "Most Jews keep out of sight; they either left town or hide. Some were frantically carrying things away and attending to some urgent business. All the scum ["*szumowiny*"] are milling around, a lot of [peasants with] wagons came from the countryside and stood waiting the entire day for the moment when they could start looting. News keeps reaching us from all directions about the scandalous behavior of segments of the Polish population who rob emptied Jewish apartments. I am sure our little town will be no different. . . . Everybody in town is very tense. Many people would like this to end one way or the other because panic among the Jews spreads around and affects all the inhabitants."[33]

And then for a few days the tension let up. There were no more passing trains to Bełżec. Until May 8, when at "about three o'clock in the afternoon all hell broke loose in town. A few armed Gestapo men arrived from Zamość. First they requested that one hundred Jews show up for work within an hour, and then, assisted by local gendarmes, they took to their bloody work. Shots were ringing continuously. People were shot at as if they were ducks; they killed also in apartments, anybody—women, children, men without discrimination. It is impossible to estimate the number of dead and wounded. There must have been over a hundred."[34] The hospital and Klukowski were forbidden to tend to the wounded Jews. He was shaken by this injunction, but afraid to break it, especially after two Gestapo agents came over looking for Jews they were told were there.

Klukowski noted at this time a general breakdown of "law and order" in the surrounding countryside. "Guerillas are all over. They take from peasants primarily food. It's impossible to tell who is who—there are Polish guerrillas among them, Soviet guerrillas, German deserters, regular bandits, what not."[35] Germans seemed unable to stop this descent into chaos. They frequently resorted to measures of collective responsibility, killing scores of randomly picked peasants for allegedly abetting bandits. And yet the Jews had nowhere to go, they could not find shelter in the midst of this deepening disorder. "On the next morning—after the murderous eighth of May . . . behavior of a certain part of the Polish population left a lot to be desired. People were laughing, joking, many strolled to the Jewish quarter looking around for an opportunity to grab something from deserted houses."[36]

A new wave of mass killings of the Jews took place in the area— in Krasnobród, again in Zamść, and in Tomaszów. In early July some 1,500 Jews of Józefów got killed on the spot.[37] On August 8, all Jews of Szczebrzeszyn were ordered to assemble in the square, near the

Judenrat, with a few belongings, in order to be taken to work in the Ukraine. Nobody showed up voluntarily. From midday on local gendarmes, gestapo, Sonderdienst soldiers, as well as Polish policemen, *Judenrat* members, and Jewish policemen went around taking Jews out from their apartments and hiding places. Terrorized Jews brought to the assembly point, remained there in complete silence. "Quite a few Poles, especially boys, eagerly help in the search."[38] When finally led out of town late in the evening, some Jews tried to run away. Shooting started in all directions. Poles in the streets panicked. The column of Jews was driven with blows and shots to the station. Some one thousand Jews from Biłgoraj and vicinity were taken out to the train station in Zwierzyniec on this day as well.

After this *Aktion* only "productive" Jews were allowed to remain in town. Every day a few Jews were shot, but people no longer paid any attention. And so it went for a couple of weeks. The final roundup began on October 21. Nine hundred Jews were led out of town in the afternoon. Some four to five hundred had been killed right away. "Nobody ever dreamed that things like that are possible. I am completely overwhelmed, I cannot find a place for myself, I cannot do anything."[39] The bloody spectacle continued for several days. Jews were being hunted down, killed on the spot, or brought to the cemetery in groups for execution. On October 26, "I saw near the hospital, in the compound of well-known rope makers named Dym, fifty Jews were found and taken out. We counted as they were led to the police station. A crowd of spectators stood around and watched. Some volunteered assistance: they ripped through walls and roofs searching for Jews, and then beat them with truncheons. . . . From opened-up Jewish apartments people grab everything they can lay their hands on. Shamelessly they carry loads of poor Jewish belongings or merchandise from little shops. . . . All of this together makes an unbelievable spectacle, hard to describe. Something equally terrifying, horrible, was never seen or heard about by anybody anywhere."[40]

And the same spectacle gets repeated all over the area. Under the November 4 entry Klukowski notes a three-day-long *Aktion* in Biłgoraj and Tarnogród. Afterward the road from Biłgoraj to Zwierzyniec where Jews were loaded on the trains was covered with corpses. Those who had scattered throughout the countryside were hunted down by everybody. "Peasants afraid of reprisals catch Jews in hamlets and bring them to town or sometimes kill them on the spot. In general some terrible demoralization has taken hold of people with respect to Jews. A psychosis took hold of them and they emulate the Germans in that they don't see a human being in Jews, only some pernicious animal, that has to be destroyed by all means, like dogs sick with rabies, or rats."[41]

Klukowski leaves an unusually comprehensive account. He makes no apologies for anything that he had witnessed or done (as when he refused, following a German prohibition, to treat wounded Jews, for example, or accepted for his hospital a "donation" of linen and household goods from the gendarmes after an *Aktion*).[42] But he does not tell us, in substance, anything we didn't know about the mechanism of destruction. What is it, then, that makes his memoirs so significant? We owe Klukowski the realization of a simple fact that easily escapes attention despite voluminous readings about the period — namely, *that Poles have witnessed the Holocaust*. And this, to my mind, is the most remarkable significance of the document he left behind. His testimony *proves that this entire process had taken place in full view of the surrounding population*. The most revealing information in Klukowski's memoir is two numbers he quotes from a conversation with Szczebrzeszyn's mayor: that 934 Jews were deported on the first day of the *Aktion* and that about 2,300 were killed in town over the next two weeks.[43]

These proportions may vary from town to town and from ghetto to ghetto. I would guess that from the largest agglomerations a greater proportion of the Jewish population was deported rather than murdered on the spot. But in countless small towns where from a few hundred to a few thousand Jews were confined to their quarters, by no means walled in and out of sight of the Gentile population, a significant proportion, if not the majority, were killed right there. Holocaust, in other words, was not confined to the pitch dark interiors of gas chambers and covered vans. It took place in full daylight and was witnessed by millions of Poles who, as we have seen, by and large did little to impede it, to slow it down, or to interfere with it. In Polish historiography the significance of these circumstances has not been evaluated and is only barely recognized. Or else the firmly held conviction that there are two separate histories (and ipso facto historiographies) of the war, one Polish and one Jewish, and that they overlap only marginally when there is talk of extortionists and of heroes (these proverbial "social margins" of wartime historiography), would have to be cast off. In light of the evidence and analysis here presented, I submit that the Holocaust of Polish Jews is a central feature of Polish history of the Second World War, and that it cannot be excised for some special treatment.

JEWS UNDER SOVIET RULE, 1939–41

That Jews welcomed the Soviet occupation of southeastern Poland in 1939 and willingly collaborated with the Communist administration set up in these territories was well known in Polish society already during the war. And this view was never subsequently challenged by historians. It thus stands out as an example of either extraordinarily self-reflective lucidity in a society under occupation, or of an uncritical dullness on the part of historians who simply incorporated into their interpretations what was believed at the time.

The stereotype of Jewish behavior under the Soviet occupation is made up of two components. First, Jews are reported to have enthusiastically welcomed occupation of southeastern Poland by the Red Army, and second, Jews are known to have developed particularly good relationships with the Soviets as evidenced by their collaboration in the local administration and the apparatus of coercion. One ought to note, in the first place, that the initial welcome of the Red Army should have made Jewish behavior, and perhaps its motivation, indistinguishable from that of other "minorities" (the Ukrainians, for example, who were a majority population in this area) and thus at least removed the odium of some special rapport with the Soviets. But, more generally, a proper evaluation of the initial response to the confusing and new circumstances requires that we reconstruct what people knew *at the time* about unfolding events, or else we won't understand their motivation or behavior. Furthermore, as the historical record will show, Jewish behavior and rapport with the Soviets *changed over time* and must be differentiated by social category. In fact, upon close scrutiny, one could contend that Jews have suffered more than other ethnic groups as a result of sovietization of southeastern Poland, and that Jews manifested their hostility toward the Soviet regime uniquely and overtly.[44]

In 1939 neither the Polish government nor the military were envisioning or preparing to fight a war with the Soviet Union. Indeed, Poland was never officially at war with the USSR, and while the country had been at war with Germany since 1 September 1939 on the western front, what eastern Poland experienced late in the month was not nearly as clear-cut and unambiguous. When informed on September 17 about the Red Army's invasion of Poland, the supreme commander, just before crossing into Romania where he was interned, issued orders not to oppose the Soviets (which didn't matter since communication between scattered Polish detachments was already broken). Local Polish authorities and officers as often as not gave orders or instructions to greet and welcome entering Soviet units. It was not clear to many whether the Soviets came as allies or as enemies. And one could easily succumb to wishful thinking in assessing their intentions, for they employed clever deception—to wit, the Red Army detachment that marched with its regimental band into the border town of Ostróg to the tune of the "First Brigade," the signal piece of Piłsudski's Legions.[45] To compound the confusion, it is not clear that the Red Army soldiers knew the specific purpose of their mission as they passed by, waved, and otherwise communicated their amicable intentions.

The friendly reception of Red Army detachments in villages, hamlets, and towns all over Western Ukraine and Western Belorussia is a well-established fact. All over the Ukrainian countryside groups of peasants hoisted flags in the blue and yellow Ukrainian national colors in joyful celebration of the long-awaited collapse of the Polish state. Occasionally a mixed crowd with church banners greeted Red Army units singing, "in the confusing elation, Communist songs mixed with religious hymns."[46] Colors, songs, and inscriptions during these welcoming episodes were a mixed bag, just as the people who were lining the roads were mixed up. Where did Jews fit into this situation? They were part of the general confusion.

Crowds lining up along the roads and greeting the Red Army soldiers were reported to have been composed predominantly of "minority" youth.[47] Not surprisingly, for one should hardly expect local youth, in some godforsaken backwater, to quietly sit at home when an army goes by their little hamlet and does not kill or rob anybody! In many instances—when the Germans were evacuating an area they had conquered, but which the Soviets had to occupy according to the Ribbentrop-Molotov agreement—welcoming ceremonies were organized on explicit instructions, and people were forced to attend.[48] We have no clear evidence to judge the size of the welcoming groups. We read repeatedly that the majority of local residents were fearful and suspicious of the Red Army and, invariably, that it was young people one could see cheering in the streets. Undoubtedly only a small fraction of the local population showed up on these occasions. But what Poles and Ukrainians reported, often with biting irony, the Jews did not deny: "Jews greeted the Soviet army with joy. The youth was spending days and evenings with the soldiers." "Jews received incoming Russians enthusiastically, they [the Russians] also trusted them [the Jews]." "The first days of the Bolsheviks' presence were very nice. People went out into the streets, kept looking over tanks, children walked after soldiers."[49]

What could have been the motivation of young Jews milling in these crowds? Undoubtedly there were Communist sympathizers among them. There were some young Zionists in the streets as well. But left-wing and secular ideologies captured only a few hearts and minds locally and were not representative of the spiritual or mental outlook predominant among the shtetl Jews. But even a few enthusiasts could make a spectacle of themselves that their neighbors would have remembered forever: "I have to say that if someone ever experienced total happiness, it was [for us] the day when the Red Army came. I imagine that Jews awaiting a Messiah will feel that way the day when that Messiah finally comes. It is hard to describe this feeling—this anticipation and this great happiness. Finally our wait was over, they came to Lwów. First tanks came—and we wondered how to express ourselves, what to do: throw flowers? Sing?"[50]

We may sympathize, in hindsight, with the cold shower that such young idealists would soon receive in ever greater doses upon confrontation with the reality of everyday life in Stalin's Russia.[51] But the vast majority of local residents responded to the Soviet presence, one way or another, on opportunistic grounds. They were motivated less by preconceived ideological notions than by immediate experiences and expectations. The Jews, for instance, had a very clear awareness as to what might have happened had the Soviets not arrived.

It took a good many days before the Red Army, moving along a sparsely developed road and transportation network, would show the flag in outlying areas. But it was there that the bulk of the population of this backward half of a relatively underdeveloped European country lived at the time. Wherever ethnic strife filled the power vacuum created in the interim period, the local minority (whatever that minority happened to be in a given place) might suffer brutal persecution at the hands of its neighbors. Many residents of these backwaters—including Polish military settlers or landowners, who were the most exposed—expressed relief at their first sight of the Soviet military, or fled into the neighboring towns where the Soviets had already established their presence.[52] In the absence of landowners, Jews provided a second best target of *jacquerie*, and as peasant crowds converged on the towns of Western Ukraine and Western Belorussia, they had innumerable shtetls to choose from. Apparently, as always in the Jewish Diaspora, only a central authority could protect it from the surrounding population.

To justify its invasion of Poland, the Soviet government announced that it was compelled to enter Polish territory in order to protect the interests of national minorities, specifically those of the Ukrainians and the Belorussians. This pretense at national liberation was of course but a fig leaf used to cover Soviet imperial ambitions. Yet initial Soviet policies (replacement of the Polish state administration with locally recruited volunteers, for instance) as well as a variety of steps taken to follow up on the promise of national liberation (immediate promotion of local languages into the public sphere, for example) created a general atmosphere of ethnic emancipation. People belonging to ethnic minorities—and one should be mindful that these so-called minorities were a significant majority in the Soviet occupied territories—lost the humiliating sense of being second-class citizens. "You wanted Poland without Jews, so now you have Jews without Poland," was an expression one woman recalled from the period, turning around a Polish nationalistic slogan from before the war.[53] Furthermore, for the entire Jewish community, this initial sense of emancipation came not solely in the context of discriminatory policies of the prewar Polish administration, but also in the context of the brutalities Jewish communities were suffering at the time from the invading Germans.

This is important to remember: Jews had been brutalized by invading Germans beginning in September 1939, and the awareness of this harsh treatment had spread to Jews in southeastern Poland by the time of the Soviet invasion.[54] Even more to the point, however, Jews had actually experienced treatment at German hands in a sizable chunk of the territories eventually occupied by the Red Army, because the Wehrmacht, as mentioned earlier, had come there first. During the following months a steady trickle of horrors would feed into the Jewish community via refugee stories.

Hundreds of thousands, perhaps millions, had been displaced by the war in September 1939, but the Jewish experience was again unique in its severity, especially in the vicinity of the shifting border separating the German and the Soviet zones of occupation. Entire Jewish communities—men, women, and children—were uprooted by the Germans and driven eastward over the river into the Soviet zone where, as often as not, they were denied entry. They would then linger for days in a no-man's land—abused, pillaged, raped, shot at until they bought their way in, or got in by stealth or good luck. Let the story recounted at the time by twenty-two-year-old Rosa Hirsz stand in lieu of many:

I spent a long time in the so-called neutral zone. Germans robbed me thrice. They even took a packet of needles, they took my coat and linen, they said they needed linen for their wives and children. There were instances when Germans took clothes away from Jewesses and gave them to Polish women. I saw how Germans took all clothing from some Jews and tore it to pieces, just to harm the Jews. Young Germans were the worst. With older ones one could manage somehow and cross the border for a few pennies. I finally managed to bribe a patrol and with some other young Jews I found myself on the other side. As soon as we moved in a little, Germans alerted the Bolsheviks and from both directions shots were fired at us. We hid in a ditch. Three in our group, including one young woman, were killed on the spot. Others miraculously survived. We spent two days in the ditch near the Soviet border without food or drink. As soon as we raised our heads shots would be fired. We could not stand it any longer and risking our lives we crawled on all fours toward the Soviet border, without food or drink. A Soviet patrol caught us. They were quite friendly. They gave us something to eat and to drink and then "assisted us" to get over to the German side. We were ready to commit suicide. We were totally exhausted mentally and physically. We were dead tired and could not see how to extricate ourselves from our predicament. A German patrol beat us with rifle butts. They thought we were trying to get in from the Soviet side. In our presence, unashamed that a lot of people were watching, Germans raped two young Polish women and then savagely beat them. We spent another ten days in the neutral zone. We witnessed horrible mistreatment of people. We saw the arrival of a group of Jewish artists with Turkov and Ida Kamińska. They were well dressed and must have thought they would be left in peace when they identified themselves as actors. Germans ordered Ida Kamińska to strip naked. They took her precious coat, all of her underwear, and her dress, and when she stood completely naked a young German officer ordered her to act. My heart was breaking when I looked at this wild scene. I admired her comportment. With a faint smile she gave away everything, her face was pale, but she did not want to show the Germans that she was afraid. The same happened to the whole group of actors who showed up on the border. Completely naked they were allowed into the border zone. We were lucky that the Gestapo enforced the principle of racial purity in the border zone. Some German military were quite eager for Jewish girls whom they wanted to make happy and in exchange smuggle across the border, but they were afraid of the Gestapo. Finally we managed to get over to the Soviet side. It was at the end of the month, during a pitch-dark night, when we got to Białystok bypassing Soviet patrols. Even though I had no place to stay and I was constantly hungry, the feeling of freedom and the return of my human dignity after weeks spent with the Germans gave me strength to bear all the discomforts. Most important was that one could freely walk the streets; Soviet bands were playing cheerful marches. Nobody was pulling Jewish beards off in the streets, and one didn't see pale, trembling people.[55]

Since the very beginning of World War II Jews were extremely vulnerable. They sensed and experienced this vulnerability and responded accordingly. They were particularly endangered by the absence of a central authority and by the German presence. Soviet occupation of southeastern Poland held both in abeyance. The sense of relief that was initially detectable in the Jewish community (and I have to caution that we have no evidence to judge how widespread it was, as there were vivid memories in the older generation of mayhem in these areas, which followed the October revolution and continued during the 1920 Polish-Bolshevik war) at the prospect of Soviet administration must therefore be properly put in context, since the only viable alternative to the Soviet occupation at the time was the establishment of the German administration, not the continuation of Polish statehood.

Local Jews and the Soviet Administrative Apparatus

Now that we have contextualized the initial Jewish response to the Soviet occupation of southeastern Poland, we can proceed to evaluate the claim of massive Jewish participation in the Soviet administration. We have very good evidence with which to do so, and it indicates, unambiguously, that Jews were not involved, except sporadically, in the Soviet-sponsored apparatus of administration in the villages (i.e., where the vast majority of the local population lived at the time).

After Hitler invaded Russia in the summer of 1941, the USSR finally joined the Allies in their war against Germany. It also recognized the Polish government in exile and signed an agreement to release Polish citizens sent to camps and forced settlement in the Russian interior in 1939–41. The Soviets also allowed the formation of a Polish army in the territory of the USSR. This army was then evacuated to Persia in 1942 and fought gallantly along the Allied troops all the way to Germany. Some 130,000 people were evacuated from Russia at the time—soldiers and their families. At the request of the Historical Bureau of the Army all the evacuees were queried about their experiences under the Soviet occupation. Several questionnaires were distributed, and some twenty thousand answer sheets collected at the time—sometimes running into dozens of pages of wide-ranging narratives—are preserved in the Hoover Institution Archives. We thus have testimonies from all over the occupied area, and from people of every profession (duly marked on each questionnaire) that permit us to reconstruct numerous details of life under the Soviet regime. Among other things, we know scores of names of members of village committees and personnel of rural militias that served all over the area—*and Jews are only infrequently mentioned among them.*[56] We also know that higher echelons of local Soviet administration—on county (*raion*), voivodeship (*oblast*), or city level—were staffed by functionaries brought in from the east and while there were Jews among them, of course, they were not any more numerous than in the administrative apparatus in the Soviet interior.

What about the shared memory of Jews lending helping hands to the Soviet invader, then? Clearly, there is a discrepancy between broadly generalizing statements provided by witnesses who speak about the ubiquitous presence of Jews among Soviet functionaries, and detailed depositions left by the very same witnesses stating the names of those who were involved, without mentioning Jews. I think that the explanation lies in the enormous expansion of the state sector under the Soviet rule, eventually encompassing all of the economy. The state was the only employer in the area and hiring was conducted without discriminating against the Jews or the Ukrainians. Members of the "minorities" could get jobs—as teachers, foremen, engineers, accountants, civil servants—that they could not have had under the Polish administration. Consequently, there *were* Jews in the Soviet administrative apparatus, in the economic bureaucracy, or in the local militia, and there is no reason to think that they would have been less rude or abusive than any other such Soviet functionary. But that they were remembered so vividly and with such scorn does not tell us that Jews were massively involved in collaboration, but rather of how unseemly, how jarring, how offensive it was to see a Jew in *any* position of authority—as an engineer, a foreman, an accountant, a civil servant, a teacher, or a militiaman. That is why this remembrance was so deeply engraved. And it was also an easy memory to carry about during these exceedingly confusing times, because it simplified matters and comfortably rested on the paradigm of Polish public opinion that associated communism and Jews (*żydo-*

komuna). I conclude, therefore, that claims concerning Jewish collaborationism draw on impressionistic evidence, and neglect an inherently complex and confusing reality of the Soviet occupation. But when they are used rhetorically as a *pars pro toto* allegedly to capture the meaning of the entire Jewish experience under the Soviet occupation, they are simply wrong and can be refuted by solid evidence.

In the first place, one reads in the testimonies of numerous Polish witnesses that all the national minorities — Ukrainians, Jews, and Belorussians — soon learned their lesson and but a few months into the Soviet occupation grew nostalgic for Poland. Standing alone this would be important evidence difficult to reconcile with the image of sustained Jewish collaborationism. But even more significantly, this change of mood was promptly followed by overt action in the face of two policies then carried out by the Soviet authorities. Here we touch upon the second misunderstanding about mutual relationships between Jews and the Soviet authorities. The conventional narrative of those years glosses over what in effect was Jewish resistance and Soviet repression of the Jews.

REPRESSIONS OF THE JEWS

In the early Spring of 1940 the signing up of all residents for Soviet citizenship (a so-called passportization) was initiated as well as registration for population transfers to Germany in accordance with one of the stipulations of the Soviet-German pact. In the only well-documented manifestation of their mass behavior under the Soviet occupation, the Jews refused to take up Soviet identity cards and signed up in droves for repatriation into what was by then *Generalgouvernement*, a part of Poland occupied by the Germans. "Never in my life have I seen such a determined resistance as when Soviet authorities wanted to force the Jews to accept Soviet citizenship," recalls a witness to these events. "Their resistance defies description."[57] And we need not even draw on archival material to document the Jews' eagerness to get away from Soviet rule. Nikita Khrushchev, then first secretary of the Ukrainian Communist Party, toured Lwów in the company of the head of the Ukrainian NKVD, the infamous Ivan Serov, and wrote in his memoirs: "There are long lines standing outside of the place where people register for permission to return to Polish territory. When I took a closer look, I was shocked to see that most of the people in line were members of the Jewish population.

They were bribing the Gestapo agents to let them leave as soon as possible to return to their original homes."[58]

Whatever judgment we might be able to pronounce about this behavior with the benefit of hindsight (presumably, that it was collective insanity—an opinion that some witnesses were lucid enough to articulate on the spot),[59] this was undeniably a collective manifestation of defiance and an open, public rejection of the Soviet regime.[60] And it was treated as such. In the arsenal of Soviet repressive measures one of the most ferocious was forced deportation. It aimed at removal of an entire category of the population (presumably inimical to the Soviet regime) into some remote part of the Soviet interior, taking all who had been targeted—including children, the sickly, or the elderly—without exception. One of the four big deportations carried out by the Soviet authorities from southeastern Poland, the June 1940 deportation, was made up of refugees from the German-occupied part of the country. It was predominantly made up of those very Jews who had queued up for repatriation to the *Generalgouvernement*.

Jews were sent into forced settlement during other deportations as well. Statistics compiled in 1944 by the Polish Ministry of Foreign Affairs on the basis of 120,000 personal files from the Polish Red Cross records in Teheran show that among Polish citizens who found themselves in the Soviet interior (for the most part forcibly deported in 1940–41), 52 percent were ethnic Poles, 30 percent were Jewish, and 18 percent were Ukrainian and Belorussian.[61] Thus, the ratio of Jews in this group was roughly three times their ratio in the total population of Soviet-occupied southeastern Poland. By that measure alone the Jews were more heavily repressed than the Poles, whose ratio among the deportees was less than double their ratio in the total population of these territories. Whatever the imprecision of statistics compiled in wartime, we may safely dismiss a view stipulating that the Jews were beneficiaries of the Soviet rule and enjoyed some special rapport with the Soviet authorities.

As perverse irony of the Jewish fate would have it, victims of deportations turned out to be the lucky ones. And it is not the death rate (some 25–30 percent) but the survival rate among them that stands out in comparison to the all-out extermination of the Jewish population that managed to stay put in the Western Ukraine and Western Belorussia. Given what the Nazis had done, it would have been best for the Jews if they all had been deported into the Soviet interior prior to the outbreak of the Russo-German war. But if the Soviets had indeed implemented such a policy, it would not have been for love of the Jews.

One final note on deported Jews: once the Polish Jews found themselves in the USSR, they could not get out. Out of some 130,000 prewar Polish citizens who had been evacuated from the USSR by the Polish authorities, Jews numbered about 8,000. They made up about 30 percent of the deportees and about 6 percent of the evacuees.[62] So much for the preferential treatment.

The third dimension of Jewish experience under the Soviet rule that needs to be mentioned has less to do with mental states, real or imputed sympathies, and police measures, but is grounded instead in the tedious reality of everyday life. Thus, a brief commentary on socioeconomic aspects of sovietization and how it affected the Jews is in order.

Soviet authorities instituted a new economic regime in the occupied territories, and property rights were effectively suspended there. Short of collectivizing agriculture (though peasantry was put under gradually more oppressive tax burdens and property use restrictions), they abolished private property. Jews were the ethnic group most affected by these measures. Not because they owned so much, but because so many Jews owned so little. Sociologically speaking, Jews were an impoverished stratum of self-employed craftsmen and tradesmen. Consequently abolishment of private property touched them strongly, for they had no reserves of accumulated possessions to draw on, and were additionally burdened by the claims for material assistance from vast numbers of destitute Jewish refugees. Despite previously unavailable employment opportunities that opened up for Jews in industry or administration, as a group they suffered material calamity under the Soviet regime.

Sovietization, naturally, affected more than the material aspects of community life. It also radically undermined what we would call today civil society. Indeed, community institutions folded up soon after the Soviet authorities established themselves in southeastern Poland. Pinchuk quotes numerous memorial books as well as Yad Vashem sources to illustrate this process. In the words of an eyewitness from Łuck: "[C]ommunity and social life of the local Jewish organizations stopped entirely. With the entry of the Red Army nobody dared to call a meeting of an organization or institution. All community or national contacts from that day on went underground."[63] In reality the situation varied significantly from one place to another since so much depended on local authorities, but the dissolution of all institutions supporting Jewish community life became universal. As a witness from Lwów stated in his deposition: "In the end the Jewish community in Lwów ceased to exist and transformed itself into a shelter for the homeless. In the final instance only the funeral *artiel* [cooperative] remained, and was put in charge of the cemetery."[64]

As Soviet authorities promoted all-out secularization, synagogues—all places of worship, irrespective of denomination—were closed up or placed under an enormous tax burden, which the already impoverished population could not long sustain. Jewish religious life was additionally affected by a ban on official use of Hebrew. Books in Hebrew were purged from public libraries, and the well-developed school systems with instruction in Hebrew—Horeb and Beth Jakov schools—were closed.[65] Yiddish, language of the toiling masses, was promoted instead, but only up to a point.[66] Only the Yiddish-language theater prospered and fared better than before the war.[67]

The dissolution of the kehillah undercut the very material ability of a host of religious, educational, and social welfare organizations to function. Political parties dissolved or were banned, their leaders and prominent members arrested, and Bundists and Zionists were hunted down with particular diligence. To quote a witness of these events from Pińsk: "Systematically and mercilessly all activists were removed from among the Jewish masses. All those who might or could have expressed opposition to the reeducation of the population were eliminated."[68] In a memorandum on the "State of European Jewry at the Beginning of World War II," sent from the relative and only temporary security of Lithuanian-administered Wilno, Moshe Sneh informed Nachum Goldman that "the spiritual elite of Polish Jewry" has now found refuge in Lithuania. "To Lithuania fled those Jews who were threatened equally by Nazi and Soviet occupation, that is, Jewish intelligentsia of Zionist and Socialist persuasion, Zionist and Bundist leaders, authors, journalists, teachers, scientists, Hasidic and non-Hasidic rabbis, whole yeshivot, and a large section of the Jewish plutocracy."[69] The Jewish population—just as the Ukrainian, Polish, or Belorussian—was both deprived of the institutional infrastructure underpinning its community life—and systematically "decapitated" as a broad spectrum of the Jewish elite was removed through arrests, deportations, or forced exile abroad.

My sense is that the social context of Jewish life in this territory over preceding decades had rendered the Jewish community particularly vulnerable to such deprivations. During the interwar years Jews could not count on favorable treatment by the Polish-dominated state and local administration, and they were simultaneously under hostile pressure from the majority ethnic group residing in a given area. Thus, they were alien to all powers and

271

therefore thrown upon themselves and their own self-reliance. Hence, the destruction of their communities' infrastructure must have been truly incapacitating.

But in the experience of the Jewish community a confusing paradox was associated with the process of sovietization. In short order, following the Soviet annexation of this area, Jewish community life as well as a dense network of cultural and political institutions were destroyed, secularization was imposed on the Jews, and leading citizens were arrested. Why would any Jews have any illusions about what the Soviet regime had in store for them, then? They did, I believe, because the Soviet approach to "nationality problems" was unusual. According to the traditional pattern of discrimination, familiar to national minorities, as long as such groups kept to themselves they were tolerated. Only when the processes of social change led segments of the minority population out of self-imposed isolation, or when they actively sought assimilation, would the dominant nationality be provoked to show anger, contempt, and frequently violence. The opposite was true under the Soviet regime: here Jewish insularity, willful Jewish separation from the rest of society, was not tolerated. Jews could acquire Soviet citizenship with all the rights and entitlements that went with the honor, but they could not sustain their community life anymore. Once again they could not be simultaneously Jews and citizens of the state that had jurisdiction over them. This reversal of the pattern of discrimination was disorienting, and initially scores of people grew to appreciate the "nationality policy" of the new regime.

Finally, especially for younger Jews, there was also another experience of emancipation. Because of its self-imposed insularity and hostile surrounding social environment, Jewish community life was all encompassing. And those for whom institutions, practices, and customs of traditional Jewish life felt oppressive and those who wanted out because they could not fit, or fell out, or had hopes, dreams, and aspirations that could not be fulfilled within the boundaries that the community drew around itself—all those, primarily young, socially marginal, unusually open minded, gifted, or sensitive—welcomed the change. They sensed that the new regime offered an easy way out of the confining limitations of the Jewish community. Not exclusively by the so-called opportunities afforded Soviet citizens but also, perhaps primarily, because under the impact of sovietization the social control mechanisms of the Jewish community were so swiftly and utterly destroyed. It was, in other words, the perspective of emancipation *from* Jewishness as much as emancipation of the Jews that drew youngsters into the streets to cheer the Red Army and later to work on behalf of the Soviet occupiers. That these images of emancipation were mostly in the eye of the beholder matters little, for people are motivated primarily by their own representation of reality.

Given the socioeconomic circumstances of the Jewish population — that refugees made up such a significant fraction of the total; that Jews were predominantly self-employed, and hence belonged to the propertied, capitalist class; that the language of Jewish religious identity and practice, Hebrew, was cast off by the Soviets who for the sake of emancipation of the common man and secularization promoted Yiddish instead — for all these reasons, even though not deliberately discriminated against as an ethnic group, the Jewish community suffered probably the heaviest adverse impact of sovietization. I am hesitant to engage in comparisons of collective sufferings by entire communities (hence the word "probably" in the preceding sentence) because each was undermined differently by different aspects of Soviet policies. Jews, for instance, were relatively unaffected by the wiping out of the Polish state institutions and administrative apparatus because they did not partake in them. Here, Poles were the primary victims, just as Ukrainians or Belorussians would have been, had forcible collectivization been implemented. But, undeniably, as individual property owners or as persons who came from a foreign country and had close relatives living abroad, Jews were singularly ill suited to be welcomed into the fold of Soviet society. Hence the sorry fate of the Jewish population that did not suffer necessarily *qua* its Jewishness, but rather *qua* the ways in which it was politically and socioeconomically unacceptable.

As we revise stereotypes about our own history — and congratulate ourselves for being able to do so — it may be prudent to remember that ideas we hold about the past or present are a potent force capable of mobilizing people to action. And whether we imagine the surrounding world in accordance with the "material of facts," or in some other way — stereotyped, prejudiced, and unrelated to facts — the consequences of our deeds that may follow are, in each case, just as real. A report was sent to the government in exile on 8 December 1939 describing as follows the mood and condition of the Polish population under the Soviet occupation: "Jews are so horribly persecuting Poles and everything that is connected to Polishness under the Soviet partition . . . that at the first opportunity all the Poles here, from the elderly to the women and children, will take such a horrible revenge on the Jews, as no anti-Semite has ever imagined possible."[70]

As a description, we know, these words were flawed, but they were, unfortunately, accurate as a prediction. When Hitler invaded Russia in the summer of 1941 the *Einsatzgruppen*, special ss detachments entrusted with the task of killing the Jews, had little trouble enticing the local population (Poles, we must be reminded were locally in the minority) to stage bloody pogroms all over the area.[71] As a prelude to the systematic German killing of them all, the Jews were brutalized by their neighbors to avenge miseries inflicted on the local people by the Soviet authorities—as if the Stalinist regime favored the Jews, and did not count them among its victims.

POSTWAR POLISH-JEWISH RELATIONS

Mental constructs, including stereotypes, have a great staying power. They linger long after the people, events, or circumstances that inspired and brought them to life have left the stage of history and are no longer with us. And so, even though most Polish Jews had been killed during the Second World War, the stereotype about the special affinity between Jews and communism, the "Judeo-commune" syndrome, survived the war. If anything, it got reinforced by a widespread consensus among the Poles that during the opening year and a half of the war, when Hitler and Stalin were de facto allies dividing the spoils and each occupied about half of Poland, Jews openly sided with the Soviets and assisted in the subjugation of southeastern Poland. And then, when the Soviet-sponsored "Lublin" government of "national liberation" got established in the closing months of the war, including a number of Polish communists of Jewish extraction who spent the war years in Russia, the stereotype was further perpetuated.[72] In popular sentiment a nefarious role was attributed to Jews—they were portrayed as particularly zealous collaborators of the security police serving the new regime.

Let me state immediately that I do not consider counting Jews in the communist apparatus of repression as a very fruitful undertaking. For one, highlighting an inordinately high number of Jewish-born members therein does not lend itself to a simple interpretation.[73] Communists of Jewish extraction, just as people of other nationalities in various countries where communist regimes were installed, worked in the security apparatus qua communists and not qua Jews—or Poles, or Georgians—and they were not forcing on the reluctant population some "Jewish, Polish, or Georgian interests," but rather the "interests of the people."

By now it is very well known to students of totalitarianism that communists had an instrumental attitude to all values and institutions, and that they also exploited ethnic prejudices to gain and establish themselves in power. Hence, it seems to me, to the question of why Jewish communists worked in the security apparatus of their respective countries, the most sensible, perhaps the only, answer is simply, "and why not." But, in view of the persistent stereotype, it behooves us to ask whether indeed the dominant postwar Jewish experience in Poland was that of partaking in the imposition of scientific socialism on reluctant fellow citizens and attendant persecution of ethnic Poles. And, if I may anticipate the following pages, I will answer this question in the negative. Rather, I am prepared to argue, the dominant Jewish experience in post–World War II Poland was that of fear.

THE CENTRAL SPECIAL COMMISSION

In the closing months of the war, as Poland's territory was successively liberated from German occupation, the remnants of Polish Jewry who miraculously survived the war were coming out of hiding and returning from the concentration or labor camps where they had been held until then. In view of the utter destruction of their communities, their own exhaustion, and the resulting massive need for all kinds of assistance, survivors promptly established an organization called the Central Committee of Jews in Poland. It was an umbrella organization put together by representatives of all prewar Jewish political parties, with territorial branches wherever a significant number of Jews tried to settle.[74] The Committee attempted as best it could to address the various needs of the Jewish population. I want to call attention to one of its less known initiatives.

Admittedly the Special Commission established by the Central Committee of Jews in Poland was an ephemeral institution. It existed only for a period of eight months, from July 1946 to March 1947. In addition to a short life span its name was also rather enigmatic. Thus, we should not be surprised that two boxes containing its files attracted little attention from scholars perusing archives of the Jewish Historical Institute in Warsaw. And yet its records tell a fascinating story. Here is a fragment of the Commission's final report dated 30 May 1947:

The main task of the Central Special Commission (CKS) was to organize the adequate protection and defense of Jewish institutions and thereby assist the authorities in their defense of the lives of the Jewish population in the country, to prevent panic, and to facilitate the peaceful constructive efforts of the Jewish society trying to rebuild its existence. The first measure of the CKS was to establish close contacts with Security Services of Democratic Poland [capital letters in original]. These services approved of our efforts and offered us comprehensive assistance. . . .

Contacts between Special Commissions (KS) and the Ministry of Public Security (MBP), Citizens' Militia (MO), and the Voluntary Workers' Citizens' Militia (ORMO) were established all over the country, and collaboration proved fruitful. . . . During their existence the KSS made over *2,000 interventions with the Authorities* [emphasis in original] in the country. . . . The work of our information network was comprehensive. We had our people in factories, in open markets, at schools, at universities, etc. Our people were going to church services.[75]

Thus, under the enigmatic label of "Special Commission," we find a Jewish organization that in defense of Jewish interests collaborated with the secret police. In this manner the stereotype pointing to close association between Jews and security police in postwar Poland finds a concrete embodiment. What did this collaboration entail and how did it come about?

The Special Commission was established in the aftermath of the 4 July 1946 Kielce pogrom, which caused panic among Jews residing in Poland at the time and prompted their massive flight from the country.[76] Jews had been leaving Poland for some months before, but after Kielce the wave of departures swelled. Still, tens of thousands of people, exhausted by the horrors of their wartime experiences, could not leave their country on a moment's notice. And many were not even contemplating a departure. So, as one consequence of the tragic events in Kielce, the Jewish community decided to establish a self-defense organization. During a discussion held at the Presidium of the Central Committee of Polish Jews about the situation faced by the Jewish community in Poland, the idea of reactivating the Jewish Combat Organization ("ŻOB," as the wartime Jewish underground was called) was broached. And when finally the Central Special Commission was established, in a symbolic gesture Itzhak Zuckerman, "Antek," the last ŻOB commander, was designated its chairman. It was not accidental that when news of the Kielce pogrom reached the Committee the very same evening Zuckerman, accompanied by Marek Edelman, set out for Kielce to bring the remaining Jews into safety.[77]

The Jewish community interpreted the Kielce pogrom as a sign of pending ultimate danger. We have no precise statistics enumerating all the Jews murdered in Poland after the war. In any case such numbers would be difficult to interpret. After all this was a time when a civil war of sorts, as well as postwar banditry, were rampant. Tens of thousands of people lost their lives due to violence in this period. Dr. Lucjan Dobroszycki, who studied this epoch and always paid meticulous attention to numerical evidence, counted some 1,500 Jewish victims. Given the general level of disorder at the time, and the fact that many victims were not killed qua Jews but as targets of political violence or armed robbery, only a fraction of these deaths can be attributed to anti-Semitism. Still, one must be careful about the circumstances of each episode for, as it turns out, even victims of robberies could be deliberately targeted because of their ethnicity. Especially dangerous for the Jews in this respect were the railroads.[78] In addition to such assaults we encounter aggression specifically directed against Jews on the occasion of pogroms, when crowds of assailants act motivated by a belief that Jews committed a ritual murder of a Christian child, and when Jews returned to their prewar domiciles. Regarding the latter, murderous threats or actions were an effort to preempt returnees' claims on property that in the meantime had been taken over by the local population.

Still, no more than a few dozen people were killed by mob violence. And since many, perhaps most, could not return to their places of origin (incorporated into the Soviet Union after the war) the numbers of returnees killed in their domiciles were also limited. Hence, it was perhaps not murders of Jews qua Jews that evoked such a panicked reaction among the Jewish population, but the atmosphere of widespread anti-Semitism they encountered after the war ended. For even though anti-Semitism was nothing new in their interaction with Polish society, after the experience of the German occupation it acquired a new meaning: in view of the just experienced Holocaust no one could be oblivious to the realization that anti-Semitism could open up the gates to an ultimate catastrophe. Let us ascertain, therefore, how widespread were anti-Jewish sentiments in Poland fifty years ago.

POSTWAR ANTI-SEMITISM

State administration acts rather slowly, as we know, and it does not send circulars in response to individual complaints. Thus, it is fair to assume that the Ministry of Public Administration must have received a good number of interventions before circulating a memorandum entitled "In the Matter of Attitude toward Citizens of Jewish Nationality" to all the voivodes (i.e., chief administrators of the largest territorial units, voivodeships), district plenipotentiaries, and presidents of Warsaw and Łódź. Dated 5 June 1945 the memorandum was issued barely one month after the capitulation of Nazi Germany:

The Ministry of Public Administration has been appraised that voivodeship and county authorities, as well as offices of general administration, do not always apply the necessary objectivism when dealing with individuals of Jewish nationality. In the unjustifiably negative attitude of the said authorities and offices when handling such cases, and especially when making it difficult for Jewish returnees to take apartments that are due to them, a highly undemocratic anti-Semitic tendency rather clearly comes to the surface. The Ministry of Public Administration calls attention to this undesirable phenomenon and emphasizes that all loyal citizens of the Polish Republic, irrespective of nationality and religious denomination, should be treated the same, and that they ought to be helped within the boundaries of existing law. Therefore the Ministry of Public Administration implores you to make sure that the authorities and offices within your jurisdiction abide by the recommendations of this memorandum.[79]

In the archives of the Voivodeship Office in Cracow one can find several complaints not unlike those that must have come to the attention of the authors of the memorandum. They were frequently passed on to the authorities through the intermediary of Jewish committees.[80] A thorough study of this matter would require a search for evidence in over a dozen voivodeship archival collections. But already a few examples from the Cracow office can give us a sense for what was at issue. Thus, at the begining of July 1945 in Chrzanów

a registration clerk at the Citizens' Militia office requested that citizen Schnitzer Gusta, who returned from a camp, prove her identity by bringing a witness who would testify as to her identity and that she lived in Chrzanów before the war. When citizen Schnitzer Gusta presented to the clerk at said office as her witness the chairman of the County Jewish Committee in Chrzanów, citizen Bachner Lesser, the clerk stated in the presence of the witness that he had no confidence in the presented witness and that he would only trust a witness of non-Jewish extraction and that he would register the citizen [Schnitzer] only when she presented such a witness.[81]

Admittedly this is a trivial matter, but for this very reason also meaningful. For we cannot even justify the awkward, offensive, language of the militia clerk by the administration's attempt to stem the tide of Jewish claims and revindications. At the time, so soon after the liberation, in the entire Chrzanów county there were altogether 105 Jews.[82]

Jewish committees all over Poland complained about the anti-Semitic attitudes of Citizens' Militia personnel. But, interestingly enough, the attitude of the Security Offices (*Urzędy Bezpieczeństwa*), the most politicized organs of the administration, also often made the Jews uneasy. In the documents of Cracow's Special Commission we find a memorandum on a theatrical "revue" put on by the sports club "Force" in, of all places, Oświęcim (Auschwitz) on 24 and 25 January 1947. "The themes and content of this show were to make fun of the Jews in various sketches and songs. We want to stress that the main part in these anti-Jewish gimmicks was played by the commander of the Security Police in Oświęcim."[83] The following is another demonstration of poor judgment and lack of sensibility again in Chrzanów, where the town office at some point began sending daily request for laborers to the Jewish Committee demanding on July 5, for example, that "twelve persons of female sex be designated for washing dirty linen of Red Army soldiers." And it mattered less, in the eyes of the Jewish Committee that filed the complaint that the town office did not honor its promise to pay the honororarium, than the very fact of its issuing the request in a form "emulating methods of the occupiers, which makes the Jewish Committee responsible if the labor contingent does not appear in designated time and place. Such requests are issued only to the Jewish population with the intermediary of the Committee. In this manner the town office in Chrzanów perpetuates traditions established by the occupiers who communicated with the Jewish population with the help of 'Judenrat.'"[84]

Of course the state administration at the time of reconstruction had other more pressing issues than pestering the Jews. And the central administration—as demonstrated, for example, by the previously quoted memorandum of the Ministry of Public Administration—was sensitive to issues of racial discrimination. But ordinary citizens dealt mostly with officials at the local level, and here very often they encountered hostile treatment. Even though they could complain and get higher levels of state bureaucracy to intervene on their behalf, such repeated difficulties added up to make a shocking impact.

Jews encountered hostility not only in governmental offices but also in their places of employment. In a detailed study of how the working class was brought into the fold of the new regime immediately after the war, Padraic Kenney describes many strikes that took place between 1945 and 1947 in the industrial city of Łódź. Some of these confrontations were over the perceived favoring of the Jews—as, for example, a strike in the old Biederman mill in June 1945 that lasted for two and a half days over only one demand: "[W]e don't want a Jew director." Interestingly, "[i]n 1945 anti-Semitic incidents or statements . . . were not yet expressing . . . hatred of the communists; attacks on Jews in 1945 at no time referred to the PPR" (acronym of the Polish Workers' Party, as the communist party was known at the time). The association between Jews and communism was firmed up in the workers' minds apparently only after the Kielce pogrom. In the immediate aftermath, between July 8 and 11, workers meetings were called in factories all over Poland to pass resolutions condemning the pogrom. In several Łódź factories, according to reports of the activists involved, the workers' response was lukewarm, and only a few signed prepared petitions. But the daily newspaper in Łódź, as part of an official propaganda campaign, published headlines about workers in several factories (which were duly named) allegedly signing the resolution and requesting the death penalty for those guilty of the pogrom. And then

> [s]trikes broke out at nearly a dozen factories. . . . Warned a Central Committee report: "The situation in Łódź is serious, as evidenced by the mood among strikers, the strikes' swift leaps from factory to factory, and the aggression of striking women in all factories; they clawed and screamed ferociously. . . . Striking workers use such anti-Semitic arguments as "A pregnant Jew gets sixty thousand zlotys, and what do I have?" [or] . . . "Why don't Jews work in factory shops? Poland is ruled by Jews." Łódź Jews described a "pogrom atmosphere" in the city; there were rumors, for example, that Jews in the Bałuty district (a large worker district and a location of the Jewish ghetto during the war) had murdered a Polish child. While the strikes themselves were easily broken up once the workers had made their demand (usually that a retraction be printed in the newspaper) the hostility lingered long after. The sentencing of the pogrom leaders sparked more protests.[85]

From provincial towns one heard in these years numerous stories about physical assaults, windows broken in Jewish houses, offensive graffiti, or verbal threats. "It is an undeniable fact," wrote Jan Kowalczyk, the Cracow Voivodeship Commissar for Productivization of the Jewish Population, to the Presidium of the District Commission of the Labor Unions "that the living conditions of the Jewish population in county towns are extremely difficult. Because of the terror of reactionary elements [a phrase often encountered in the official language of the time whenever social phenomena disapproved by the administration took place] the Jewish population runs away from those locations in order to save their lives and concentrates in larger towns."[86] Indeed, county and voivodeship Jewish committees urged the Jewish population to move to larger towns where the committees tried to provide support in finding adequate living accomodations and employment. But even in larger towns Jews were not safe.

On Friday evenings after dark, according to Jewish religious custom, the shabbat service takes place. The services are held in one synagogue at 27 Miodowa Street, which also has an entrance from 8 Warszauer Street. After the service begins a crowd of hoodlums and teenagers assembles and, primarily from the direction of Warszauer no. 8, attacks the synagogue, throws stones, and with special bottles ruins the roof and breaks the windows. And so it goes every Friday, each time from a different side. These acts of public violence are accompanied by frightening screams, verbal abuse, laughter, and often attempts to enter the synagogue. Because these attacks take place every Friday and twice the rabbi was hit with a stone when he was praying at the altar, so not being able anymore to take this in stride, we call this to your attention, citizen voivode, as well as to the attention of the Public Security Office [UB] with a request for an immediate regulation, which would permit the Jewish population to finally worship in peace.[87]

One could try to pass over these episodes because in the old Jewish section of Cracow, Kazimierz, a sort of demimonde and lumpen proletariat resided for many decades after the war. But this was far from an isolated case. In fact Jewish orphanages, old people's homes, summer camps, or buildings housing Jewish returnees were frequently targets of similar attacks. And indeed, three weeks after this complaint was sent to the voivode's office, on 11 August 1945, a pogrom took place in Cracow, this time in other parts of the city as well. One of the badly beaten victims reported later on attitudes of various witnesses to these dramatic events—soldiers, militiamen, railroad workers, health service personnel, in other words, people whose opinions could not be dismissed as confined to socially marginal elements.

> I was carried to the second precinct of the militia where they called for an ambulance. There were five more people over there, including a badly wounded Polish woman. In the ambulance I heard the comments of the escorting soldier and the nurse who spoke about us as Jewish scum whom they have to save, and that they shouldn't be doing this because we murdered children, that all of us should be shot. We were taken to the hospital of St. Lazarus at Kopernika Street. I was first taken to the operating room. After the operation a soldier appeared who said that he will take everybody to jail after the operation. He beat up one of the wounded Jews waiting for an operation. He held us under a cocked gun and did not allow us to take a drink of water. A moment later two railroadmen appeared and one said, "[I]t's a scandal that a Pole does not have the civil courage to hit a defenseless person," and he hit a wounded Jew. One of the hospital inmates hit me with a crutch. Women, including nurses, stood behind the doors threatening us that they were only waiting for the operation to be over in order to rip us apart.[88]

From today's perspective we would not consider as an extenuating circumstance the fact that the invalid using his crutch as a weapon, the nurse, soldier, or railwaymen were all speaking and acting blinded by a passion, firmly convinced that Jews murdered Christian children in order to use their blood for matzoh.[89]

This medieval prejudice brought people into the streets in postwar Poland on many occasions and in many different towns—in Cracow, in Kielce, in Bytom, in Białystok, in Szczecin, in Bielawa, in Otwock, and in Legnica. And the whole matter was treated on occasion, one is tempted to say, with a disarming simplicity: on 19 October 1946 a few tipsy fellows were looking for a child in a building where Jewish returnees lived in Cracow, at Stradom Street no. 10. A small crowd began to assemble in the street, and when the guards of the building proceeded to disperse it, "the head of milita patrol [which in the meantime had been called by alarmed residents] told one of our guards that 'if your child got lost, citizen, you would also be searching around' ["*gdyby obywatelowi zginęło dziecko, to obywatel też by szukał*"].[90] That simple. This may allow us to better understand what was on the mind of Cracow's voivode when he wrote his June 1945 situational report: "There were no serious anti-Jewish demonstrations of any kind in the Cracow voivodeship last month. Despite this, however, there are no indications that attitudes toward Jews in society have changed. They are still of such a kind that a smallest incident is sufficient to generate the most outrageous rumors, and to provoke a serious outburst."[91]

So much for attitudes of the general public. And what were the views on this matter of the local elites, one might want to know. Luckily, we may shed some light on this issue as well, thanks to the record of a meeting held on 19 August 1945 in the cinema "Raj" ("Heaven") in Bochnia. This is where delegates of the Peasant Party assembled for a county meeting, about one thousand people in all according to an anonymous rapporteur who submitted this account to the Voivodeship Office. The gathering by invitation only ("*za zaproszeniami imiennymi*") brought together local activists, the elite of Stanisław Mikołajczyk's opposition Peasant Party.

> In turn the third speaker took the rostrum (his name unknown), and by analogy to a thesis from Kiernik's speech that Poland must be a monoethnic state [the matter previously discussed concerned expulsion of the German population from newly incorporated territories], put out a resolution that Jews should also be expelled from Poland, and he also remarked that Hitler ought to be thanked for destroying the Jews (tumultuous ovation and applause). Citizen Ryncarz Władysław, who was presiding at the time, immediately reacted to this speech by cutting it short and condemning what was said.[92]

In line with a tradition of Jewish humor, one could comment on this episode by pointing out that it contained both good news and bad news for the Jews.

These were the circumstances, the overall context in which the Central Special Commission (cκs) was established. After the Kielce pogrom it became clear that entire Jewish communities—and not only isolated individuals in secluded villages, in the privacy of their apartments, or when traveling by night trains—were imperiled with loss of life. During the month of July, after the decision to establish the cκs was made in Warsaw, special commissions were set up by voivodeship Jewish committees and then by their local branches. All political parties collaborating on the Jewish committees participated in this endeavor. Lists were drawn of all the apartment buildings housing refugees, all the old people's homes, Jewish party headquarters, orphanages, and other Jewish institutions that needed protection, and they were put under guard. About half of the personnel worked pro bono. The remainder were paid from the budget of the Central Special Commission. Over three million zlotys (a substantial sum at the time) were paid out each month in salaries for security guards. Some 2,500 people were issued weapons.

Special commissions in principle were subordinate to the ORMO (the Voluntary Workers' Citizens' Militia), but in practice functioned under the authority of Jewish committees and the Central Special Commission in Warsaw. Their principal tasks in the field were two-fold: to put up armed guards at designated locations, and to establish a system of communication that would alert the nearest outpost of the militia, or the security service of impending danger. Telephones were installed wherever possible or procedures established for main-taining contact by sending out messengers. Plans of all the protected buildings were drawn, together with a sketch of neighboring streets including the closest outpost of Security Services (UB) or the militia. One can find these sketches today in the CKŻP documents deposited at the Jewish Historical Museum.

One should not, however, exaggerate the professionalism of the special commissions personnel or procedures. The armed organs of the Jewish committees were far from an awesome sight. "In reality these were doormen, caretakers, and other workers used for various menial tasks. . . . Heads of various Jewish institutions and depart-ments claimed the right to use these guards since it was not clear who was in charge of them, the committee or the special commission. . . . Their condition was pitiful. They were dirty, unshaven, unkempt, al-together pretty disgusting to look at."[93] But at least someone with a weapon was patrolling the premises.

Fortunately, they had only rare opportunities to use their weapons. The final report of the CKS notes two such episodes, in Rabka and in Białystok, without mentioning details. The list of 108 employees of special commissions presented for a special award after the commis-sions were abolished on 1 April 1947 includes the names of two individuals who had lost their lives in the line of duty—in Ząbko-wice and in Łódź.

As to denunciations filed by special commission members and em-ployees, for the most part they were about circumstances or develop-ments that could endanger Jews or buildings in their custody. But this mandate could be interpreted broadly. Thus, for instance, after a meeting to elect a workers' council in a knitting factory in Nowa Ruda, a denunciation was sent to the local security service office about a speaker (a member of the Communist Party, as was duly noted) who requested that no Jews be allowed on the council after a candidacy of a Jewish female worker was put up from the floor. The chairman of the meeting, we read in the denunciation filed by the Jewish committee in Nowa Ruda, assured the assembled, who cheered him wildly, that he would certainly see to that.[94]

There are other instances of denunciations with dire consequences. The final report of the Central Special Commission, which I already quoted, includes a sentence: "On the basis of our information the Authorities [emphasis in original] have liquidated four gangs of NSZ [National Armed Forces, a nationalist underground organization] and WIN [Freedom and Independence, an illegal underground continuation of the wartime Home Army] in Wrocław and Szczecin." What human tragedies are covered by these few words we could tell perhaps if we had access to the archives of the Ministry of Public Security, for the CKŻP documents contain no further details. One can only hope that the designation of "four gangs" was a self-congratulatory report padding, as was another "success" described in glowing terms in the final report—"Special Commission in Włocławek discovered a center of propaganda and agitation that was distributing anti-Semitic literature. The center was liquidated." A memo preserved in the archives gives us a closer insight into what had actually happened:

> To the county UBP [Security Office] in Włocławek, Włocławek 1 February 1947. In the middle of December 1946 or thereabout, when I was in a certain establishment in a company, I found out that in the town library in Włocławek there are books with anti-democratic content. We decided to clarify this matter by sending as members of this library members of our committee, citizens ŁEPEK ICEK and ŁEPEK HELCZE [capitals in original]. Our members, after looking through the catalog, spotted a book with especially anti-Jewish content, entitled *Jewish Danger*, which we enclose with the above. We want to add that our members also noticed that in the aforementioned library there are also books with anti-Soviet content.[95]

Unfortunately, in those days books could be denounced by semi-literates, with dire consequences, and as a result of the Łepek siblings' report the town library was closed in Włocławek and its librarian arrested. Energetic activists from Włocławek pleaded with the CKS that it assign the task of cleansing public libraries and reading rooms to special commissions all over Poland. Thankfully, there are no traces in the archives that their advice was heeded. This, in a nutshell, is the balance sheet summarizing the activities of the only

Jewish institution in postwar Poland that in defense of Jewish interests collaborated with the secret police.

Concluding Remarks

The history of the Special Commission established by the Central Committee of Polish Jews is but a small episode in the long history of Polish-Jewish relations. But it is an episode situated in the focal point of an extraordinary phenomenon: massive emigration of the Jews from Poland after the Second World War. And, after all, an exodus from their fatherland by a quarter million people (this is, more or less, how many Jews left Poland by the end of 1948) not compelled to do so by government order or by administrative pressure is a real challenge and intellectual puzzle that has been taken up neither by Polish historiography nor by public interest journalism.[96] The Jews left behind everything—their dead ancestors, their belongings, and a material culture accumulated over centuries. Barely alive, literally, they left for a devastated Europe, not knowing where they would end up. And what they knew makes the whole matter even more of a mystery—for they went, in the first place, into camps for displaced persons situated in Germany! Was this another wave of emigration in search of better material living conditions? And if not, if it was a flight of a whole people from the threat of persecution, how do we come to terms with this, how is this to be written into a narrative of postwar Polish history? In a frequently quoted phrase Theodor Adorno declared the impossibility of writing poetry after Auschwitz. By this measure we are faced with an intellectual problem of staggering dimensions—how was anti-Semitism possible in Poland after the war?

War spawns heroic narratives and offers rich myth-producing material. Certainly for the self-awareness of the Polish nation in the twentieth century it has been of primary significance. It had all the elements that have ever served to forge Polish national identity: treacherous neighbors, unreliable allies, territorial partition, staggering human loss among the elites, deportations, even a national uprising staged against overwhelming odds. But through this rich material—a formidable national calamity transcended by exemplary heroism—there runs a fault line, an unspeakable "heart of darkness." It was too dangerous to help the Jews any more than they had been helped by their fellow Polish citizens—in other words, "we were scared" by the threat of German sanctions—runs the most spirited defense of Polish attitudes toward the Jews during the war. Cer-

tainly not the stuff from which legends are made. The Polish population took advantage of the opportunities created by the Germans to
exploit the Jews and thus shares responsibility for the Holocaust,
write critics of the Poles' behavior whose voices are barely audible in
Poland. Either way, the myth-producing quality of the war period is
shattered. And, as a result, the whole experience gets compartmen-
talized in the collective memory of the nation, and in the works of
historians as well.

The history of Polish Jews during the war became a specialized
subject, for the most part neglected. Fifty years after the war even
monographs about the principal ghettos—the Warsaw ghetto, the
Łódź ghetto, or the Białystok ghetto—remain to be written. Holocaust studies have not made it into the curricula of Polish universities.[97] But can one tell about the war and occupation in Poland
without the mass murder of Polish Jews being a central part of the
story? It is, after all, a chapter of Polish history as much as an epi-
logue in the history of the Jews in Europe. Indeed, one may ask—
given the place increasingly occupied by the Holocaust in critical self-
reflection about "Western civilization"—are there many other episodes of Polish history endowed with equally universal significance?

The spiritual legacy of Polish Romanticism contains two powerful
ideas: a conviction about righteousness and the exemplary destiny of
the oppressed, and a belief in the universality of freedom. The national poet Adam Mickiewicz wrote: "*Ibi patria, ubi male*: whenever
in Europe liberty is suppressed and fought for, there is the battle of
your country."[98] "For your freedom and ours" has been the traditional watchword of Polish patriots, derived from a belief in the
brotherhood of victims. Both ideas—that the persecuted weak are
right until proven otherwise, and that liberty of mankind is indivis-
ible—were embedded in the poetic interpretation of Poland's fate
worked out throughout the nineteenth century in an unprecedented
accumulation of creative genius, by Adam Mickiewicz, Juliusz
Słowacki, Zygmunt Krasiński, and Cyprian Kamil Norwid, while the
country was partitioned by more powerful neighbors and when its
patriots also fought continuously against the oppression of other
peoples. This fate, according to the Romantic mythos, preordained
Poland to an exemplary destiny: to become, as Polish messianism
would have it, "the Christ of Nations." And suddenly, during the
Second World War—also a paradigmatic time, stigmatized by a calamity of partition and loss of national independence, the sacrifice of
its best sons on the altar of patriotism, and the bloody defeat of a
national uprising—Poles failed to recognize a fellow victim, not in

some faraway land but in the neighbor living right across the street. Have they not, by this failure, betrayed their own destiny? Whatever the answer, a yet to be written definitive history of the German occupation of Poland would have to discuss how a combination of anti-Semitic prejudice among the Poles and deliberate, skillful Nazi policies leading to dehumanization of ghetto residents, resulted in excluding the Jews, in Polish eyes and practice, from the brotherhood of victims.[99]

ABBREVIATIONS AND ACRONYMS

AC	Anders Collection, Hoover Institution
AK	Armia Krajowa (Home Army) (earlier zwz)
AWBD	Archiwum Wewnętrzne Biura Dokumentów (Internal Archives of the Bureau of Documents)
CKS	Central Special Commission
CKŻP	Centralny Komitet Żydów w Polsce
CSYP	*Concise Statistical Yearbook of Poland, IX. 1939–VI. 1941*
DGFP	*Documents on German Foreign Policy*
DPSR	*Documents on Polish Soviet Relations*
GSHI	Instytut Historyczny imienia Generała Władysława Sikorskiego (General Sikorski Historical Institute), London
GUS	Główny Urząd Statystyczny (Main Statistical Office)
HI	Hoover Institution Archives, Stanford, California
KOP	Korpus Obrony Pogranicza (Frontier Defense Corps)
KS	Komisja Specjalna
KWZ	Jewish Voivodeship Committee
MSZ	Ministerstwo Spraw Zagranicznych (Ministry of Foreign Affairs)
NKVD	Soviet State Secret Police (earlier Tcheka and GPU)
OUN	Organization of Ukrainian Nationalists
PGC	Polish Government Collection, Hoover Institution Archives
PIA	Piłsudski Institute of America, New York
PSZ	Polskie Siły Zbrojne Collection, Hoover Institution Archives
ROU	*Russian Oppression in the Ukraine*
RSHA	Reichssicherheitshauptamt (Main Reich Security Office), Berlin
SAC	State Archive in Cracow
SD	Sicherheitsdienst (Security Service in Nazi Germany)
UPST	Studium Polski Podziemnej (Underground Poland Study Trust), London
UW	Urząd Wojewódzki
YV	Yad Vashem, Jerusalem
ŻIH	Żydowski Instytut Historyczny
ZWZ	Związek Walki Zbrojnej (Association of Armed Struggle) (later AK)

NOTES

THE COUNTY REPORTS referred to throughout this study are stored in the Polish Government Collection of the Hoover Institution. They are titled by county name and, usually, paginated consecutively. Instead of repeating the name of the collection in references to these reports, I simply give county names and page number (e.g., dobromil, 25). Several reports have been divided into sections marked by Roman numerals and are paginated consecutively within each section; only one report, from Oszmiana, is not paginated.

Also stored in the Hoover Institution are a few preliminary reports that combine data from several contiguous counties. I have used a dagger to distinguish these from individual county reports whenever the same county name appears as the title of both.

Archival holdings in the Hoover Institution are slowly being catalogued. In particular, since I last consulted it, the mammoth Polish Government Collection (PGC) has been broken into, primarily, two collections: the Poland. Ministerstwo Informacji i Dokumentacji Collection, and the Poland. Ministerstwo Spraw Zagranicznych Collection. With the help of the old register and/or the assistance of a Hoover archivist, any material that I have referenced to the Polish Government Collection can be located in these two places.

PREFACE

1. Namely, the General Sikorski Historical Institute in London, the Underground Poland Study Trust in London, the Public Record Office in London, the archives of the Ministère des Affaires Etrangères in Paris, the Bundesarchiv in Koblenz, the Yad Vashem in Jerusalem, and the Piłsudski Institute of America in New York.

2. I received this document from Professor Wiktor Sukiennicki, together with some other materials from his private archives. Sukiennicki (1897–1983) was an eminent lawyer and historian who specialized in Soviet affairs, among other fields. He was one of the founders of the Institute of Eastern Affairs established in Wilno in the 1930s, and he wrote about Soviet law at the time. He was arrested in Wilno during the Soviet occupation and deported to a labor camp. Upon release from detention in 1941, he joined the staff of the Polish embassy in Moscow and then the Ministry of Information and Propaganda in London. He was put in charge of, set up, and directed for its first six months

the Research Center (Ośrodek Studiów) established to analyze the various materials concerning Polish-Soviet relations that had been assembled by the Polish authorities.

3. In the spring of 1943 mass graves of about one-third of the missing men were dug up in a little forest near Katyń, where they had been executed by the NKVD in 1940. The bodies or whereabouts of the remaining 10,000 were never discovered. See Zawodny, *Death in the Forest.*

4. HI, AC, AWBD, note by Lt. Telmany, Dec. 6, 1943; see Kot, *Listy z Rosji do Generała Sikorskiego,* 58.

5. Thus a number of questionnaires are answered in the same handwriting, but not many. People really made an effort to write what they had to say by themselves. Perhaps there was no one who could spare time to take their depositions, or perhaps they felt the urge to express their anguish as soon as the opportunity presented itself. In any case, my impression is that friends or those who shared the bunk or the tent would help one another, rather than some clerks or specially designated personnel. Successively numbered protocols are sometimes written in the same handwriting, but they are not sufficiently numerous to worry that the individual remembrances were somehow screened in the process.

6. Gross and Gross, eds., *"W czterdziestym nas matko na Sybir zesłali,"* doc. 57.

7. HI, PGC, Box 100.

8. Kot, *Listy z Rosji do Generała Sikorskiego,* 58–59.

9. Sukiennicki's Archive, "Notatka dla Pana Ministra odnośnie rejestracji dokumentów i materiałów w sprawach polsko-sowieckich."

10. Col. Okulicki had been arrested two years earlier by the NKVD as he crossed into the Soviet zone of occupation from the Generalgouvernement to establish and take command of the Polish government-sponsored military underground network, the Association for Armed Struggle (ZWZ), later to be renamed the Home Army (AK).

11. HI, PSZ, Box 5, Folder 36/838.

12. HI, PSZ, Box 2, Folder 12/278; Box 77, Folder 77/6.

13. HI, AC, AWBD, note dated Dec. 6, 1943.

14. Report dated Apr. 13, 1944; Sukiennicki's Archive.

15. HI, AC, AWBD.

16. Soviet authorities consistently refused to recognize claims to Polish citizenship by non-ethnic Poles who were deported from the Western Ukraine and Western Belorussia throughout 1939–1941. In a note to the Polish embassy, dated Jan. 16, 1943, the People's Commissariat for Foreign Affairs summarized its position on the issue:

"In connection with the exchange of Notes in the years 1941–42 between the People's Commissariat for Foreign Affairs and the Embassy, concerning the citizenship of persons who previously lived in the Western districts of the Ukrainian and White Ruthenian Soviet Socialist Republics, the People's Commissariat for Foreign Affairs informed the Embassy on 1 December 1941, that all inhabitants of the above mentioned districts who found themselves on the territories of these districts at the time of their entry into the Union of Soviet Socialist Republics (November 1–2, 1939) had acquired Soviet citizenship in accordance with the decree of the Supreme Council of the USSR dated November 29, 1939, and the Citizenship Act of the USSR of August 19, 1938.

"In its note of December 1, 1941, the People's Commissariat for Foreign Affairs informed the Embassy that the Soviet Government was prepared, by way of exception, to regard as Polish citizens persons of Polish origin living in the territories of the above-mentioned districts on November 1–2, 1939. The People's Commissariat for Foreign Affairs is bound to state that despite the good will of the Soviet Government thus manifested, the Polish Government has adopted a negative attitude to the above statement of the Soviet Government and has refused to take the appropriate steps, putting forward demands contrary to the sovereign rights of the Soviet Union in respect to these territories.

"In connection with the above, the People's Commissariat for Foreign Affairs, on instruction from the Soviet Government, gives notice that the statement included in the Note of December 1, 1941, regarding the readiness to treat some categories of persons of Polish origin on an exceptional basis must be considered invalid and that the questions of the possible nonapplication to such persons of the laws governing citizenship of the Union of Soviet Socialist Republics has ceased to exist." (*DPSR*, 1: 473–474).

17. Many such confiscations are noted in the summary daily reports (the so-called Ereignismeldungen UdSSR) prepared by the Reichssicherheitshauptamt in Berlin on the basis of field reporting by the SS Special Commandos (Einsatzgruppen). Thus, for example, the reports numbered 3, 9, 10, 13, 14, 15, and 21 mention the capture of Soviet documents from NKVD offices in various towns of the Western Ukraine and Belorussia (Bundesarchiv, R 58/214, fol. 1–268).

INTRODUCTION

1. The following voivodeships were incorporated into the Soviet Union in 1939: Tarnopol, Stanisławów, Lwów, Wołyń, Polesie, Nowogród, Wilno, and Białystok (which was classified in the interwar statistics as one of the so-called central voivodeships). Białystok and Lwów voivodeships were split between the German and the Soviet occupiers. Thus, Suwałki county and parts of Augustów, Ostrołęka, and Ostrów Mazowiecki counties of Białystok voivodeship were under German administration. From Lwów voivodeship, counties Krosno, Łańcut, Rzeszów, Przeworsk, and Nisko came under the Germans, as well as parts of Brzozów, Jarosław, Lesko, Lubaczów, Przemyśl, Sanok, Rawa Ruska, Turka, and Sokal counties. See HI, Poland. Ministerstwo Prac Kongresowych Collection, Box 5, "Ziemie Wschodnie Polski," London, March 1943, pp. 18, 23.

2. Contemporary official Polish statistics inflate the numbers of ethnic Poles;

see, for example, Żarnowski, *Społeczeństwo Drugiej Rzeczypospolitej*, 372–376, and Horak, *Poland and the National Minorities*, 88, 89, 101. Furthermore, the boundaries of the area occupied by the Soviets in 1939 do not overlap exactly with units of statistical reporting. Finally, there was considerable spontaneous migration throughout the area in September–December 1939 that cannot be accounted for with any accuracy. I therefore use only approximations; these, I feel, are sufficient to give the reader a general understanding of the socio-political context of events described in the rest of this book.

3. Indeed, the 19th-century partitions of Poland probably weighed most heavily on the Ukrainians in this area by breaking their spiritual unity along the so-called Sokal line—the old Russo-Austrian frontier (see, for example, Żarnowski, *Społeczeństwo Drugiej Rzeczypospolitej*, 382, 385). Not only did a century of Hapsburg rule in Eastern Galicia permit the religious link with Rome to continue, but the political autonomy that the province had enjoyed also allowed for substantial growth of national self-awareness and cultural renaissance. Ukrainian nationalism was nurtured in the area as a result, and its aspirations could not be reconciled with the claims of Polish national interests pursued by successive administrations throughout the interwar period. The Wołyń Ukrainians, on the other hand, subjects of heavy-handed Romanov rule throughout the 19th century, were in consequence Orthodox and less nationalistically minded. It also mattered that throughout most of the interwar period a thoughtful (though most of the time helpless) Polish advocate of accommodation with the Ukrainians, Henryk Józewski, was Wołyń's voivode.

4. Żarnowski, *Społeczeństwo Drugiej Rzeczypospolitej*, 384.

5. See *CSYP*, p. 4, table 10.

6. For example, yields of major crops—wheat, rye, oats, barley, potatoes, and sugar beets—were lower by 10–20% there than in the rest of the country (*CSYP*, pp. 36–37, table 12). The fragmentation of farm holdings, except in Białystok and Wilno voivodeships, was greater; in the worst-affected area, Eastern Galicia, the majority of farms embraced less than 2 hectares (GUS, *Polska—dane skrócone*, p. 60, table 16). Infant mortality was substantially higher in southern and eastern voivodeships than anywhere else in Poland (GUS, *Zagadnienia demograficzne Polski*, 109). Meat consumption was considerably below the national average of 20 kilograms per person per year; in Stanisławów and Tarnopol voivodeships it was reduced by half, and in some counties—Turka (in Lwów voivodeship), Buczacz (in Tarnopol voivodeship), and Tłumacz (in Stanisławów voivodeship)—it was 4.3, 5.0, and 5.1 kilograms, respectively (GUS, *Okręgi hodowlane, produkcja i spożycie mięsa w Polsce*, pp. 76–77, table 26). A monograph entitled *The Child of the Polish Countryside* (Warsaw, 1934) concluded that children's nourishment in "Eastern Little-Poland" was worse than in any other of the country's regions (Żarnowski, *Społeczeństwo Drugiej Rzeczypospolitej*, 147).

7. GUS, *Polska—dane skrócone*, p. 7, table 2; *CSYP*, p. 29, table 6.

8. Gross, *Polish Society under German Occupation*, 15–16.

9. GUS, *Polska—dane skrócone*, p. 47, table 12.

10. Polish counter-terror included the notorious "pacification" of Eastern Galicia by the police and the army in September–November 1930 and by the Frontier Defense Corps (KOP) in 1938, and the setting up of the concentration camp at Bereza Kartuska in Polesie following the murder of Interior Minister Bronisław Pieracki by the Ukrainian underground in June 1934.

11. For information about Ukrainian communities, see the 30 volumes of the Ukrainian Archive published so far by the Shevchenko Scientific Society. Jewish life has been memorialized in some 400 volumes. Jack Kugelmass and Jonathan Boyarin have published a one-volume digest in English: *From a Ruined Garden: The Memorial Books of Polish Jewry*. In Appendix 1 they thoughtfully include a bibliography of Eastern European memorial books compiled by Zachary M. Baker.

12. The Communist Party of Western Belorussia and the local Association of Communist Youth, for example, were numerically stronger than their counterparts in the Western Ukraine throughout the interwar years, even though there were four to five times as many Ukrainians living in Poland at the time. See Kowalski, *Trudne Lata*, 61.

13. Kubijovych, ed., *Ukraine: A Concise Encyclopedia*, 2: 985.

14. The data for the year 1931 reflect the heavy toll of the Great Depression, which had already eliminated ephemeral publications. In Wilno, for example, in 1928 there were 28 Belorussian periodicals; three years later only 9 were left. Any periodical that survived until 1931 must have served some important need and had a devoted readership in the community.

15. GUS, *Statystyka Druków, 1931*, p. 8, table 3; p. 11, table 5; pp. 14–15, table 8; p. 20, table 14; p. 23, table 17; pp. 24–25, table 18.

16. DGFP, 7: 157. See also Ulam, *Expansion and Coexistence*, 260–279.

17. DGFP, 7: 295–296.

18. DGFP, 7: 363, 380.

19. DGFP, 7: 494, 509.

20. DGFP, 7: 480.

21. DGFP, 7: 540–541; 8: 4.

22. DGFP, 8: 34, 44, 60–61.

23. DGFP, 8: 68–70.

24. DGFP, 8: 77.

25. DGFP, 8: 79–80.

26. DPSR, 1: 47, 71–90. The Soviet note, though it muted the point that jarred German sensibilities, was still unacceptable to the Poles. It read:

"La guerre germano-polonaise a montré la faillite intérieure de l'État polonais. Au cours de dix jours d'opérations militaires la Pologne a perdu tous ses basins industriels et ses centres culturels. Varsovie, en tant que capitale de la Pologne, n'existe plus. Le gouvernement polonais s'est effondré et ne manifeste aucun indice de vie. Cela signifie que l'Etat polonais et son Gouvernement ont, de fait, cessé d'exister. Par cela même, les traités conclus entre l'URSS et la Pologne ont perdu leur valeur. Abandonnée à son propre sort et privée de ses dirigeants, la Pologne est devenue un champ d'action facile pour toutes sortes de menées et de surprises susceptibles de devenir une menace pour l'URSS. C'est pourquoi, ayant observé la neutralité jusqu'à présent, le Gouvernement soviétique ne peut plus rester neutre en présence de ces faits.

"Le Gouvernement soviétique ne peut pas non plus rester indifférent alors que ses frères de sang Ukrainiens et Blancs-Russiens, habitant le territoire de la Pologne, abandonnés à leur sort, sont restés sans défence.

"Prenant cette situation en considération, le Gouvernement soviétique a donné des instructions au Commandement Suprême de l'Armée Rouge d'ordonner aux troupes de franchir la frontière et de prendre sous leur protection, la vie et les biens de la population de l'Ukraine et de la Russie-Blanche Occidentale.

"Dans le même temps, le Gouvernement soviétique a l'intention de faire tous ses efforts pour libérer le peuple polonais de la malheureuse guerre où l'ont jeté ses dirigeants insensés et pour lui donner la possibilité de vivre d'une vie paisible."

Ambassador Grzybowski "refused to take it into cognizance" (*DPSR*, 1: 47). It was sent back and forth a few times between the Commissariat for Foreign Affairs and the Polish embassy: "The Ambassador ... refused to accept the note which he left on the table. The note was returned to his Embassy, when the Ambassador sent it back by hand to the People's Commissariat of Foreign Affairs, whence it was sent back to the Polish Ambassador who then re-addressed it to the People's Commissariat of Foreign Affairs by post" (Public Record Office, FO 37/23103).

27. *DGFP*, 8: 95. The final version read: "In order to avoid all kinds of unfounded rumors concerning the respective aims of the German and Soviet forces which are operating in Poland, the Government of the German Reich and the Government of the USSR declare that the operation of these forces do not involve any aims which are contrary to the interests of Germany and of the Soviet Union, or to the spirit or the letter of the Non-Aggression Pact concluded between Germany and the USSR. On the contrary, the aim of these forces is to restore peace and order in Poland, which had been destroyed by the disintegration of the Polish State, and to help the Polish population to establish new conditions for its political life" (*DGFP*, 8: 97).

28. *DPSR*, 1: 65.

29. The original demarcation line agreed upon, splitting Warsaw in half, appeared in the September 25, 1939, issue of *Pravda*.

30. *DGFP*, 8: 105, 109, 130.

31. *DGFP*, 8: 92. As it was, even after the alteration of the frontier, large areas had to be evacuated by the Wehrmacht and handed over to Soviet jurisdiction to comply with the provisions of the Russo-German Boundary and Friendship Treaty of September 28, 1939.

32. *DGFP*, 8: 164–166.

33. *DGFP*, 8: 212.

ONE: CONQUEST

1. *Czerwony Sztandar*, Nov. 4, 1939.

2. GSHI, Gen. Orlik Rückemann, "Sprawozdanie z działalności podczas wojny," Stokholm, Mar. 27, 1940, File "KOP, Dowództwo" (hereafter GSHI, Rückemann). KOP contingents were stationed in guardposts, each manned by eleven soldiers. Three guardposts and a separate command post made a KOP company. There was supposed to be communication between the compounds, but field communication equipment was lacking (GSHI, Rückemann). Thus, activities of KOP detachments could be monitored only via their guard or command posts. Once forced to abandon them, KOP soldiers were more or less on their own.

3. GSHI, Capts. Stanisław Kwasnowski and Jerzy Gędzierski, File "KOP, Pułk 'Wilno.' "

4. GSHI, Rückemann; *PSZ*, vol. 1, pt. 1, table 24.

5. GSHI, Rückemann; Kazimierz Kardaszewicz, File "KOP, Pułk 'Wilno.' "

6. GSHI, Capt. Jan Witkowski, File "KOP, Pułk 'Głębokie' "; Lt. Józef Leja, File "KOP, Pułk 'Wilejka.' "

7. GSHI, Rückemann; File "KOP, Pułk 'Wilno' "; HI, AC, Józef Tryjankowski, "Mój Pamiętnik"; PGC, 2921.

8. A Mr. Borejsza, who was then in Wilno and later joined the Polish underground, maintained that this news was inspired and authorized for dissemination by Wilno's military commander in order to boost the morale of the city's population. Interview, Stanford, Spring 1980; see also GSHI, A 9 III 2c/24, Ks. Kazimierz Kucharski, "Konspiracyjny ruch niepodległościowy w Wilnie od września 1939 do 25 maja 1941"; Studnicki, *Polska za linią Curzona*, 167, 168. As to Pińsk, a certain Telesfor Kaczmarek reports: "The danger [from groups of armed peasants converging on the town] was averted by a group of people with Regina Chodoniuk, employed at the city administration, who spread rumors that there was a revolution in Germany, that Italy signed an alliance with England, etc. This news was broadcast from loudspeakers all over town and saved the city from pillage and murder" (HI, AC, 10688).

9. For example, near Dzisna (dzisna, 2, 3); in Smolicz and near Łozowicze (nieśwież, 11); in Ludwikowo, Różana, Dobre, and Miesin (łuniniec, 4); in gmina Nowosiółki and Antopol (kobryń, 1, 2); in Łanowce (krzemieniec, 2); near Skałat (skałat, 2); near Niżniów (tłumacz, 1); near Dubrowlany and Sokołowa (stryj, 9); and in Mołodeczno county (mołodeczno, 3, 4).

10. "The Red Army took the village on September 20 after heavy fighting with KOP detachments assisted by many volunteers" (lida, 2). To this recollection from Papiernia may be added many others: from gmina Nowosiółki in Kobryń county (kobryń, 12); from Chodorów in Bóbrka county (bóbrka, 1); from Równe (równe, 3); from Siedliszcze and Kowel (kowel, 23); from Ostróg (zdołbunów, 3); from Kamionki (skałat, 3); from Łuck (łuck, 3); from Włodzimierz Wołyński (włodzimierz wołyński, 2); and from Sarny (sarny, 52).

11. GSHI, Rückemann; see also HI, PGC, 7038, 8531, and *Pravda*, Sept. 25, 1939.

12. The final "Count of the Polish Population Deported into the Soviet Union between 1939 and 1941," prepared by the Polish Ministry of Foreign Affairs in London on March 15, 1944, specifies one category as prisoners of war—180,000 of them (HI, PGC, Box 588, "Obliczenie ludności polskiej deportowanej do ZSSR w latach od 1939 do 1941"). Many Polish army soldiers successfully evaded capture in September 1939 in the territories occupied by the Soviets; many were captured and released before the outbreak of the Soviet-German war; and finally, many escaped across the frontier. Altogether, I think, we could double the POW estimate from the Foreign Ministry document and take 360,000 as a reasonable, even conservative, approximation of the total number of Polish soldiers who were at one time or another within the area of Red Army operations in September 1939.

13. HI, PGC, 2628.

14. Łuck, 2.

15. HI, PGC, 747.

16. GSHI, File "KOP, Pułk 'Sarny.' "

17. GSHI, File "KOP, Brygada 'Polesie.' "

18. Kazimierz Klidzia's adventure near Skidel (Białystok voivodeship) must have been fairly typical of these early days. Some soldiers, an officer, and civilians were traveling in a few cars toward Grodno. Near Skidel they were stopped by a mob of 300 peasants. Shots were fired; they were dragged from the automobiles and brought to town. On the way a young lieutenant was struck periodically, but a man in the crowd wielding a revolver appealed for calm, and the officer was not lynched. They were then held under guard in the gmina seat. Tension subsided somewhat, peasants passing by came to look them over, to strike up a conversation, and the prisoners were even fed. On the afternoon of the next day, September 19th, a unit of the Polish army came into town. Set free, the soldiers joined with the army in wiping out "the band" (HI, AC, 11233). See also YV, 03/1284, for an episode from Kruszówka near Kowel, where a number of Belorussian peasants were killed by a Polish army detachment that was passing through.

19. Interview with Mirosław Łabuńka, Philadelphia, Spring 1981.

20. HI, PGC, 8120.

21. HI, PGC, 10094.

22. Zdołbunów, 3.

23. HI, AC, 12644. Ogoński continues his account: "The mayor didn't call us anymore because, as it later turned out, he was arrested immediately after the Bolsheviks came into town. . . . Around nine in the morning one of the voyts from a gmina on the Soviet border called to tell about a column of the Red Army marching gaily and singing, and the soldiers greeting the population with gestures of friendship and fraternity. So the whole population received the Soviet army as if it had come to help the Polish army, and on a few occasions flowers were handed to Soviet commanders." On deliberate deceptions

practiced by the Red Army, including its marching preceded by military bands, see the excellent study of Polish-Soviet relations in 1939–1941 by Col. Roman Umiastowski, *Russia and the Polish Republic, 1918–1941*, esp. pp. 173–174.

24. HI, PGC, 4102, 7568, 10015, 10204, 3435, 7557, 10204; AC, 4307.

25. HI, PGC, 3435.

26. Drohobycz, 1. See also Gross and Gross, *War Through Children's Eyes*, doc. 2, 77.

27. See, for example, wilno-troki, 3; mołodeczno, 2; postawy, 3, 6; dzisna, 1; brasław, 1; nieśwież, 10; łuniniec, 3; wilno, 4; wilejka, 3; kosów poleski, 1; równe, 2; kowel, 1; zdołbunów, 4; skałat, 1; łuck, 2; włodzimierz wołyński, 2; pińsk, 2; święciany, II.1; kobryń, 2; dubno, 3; krzemieniec, 2; nadworna, 15.

28. See, for example, nowogródzki, 11; prużana, 1; święciany, II.1; mościska, 3; nadworna, 15; dzisna, 3; oszmiana; nieśwież, 10.

29. Such episodes are reported, for example, from Katrynburg and Krzemieniec in Krzemieniec county (HI, AC, 12394; krzemieniec, 3); from Broszniów (HI, PGC, 7147; dolina, 13); from Kałusz and Stefanówka (HI, PGC, 2650, 8933; kałusz, 1); from Worochta and Jaremcze (nadworna, 18); from Chodorów and Borusów (HI, PGC, 2655; bóbrka, 2); from Złoczów (HI, PGC, 7135); from Radziechów county (HI, PGC, 7159); and from Gaje in Lwów county (UPST, BI/333/2).

30. An interesting account of administrative disorganization and efforts to overcome it was left by a Łańcut county prefect, Józef Mieczysław Staszko, who was evacuated east toward Sokal and attempted to take in hand Sokal county affairs: "Once I realized that everything was falling to pieces and that people had completely lost their heads I decided to safeguard whatever was left, and since the county prefect and the commandant [of the police?] had left Sokal county I assumed authority over the county by telephone from Tartakowo [an estate nine kilometers from Sokal] since there was a telephone on the estate and I could not reach Sokal anymore because I had no means of transportation, no gasoline, and anyway Ukrainian bands were already terrorizing the countryside. When I found out that Ukrainians, having armed themselves, ambush and disarm on the roads small military and police units, that they rob and kill the refugees and even assault police stations I ordered the police—wherever there was a substantial Polish population—to stay in their compounds. I instructed them also to cease patrolling because there were not enough of them. In addition, in order to fight the bands, I was trying to establish larger groups from police units that were passing by, but I was not obeyed. In any case, until the arrival of regular Bolshevik units, those colonies where police stations were manned had not been assaulted by the bands" (HI, AC, 8027).

31. HI, AC, "Mój pamiętnik."

32. HI, PGC, 4047, 4599, 5313, 6932; AC, 6941.

33. See, for example, HI, PGC, 4047, 4106, 6923, 7606; AC, 6941. In Horochów (Wołyń voivodeship) this concern, we are told, united Polish and

Ukrainian intelligentsia ("though the latter was not very numerous") into the town's Citizens' Guard. High school youth were active in it too (HI, PGC, 7606).

34. HI, PGC, 986, 5313, 9722; Poland. Ambasada USSR, Box 33, Franciszek Pawlak, Box 46, Piotr Halicki; UPST, BI/3333/2, BI/104.

35. Edward Skowron, a student at the Lwów Polytechnical School, joined the Citizens' Guard on September 11 and stayed in what was by then already a militia until October 31, when he escaped from Lwów altogether. HI, PGC, 986, 5313; UPST, BI/104.

36. HI, PGC, 4047.

37. HI, AC, 14463; Poland. Ambasada USSR, Box 48, illegible signature.

38. See, for example, HI, PGC, 3818; GSHI, Polskie Siły Powietrzne Collection, File 9, Tadeusz Nowiński.

39. HI, PGC, 7301, 8920, 9039; AC, 10685; YV, 03/1178.

40. See, for example, białostocki, 4; mołodeczno, 7; postawy, 6; dzisna, 5; nieśwież, 14; szczuczyn, 3; wilejka, 5; kosów poleski, 3; dobromil, 2; drohobycz, 2; krzemieniec, 3; skałat, 6.

41. See, for example, białostocki, 3; Białystok, 3, 4; sokolski, 9; mołodeczno, 5, 9; postawy, 5; dzisna, 4; brasław, 3; prużana, 2; nadworna, 17; dubno, 3; łuck, 5; lida, 2, 3 (Jews); szczuczyn, 1; postawy, 5; nowogródzki, 10, 11; wilejka, 5 (Belorussians); mościska, 2; sambor, 6; bóbrka, 2; kowel, 7; horochów, 2; skałat, 5; luboml, 2; stryj, 10 (Ukrainians).

42. HI, Poland. Ambasada USSR, Box 46, Stanisława Kwiatkowska; Box 47, Alicja Sierańska; PGC, 3194, 4060, 7508; nieśwież, 13; postawy, 5; wilejka, 5; sokolski, 9; kołomyja, 22; kostopol, 5.

43. HI, AC, 12463. See also, for example, HI, AC, 12459, 12460, 12461, 12462, 14458; interview with Omeljan Pritzak, Cambridge, Mass., Spring 1981; YV, 03/1293.

44. Interview with Lev Shankovsky, Philadelphia, Spring 1981. See also HI, AC, 4179, 15543, 15545; PGC, Box 131, palestinian protocol no. 123; turka, 2; interview with Mirosław Łabuńka, Philadelphia, Spring 1981.

45. Kubijovych, *The Ukrainians in the Generalgouvernement, 1939–1941*, pp. 47, 60, 182; drohobycz, 2; przemyśl, 5; YV, 03/2309.

46. HI, PGC, 8570.

47. YV, 03/2309, 03/1791; drohobycz, 2; HI, PGC, Box 131, palestinian protocol no. 187. See also *Sefer Sokolkah*, p. 344.

48. HI, PGC, Box 131, palestinian protocol no. 120, 123; YV, 03/666, 03/1327, 03/2148, 03/2127, 03/1323; Gross and Gross, *War Through Children's Eyes*, doc. 118, 120; *Sefer Sokolkah*, p. 346; HI, AC, 15545.

49. HI, AC, 15543.

50. HI, Poland. Ambasada USSR, Box 48, Barbara Lejowa.

51. HI, PGC, 3093.

52. HI, PGC, 3584, 3930; włodzimierz wołyński, 4; mołodeczno, 5; dzisna, 3; oszmiana; Wilno, 6.

53. See, for example, białostocki, 3; Białystok, 4; wilno-troki, 2;

mołodeczno, 5, 6; postawy, 5; nieśwież, 13; lida, 3; pińsk, 7; łuniniec, 5; święciany, I.1; wilejka, 5; sambor, 6; Gross and Gross, *War Through Children's Eyes*, doc. 15, 39.

54. HI, PGC, 3930.

55. HI, PGC, 6368, 7141, 8694, 8810; AC, 12461; Poland. Ambasada USSR, Box 47, Tadeusz Dworakowski; Box 51, Marian Siedlecki; przemyśl, 4; święciany, II.2.

56. See, for example, mołodeczno, 5; oszmiana; nowogródzki, 10; kołomyja, 22; dubno, 3; łuck, 5; kałusz, 1, 2; horochów, 2.

57. Interview with Celina Konińska, Tel Aviv, Winter 1980.

58. As soon as news of the Red Army's crossing of the frontier reached Mirosław Łabuńka's village in Brzeżany county, several young men from OUN appeared at his father's farm, armed with scythes, knives, and pitchforks, on their way to slaughter ("rżnąć") the Poles. They almost killed the old peasant when he refused to go along (interview with Mirosław Łabuńka, Philadelphia, Spring 1981). In Brzeżany county and the counties of Luboml and Nowogródek there was somehow more violence than in other parts of the invaded territory.

59. The original text of such a leaflet from the commander of the Belorussian front, with its misspellings, grammatical errors, and Russicisms, is reproduced in J. T. Gross, "W zaborze sowieckim," pp. 20–21.

60. HI, PGC, 1325, 2713, 8486; łuck, 9; Gross and Gross, *War Through Children's Eyes*, doc. 85.

61. Mołodeczno, 10. In a Łuck county village Lucjan Malinowski witnessed a speech by a Soviet political commissar who arrived with the first wave of Red Army soldiers: " 'Listen citizens, you shouldn't kill people or rob them. With us all citizens are equal, irrespective of ethnicity.' And when he was leaving he threw tracts from his car which read like this: Grazhdane nastupilo vashe vremia kto komu vinovat s nim roschitaites' za to nichevo ne budet [Citizens, your time has come. If you have a grudge against anybody, square your accounts. You will not be held responsible]. And from this moment robberies and killings began" (HI, PGC, 2413). For other episodes depicting distribution of tracts, consult kostopol, 4; krzemieniec, 6; horochów, 1; luboml, 2; skałat, 1; and łuck, 2.

62. Babii, *Vozzyednanya Zakhidnoi Ukraini s Ukrainskoyu RSR*, pp. 58–59.

63. HI, AC, 7426.

64. HI, Poland. Ambasada USSR, Box 48, Zofia Andruszko. Promptly, two Polish policemen were dragged from their apartments and killed. Their corpses were left for two days at the site of execution, and grieving families were not allowed to touch them. See also HI, PGC, 2685, 2887, 2976, 3306.

65. HI, PGC, 5137.

66. HI, PGC, 5531.

67. HI, AC, 7758.

68. Here, for example, is a story reported from Moscow by a naturalized

American who visited his native Russia during collectivization: "There was a well known merchant's son whose wife was on the point of giving birth to a child. The husband went to the chairman of the house committee, a former janitor of his, with the request that they be allowed to remain in the apartment long enough for their baby to be born. Whereupon the former janitor replied: 'Citizen L., all these years you have been drinking our blood, now it is about time we drink a little of yours' " (Hindus, *Red Bread*, pp. 96–97).

69. HI, PGC, 2823.

70. HI, PGC, 2413.

71. See also mołodeczno, 10, 11; postawy, 6; dzisna, 6, 8; nowogródzki, 11; nieśwież, 10, 15; lida, 4; święciany, II.3; kobryń, 16; kosów poleski, 4; kowel, 10; skałat, 6; horochów, 3; łuck, 7; włodzimierz wołyński, 5; kałusz, 8; dolina, 16; stryj, 12.

72. HI, PGC, 10542.

73. HI, Poland. Ambasada USSR, Box 47, Teresa Mickiewiczowa.

74. HI, Poland. Ambasada USSR, Box 46, Józefa Krupa; see also HI, PGC, 2854, 674, 4790, 4158, 9045, 2173, 5028; AC, 1412.

75. HI, Poland. Ambasada USSR, Box 33, Jadwiga Mateuszak.

76. HI, PGC, 615, 985, 3134, 4158, 5214, 6224, 7967, 8536; Poland. Ambasada USSR, Box 46, Zofia Rutyna; AC, 4533; kosów poleski, 5.

77. HI, PGC, 985, 2611, 6224, 7874, 9222, 14290. See also HI, PGC, 11295, as well as reports about villages Nawóz, Sokół, and Prusiatyn in Łuck county (łuck, 9–11); about gmina Werba (dubno, 5); Włodzimierz Wołyński county (p. 8); Jamno (nadworna, 16); Kołomyja county (p. 28); Skidel (szczuczyn, 4); gmina Porzecze and Pohost Zahorodzki (pińsk, 10, 11); gmina Antopol and Dziatkowice (kobryń, 5, 6); gmina Piaski and village Różana (kosów poleski, 4, 5); Kupiatycze (przemyśl, 7); gmina Buhryn (równe, 6). A group of soldiers was killed near Poworsk, 37 settlers near Mokrany, 8 in gmina Hołoby, and 12 in gmina Rożyszcze—all from Kowel county (pp. 5, 13, 14, 15). There were killings also in gmina Kostopol (kostopol, 4). In addition, victims specifically identified as policemen or foresters were killed in Hołody (Bielsk-Podlaski county) (HI, PGC, 8107); in Toporów (Radziechów county) (HI, PGC, 10129); near Choroszcz (białostocki, 6); in Mołodeczno (p. 11); in Polanica (dolina, 18); and in Dołpatów and Podhorki (kałusz, 11, 12).

78. A civil servant, caught fleeing on a country road, was brought by a local militia to a makeshift jail in the village of Indury (Szczuczyn county). With many others he was held in the basement of a bank cooperative. Each night some prisoners were led away for a beating. "Finally, on the night of 23/24 of September, around midnight, they gave us Soviet justice—they started to shoot us one after another. In a few minutes the whole basement was covered with blood and innocent people were dying on the floor. After superficial inspection whether we were still alive and taking all valuable parts of our garments, our killers left. By some miracle I managed to come out of this grave. Till today I have a bullet in the roof of my mouth, and as a souvenir of Soviet friendship I lost my left eye" (HI, PGC, 2820). On killings perpetrated by militias, see

białostocki, 5; sokolski, 21; mołodeczno, 11; oszmiana; nowogródzki, 16, 17; nieśwież, 16, 20, 21; lida, 13; łuniniec, 9; krzemieniec, 3; luboml, 4; łuck, 4; dubno, 4.

79. Dolina, 19; HI, AC, 11922; PGC, 3106. See also HI, Poland. Ambasada USSR, Box 47, Maria Lewandowska; PGC, 5135; Gross and Gross, *War Through Children's Eyes*, doc. 78.

80. See, for example, kobryń, 16; sarny, 7; stryj, 14; skałat, 18; przemyśl, 15.

81. Równe, 8.

82. An exasperated local resident remembered the beginnings of Soviet administration in Nieśwież: "When somebody complained that he didn't have a cow, [Sirotko] would say go to a landlord or a settler and take one. When a settler came complaining that a cow or a sheep was taken from him, Sirotko said 'why didn't you kill him?'—in a word, he wanted to create the semblance of a revolution" (HI, PGC, 3129; see also PGC, 3162, 10516). On rumors about impending attacks by Poles on Ukrainians and vice versa, see HI, AC, 12642, 12698; PGC, 4451.

83. Mołodeczno, 10; HI, Poland. Ambasada USSR, Box 47, L. Szwacka; PGC, 4842; dzisna, 9.

84. HI, PGC, 688, 2179, 4968, 10688, 11253.

85. See, for example, HI, PGC, 2325, 4286; AC, 12645; dzisna, 5; krzemieniec, 3; dubno, 3; kołomyja, 22, 23; kowel, 9; Białystok, 5, 6; białostocki, 4; sokolski, 10; mołodeczno, 7; postawy, 6; nieśwież, 14; szczuczyn, 3; pińsk, 8; łuniniec, 6; prużana, 2; Wilno, 8; święciany, 1.1; wilejka, 5; kobryń, 3; dobromil, 2; lesko, 2; Zdołbunów, 4; luboml, 2; łuck, 6; włodzimierz wołyński, 5; stryj, 11.

86. HI, PGC, 4067. "Only after the colonists were completely robbed, the order was issued to leave them in peace and to force them to plant crops, and the Soviet authorities will know what to do with them," wrote a farmer from Luboml county (HI, PGC, 8846).

87. Mołodeczno, 6. See also białostocki, 4; HI, PGC, 4107.

88. HI, PGC, 7595.

89. J. T. Gross, *Polish Society under German Occupation*, p. 68.

90. See, for example, HI, PGC, 2253, 4018, 7600, 8925; AC, 12657; mołodeczno, 8; UPST, 3.1.2.1, Januszajtis's report; 3.3.1/5, Macielinski's report.

91. YV, 033/1213.

92. See, for example, HI, PGC, 2611, 3134, 3356, 4032, 8032, 9222.

93. Gross and Gross, *War Through Children's Eyes*, doc. 70.

94. GSHI, File "KOP, Brygada 'Polesie.' "

95. HI, AC, 3510.

96. HI, AC, 4337; also AC, 3352.

97. HI, AC, 4424.

98. HI, AC, 4835.

99. "On the 29th of September, near Szack, Bolsheviks machine-gunned

about 200 officers from various units who were marching together with regiment 'Kleck' and fell into Bolsheviks hands" (GSHI, File "KOP, Pułk 'Sarny' "). "I saw with my own eyes how Soviet soldiers caught a Polish colonel in the street [in Równe], took out his revolver from the holster, shot him with his own revolver, and then left his body lying in the street and went away" (równe, 7). A Soviet tank stopped a car carrying two Polish officers near Jasienów Polny (Horodenka county). They were ordered out, hands up; a Soviet officer came down from the tank and shot them point blank with his revolver. He searched them, took what he liked, mounted the tank, and was on his way in no time (HI, PGC, 7801). See also HI, AC, 1448; Dr. Tadeusz M. Wieliczko, "Okupacja ziem polskich przez Związek Sowiecki;" PGC, 2847, 4367, 5945; mościska, 6; przemyśl, 7; bóbrka, 3; kałusz, 12; zdołbunów, 5; mołodeczno, 4.

100. HI, PGC, 1976, 7107; brasław, 2; nieśwież, 10; wilejka, 3. A captain lying wounded in a Równe hospital was killed in bed when he agreed to turn in his revolver through the intermediacy of a superior officer lying in the same room (krzemieniec, 5).

101. Interview with Mirosław Łabuńka, Philadelphia, Spring 1981.

102. Gross and Gross, *War Through Children's Eyes*, doc. 33.

103. Headquarters of a Soviet regiment stopped for the night on an estate near Chełstowo (Wołkowysk county). "At 5:30 in the morning they brought my aunt [who owned the estate] in front of the porch, they put her against the wall and two officers, one a colonel, stood in front of her. Our entire family— my mother, two sisters, and myself—was ordered to witness the scene from the porch. . . . The colonel first fired his revolver followed by the other officer. My aunt was still standing. Then each fired one more shot and said 'this Polish bitch has a sturdy life' " (HI, AC, Dr. Wieliczko, "Okupacja wschodnich ziem Polski przez Związek Sowiecki," pp. 42–43). For other episodes, see HI, PGC, 4367, 6316, 7789, 8737; AC, 5102; mołodeczno, 4; nowogródzki, 12; szczuczyn, 5; święciany, II.4; lida, 5; bóbrka, 3, 4; krzemieniec, 7; równe, 6; sarny, 52; Gross and Gross, *War Through Children's Eyes*, doc. 3, 56.

104. Gross and Gross, *War Through Children's Eyes*, doc. 17, also 19, 43, 107, 110. See also HI, PGC, 6089; łuniniec, 2; wilejka, 4; skałat, 5; dolina, 13.

105. See, for example, wilejka, 10; horochów, 11; śniatyń, 19; lida, 9; postawy, 13; HI, PGC, 611, 8160; Poland. Ambasada USSR, Box 47, Janina Zawiasa, Aleksandra Nowak; Gross and Gross, *War Through Children's Eyes*, doc. 110.

106. HI, PGC, 8823; AC, 12643; gródek jagielloński, 4.

107. HI, Poland. Ambasada USSR, Box 51, Karol Bartosz; Chudy, "W sowieckim więzieniu w Brześciu nad Bugiem," p. 117.

108. They were not completely reluctant, however. A peasant from Kowel county remembers how the NKVD took away a truckload of Red Army soldiers from in front of a local store (HI, PGC, 6689).

109. GSHI, Polskie Siły Powietrzne Collection, File 11, Marian Siekierski.

110. Gross and Gross, *War Through Children's Eyes*, doc. 46.

111. HI, PGC, 7997, 2380, 7604. "I myself saw," writes another twelve-year-old boy who observed the Soviets' behavior in Dzisna county, "a political officer who went into a store with his wife and she didn't know what to buy. First she bought eight kilograms of sausage. So, how was it? When they first came in, they both couldn't get their fill of the smell; like dogs on the track of a hare, the two of them kept smelling that sausage. He couldn't control his appetite for that sausage very long, he totally lost patience and broke off half for himself and gave half to his wife. As soon as he bit into it his eyes lit up and he said 'vkusnaya kielbasa' [delicious sausage].' But his wife didn't say anything because the sausage made her eyes bulge as she stuffed it down and she only nodded her head three times yes. Not half a minute went by and he ate half the sausage and asked for another one. 'Please if I could have another one,' and the lady who was selling it said, 'Why not, you can have more than two.' Then both of them jumped with joy and she said: 'Eight kilos worth, please.' The saleswoman gave it and he put it anywhere he had room, even inside the top of his boots. She bought calves' feet too, which she carried in her hands because she had no place to put it and maybe just because she wanted to show off" (Gross and Gross, *War Through Children's Eyes*, doc. 78, also doc. 19, 67).

112. HI, PGC, 7301, 7615, 8154; GSHI, Polskie Siły Powietrzne Collection, File 7, Kazimierz Gajda; File 9, Tadeusz Nowiński.

113. See for example Gross and Gross, *War Through Children's Eyes*, doc. 77.

114. HI, AC, 10718.

115. HI, PGC, Box 234, Józef Weleszczuk. See also Rudnycka, *Western Ukraine under the Bolsheviks*, pp. 74, 80.

116. Rudnycka, *Western Ukraine under the Bolsheviks*, pp. 34–52; HI, PGC, 7301.

117. HI, PGC, 8925.

118. UPST, 3.1.2.1, Januszajtis's report, Dec. 8, 1939; 3.3.1/5, Macieliński's report, July 4, 1940; HI, PGC, 4018. The truth of these words was demonstrated less than two years later when millions of Red Army soldiers surrendered to the Wehrmacht in the first months of the German offensive.

119. HI, AC, 10685, 14458, 14461; GSHI, Polskie Siły Powietrzne Collection, File 7, Zygmunt Grzesiak; UPST, 3.1.2.1, Januszajtis's report, Dec. 8, 1939; HI, Stanisław Mikołajczyk Collection, "Białystok. Areszty, więzienie, śledztwo, obozy, amnestia"; AC, Dr. Wieliczko, "Okupacja wschodnich ziem Polski przez Związek Sowiecki," p. 24. The Red Army contingent in the Western Ukraine and Western Belorussia was drafted primarily from the adjacent territory of the Soviet Ukraine and Belorussia. Jews, Ukrainians, Poles, and Belorussians sent westward wearing Soviet uniforms frequently attached themselves to their "blood brothers" (a theme, ironically, underlined by Soviet propaganda) to give and receive comfort and help, or at least to commiserate, for each ethnic group could look into the past or into the present and see itself as exposed and vulnerable (HI, PGC, 688, 7600).

120. *Nowe Widnokręgi*, no. 2 (1941), p. 3–8.

121. Interview with Celina Konińska, Tel Aviv, Winter 1980.

122. HI, PGC, 10204.

123. Interview, Tel Aviv, Winter 1980. In Łomża, the Soviets immediately "took over the government and municipal buildings together with all the records and documents. Arrests of leading personalities began immediately because the Address Bureau of the City Council was taken over virtually intact" (łomża, 22; see also sokolski, 16).

124. HI, PGC, 1594, 8656; równe, 10; zdołbunów, 17; kowel, 55; Białystok, 8, 13.

125. Ostrovski, *How the Steel Was Tempered*, pp. 229–230

126. For example, in Lipina (sokolski, 10), Jaszuny (wilno-troki, 2), Smorgonie (oszmiana), Brasław (brasław, 3), Siniawka (nieśwież, 16–18), Sielec (lida, 4), Dywin (kobryń, 3), Różana (kosów poleski, 2), Chodorów (bóbrka, 2), Opalin (luboml, 3), Horochów (horochów, 2), Cuman (łuck, 13)—to mention just a few villages and small towns in different counties and voivodeships.

127. "At the beginning the local authorities (the committee and the militia) changed constantly and many members fled to Germany," wrote a locksmith from Potylicz (Rawa Ruska county) (HI, PGC, 11132). "Committees changed several times during the first month—90 percent of them were arrested" (Brasław county) (HI, PGC, 1036). "At the time of my arrest, only the worst individuals still remained in the militia. The majority of the local people who had joined it originally had been arrested and deported along with everybody else" (łomża, 16). See also HI, AC, 12655; mościska, 4; dolina, 30.

128. See, for example, HI, PGC, 1188, 3316, 3593.

129. YV 033/1312.

130. Sokolski, 16.

131. Babel, "Berestechko," in *The Collected Stories*, pp. 119–121

132. HI, PGC, 3426; pińsk, 12.

133. Sokolski, 16, 19; krzemieniec, 12; nieśwież, 31.

134. Interview with Petro Mirchuk and Mirosław Łabunka, Philadelphia, Spring 1981. See also HI, PGC, 4108; AC, 4843; nadworna, 22; lesko, 10; Babii, *Vozzyednanya Zakhidnoi Ukraini s Ukrainskoyu RSR*, p. 63. "Ukrainians were trying to use the opportunity by collecting weapons thrown away by the army and joining the militia in large numbers. Within the militia, confrontations were taking place between Poles and Ukrainians, sometimes more than only verbal" (UPST, BI/333/2).

135. See, for example, HI, AC, 9606, 12463, 12656; PGC, 10049; szczuczyn, 14; sokolski, 19; mościska, 4; łomża, 11; dobromil, 8.

136. Dobromil, 8.

137. See, for example, HI, AC, 12655; PGC, 9606, 10047, 10049; sambor, 10; szczuczyn, 14; łomża, 11; mościska, 4; białostocki, 10.

138. HI, PGC, 9606, 6307; nowogródzki, 25; mościska, 4; Babii, *Vozzyednanya Zakhidnoi Ukraini s Ukrainskoyu RSR*, p. 62.

139. *Pravda*, Oct. 2, 4, 5, 1939; Babii, *Vozzyednanya Zakhidnoi Ukraini s Ukrainskoyu RSR*, p. 64.

140. "The Red militia was mostly composed of scum and craftsmen's helpers" (HI, Poland. Ambasada USSR, Box 47, Jan Katarzyński). "In the militia there were a newspaper boy and street urchins" (sambor, 9). "The local militia had no education, and when they checked documents they would hold them upside down and then return them very pleased with themselves" (HI, PGC, 7434). "In the revkom sat and ruled youngsters with absolutely no education, morals, or scruples. In normal times their place would be in a juvenile detention center" (HI, PGC, 8449). About minority youth in village committees and militias, see, for example, mołodeczno, 13; oszmiana; nieśwież, 17; prużana, 2, 8; wilno, 17; równe, 10; święciany, 1.3; nowogródzki, 16; lesko, 9; krzemieniec, 39; zdołbunów, 8; horochów, 5.

141. In his Lwów prison cell Aleksander Wat met a Ukrainian safecracker, a lawyer by training, who had volunteered for the militia with a group of associates immediately after the Soviets entered Lwów. He was appointed deputy commander of the Zamarstynów precinct under a Soviet officer who was taken on the group's payroll. They would go around town at night, like a squad of militia on assignment, and remove merchandise from sealed warehouses filled with goods impounded by the Soviet authorities (Wat, *Mój Wiek*, 1: 353–354). For evidence about criminals in the militia and village committees, see, for example, białostocki 9; Białystok, 11; mołodeczno, 16; postawy, 7; dzisna, 8; brasław, 11; nowogródzki, 14; nieśwież, 18; szczuczyn, 4, 12, 13; łuniniec, 7, 8; kobryń, 9; lubaczów, 5; sambor, 9; krzemieniec, 12; kostopol, 7; horochów, 4, 5; łuck, 12; sarny, 6; dubno, 8; kołomyja, 32; dolina, 30.

142. UPST, 3.3.1./5, Macieliński's report, July 4, 1940.

143. See, for example, HI, AC, 14458; PGC, 2614, 6142, 7897, 10026; zdołbunów, 6; białostocki, 9. Khrushchev deplored that Soviet authorities had released Ukrainian nationalists from Polish prisons—the very political prisoners whose cause the Red Army was to champion, according to the "national liberation" justification of the invasion (*Khrushchev Remembers*, pp. 139–141.

144. HI, PGC, 2524.

145. HI, PGC, 3426, 2727, 1597, 6634.

146. See, for example, HI, PGC, 9648, 2609, 6817, 8032, 9156, 9345, 10026, 10273, 2614, 4169, 6142, 7897; AC, 14458; gródek jagielloński, 5; białostocki, 9, 10; sambor, 10; łomża, 11. See also Umiastowski, *Russia and the Polish Republic*, p. 248.

147. HI, PGC, 6689.

148. See, for example, łomża, 18; białostocki, 13; sokolski, 15; ostrołęka, 4; wilno-troki, 6; postawy, 12; brasław, 6, 7; nieśwież, 26, 27; lida, 8; pińsk, 17; łuniniec, 15, 16; wilno, 17; święciany, II.7; wilejka, 15; kobryń, 11, 12; mościska, 10; sambor, 14, 15; przemyśl, 16; kowel, 21; krzemieniec, 15; horochów, 10; dolina, 24.

149. Among the first ordinances routinely announced immediately after the entrance of occupation forces into any locality was the call to surrender weapons, and by the time of the first house search people had usually either complied with it, thrown the weapons away, or hidden them. See, for example, lida, 8; lubaczów, 7; zdołbunów, 10; skałat, 11; horochów, 10; łuck, 23; dubno, 11; nadworna, 24; krzemieniec, 14; sanok, 5.

150. Szczuczyn, 8.

151. Kobryń, 12.

152. HI, PGC, 5003.

153. Postawy, 12. From Władysław Szpak's house in Olszanica (Lesko county) eight pillows and two blankets were taken during a search; from a railroadman in Wilno, "2000 złoty and other golden trinkets," and from a shoemaker's home, "a bicycle and a suitcase"; from somebody else's house, wedding rings. Piotr Krot on a similar occasion lost "2000 złoty, 10 pairs of silk stockings, and 2 Roskop watches"; and such complaints could be heard from all over the Western Ukraine and Western Belorussia (kosów poleski, 8; wilno, 17; białostocki, 13; HI, PGC, 6618, 10451).

154. Gródek jagielloński, 9; łuniniec, 8; wilejka, 15.

155. Kosów poleski, 9.

156. Dolina, 24.

157. Expropriations in these days were very thorough: people had the boots taken off their feet and the shirts off their backs. Anna Wiltowska saw her household stripped of all valuables over a six-week period following her husband's arrest. In the end they even took his boots, which she was wearing, threw her and the children out of the house, and ordered her to live in the chicken coop (HI, Poland. Ambasada USSR, Box 46). See also, for example, HI, PGC, 5231, 7954, 9073; lida, 8; zdołbunów, 9; horochów, 9; nadworna, 24; wilno, 17; kołomyja, 32; wilno-troki, 6; równe, 13, 14; Białystok, 14; żydaczów, 11; kowel, 20; śniatyń, 18; kałusz, 17; pińsk, 17; łomża, 16, 18; łuniniec, 8; łuck, 23.

158. Nieśwież, 25.

159. See, for example, dzisna, 11; święciany, II.6; dobromil, 6; sambor, 12, 13; gródek jagielloński, 8, 9; bóbrka, 9; krzemieniec, 9; kostopol, 6; śniatyń, 17; włodzimierz wołyński, 9, 10; wilejka, 13, 14; rudki, 7; ostrów, 7; łomża, 22.

160. See, for example, białostocki, 14; dzisna, 12; przemyśl, 21; równe, 5; kowel, 19; ostrów, 7.

161. Białystok, 17.

162. HI, Poland. Ambasada USSR, Box 48, Józefa Pożogowa, Wanda Kotowska; PGC 4782.

163. HI, Poland. Ambasada USSR, Box 48, Witold Białkowski; PGC, 7980.

164. Łomża, 7–9.

165. See, for example, HI, PGC, 6589; postawy, 10; łuniniec, 10; rudki, 5.

166. See, for example, HI, Poland. Ambasada USSR, Box 48, Witold

Białkowski; PGC, 6590, 10283; wilno-troki, 3; rudki, 6; łomża, 7–9; Białystok, 7, 8; drohobycz, 5.

167. "I personally witnessed how the TSL's [Society of People's School] and the school library were burned in the fields out of town [Rudki]" (HI, PGC, 6589). "Then they announced that within five days everybody must bring all Polish books, newspapers, and periodicals, which were later burned in front of the gmina seat in the politruk's presence [Barany, Horochów county]" (HI, PGC, 10336). See also HI, PGC, 6590, 10283; wilejka, 11.

168. HI, PGC, 8669.

169. HI, PGC, 1137.

170. HI, Poland. Ambasada USSR, Box 48, Witold Białkowski; wilejka, 11; łomża, 7–9; mołodeczno, 13; białostocki, 6, 7; rudki, 6; wilno-troki, 3; ostrów, 7.

171. Święciany, II.2.

172. HI, PGC, 611; wilno-troki, 7; dzisna, 14; ostrów, 4; lida, 9. "On September 24, the day after they took over, our village was ordered to send baked bread and cloth for the army. We complied with the order, every house baking a loaf and sending two meters of cloth. From that day quotas were imposed on our village—for foodstuffs, meat, milk, etc." (HI, PGC, 4899). See also, for example, łomża, 15; ostrów, 4; lida, 9; szczuczyn, 9.

173. HI, PGC, 2484.

174. HI, PGC, 2062, 2426, 8816; postawy, 13.

175. Throughout the early 1930s, forced collectivization devastated the countryside in the USSR, causing, among other calamities, hunger in the Soviet Ukraine, which claimed several million victims. See also Robert Conquest, *The Harvest of Sorrow*.

176. Even when their lives were spared, those whose land was taken away were brutalized, sometimes beyond endurance. Thus, a certain Andrzej Safron who owned 12 hectares in Borowo village (Postawy county) and had a family of 10 to provide for lost his mind when stripped of the farm on October 3, 1939 (HI, PGC, 6126).

177. See, for example, HI, AC, 6331. Not that the people's verdicts were necessarily implemented. In Nesterowce (Zborów county, Tarnopol voivodeship), for example, the Soviet commander asked an assembled group of farm laborers on such an occasion what to do with the landowner: " 'Do you want us to leave him here, or shall we take him away?' and the assembled crowd unanimously asked that he be left in his place. Then the Soviet stood up and said: 'kak vy khochete eyo ostavit', tak my eyo zavtra utrom zaberiom' [if you want him to stay, then we will take him away tomorrow morning]" (HI, PGC, 1876). And he was true to his word.

178. HI, PGC, 631, 8579.

179. HI, PGC, 10094.

180. See, for example, HI, PGC, 1876, 2287, 7900, 9365, 10049; sokolski, 25; łomża, 34, 36; wilno-troki, 9; nowogródzki, 26; nieśwież, 35.

181. See, for example, HI, PGC, 968, 5058, 10554; mościska, 13; mołodeczno, 11; oszmiana.
182. Luboml†, 10.
183. HI, PGC, 2788.
184. Kołomyja, 26.
185. Białostocki, 10; see also HI, PGC, 6618.
186. HI, PGC, 2651, 5010, 2599; luboml, 3.
187. Babii, *Vozzyednanya Zakhidnoi Ukraini s Ukrainskoyu RSR*, p. 65.
188. HI, PGC, 6035.
189. HI, PGC, 14.
190. HI, PGC, 2738, 8007, 9056; AC, 12645; sarny, 6.
191. HI, PGC, 9436.
192. HI, PGC, 5010.
193. HI, PGC, 4856. See also HI, AC, 14461; PGC, 6035; zdołbunów, 6.

Two: Elections

1. The sequence of elections in the Wilno district was different, conforming to the timetable for incorporation of the Baltic states.

2. In this respect they succeeded brilliantly. Not even the Polish government declared war on the Soviet Union. Why, I cannot tell with certainty, for an open act of war had been committed by the USSR against Poland. The decomposition of the Polish government in the days immediately following its flight to Rumania on September 17, the very day of the Soviet invasion, may have been partly responsible for the lack of immediate reaction. Then, too, pressure from Poland's allies may have been a factor. Upon learning of the Soviet invasion of Poland, Sir William Seeds, the British ambassador in Moscow, cabled the Foreign Office: "I do not myself see what advantage war with the Soviet Union would be to us, though it would please me personally to declare it on Mr. Molotov" (PRO, 371/23103). His advice was followed in London; and the Poles, when they finally reorganized the government, may have been pressed to do likewise.

3. Unfortunately I have been unable to obtain any newspaper from Western Belorussia, only the *Czerwony Sztandar* (Red Banner) printed in Lwów (Western Ukraine). Thus my references to the official history of the elections in Western Belorussia are derived either from the information appearing in the all-union newspaper *Pravda* or from secondary sources, in particular Edward Bonatt's "International Law and the Plebiscites in Eastern Poland, 1939," and Wiktor Sukiennicki's "The Establishment of the Soviet Regime in Eastern Poland in 1939."

4. Eduardas Turauskas, who was director of the Political Division in the Lithuanian Ministry of Foreign Affairs, wrote that Soviet-Lithuanian negotiations concerning the stationing of Soviet garrisons on Lithuanian territory and the return of Wilno and adjoining areas were difficult. A Lithuanian delegation that went to Moscow on October 3 flew back home the next day, discouraged

by Moscow's insistence on stationing troops in Lithuania. It returned on the 7th with a counterproposal, met with Stalin on the 8th, but failed to persuade him. On the 9th some members of the delegation flew back to Kaunas, and later the delegation was authorized by the cabinet in Kaunas to sign the treaty with the Soviet Union. They returned to Moscow on October 10. Turauskas, "Communist Diplomacy Exposed."

5. Bonatt, "International Law and the Plebiscites in Eastern Poland," pp. 384–385.

6. A few requirements were violated, especially those concerning the statutory lapse of time between some preliminary steps (such as the formation of election precincts and official confirmation of central election commissions) and the scheduled election date. Vyshinskii, ed., *The Law of the Soviet State*, pp. 703–705.

7. Ibid. pp. 672, 685, 693.

8. *Czerwony Sztandar*, Oct. 14, 19, 1939.

9. This assignment was not prescribed by electoral law, but organizers seemed to hope that the example of these agitators would inspire a spontaneous initiative on the part of politically conscious citizens. "Not only trained agitators but everybody who feels up to it should go among the workers, peasants, and the working intelligentsia and talk with everybody about the Soviet constitution," appealed J. Stein in "Everybody's Duty" (*Czerwony Sztandar*, Oct. 15, 1939).

10. Witnesses from many localities report that neighbors were forcibly put on electoral commissions; see, for example, łomża, 45; brasławski, 16; lida, 21; szczuczyn, 21; lesko, 15; sanok, 14. For candidates who were nominated against their will, see HI, PGC, 4327, 4849; szczuczyn, 23. See also HI, PGC, 2965, 3036.

11. *Czerwony Sztandar*, Oct. 6, 1939. See also *Pravda*, Oct. 5, 1939.

12. Vyshinskii, ed., *The Law of the Soviet State*, p. 724.

13. *Czerwony Sztandar*, Oct. 6, 1939.

14. Równe†, 12; HI, PGC, 9738. See, for example, Białystok, 33; łomża, 26; pińsk, 33; skałat, 22; łuck, 41; łuniniec, 25; kosów poleski, 19; kobryń†, 24; ostrołęka, 7; wilejka, 24; drobhobycz, 25; dobromil, 13; prużana, 17; mościska, 18. Józef Syćko, a worker from Budy near Baranowicze, recalls a pre-election meeting: "A disfigured eagle with downcast wings was put on stage, and a drawing of General Sikorski [prime minister of the Polish government-in-exile] climbing a ladder and begging assistance from 'a whore,' France. In the next drawing Sikorski was on the floor next to a broken ladder, without any help of course. These drawings were supplemented by a teasing and malicious narrative. Then a Communist activist, Szejko Stefan, came on stage and swept the eagle, drawings, and the Polish flag with broom, and the Soviet flag and portraits of Lenin, Stalin, and others were brought in. Such meetings, organized by Communist activists and stage-managed by the NKVD, were rather often shown in factories" (HI, PGC, 2960).

15. Wilejka, 23; bóbrka, 16; jaworów, 19; kowel, 33; skałat, 23.

16. See, for example, *Pravda*, Oct. 13, 14, 1939, and *Czerwony Sztandar*, Oct. 15, 18, 1939, for coverage of large meetings in the movie theater Apollon in Białystok and in the Collegium Maximum, the City Theater, and the Great Theater in Lwów. They were usually well managed, and not much was allowed to happen there besides a string of prepared speeches. But at least one such meeting, at the Lwów Polytechnical School, ended in a bloody confrontation. Probably the audience was deliberately set up. In any case, after a shouting match between some speakers and the audience, a fistfight erupted, which led to the brutal intervention of Red Army soldiers and NKVD operatives, who turned out to be present in large numbers. Many people were arrested, and it appears that even some shots were fired in the room (HI, PGC, 3458).

17. Nieśwież, 30.

18. HI, Poland. Ambasada USSR, Box 48, Maria Saja; nowogródzki, 29.

19. In the March 1940 elections, in the Western Ukraine alone, there were "over 100,000 agitators," according to Soviet historian I. Ia. Kosharnyi (*U suziri sotsialistichnoi kulturi*, p. 39).

20. HI, PGC, 2318, 4887, 6581; dolina, 39. Even during the time of Polish sovereignty, teachers as well as the employees of state and local administrations had been important instruments for getting the government's message to the electorate.

21. Among other things, notes were made of people's education, religion, ethnic affiliation, employment history, and military record, though I am not sure that this was a standard procedure everywhere. See HI, PGC, 4887; dolina, 39; postawy, 22; pińsk, 38.

22. HI, PGC, 2318.

23. See, for example, HI, PGC, 7579, 7997, 8449; Poland. Ambasada USSR, Box 46, Stefan Ogrodnik; pińsk, 34; gródek jagielloński, 15; zdołbunów, 54.

24. Jędrychowska, *Zygzakiem i po prostu*, pp. 291ff.; Naszkowski, *Lata próby*, pp. 115, 116, 121; Turlejska, *Prawdy i fikcje*, p. 275; interview with Włodzimierz Brus, Oxford, Summer 1980.

25. Sambor, 23. A lazy postmaster at post office No. 1 in Stanisławów distributed the text of the Soviet constitution to his employees and ordered them to learn it by heart. Later he quizzed them, promising pay hikes to those who passed the exam well (HI, PGC, 7743).

26. Sambor, 24. "They ordered some Pole to come out and tell how he lived and in what conditions he worked in Poland, and if it seemed from his speech that he didn't do so badly, he was arrested a few days later" (HI, PGC, 6130).

27. Interview with Lew Wasyl, New York, 1981. See also, przemyśl, 39; łuck, 41; mołodeczno, III.3.

28. HI, PGC, 7579.

29. See, for example, Białystok, 24; żydaczów, 17; sambor, 26; drohobycz, 28; przemyśl, 43; zdołbunów, 64; pińsk, 38.

30. Jaworów, 22.

31. See, for example, łomża, 47; białystok, 39; wilejka, 29; lida, 22; sambor,

27; lubaczów, 21; brasławski, 17; mołodeczno, III.9; drohobycz, 30; przemyśl, 43; zdołbunów, 64.

32. Minors were registered in gmina Jasienica (ostrów, 14), in Kapce (wilejka, 29), in gimna Brodnica (pińsk, 38), in gmina Rudniki (prużana, 20), in Laszki (lubaczów, 32), in Bar (gródek jagielloński, 18), in Wolica and Wawelówka (skałat, 28), and in gmina Dederkały (krzemieniec†, 21).

33. Białystok, 38; lida, 32; przemyśl, 43.

34. Białystok, 39. See also for Lwów, HI, PGC, 7047; przemyśl, 61; horochów, 27.

35. Łuck, 45; dolina, 38; pińsk, 38; oszmiana.

36. Sanok, 16.

37. Śniatyń, 28; nowogródzki, 29; dubno, 58; drohobycz, 24.

38. HI, PGC, 1401; łomża, 40; postawy, 9; nieśwież, 39; sambor, 23.

39. Łomża, 43; przemyśl, 39; śniatyń, 29.

40. Dzisna, 22; pińsk, 33; bóbrka, 16; krzemieniec, 56; Białystok, 34; drohobycz, 24.

41. See, for example, wilejka, 25; mołodeczno, III.5; nowogródzki, 29; szczuczyn, 17; pińsk, 33; gródek jagielloński, 15; mościska, 18; równe†, 24.

42. Kostopol†, 13; równe†, 24; skałat, 23, 24; oszmiana; krzemieniec†, 19. On a few occasions Polish colonists were explicitly *excluded* from pre-election meetings. "This produced among the Poles an atmosphere of being condemned to death or at least of having been excluded from normal life and thrown to a mob to be done away with" (HI, PGC, 688; see also nowogródzki, 30).

43. Łomża, 40; Białystok, 33; dobromil, 13; brasławski, 15; kobryń, 24; postawy, 19; białostocki, 21; ostrołęka, 6; mołodeczno, III.5, 6; dzisna, 23; szczuczyn, 18; lida, 19; łuniniec, 25.

44. Białystok, 43; białostocki, 22; równe†, 22; sambor, 23; bóbrka, 16; łuck, 43; horochów, 21; nadworna, 31.

45. Kobryń, 25; przemyśl, 38; kowel, 35; nieśwież, 38.

46. Oszmiana; kobryń, 35.

47. Drohobycz, 24. See also Białystok, 24; żydaczów, 17; sambor, 26; drohobycz, 28; przemyśl, 43; zdołbunów, 64; pińsk, 38.

48. Krzemieniec†, 20; sokolski, 28; włodzimierz wołyński, 20.

49. *Czerwony Sztandar* (Oct. 21, 1939) printed an utterly surrealist description of a pre-election meeting. As with all idealizations, it unwittingly discloses the frightening character that meetings must have had in reality:

"A knock on the door. Somebody enters the apartment. He is a worker, or maybe from the intelligentsia. He asks for everybody who lives on this floor to be brought over to the apartment. It's the neighborhood man of confidence who organizes a building's meeting.

"It's worth seeing how briskly all floor residents come together. Housewives, civil servants, students, the superintendent get into the room. They all sit around the table and the man of confidence begins his talk. They listen carefully because they know that here is a man of confidence in the neighborhood to whom this noble task was entrusted by thousands of people. He doesn't deliver a matter-of-fact speech. He speaks as if with friends about the new life, about voting procedures, about nationality problems. And words flow as if directly from his heart and to the hearts of the listeners. A building meeting is general conversation, where everybody speaks. It is not that the man of confidence simply answers some questions. One person answers another, and they share thoughts.

"The sincere wish to remove the ruins remaining after the brutal rule of the Polish bourgeois clique dominates the conversation. Harsh words of criticism and denunciation of the hated Polish masters are often heard during these meetings. People are reluctant to talk about this anymore, they want to forget everything as soon as possible. New times have arrived, awaited for so long. Let us build and celebrate.

"The atmosphere of apartment house meetings is friendly. People from different milieus meet to discuss together matters that affect them all. We are all going to vote fully aware that we are building a new, happy life. We want to unite with the Soviet Ukraine—this is the conclusion of all building meetings."

50. HI, PGC, 2594.

51. HI, PGC, 6590.

52. HI, PGC, 4450, 5146 (Lwów); drohobycz, 24; łomża, 41; Białystok, 32.

53. HI, PGC, 4796.

54. HI, PGC, 7624.

55. As Bronisław Kender from Brześć put it, "There were always quarrels and arrests during propaganda meetings because of protests against the speeches of politruks" (HI, PGC, 2198; see also PGC, 2181; Białystok, 43; sokolski, 29, 35; nieśwież, 38; mołodeczno, III.5; nowogródzki, 30, 35; przemyśl, 38; lesko, 13; łuck, 43; śniatyń, 27). Such confrontations were not uncommon, though to say that "there were always quarrels" is certainly an exaggeration. But in gmina Widze (Wilno viovodeship), for example, the NKVD had to send a second team of propagandists after the first group made fools of themselves (HI, PGC, 11074). In Wołkowysk (Białystok viovodeship), a well-known horse thief was teaching Stalin's constitution at propaganda meetings. "He made a fool of himself and of the Soviet authorities that had appointed him. And there were many like that" (HI, PGC, 1990). A miller from Mościska county (Lwów voivodeship) recalled an amusing episode: "When one of the local speakers started to praise the USSR, his wife, who was in the audience, grabbed a fence pole and gave him a solid beating, after which the humiliated and laughed-at husband called the militia. She was arrested and got a two-year sentence as a result" (HI, PGC, 2224). Clearly, the lot of a propagandist was not always enviable.

56. See, for example, białostocki, 21; nowogródzki, 29; szczuczyn, 17, 18; rudki, 13; nieśwież, 39; sambor, 24; zdołbunów, 56; drohobycz, 25, 26; lida, 17; pińsk, 33; prużana, 17. *Czerwony Sztandar*, Oct. 18, 21, 1939.

57. Prużana, 17; łuniniec, 25; łuck, 44; dolina, 37; horochów, 21; HI, PGC, 1025, 6708.

58. Sambor, 23; gródek jagielloński, 16; zdołbunów, 56; skałat, 24. This

may have been a more or less routine form of assessment by the Soviet authorities. For an episode from the vicinity of Stołpce, where an identical procedure was followed, see HI, Stanisław Mikołajczyk Collection, Box 9, File "Correspondence, February–May 1940."

59. Horochów, 19; mołodeczno, III.6; HI, PGC, 6844, 7325.

60. Dobromil, 22.

61. See, for example, kałusz, 30; przemyśl, 38; drohobycz, 24; wilejka, 23, 24; nowogródzki, 28; kobryń, 25; krzemieniec, 26.

62. HI, PGC, 2822, 10268; lida, 19; pińsk, 34; kowel, 34; równe†, 20.

63. HI, PGC, 898, 6026, 12461.

64. Nieśwież, 39.

65. HI, PGC, 2376.

66. Lida, 20.

67. HI, PGC, 2212.

68. Kosów poleski, 17; dubno, 52; równe†, 22; nieśwież, 53; bóbrka, 17; łuck, 59; włodzimierz wołyński, 31.

69. Every county report bears witness to the totality of this ignorance. See, for example, łomża, 56, 57; Białystok, 55, 56; wilejka, 40; dzisna, 36, 37; nowogródzki, 39, 40; lida, 16, 17; szczuczyn, 30, 31; pińsk, 29, 30; łuniniec, 39; sambor, 36, 37; przemyśl, 62, 63; bóbrka, 17; skałat, 31; and many others. See also Umiastowski, *Russia and the Polish Republic*, p. 222.

70. Postawy, 25.

71. See, for example, łomża, 49; białostocki, 26; ostrołęka, 9; postawy, 23; mołodeczno, III.8; jaworów, 23; stryj, 29; drohobycz, 33; gródek jagielloński, 19; kowel, 41; dobromil, 15; nowogródzki, 33; kobryń, 30; kosów poleski, 24; prużana, 22; sambor, 28.

72. Szczuczyn, 22.

73. Łuck, 50.

74. Krzemieniec, 67.

75. HI, PGC, 11262; see also PGC, 2577.

76. HI, PGC, 9926.

77. HI, PGC, 2965.

78. HI, PGC, 3063.

79. HI, PGC, 7991.

80. HI, PGC, 615, 2541, 6263, 7174, 7198.

81. HI, PGC, 6263; see also brasławski, 18.

82. See, for example, łomża, 50, 51, 52; białostocki, 25; rudzki, 17; nowogródzki, 33, 34; drohobycz, 31; łuniniec, 30, 31; sambor, 28; łuck, 50; stryj, 29.

83. See, for example, Białystok, 40, 42; białostocki, 25; brasławski, 18; nowogródzki, 23; dobromil, 51; kosów poleski, 25; mościska, 21; łuck, 49; lida, 23; kobryń, 31; skałat, 29; dolina, 41.

84. See, for example, łomża, 48, 49; przemyśl, 45; włodzimierz wołyński, 24; Białystok, 40; lida, 23; łuniniec, 30, 31; kowel, 41; dobromil, 15; prużana, 22; kosów poleski, 24; drohobycz, 31; łuck, 49.

85. For example, łomża, 50, 51; łuniniec, 30; rudki, 17.

86. HI, PGC, 10585.

87. HI, AC, 4491.

88. HI, Poland. Ambasada USSR, Box 51, Feliks Dziewicki; Box 47, Stefania Żurowska; PGC, 707, 1204, 6425, 8695.

89. HI, PGC, 885, 859, 4327; szczuczyn, 23; see also PGC, 7949.

90. The first secretary of the Belorussian CP, Ponomarenko, was in Białystok throughout the election day (*Pravda*, Oct. 23, 1939), and electoral district committees were in *hourly* contact with all precincts, monitoring the fulfillment of voter quotas (pińsk, 48; GSHI, A.9.III.2a, file 58).

91. An almost unique exchange took place at the end of a big meeting in Postawy county when the audience was invited to come forward and speak up. "Dymon, from a neighboring village, stood up and gave a list to the presiding commissar. When asked what this was, he said this was a list of bad people who ought to be removed because they were Polish patriots. The commissar took the list and after a long pause for thought said if there was a State there had to be patriots . . ." (postawy, 20).

92. HI, PGC, 4849; szczuczyn, 23.

93. See, for example, HI, PGC, 2577; łomża, 41; lida, 23; kobryń, 30; prużana, 23; krzemieniec†, 23; równe†, 26; łuck, 49; horochów, 27. Collectivization in the USSR during the 1930s was also "unanimously" endorsed at numerous peasant meetings by silence in response to the question "Who is against Soviet power?" (Davies, *The Socialist Offensive*, pp. 221–222).

94. See, for example, Białystok, 44; dubno, 68; kowel, 44; zdołbunów, 69; postawy, 26; dzisna, 29; szczuczyn, 25; nieśwież, 47; łuniniec, 32; kosów poleski, 25; luboml, 69, 70.

95. HI, PGC, Box 10, Stanisław Widomski; równe†, 29; ostrów, 12.

96. HI, PGC, 10585 (Włodzimierz Wołyński); horochów, 21; łomża, 63, 64; jaworów, 28; Białystok, 51, 52; wilejka, 37; pińsk, 51; nowogródzki, 30; kobryń, 38; brasław, 16.

97. "A więc jutro droga Franiu spotkaj mnie przy głosowaniu"; "każdy dom i każda chata wybierają delegata."

98. See, for example, HI, PGC, 10193, 11316 (Lwów); dubno†, 25, 27; pińsk, 42, 44; wilejka, 34; nowogródzki, 37; lida, 25; kobryń, 32; łuniniec, 33.

99. Ostrów, 17.

100. Równe†, 28.

101. See, for example, równe, 61; łomża, 63; Białystok, 51, 52; ostrów, 20; sokolski, 40; wilejka, 37; dzisna, 33; brasławski, 20; nowogródzki, 37, 38; lida, 27; kobryń, 38; łuniniec, 36; kosów poleski, 32; sambor, 35.

102. See, for example, Białystok, 45, 46; białostocki, 28; ostrów, 17; sokolski, 36; postawy, 27; mołodeczno, III.15; dzisna, 30; nieśwież, 50; nowogródzki, 37; pińsk, 44; kobryń, 32; łuniniec, 33; prużana, 25; sambor, 32; lubaczów, 26; mościska, 23; drohobycz, 37; przemyśl, 48; jaworów, 25; kowel, 45, 46.

103. See, for example, łomża, 54–57, 62; Białystok, 46, 49; białostocki, 31, 32; postawy, 27; dzisna, 24, 25, 30; brasław, 19; nowogródzki, 36; lida, 25; prużana, 25; kosów poleski, 27; dobromil, 17. A ballot box was brought to a group of Jews praying in the Lwów synagogue on Żółkiewska Street, and some 200 votes were thus taken in less than an hour (HI, PGC, 9663).

104. Białostocki, 28.

105. Włodzimierz wołyński, 26.

106. See, for example, łomża 57; pińsk, 55; brzozów, 18; rudki, 18; stryj, 30; luboml†, 12; kostopol†, 18.

107. Kołomyja, 43; równe, 75; wilejka, 25; nieśwież, 52; pińsk, 43; białostocki, 28; ostrów, 9; sambor, 33; krzemieniec, 71; HI, PGC, 2375, 3874, 10396.

108. Kostopol†, 17; szczuczyn, 27. See also łomża, 61; Białystok, 47, 48; białostocki, 30; sokolski, 37, 38; ostrołęka, 11; wilejka, 35; mołodeczno, III.15; brasławski, 19; nowogródzki, 36; szczuczyn, 27; pińsk, 48; sambor, 34; drohobycz, 39; kobryń, 35, 36; dobromil, 19. I know of only one instance—Kiełbasicze, in gmina Kleck, Nieśwież county (nieśwież, 50)—where the polling station was actually destroyed by the local population. Undoubtedly, had this happened anywhere else it would have been eagerly reported, if only to show that one either participated or at least witnessed such a commendable outpouring of patriotism.

109. Horochów, 32.

110. See, for example, łomża, 44; białostocki, 24; sokolski, 31; łuniniec, 27; nowogródzki, 32; nieśwież, 42; oszmiana; brasław, 16; mościska, 19; przemyśl, 41; lubaczów, 20; pińsk, 36; kobryń, 27; skałat, 26, 27; łuck, 46; włodzimierz wołyński, 23.

111. Wilejka, 36.

112. Dzisna, 31.

113. Żydaczów, 19.

114. See, for example, HI, PGC, 2375, 2786; kowel, 48; szczuczyn, 27; nieśwież, 51; kobryń, 36; przemyśl, 53; łuck, 55. A peasant from Kołki (in Łuck county) recalled: "People were brought to places where there was voting by whole villages, but into the polling station they were ushered one by one and asked, 'Will you vote?' " (łuck, 55). In Szczuczyn county "there was one politruk, one NKVD, and one devil with a rifle and some local communists. In addition there was a buffet, selling tea and rolls, musicians with an accordion playing for the voters. Outside a militia armed with rifles was posted. People were let into the voting station one by one. . . . Afterwards one was ordered to drink a cup of tea in the buffet" (szczuczyn, 37).

115. Łuniniec, 37.

116. Łomża, 46; bóbrka, 16; dubno, 74; łuck, 58; przemyśl, 56; HI, PGC, 3149 (Bielsk Podlaski), 7102 (Lida).

117. Pińsk, 47.

118. Inhabitants of Rogowo (białostocki, 30), Tymianki (ostrów, 19), Kulbaczno (wilejka, 36), Adampol (nowogródzki, 37), Kolby (pińsk, 47), Batcze

(kobryń, 35), Pieszczanka (łuniniec, 34), Różana (kosów poleski, 30), Łanowice (sambor, 34), Ryszkowa Wola and Sieniawa (lubaczów, 30), Sułkowszczyzna (mościska, 26), Tuligłowy (rudki, 19), Magdałówka (skałat, 33), Wiśniowiec (krzemieniec†, 27), Rożyszcze (łuck, 56, 57), Orlęta (włodzimierz wołyński, 28), Zuzanówka (żydaczów, 19), and perhaps of many more places all shared this experience.

119. There were quite a few of such precincts, notably in gmina Chotiaczów, Włodzimierz Wołyński county (HI, PGC, 2786), in gmina Boguty (ostrów, 20), in gmina Dzisna (dzisna, 32), in a Pińsk hospital and in gmina Pohost Zahorodzki (pińsk, 47, 49), in Łomża (łomża, 58), in gmina Rudniki and Prużana (prużana, 26), in Nowosiółki (przemyśl, 53), in Omelna and Kolońsk, and in gmina Święta Wola (kosów poleski, 28).

120. Dobromil, 19.

121. Skałat, 35.

122. See, for example, HI, PGC, 6571, 7612, 8722, 9964, 10035, 10047; łomża, 58–60; Białystok, 47; białostocki, 26, 29; ostrów, 19; śniatyń, 36; kałusz, 39; stryj, 32; żydaczów, 19; sokolski, 37; postawy, 29; wilejka, 35, 36; mołodeczno, III.14; dzisna, 33; brasław, 19; nowogródzki, 38; szczuczyn, 27; pińsk, 47; prużana, 27; kosów poleski, 29; sambor, 33, 34; lubaczów, 30; mościska, 25; dobromil, 19; drohobycz, 41; przemyśl, 54; bóbrka, 20; kostopol, 73; zdołbunów, 74; kowel, 50; krzemieniec†, 24; luboml†, 11; dubno†, 27; łuck, 54; sarny, 13; włodzimierz wołyński, 27.

123. See, for example, HI, PGC, 7745; Białystok 48, 57, 58; białostocki, 38; sokolski, 43; wilejka, 42; mołodeczno, III.17; dzisna, 37, 38; brasławski, 22; nowogródzki, 37; lida, 29; szczuczyn, 32; nieśwież, 54; pińsk, 55; łuniniec, 40, 41; kosów poleski, 35; mościska, 27; dobromil, 24; gródek jagielloński, 24; bóbrka, 25; rudki, 21; równe†, 32; dubno†, 30; kowel, 53; łuck, 54, 55, 61; stryj, 39.

124. Łuniniec, 35.

125. Wilejka, 42; oszmiana; dolina, 43.

126. Postawy, 29. As a woman from Radków put it: before a voter could drop his or her ballot into the box, "one of the local Jews took it, read it, and then deposited it himself" (nieśwież, 49). In a similar fashion people voted in gmina Annapol (prużana, 26), in Różana (kosów poleski, 27), in Jaksmanica (przemyśl, 54), in Majdan (drohobycz, 37), somewhere in Gródek Jagielloński county (p. 22), and in gmina Dederkały (krzemieniec†, 27).

127. HI, PGC, 2810; dzisna, 32. See also lubaczów, 30.

128. HI, AC, 78.

129. Kostopol†, 17.

130. See, for example, wilejka, 35; mołodeczno, III.14, 15; drohobycz, 37; krzemieniec, 74; kowel, 48; lida, 26; szczuczyn, 27.

131. Lubaczów, 29.

132. HI, PGC, 8160.

133. "When I entered behind such a partition [in a Złoczów precinct], I noticed that through a hole in the cloth an agent spied on me" (HI, PGC, 3429).

See also łomża 59; Białystok, 48, 49; sokolski, 37; łuck, 54; wilejka, 35; mołodeczno, III.13, 14; pińsk, 47; łuniniec, 35; przemyśl, 53.

134. Three local boys entered the hall through a back door and found them posted there (HI, PGC, 5927).

135. Włodzimierz wołyński, 27; mołodeczno, II.13; dzisna, 32; przemyśl, 55; prużana, 26; kosów poleski, 28.

136. Białostocki, 31; horochów, 32; mołodeczno, III. 14. In Bogusze (Sokółka county), voters kept going behind the partition one after another. A Soviet supervisor finally went in to break all the pencils. But another commission member, Feliks Zarzecki, who had been put on the commission against his will, proceeded to sharpen them. He was told not to interfere, but it did not really matter because people brought their own pencils (HI, PGC, 8835). In one of Szczuczyn precincts a pen and an inkpot were placed on a table behind a partition, but the inkpot was empty (HI, AC, 96).

137. HI, PGC, 8705.

138. Kałusz, 39.

139. To compound their confusion, many voters complained, candidates' names on the ballot were written in Russian, a tongue and alphabet they did not understand. See, for example, prużana, 26; kosów poleski, 28, 29; horochów, 32; przemyśl, 53; drohobycz, 42; krzemieniec†, 27; stryj, 33; lubaczów, 28, 29; dobromil, 18.

One great authority on these matters summarized the voting experience in a lengthy statement that I shall quote here in excerpts: "Particularly illusory is the secret voting . . . electors are persecuted . . . if they take into their heads to discuss the candidates of the official . . . list, to say nothing of proposing candidates of their own. Those who avoid 'elections' are accused of treason and subjected to torture. . . . voters in many districts were given ballots already marked 'Yes,' and in other cases transparent envelopes were used through which their votes could be seen. There was also a practice of giving numbered envelopes whereby it was possible to determine who voted for whom, inasmuch as the envelopes were given out according to a list. Ballot boxes were so constructed that the ballots dropped in them formed in the order in which the votes were given, thus making it possible to establish how a given voter had voted. . . . From information published . . . it is clear that . . . in the election room [there is] one booth, guarded. . . . It is so constructed that [those] who 'guard' it can look freely over the shoulder of the voter and see how he votes . . . and when certain workers voted against . . . they were cruelly beaten."

Who should know better than Andrei Vyshinskii, the former prosecutor general and then deputy commissar for foreign affairs who was the Soviet government's plenipotentiary sent to supervise Lithuania's incorporation. His expertise came from a long career in police apparatus combined with responsibilities in the foreign field. Although he wrote this passage about the 1933 German elections (my deletions were mostly of the words "German," "fascist," and, in one instance, "English paper"), I am sure he did not have to stretch his imagination very much. It is standard occurrence in Communist propaganda to vilify the enemies of the moment by attributing to them precisely what has been practiced by the Communist regime itself. Truly, the sense of déjà vu is uncanny when one compares the Soviet record in 1939 with Vyshinskii's description of Hitler's Germany published in 1938 (the date of the Russian-language Soviet edition of his *Law of the Soviet State*; quotation from p. 694).

140. HI, PGC, 7819.

141. Kobryń, 35.

142. Dobromil, 19; oszmiana.

143. Here follows a list of precincts, undoubtedly incomplete, that had more than one candidate on the ballot, as well as the voting instruction: gmina Poczajów, 3 candidates (nowogródzki, 38); Piotrowicze (lida, 28), 3 candidates; Kołki (nieśwież, 45), 2 candidates; Kuchczyce (nieśwież, 45), 3 candidates; Pińsk (p. 46), 4 candidates; Kobryń (p. 31), 8 candidates, 6 to be crossed out; Malkowicze (łuniniec, 34), 3 candidates, 2 to be crossed out; Lubaczów (p. 30), 4 candidates; Lacka Wola (mościska, 25), 3 candidates, 1 to be underlined; Podliski (mościska, 25), 2 candidates, 1 to be crossed out; Złotkowice (mościska, 25), 3 candidates, 2 to be crossed out; Trzcianiec (dobromil, 19), 3 candidates, 1 to be underlined; Leszczawa Dolna (dobromil, 19), 3 candidates, signature to be put next to the chosen one; Medyka (przemyśl, 46), 2 candidates, 1 to be crossed out; Rozobowice (przemyśl, 53), 3 candidates, 2 to be crossed out; Chodorów (bóbrka, 21), 2 candidates, 1 to be crossed out; Stare Sioło (bóbrka, 21), 5 candidates, 2 to be underlined; Nowosielce (bóbrka, 22), 4 candidates; Jaworów (p. 26), 3 candidates, 2 to be crossed out; Skałat (pp. 31, 32), 2 candidates; Krzemieniec (p. 74), 3 candidates; gmina Malin (dubno, 74), 3 candidates; Borki (luboml, 80), 3 candidates; gmina Mizocz (zdołbunów, 81), 4 candidates, 2 to be crossed out; Piszczotyńce (krzemieniec†, 24), 3 candidates, 2 to be crossed out; Krzywczyki (krzemieniec†, 26), 3 candidates, 1 to be underlined; Równe (pp. 29†, 30†), 3 candidates in one precinct and 4 candidates, two to be crossed out, in another; Hużby (zdołbunów†, 22), 3 candidates, 2 to be crossed out; Chorów (zdołbunów†, 23), 2 candidates; Zdołbica (zdołbunów†, 23), 5 candidates, 3 to be crossed out; Opalin (luboml†, 23), 3 candidates; Ułaniki (łuck, 55), 3 candidates, 2 to be crossed out; Kałusz (p. 38), 5 candidates, 1 to be underlined; Delatyn (nadworna, 34), 5 candidates, 2 to be crossed out; Kołomyja (p. 41), 3 candidates; Tłumacz (p. 15), 3 candidates.

144. Why election organizers, who at other places went to the opposite extreme, would be so casual and careless, I am not sure. No better explanation comes to mind but to guess that local organizers were more or less left alone to do the job as they saw fit, and that many were inexperienced, naive, or trusting, or dependent on their local assistants, who were emulating, in a way, what they had seen practiced here in the past.

145. Szczuczyn, 31; postawy, 30. In one of Kobryń's precincts people who did not vote as they were told (i.e., by underlining the only candidate's name on the ballot) were later called back individually (apparently each person's

ballot could be verified) and ordered to vote for a second time (kobryń, 39). A second round of voting was organized also in Kozin, Dubno county (dubno†, 29, 30), in Chodorów, Bóbrka county (p. 25), and in gmina Katerburg, Krzemieniec county (p. 85).

146. *Pravda*, Oct. 25, 1939.

147. A detailed account from one voting station of the 3rd precinct in Mołodeczno (Wilno voivodeship) reveals that only 63 eligible voters out of 820 actually voted. "These are exact numbers, because in Wasilewicz's house [where the voting station was set up] lived the train conductor Korybut Władysław, with whom I had a secret talk a day before the elections. Since Korybut was my closest friend . . . , his wife agreed to count all coming for the vote and to write down names of acquaintances. So, except for a school which was brought in to drop ballots into the box, only 63 people voted, mostly Jews . . ." (HI, PGC, 8735).

148. See Łomża, 65, 88; Kamionka Nadbużna and Ciechanowiec (ostrów, 21, 22); Zamorze (łuniniec, 37, 40); Drejżyce (drohobycz, 46); Eleonorówka (skałat, 34); Kupiatycze (przemyśl, 59); gmina Mizocz (zdołbunów, 81); Daniczów (równe, 81); Kudłajowo (krzemieniec, 71); Krzeczkowo (białostocki, 34); gmina Janów (gródek jagielloński, 20), Jachnowszczyzna (nowogródzki, 36, 37); Strzeżuny (lida, 28).

149. HI, PGC, 4364; zdołbunów, 81; oszmiana; lida, 28.

150. Białostocki, 34.

151. Śniatyń, 37.

152. See, for example, Białystok, 53; wilejka, 38; dzisna, 34; brasławski, 21; nowogródzki, 39; nieśwież, 50, 54; łuniniec, 37; sambor, 35; dobromil, 23; gródek jagielloński, 23; przemyśl, 58, 59; rudki, 19; łuck, 58; kołomyja, 44; dolina, 45; stryj, 35; łomża, 66–68; pińsk, 52; mościska, 26; kobryń, 39.

153. Oszmiana.

154. HI, PGC, 5665 (Złoczów), 7364, 9903; lubaczów, 33; mościska, 26. Vincenz, *Dialogi z Sowietami*, p. 174.

155. See, for example, kosów poleski, 34; dobromil, 24; Białystok, 57; brasław, 21.

156. See, for example, HI, PGC, 10003 (Lwów); PGC, 2157 (Mołodeczno county); łomża, 72; białostocki, 34; ostrów, 22; oszmiana; lida, 29; mościska, 27; dobromil, 24; przemyśl, 64; równe, 80; sokolski, 43; postawy, 31.

157. Dobromil, 24; HI, Poland. Ambasada USSR, Box 47, Maria Ostrowicz; PGC, 3826. "There were no invalid votes. When all [four] names on the ballot were crossed off, it was counted as if the first and the third candidate got the vote. As village head [of Pakulnia, Brasław county], I was present when the ballot box was opened" (HI, PGC, 6016).

158. HI, PGC, 8835.

159. Holszany (oszmiana); HI, AC, 93.

160. HI, PGC, 8579.

161. GSHI, A.9.III.2a, File 58.

162. Rigby, "A Conceptual Approach to Authority, Power, and Policy in the Soviet Union," pp. 17–20.

163. Lewin, *The Making of the Soviet System*, pp. 266–268.

164. See, for example, łomża 69; Białystok, 54; postawy, 31; wilejka, 39; dzisna, 35; pińsk, 53; łuniniec, 38; kowel, 54; zdołbunów†, 21.

165. See, for example, łomża 69, 70; ostrów, 21; lida, 28; szczuczyn, 29; łuck, 58; brasław, 21; bóbrka, 24; stryj, 37. *Pravda* (Oct. 25, 1939) reports the following conversation as having allegedly taken place in the 6th precinct in Łuck: " 'Please, let me vote for my wife. She has no shoes, you see, and it's cold and muddy in the street.' 'Impossible, comrade. Everybody must vote only in person. We will send a car for your wife.' " Michał Jaremczuk from Zielona, on the other hand, was ordered to vote for his parents, who had been dead for years but who were somehow put on the electoral list (nadworna, 37).

166. HI, PGC, 9356 (Nowogródek); łomża, 69; łuniniec, 38; przemyśl, 60; bóbrka, 24; rudki, 18; łuck, 59.

167. HI, PGC, 2942 (Lwów); kosów poleski, 33; włodzimierz wołyński, 30.

168. Wasilków (białostocki, 35); Gdeszyce (przemyśl, 60); kobryń, 40; łuniniec, 38; dobromil, 23; Konotop (pińsk, 53); Różana (kosów poleski, 33); Bartkówka (brzozów, 22); Łomna (turka, 22); Czechowszczyzna (łuck, 59); Łobaczowka (horochów, 33); Kołomyja (p. 45).

169. Pińsk, 51.

170. Szczuczyn, 28.

171. See also zdołbunów†, 23; dubno, 76; nadworna, 35, 36; żydaczów, 20; drohobycz, 43; równe, 77; krzemieniec, 85.

172. *Pravda*, Oct. 25, 1939.

173. *Czerwony Sztandar*, Nov. 3, 1939.

174. *Czerwony Sztandar*, Nov. 17, 1939.

175. *Pravda*, Oct. 26, 31, 1939.

176. *Czerwony Sztandar*, Nov. 3, 1939.

177. The four main speakers in order of appearance during deliberations of the National Assembly of the Western Ukraine were Dr. Panchishin, Prof. Studyński, a peasant woman (Shkalubina), and a worker (Sadovy). During the debate in Białystok, the nature of state authority was presented by a Communist (Pritickii), confiscation of landholdings by a peasant (Shig), and nationalization by a woman worker (Diachuk). I was unable to establish the identity of the speaker presenting the declaration of intent on the part of the Western Belorussian population to join the Soviet Belorussian Republic (*Pravda*, Oct. 27, 28, 1939).

178. *Pravda*, Oct. 27, 30, 1939.

179. Równe†, 33; Bonatt, "International Law," p. 390; *The Tchortkiv District*, p. 367. Umiastowski also mentions Vinnichenko as the lonely dissenter (*Russia and the Polish Republic*, p. 222). A school principal from Dymytrów (Tarnopol voivodeship) met a former deputy to the Lwów Assembly in a cell of the Brygidki prison and learned from him that the delegates were actually flanked from both sides by security men. That would mean that there were as

many NKVD agents as there were deputies in the hall and that only every other seat was occupied by a deputy (Gross and Gross, *W czterdziestym,* doc. 138).

180. *Czerwony Sztandar,* Nov. 17, 1939.

181. *Pravda,* Nov. 16, 1939.

182. See, for example, Białystok, 48, 57, 58; białostocki, 38; sokolski, 43; wilejka, 42; mołodeczno, III.17; dzisna, 37, 38; brasław, 22; nowogródzki, 37; lida, 29; szczuczyn, 32; nieśwież, 54; pińsk, 55; łuniniec, 40, 41; kosów poleski, 35; mościska, 27; dobromil, 24; gródek jagielloński, 24; bóbrka, 25; rudki, 21; równe†, 32; kowel, 53; dubno†, 30; łuck, 54, 55, 61; stryj, 39.

183. HI, PGC, 6725 (Tarnopol); oszmiana; szczuczyn, 33.

184. A simple but effective population control procedure was introduced on the occasion of the July 14 elections: identity cards were stamped at the voting stations, thus establishing a permanent record that each person had to carry at all times.

185. The decree specifying that elections were to be held on the 24th of March was issued jointly by the all-Union Supreme Soviet and the Republican Supreme Soviets (*Czerwony Sztandar,* Jan. 22, 1940).

186. See, for example, *Czerwony Sztandar,* Jan. 22–28, 1940.

187. HI, AC, 7846.

188. *Czerwony Sztandar,* Feb. 20, 1940.

189. *Czerwony Sztandar,* Mar. 18, 22, 1940.

190. Kosharnyi, *U suziri sotsialistichnoi kulturi,* p. 39.

191. *Czerwony Sztandar,* Mar. 20, 29, 1940.

192. *Czerwony Sztandar,* Mar. 6, 1940.

193. *Czerwony Sztandar,* Mar. 15, 16, 1940.

194. HI, AC, 7473.

195. HI, PGC, 9491; Poland. Ambasada USSR, Box 48, Eugenia Krakowska; AC, 7846.

196. HI, AC, 11940.

197. HI, Poland. Ambasada USSR, Box 46.

198. HI, PGC, 8038, 9510. "At the first table they took the voter's name and his number [presumably from the list of eligible voters], at the second table one was given the ballot and its number was also recorded on a list. Alongside stood the ballot box and a box with tobacco. Behind the boxes, for appearance's sake, a curtain was hung" (HI, AC, 12574).

199. *Czerwony Sztandar,* Mar. 17, 1940.

200. HI, PGC, 1248.

201. *Czerwony Sztandar,* Mar. 26, 1940.

202. See, for example, *Izvestia,* Mar. 28, 1940.

203. Babii, *Vozzyednanya Zakhidnoi Ukraini s Ukrainskoyu RSR,* p. 126; *Czerwony Sztandar,* Dec. 18, 20, 24, 1940.

204. *Czerwony Sztandar,* Oct. 30, Nov. 1, Dec. 14, 24, 1940.

205. *Czerwony Sztandar,* Oct. 15, 1940.

206. Scott, *Duel for Europe,* p. 78.

207. HI, PGC, 7643.

208. HI, PGC, 7101.

209. HI, PGC, 7456.

210. *Pravda*, Oct. 23, 1939.

211. See Juan Linz's characterization of voting in totalitarian countries in "Non-Competitive Elections in Europe," p. 44.

THREE: THE PARADIGM OF SOCIAL CONTROL

1. Davies, *The Socialist Offensive*, p. 197. Robert Davies, a collaborator of E. H. Carr and a sympathizer of the cause of socialism, wrote this history of the collectivization of Soviet agriculture almost exclusively from official Soviet materials printed at the time in the local and central press.

2. Ibid., p. 235.

3. Ibid., p. 245. "An okrug official in the Black-Earth region is reported to have told his subordinates: 'remember comrades, our approach is that it is better to overstep the mark than to fall short . . . remember that we will not condemn you for an excess, but if you fall short—watch out' " (ibid., p. 218). An essay in Moshe Lewin's *The Making of the Soviet System* is devoted to the single question; "Who was the Soviet kulak?" The arbitrariness with which this social category was defined is striking. In the end, the only definition seems to have been that a kulak was any person "who is declared to be such by the authorities" (Lewin, p. 126).

4. Davies, *The Socialist Offensive*, p. 246.

5. Ibid.

6. Fainsod, *Smolensk under Soviet Rule*, p. 246. Only five days later, on February 28, 1930, the Smolensk secret police further refined the picture: "In many villages 'certain members of the workers' brigades and officials of lower echelons of the Party-Soviet apparatus' deprived members of kulak and middle peasant households of their clothing and warm underwear (directly from the body), 'confiscated' headwear from children's heads, and removed shoes from people's feet. The perpetrators divided the 'confiscated' goods among themselves; the food they found was eaten on the spot; the alcohol they uncovered was consumed immediately, resulting in drunken orgies. In one case a worker tore a warm blouse off a woman's back, put it on himself with the words, 'You wore it long enough, now I will wear it.' The slogan of many of the dekulakization brigades was: 'drink, eat—it is all ours.' One commune in search of more and richer 'confiscations' commenced to dekulakize kulaks of the bordering village soviet. As the kulaks in question were administratively under the 'jurisdiction' of another kolkhoz, a struggle ensued between the communards and the kolkhozniks. The communards under the direction of their party secretary absconded with much of the money and property of the kulaks before the kolkhoz could act. In the process even eyeglasses were torn from the peasants' faces; kasha was 'confiscated' straight from the oven and either eaten or used to smear the ikons" (ibid., pp. 245–246).

7. See, for example, HI, PGC, 2611, 3134, 3356, 4032, 8032, 9222.

8. HI, PGC, 7648, 6673, 9905.

9. See, for example, HI, AC, 3685; PGC, 2376, 2999, 7654, 8692; gródek jagielloński, 5; łuck, 13, 14.

10. "The militia and the local committee didn't do much; they were mostly drinking hooch and eating stolen geese, turkeys, pigs, and lambs. I remember how they stole a pedigreed ram from Mrs. Szyrynowa, and they couldn't agree what to do with it because three of them wanted it. In the end they killed it and six of them ate it in one night" (HI, PGC, 3660).

11. Here are some more names: Grzegorz and Aleksander Kościukiewicz, three Nikitiuk brothers, and two Buchoński brothers in Sutkowszczyzna (Horochów county, Wołyń; HI, PGC, 3302); Iwan, Dymian, and Marta Maciocha, and Michał and Teodor Janusz in Wołczek (Włodzimierz Wołyński county, Wołyń; HI, PGC, 3934); Antoni, Stefan, and Mikołaj Kiryczuk in gmina Szumsk (Krzemieniec county, Wołyń; HI, PGC, 11239); Kondrat and son in Bytyń (Kowel county, Wołyń; HI, PGC, 5809); Jan and Michał Kłok in Krolin (Mościska county, Lwów voivodeship; HI, PGC, 4426); three brothers Konaczuk in Armatniów (Łuck county, Wołyń; HI, PGC, 7468); Stefan and Karp Sacharczuk, and Wasyl and Prokop Mielniczuk in Nawóz (Łuck county, Wołyń; HI, PGC, 2659); Zbigniew Dziekoński and father, and Margules brothers in Zimna Woda (Lwów county, Lwów voivodeship; HI, PGC, 5871); Maria and Michał Hupało, and Stefan, Jan, and Michał Tarnawski in Stare Sioło (Bóbrka county, Lwów voivodeship; HI, PGC, 3922); Aleksy, Aleksander, and Piotr Kuncewicz, Sylwester and Wincenty Mieleszkiewicz, Jan and Szymon Jesis, Szymon and Piotr Sienkiewicz, Józef and Antoni Szmienko, Antoni and Wincenty Duduk, and Sergiusz and Michał Wójcik in Sieniawka (Nieśwież county, Nowogród voivodeship; nieśwież, 16, 17); Hipolit Kilczewski and two sons in gmina Lipniszki (Lida county, Nowogród voivodeship; lida, 6); Aleksander and Piotr Bubin, and Aleksander and Mikołaj Czajkowski in Brodówka (Lida county, Nowogród voivodeship; lida, 13); Mikołaj and Ignacy Awruszewicz in gmina Święta Wola (Kosów Poleski county, Polesie voivodeship; kosów poleski, 7); Stefan and Jan Budryło in Wola Bartatowska (Gródek Jagielloński county, Lwów voivodeship; gródek jagielloński, 5); Marian Święty and brother in Chłopy (Rudki county, Lwów voivodeship; rudki, 5).

12. Once again, the Smolensk archives offer corroborating evidence concerning a similar organization of authority in the kolkhozes of the 1930s, the frontier of sovietization, so to speak. The kolkhoz management was tantamount to Soviet authority. As Fainsod reports: "Sometimes the ruling clique was literally a close-knit family group, [as in] a kolkhoz near the village of Vasinichi where the wife was chairman of the kolkhoz, the husband the accountant, and the father the business manager. . . . Nor was this case an isolated exception. . . . In Dorogobuzh raion [in] a kolkhoz (named after Voroshilov) the son of the chairman was the accountant, the wife the milkmaid, the mother the receiver of milk, and the father the guard of the kolkhoz" (Fainsod, *Smolensk under Soviet Rule*, pp. 270–271; see also p. 239).

13. HI, PGC, 1167, 2229, 3062; HI, Poland. Ambasada USSR, Box 46, Halina Borowikówna; HI, PGC, 5966.

14. Reinhard Mann, who studied Gestapo files from Düsseldorf, found that "in the majority of cases, denouncements were generated by private conflicts . . . they were intended to 'solve' these conflicts, i.e., the complainant tried to eliminate his enemy indirectly by means of the Gestapo. Quarrels between spouses, differences between landlords and tenants, conflicts within a neighborhood, rivalries in professional spheres, failed love affairs—all produced denouncements" (Mann, *Zur Soziologie des Widerstandes in nationalsozialistischen Deutschland*, p. 233).

15. See, for example, Vassili Grossman, *Tout passe . . .*, ch. 13.

16. HI, PGC, 8461.

FOUR: SOCIALIZATION

1. Interview with Jerzy Kulczycki, London, Summer 1977.

2. See, for example, dubno, 31; sambor, 44; rudki, 25; nowogródzki, 46.

3. Horochów, 45; sarny, 21; równe, 35; lubaczów, 41; łuniniec, 49; łomża, 100.

4. Szczuczyn, 41.

5. Śniatyń, 43; see also HI, PGC, 3963, 4267, 7742, 10094.

6. HI, AC, 12676, 14267; równe, 36; kosów poleski, 39; *The Tchortkiv District*, p. 736.

7. *Czerwony Sztandar*, Dec. 12, 29, 1939; HI, PGC, 3046; Poland. Ambasada USSR, Box 46, Stefania Kurianowicz.

8. Brasław, 28.

9. Take, for example, information provided by Khrishchuk, the secretary of the Lwów Oblast (District) Committee of the Ukrainian Communist party. On the eve of the 1940/1941 school year, in the summer of 1940, there were 1,003 Ukrainian-language schools, 314 Polish-language schools, 7 Russian-language schools, and 20 Yiddish-language schools in the Lwów district (*Czerwony Sztandar*, Aug. 20, 1940). Ethnically, the area was divided more or less equally into groups of Poles and Ukrainians (some 44–45% of the total for each nationality); the remainder, 10–12%, was Jewish. These numbers do not reflect the influx of refugees, predominantly Jewish, who dramatically swelled the population of Lwów and other towns in the district. Thus 20 Yiddish-language schools among a combined total of 1,344 (i.e., about 1.5%) means underrepresentation by a factor of nearly 10—a result of deliberate policy, no doubt, rather than a mere oversight. And by January 1941 the total number of Yiddish-language schools in the Lwów district had further declined to 14 (*Czerwony Sztandar*, Jan. 5, 1941). See also Dov Rabin, "Two Years of Soviet Rule in Grodno," p. 506.

10. Horochów, 45; kostopol, 19; zdołbunów, 26; łuck, 64; włodzimierz wołyński, 41; przemyśl, 82; kałusz, 53; szczuczyn, 41; postawy, 40; święciany, 35; Gross and Gross, *W czterdziestym*, doc. 90.

11. Mościska, 32.

12. Pińsk, 70; Rabin, "Two Years of Soviet Rule," p. 506; [Hashomer Hatzair], *Youth Amidst the Ruins*, p. 96.

13. Białystok, 48.

14. Another episode in the saga of introducing Soviet versions of various commodities may be worth recording here. On August 11, 1940, we read in *Czerwony Sztandar* about a new school opened in Lwów, a school of Soviet calisthenics. Physical education as it had been taught in Polish schools also needed revision, it seemed. But as there were no instructors of "Soviet calisthenics," a special school was set up to train them; 28 in all were admitted in the first year. "Soviet calisthenics is significantly different from calisthenics as it was practiced in Lwów until recently," according to the report, "because along with physical development it also strives to prepare for exercises useful for defense purposes."

15. Bóbrka, 30; rudki, 25; dzisna, 46; gródek jagielloński, 29. "A teacher's situation became very difficult, one lived in constant nervous tension, several times a month a school inspector or some other commissar or a politruk came on an official visit. Often the teacher would be asked to leave the classroom, and the commissar stayed alone with the children and questioned them about various school matters—how is the teacher doing his job and what is he saying? does he speak Polish? does he conduct prayers or is he making antireligious speeches? does he go to church? does he meet with the local priest? whom does he visit and who comes to visit him? does he allow children to address him with 'Pan'? A teacher's fate depended on the children" (HI, PGC, 4487).

16. HI, PGC, 5097; gródek jagielloński, 29.

17. Interview with Lew Wasyl, New York, Spring 1981.

18. HI, AC, 1858.

19. Nowogródzki, 46.

20. HI, AC, 1858; PGC, 7458.

21. *The Tchortkiv District*, p. 139.

22. HI, PGC, 7432; kołomyja, 57; jaworów, 38; Gross and Gross, *W czterdziestym*, doc. 113; Pinkas Hakehillot, *Encyclopedia of Jewish Communities*, vol. 2, *Eastern Galicia*, p. 23.

23. Thus a physician from Łomża, Kacper Latała, writes: "When the school board ordered that classes are to be held on Sundays, all schoolchildren boycotted the regulation, and after a few failed attempts the Soviet authorities were forced to change their position and the youth has won Sunday for the holiday free of classes" (HI, PGC, 668).

24. HI, PGC, 3664, 4761, 4904, 6612, 6748, 6765, 7774, 8135, 11265; kałusz, 54; nieśwież, 64; postawy, 40; Białystok, 79; łomża, 99.

25. Gross and Gross, *W czterdziestym*, doc. 34.

26. Sambor, 45.

27. HI, PGC, 9658.

28. Grownups, of course, also celebrated in a myriad of officially sponsored

parties. An article published in *Czerwony Sztandar* on January 3, 1940, conveyed the cheerful mood of the period through a quantitative measure: "The Central Lwów Telegraph Office was crowded on December 31 and January 1. Lwów's inhabitants were sending out telegrams on those days to their kin, friends, and acquaintances . . . 34,575 were sent out in just two days. . . . The working people extended their friendly greetings to mailmen who worked around the clock delivering telegrams." See also *Czerwony Sztandar*, Dec. 31, 1939.

29. Bóbrka, 30. The most complete and sophisticated articulation of this new ritual inserted into the calendar of festivities came in the feature article of the New Year's edition of *Czerwony Sztandar*. Its author, Adam Ważyk, later rose to prominence in the Polish intellectual firmament, initially as one of the stalwarts of the postwar Stalinist cultural establishment and, after the Great Helmsman's death, as a beacon of liberalization. The following piece, then, is of historical interest also because of its author. The article is entitled "The Soviet Tree," or rather "The Soviet Christmas Tree." The word *choinka*, by which Poles designate the trees they buy during the Christmas season, has, as it were, no religious phonetics. There is no common root with "Christmas" in the sound, and therefore it can be used in a secular combination, such as "Radziecka choinka" ("The Soviet Christmas Tree"), without actually saying "Christmas." I shall refer in what follows to the "Soviet tree" precisely because the whole idea behind introducing it was to abolish Christmas; besides, to say "Soviet" and "Christmas" in one breath at that time was inconceivable.

Today for the first time workers, peasants, and all the laborers of the Ukraine's western districts partake in a happy new year celebration, together with all peoples of the multinational Soviet Union. Children and youth gather around the Soviet tree. Let us understand the character of this celebration and the meaning of the Soviet tree which embraces in its widely extended arms children in kindergartens, schools, factories, and industrial enterprises. . . .

A New Year tree once was part of rituals indulged in by peoples settled in moderate climes, where conifers grow. Cut in the woods and brought to the family hearth, the tree symbolized, as an element of nature, the constant renewal of life. Christian clergy substituted for this new year ritual its own religious myth and, in order to satisfy the myth's requirement, disconnected the tree from the new year and tied it to the legend about the birth of God's son, so that until today children brought up in the capitalist countries have such ideas as annunciation, the magic star, the peregrination of king-magicians, and many other details implanted into their minds. The clergy presents these ideas simultaneously as historical facts and as supernatural phenomena. Thus at the same time history is falsified and the human mind warped from earliest childhood. And the myth is not even an original invention of Christianity but was articulated in the middle of the second century from myths borrowed from other religions, and in the light of extensive studies of religious texts it turns out that the one whom the clergy associated with the Christmas tree had never been born.

The Soviet nation, associating the tree with the New Year's Day, does not at all return to some pagan beliefs, because it rejects all religious beliefs as false concepts in contradiction with the fundamentals of materialistic thought, as concepts overcome in the epoch of socialism. It only renews a beautiful popular custom, which brings so much direct happiness to children, and links it with the day of the stormworker, thus giving the joy of life a new basis—not a religious one, but socialist; the basis of work and the noble competition of work. . . .

30. HI, PGC, 10861, 11281; Poland. Ambasada USSR, Box 46, Stefania Gołaszewska; równe, 35; kobryń, 48. Umiastowski reports that 25,000 activists of the League of the Godless were sent to the newly incorporated territories in January 1941. "The Moscow branch of the 'League of the Godless' held 14,000 meetings during March in Poland" (*Russia and the Polish Republic*, p. 252).

31. HI, PGC, 9093; Poland. Ambasada USSR, Box 46, Stefania Gołaszewska; kostopol, 19; równe, 35, 36; sambor, 45; jaworów, 38; zdołbunów, 26; krzemieniec, 41; łomża, 101; kobryń, 48; Gross and Gross, *W czterdziestym*, doc. 16, 98, 113. Books in Hebrew were destroyed as well; see Rabin, "Two Years of Soviet Rule," p. 506.

32. Jerzy Hurwic, "Podręczniki z matematyki, fizyki i chemii dla szkół z polskim językiem wykładowym," *Nowe Widnokręgi*, no.1 (1940).

33. HI, PGC, 4487.

34. It had been the custom especially in primary schools, where it would be inappropriate to call one's teacher "a professor," the latter title being reserved for university or high school teaching staff.

35. HI, PGC, 4487; AC, 14267; kałusz, 57; Gross and Gross, *W czterdziestym*, doc. 113.

36. Dolina, 65.

37. HI, PGC, 9138.

38. Skałat, 41; see also HI, Poland. Ambasada USSR, Box 46, Dominik Pytel.

39. Horochów, 45; kostopol, 19; łuck, 64, 65; łuniniec, 50; dzisna, 46; wilejka, 54; równe, 35; włodzimierz wołyński, 41; nadworna, 48. From mid-October 1939, *Czerwony Sztandar* writes about and advertises new job opportunities for unemployed teachers; see, for example, issues of October 14 and November 22.

40. HI, AC, 10747; see also przemyśl, 81; kałusz, 53; dolina, 63, 65.

41. Kowel, 64; włodzimierz wołyński, 41; sambor, 41; żydaczów, 27; lida, 40; pińsk, 70; dzisna, 46; wilejka, 54; Białystok, 81; łomża, 101.

42. Apparently, 5,833 of the students had not made "satisfactory progress" by May 6, 1940, as we learn from his speech (printed in *Czerwony Sztandar*). Another 6,133 had "not been graded yet."

43. Indeed, the problem was recognized at the time in Moscow as well. At a

conference held in the Soviet capital on January 6, 1941, a professor, the president of Moscow University, and the director of the Steel Institute all denounced the widespread practice among university professors of giving their students better grades than they deserved. There was even a special resolution of the Central Committee of the Bolshevik Communist Party that addressed the issue (*Czerwony Sztandar*, Jan. 7, 1941). On socialist competition at Lwów University, see *Czerwony Sztandar*, Oct. 15, 1940.

44. YV, 033/1213. See also Rudnycka, *Western Ukraine under the Bolsheviks*, pp. 167–169, 186–189.

45. HI, PGC, 4651. See also HI, AC, 7629, 9051; PGC, 6590; pińsk, 70; dolina, 63; kowel, 64; Gross and Gross, W *czterdziestym*, doc. 111.

46. HI, PGC, 6698.

47. HI, PGC, 11281; AC, 10747; horochów, 45; dubno, 31; sarny, 22; krzemieniec, 41; łuck, 65; drohobycz, 65; kałusz, 53; nadworna, 48; nowogródzki, 45; lida, 39, 40; nieśwież, 64; Białystok, 80.

48. Interview with Mrs. Łabuńka, Philadelphia, Spring 1981.

49. *Czerwony Sztandar*, Nov. 13, 1940.

50. From a letter dated July 13, 1940, by a high school friend of Danuta Polniaszek Kossakowska, we learn about the frustration of a Lwów high school orchestra that had just won first place in the local olympiad. An excursion to Kiev was offered as the first prize, but arrangements were made for only 30 people to go on the trip, while there were 150 deserving laureates in the competition. Interview, London, Summer 1977. See also *Czerwony Sztandar*, Mar. 21, 27, Apr. 24, May 6, July 5, 1940; Jan. 5, 12, 1941. Adam Ważyk reported on one such olympiad held in March 1940. In it "a musician-eccentric Comrade Apt performed Tchaikovsky and Paganini on an ordinary pencil" (*Czerwony Sztandar*, Mar. 27, 1940). And why not? After all, as one of the propagandists in Słonim county revealed, Soviet watches are the best, the fastest in the world (HI, PGC, 2169).

51. *Czerwony Sztandar*, Dec. 19, Oct. 15, Sept. 1, 1940.

52. In Tarnopol, Piłsudski was not so lucky: hoofs on a pedestal were all that remained of his monument one morning (HI, PGC, 9200). See also HI, AC, 11943; Gross and Gross, W *czterdziestym*, doc. 1.

53. As early as October 2, 1939, *Pravda* reported that 28 editorial teams, ready to set up town newspapers, were dispatched into Western Belorussia. For listings and comments about the function of county-level newspapers, see for example *Czerwony Sztandar*, Jan. 18, Apr. 24, 27, May 5, Aug. 1, Oct. 13, 1940; Jan. 18, 1941. On literary periodicals put out at the time, see *Czerwony Sztandar*, Oct. 1, 1940; Feb. 12, 16, May 5, 14, 1941. About factory wall-newspapers and special seminars organized for their editors, see *Czerwony Sztandar*, Jan. 18, Apr. 20, 27, Aug. 1, 1940.

54. On January 9, 1940, *Czerwony Sztandar* carried a story about the Oblast Lectures Office in Lwów. From November 6 through December 31, 1939, it provided 257 lectures in various schools, clubs, and factories of the oblast, and it was planning 13 lecture series for the year 1940. The most com-

prehensive series (91 presentations) was on "world, Russian, Ukrainian, and other Soviet Union's nations" literature, followed by series on the history of the Bolshevik party (62 lectures), the history of the Soviet Union (50), art and music (43), and so on. "The range of topics," concluded the journalist, "has a truly all-humanities encompassing breath." And there were also concerts, tours of provincial towns by the Lwów Philharmonic, theater companies, road shows, traveling cinemas, authors' readings, and the like. See, for example, *Pravda*, Oct. 12, Nov. 27, 1939; *Czerwony Sztandar*, Dec. 12, 21, 1939; Jan. 1, Mar. 24, Oct. 19, Nov. 6, 7, 1940.

55. HI, AC, 12403. See also HI, Stanisław Mikołajczk's Archive, Box 15, File "Poland Under Soviet Occupation. Wilno and Lwów regions, 1940–43," ms. "Okupacja sowiecka. Stosunki wewnętrzne w kraju." A certain Zbigniew Mackiewicz put forth a far more drastic formula: "One of their educational methods was teaching disrespect for parents, awakening sexual instincts, and slandering all that human nature was accustomed to consider as sacred" (GSHI, Polskie Siły Powietrzne Collection, File 9).

56. HI, PGC, 10015.

57. Liuba Prokop (L.K.), "U sorokovi rokovini protsesu 59–i"; *The Tchortkiv District*, pp. 116, 445; interview with Mykoła Lebed, New York, Autumn 1981; interview with Petro Mirchuk, Philadelphia, Spring 1981.

58. Hakehillot, *Encyclopedia of Jewish Communities*, p. 22; Hasia Blitzka, "Zionist Youth Maintains Contacts," Moshe Nots, "Beitar," Tuvia Berger, "My visit to Grodno," all in *Encyclopedia of Diaspora*, ed. Rabin, 9: 507–512; Ezriel Shockat, "World War II until the Nazi Occupation," p. 288; Shimon Redlich, "The Jews in the Soviet Annexed Territories 1939–1941," pp. 86–88; [Hashomer Hatzair], *Youth Amidst the Ruins*, esp. pp. 104–117.

59. See, for example, Gross and Gross, *W czterdziestym*, doc. 128; Y. Margolin, "The Days of Soviet Occupation," p. 312; D. Bilii, "Bolshevitske pridooshivania religiinykh proiaviv u drogobitskikh shkolakh," p. 61.

60. On the activities of various political parties in Wilno, see GSHI, A 9 III 2c/24, ms. by Rev. Kazimierz Kucharski. For Lwów, see UPST, B I/104, statement by docent Władysław Zych; B II/5406, statement by Lt. Jan Jaworski; B I 3333/3, statement by Franciszek Wilk; B I 3333/1, "Sprawozdanie Rewolucyjnego Związku Niepodległości i Wolności na terenie okupacji rosyjskiej," by Michał Lang; HI, Poland. Ambasada USSR, Box 51, Julian Hochfeld.

61. Captain Jerzy Antoni Niezbrzycki was called that day to the headquarters of the supreme commander in Kołomyja, where he was ordered to set up a clandestine military organization in the eastern territories of the Polish republic. It was his impression then that several other officers received similar orders. He was sent to Bucharest to consult with Polish intelligence as well as with one of the most influential politicians of the last prewar decade in Poland, Colonel Zygmunt Wenda. On the colonel's orders, Niezbrzycki collected $100,000 from the Polish embassy in Bucharest on September 21. An attack of kidney stones incapacitated him soon afterward, however, and he was unable to organize the transfer of money to Poland.

62. Ivan Serov, the head of the Ukrainian NKVD who held several conversations with the defeated Lwów garrison commander, General Władysław Langner, queried him in late October about Januszajtis's whereabouts (GSHI, Memorandum from Gen. Władysław Langner, "Treść rozmów przeprowadzonych we Lwówie z szefem GPU na Ukrainie i jego zastępcą w dniach 7.X, 21.X, i 16.XI, 1939"). Januszajtis was also recognized by the Polish government-in-exile as an eminent organizer of the military underground. The first "Instruction" co-signed by Generals Kazimierz Sosnkowski and Władysław Sikorski on December 4, 1939, which laid out the blueprint for the military underground conspiracy in Poland, was sent to the commander of the ZWZ in Warsaw, Colonel Stefan Grot-Rowecki, and to General Januszajtis in Lwów. A special courier was dispatched with the "Instruction" from Paris on Christmas Eve, 1939. Unbeknownst to the Polish authorities in France, General Januszajtis had been in a Soviet jail since October 27 (*Armia Krajowa w Dokumentach*, 1: 10, 21).

63. When one month later Jaworski accidentally met Colonel Władysław Zebrowski, whom he had known before the war, he could put at his disposal the entire group. Then, as Zebrowski's aide, he continued to build the organization, incorporating in it "a spontaneous" influx of soldiers. In February 1940 the estimated total membership of their organization was about 6,000 in Lwów alone and another 4,000 in the countryside (UPST, B II/5406, statement by Lt. Jan Jaworski).

64. UPST, B I/165–1(5).

65. The Macieliński affair is rather intricate, and some of its details may be gleaned from printed documents in *Armia Krajowa w Dokumentach*, vols. 1 and 2. In the end, he was charged before an underground Polish military tribunal, sentenced to death, and executed on December 17, 1941. For his indictment, see *Armia Krajowa w Dokumentach*, 2: 135–137.

66. HI, AC, 1512, 1841, 1734, 4100, 8719, 12556; PGC, 9338, Box 234, Edward Mucha; UPST, B I, Józef Boruta-Skowronek, Jan Organista; B I/370, Jan Bieniowski; GSHI, Polskie Siły Powietrzne Collection, File 4, Tadeusz Marian Baczała; File 9, Tadeusz Pendlowski; File 23, Michał Konon.

67. After all, how long can one maintain "organizational readiness," presumably to stand up when ordered to join in an uprising, without ever finding out who is empowered to call one? And as to the financial situation, it can be gauged from the reports of Colonel Sulik (the commanding officer of the Wilno district of the ZWZ) to London in September 1940. In the past year he had received altogether the sum of $820 from the Supreme Headquarters. As a result, he was obliged to finance his organization from other sources. In mid-September 1940 the Wilno ZWZ had 1,000 American dollars, 275 English pounds, and 2,000 Lits (Lithuanian currency) in its treasury, but monthly expenses ran from $2,000 to $3,000, not counting the $15,000 to $20,000 needed for assistance to the civilian population (UPST, 3.1.1/4 Raport Sulika, Sept. 1 and 16, 1940.

68. HI, AC, 691, 1249, 1264, 2089, 2107, 4363, 5498; PGC, 4840, 9338; UPST, B I, Henryk Pyptiuk; B I/3462.

69. The Soviet-Finnish war had started, and the Red Army was doing poorly. All kinds of rumors circulated—for instance, that a joint Polish-French expeditionary force might be coming on a rescue mission through Rumania. Some heard that there was to be a general uprising in February. It seems that two junior officers, Lieutenants Kowalski and Woszczyński, arrived into town in December claiming plenipotentiary powers from the Lwów headquarters of the zwz to take over the organization. In January 1940, apparently, Soviet army units were sent from Czortków to the Finnish front. Also, the conspirators feared for some reason that their clandestine activities might be soon compromised. In those circumstances they decided to call an armed uprising, take over the town, and then fight their way to Rumania.

70. GSHI, Polskie Siły Powietrzne Collection, File 6, Tadeusz Bańkowski; HI, Mikołajczk's Archive, Box 9, Folder "General Sosnkowski's File. London. 1940–1941."

71. HI, AC, 1254, 2056, 8462, 8593, 9562, 10752; PGC, 3559, 10352; Poland. Ambasada USSR, Box 47, Stefania Mikołajczyk; Mikołajczk's Archive, Box 9, Folder "General Sosnkowski's File"; GSHI, A 9 III 2a/58, Maria Kozkowa; Polskie Siły Powietrzne Collection, File 6, Tadeusz Bańkowski.

72. Here I am merely referring to a sample of conspiratorial initiatives in the places indicated. See HI, AC, 132, 2423, 5700, 7746, 8462, 8719, 8877, 10746, 10752, 14458; PGC, 7607; PGC, Box 234, Edward Mucha; Poland. Ambasada USSR, Box 46, Stanisław Chruściel; UPST, B II/5406, Jan Jaworski.

73. HI, PGC, 4713; AC, 10686; interview, London, Spring 1977.

74. HI, PGC, 9184; AC, 10686, 14458.

75. HI, AC, 12609.

76. HI, PGC, 1135, 8220, 9184, 9265; Box 234, Irena Szadnik; AC, 5700, 10686, 12696; łuck, 66; przemyśl, 80; jaworów, 38; szczuczyn, 40; wilno, 74; wilejka, 55; Białystok, 80; *The Tchortkiv District*, pp. 116, 445.

77. In October 1940 tuition was charged for all but the first seven grades of school. Ten days after the original announcement, this decision was revoked for the Western Ukraine and Western Belorussia, postponing the imposition of tuition there for two years (until 1942/1943). But one exception was made: there were fees for children "whose parents do not work for a living" (*Czerwony Sztandar*, Oct. 3, 13, 1940).

78. HI, PGC, 7557. See also PGC, Box 234, Józef Kuhn; Poland. Ambasada USSR Collection, Box 46, Jadwiga Pogorzelska; *Czerwony Sztandar*, Nov. 21, 1939; Jan. 8, July 31, 1940.

79. *Czerwony Sztandar*, Dec. 8, 1940.

80. *Czerwony Sztandar*, Sept. 18, 1940.

FIVE: PRISONS

1. Vincenz, *Dialogi z Sowietami*, p. 125; HI, PGC, 8459.

2. HI, PGC, 7557.

3. HI, PGC, 7718. "Soon after the elections began mass arrests, house

searches, and deportations to Russia. Men who had to go into town on some business were always prepared for the eventuality of arrest in the street, so everybody wore two or three pairs of underwear, and carried some necessary items—like towel, soap, or toothbrush—in the briefcase" (HI, PGC, 7366). Perhaps this shoemaker from Lwów cared more about personal hygiene than the average person; but he, and apparently others he knew, evidently thought that arrest might come at any moment.

4. HI, PGC, 3443, 3888, 7101, 9794. "Numerous officers' wives are collaborating with the Soviet secret police" (GSHI, Collection no. 88, File A, "Conversation with General Langner held on December 12, 1939," filed by Col. Wasilewski).

5. Some such letters, in Lwów at least, were plucked out by postal employees working for the Polish underground (UPST, B I/165–1) [5].

6. A revealing document signed by Guzevicius, the head of the Lithuanian NKVD in 1940, was published by the Lithuanian American Information Center in New York in August 1944: *An Appeal to Fellow Americans on Behalf of the Baltic States.* I am convinced of its authenticity, having found a mention of its capture on July 20, 1941, together with translated excerpts, in the Ereignismeldung UdSSR, no. 28 (Bundesarchiv, R 58/214, fol. 1–268). It is a local version of order 001223 of the NKVD of the USSR "about the accounting concerning anti-soviet and socially alien element" (p. 19). Issued in Lithuania on November 28, 1940, it orders the preparation within ten days of "the index account covering all those persons who by reason of their social and political past, national-chauvinistic opinions, religious convictions, moral and political inconstancy, are opposed to the socialist order and thus might be used by the intelligence services of foreign countries and by the counter-revolutionary centers for anti-soviet purposes. These elements include:

(a) All former members of anti-soviet political parties, organizations, and groups: trotskyists, essers (socialist revolutionists), mensheviks, social democrats, anarchists, and the like;

(b) All former members of national-chauvinistic anti-soviet parties, organizations, and groups: nationalists, Young Lithuania, voldermarists, populiata, christian democrats, members of nationalist terroristic organizations ("Iron Wolf"), active members of student fraternities, active members of Riflemen's Association, Catholic terrorist organization "White Horse";

(c) Former gendarmes, policemen, former employees of political and criminal police and of the prisons;

(d) Former officers of the czar, Petliura, and other armies;

(e) Former officers and members of military courts of the armies of Lithuania and Poland;

(f) Former polit(ical) bandits and volunteers of the white and other armies;

(g) Persons expelled from the Communist Party and Comm-youth for offences;

(h) All deserters, polit(ical) emigrants, re-emigrants, repatriates, and contrabandists;

(i) All citizens of foreign countries, representatives of foreign firms, employees of offices of foreign countries, former citizens of foreign countries, former employees of legations, firms, concessions, and stock companies of foreign countries;

(j) Persons having personal contacts and maintaining correspondence abroad with foreign legations and consulates, esperantists, and philatelists;

(k) Former employees of the departments of ministries (from referents up);

(l) Former workers of the Red Cross and Polish refugees;

(m) Religionists (priests, pastors), sectants, and active religionists of religious communities;

(n) Former noblemen, estate owners, merchants, bankers, commercialists (who availed themselves of hired labor), shop owners, owners of hotels and restaurants. (pp. 20–21)

The document includes a sample form in eight sections for *daily* reports on arrests. The first section concerns Lithuanian, Polish, Jewish, Ukrainian, and Belorussian "National Counter Revolution." Regular contributors to the press of any political party and the leadership personnel ("starting with county committeemen") are to be accounted for within each of these national categories. Section two covers in great detail police and prison personnel; section three, "former large landlords, manufacturers, and state employees" (each subsection divided into about twenty specific categories); section four, "former officers of the armies of Poland, Lithuania, and White bands." Finally, section eight singles out "members of families of the persons indicated in the first, second, third, and fourth sections." Section five, I might add, refers to common criminals, section six to prostitutes, and section seven to repatriates from Germany. These guidelines translated into the observation of an engineer who had been held under arrest since September 1939 in Kowel: "At the beginning, among the prisoners, there were mostly leadership cadres, the military, and the police; later, middle-level Polish intelligentsia appeared; and then the settlers and Ukrainian peasants" (HI, AC, 2402). In other words, there was hardly anybody who could not be subsumed under one or another category on the list.

7. In one respect, the postelection arrests were unlike other mass arrests, because they affected primarily people whose behavior had been monitored. These people were incarcerated for what they had done (or, more accurately, had *not done*,, i.e., voted), while others were taken primarily for what they had *been*.

8. It is difficult to give more precise estimates because of population movements across the frontiers due to the war. Many people, primarily Jews, escaped from German occupation to the Soviet-occupied territory. Others—Ukrainians, Poles, and eventually Jews as well—went in the opposite direction. Similarly, there was substantial illegal traffic across the frontier to Lithuania, Hungary, and Rumania. For the most careful estimate of the number of deported, see a memorandum prepared by the Polish Ministry of Foreign Affairs in London on March 15, 1944, "Obliczenie ludności polskiej deportowanej do ZSSR w latach od 1939 do 1941" (HI, PGC, Box 588).

9. In February 1940, a student in an underground officers' course is reported to have shot himself to death in Lwów after a car with NKVD operatives stopped near the apartment building where he had a flat. "He was sure he

would be arrested, but by some strange coincidence the Soviets did not hear the shot and left after taking along some other person, who had no connection with the ZWZ [Association of Armed Struggle] and whom they had come to arrest" (UPST, B II, 5406).

10. Why interrogations were conducted at night is easy to explain. It was a simple device to weaken prisoners by depriving them of sleep. Also, the secret police may have spread their workload over twenty-four hours once prisons facilities were inadequate for the higher volume of arrests. Interrogations often had to be conducted on some other premises, such as NKVD buildings, which were separate and sometimes quite distant from local prisons. Since even the NKVD did not have enough motor transport, especially in small localities, prisoners and their escorts would be seen if they were walked through town in broad daylight (HI, PGC, 4343); this would make for bad public relations, given the physical tortures the prisoners had routinely suffered. Finally, it may have occurred to someone that a praetorian guard of the regime ought to be kept separate from the rest of society and that the NKVD men who worked nights would sleep during the day and thus keep to themselves. Last but not least, Stalin kept late hours, and offices of the state, particularly in Moscow, had to accommodate themselves to his working habits (remember, for example, the timing of Ambassador Grzybowski's interview in the Commissariat for Foreign Affairs). This schedule must have also affected the nervous system of the regime—the political police—down to the local, provincial offices. An engineer from Równe, I may add for the record, found out that "hourly wages for night shifts were much higher in the NKVD and so they preferred to work nights" (równe, uzupełnienie, 2). If this is true, we ought to add pecuniary considerations to all the other hypothetical explanations.

11. See Chapter 3.

12. Interview with Michał Borwicz, Paris, Autumn 1980. See also Wasilewska, "Wspomnienia," pp. 342, 344, 346, 347, 351, 357, 369, 370, 400. Khrushchev as well befriended Wasilewska. "She was later one of the few people who could talk back to Stalin and still keep in his good graces" (*Khrushchev Remembers*, p. 145). See also Ola Watowa, *Wszystko co najważniejsze*, pp. 30, 52–56; Torańska, *Oni*, p. 237.

13. "Personal life lost its private character. The living space designated for one person was strictly limited. The rest of the apartment was assigned by the residential building office to some visitor from the East. Solitude, personal freedom, and the possibility to rest after work were all gone. Under constant observation and being eavesdropped on, one feels like in a prison cell . . ." (UPST, B I, 3859). In villages or small towns where all residents knew each other at least by sight, an unknown, anonymous visitor would be picked up immediately by the local militia. Thus, neither prominence nor the definite lack thereof offered any protection.

14. HI, PGC, 3852, 8770, 8948; Poland. Ambasada USSR, Box 46, Grabiec.

15. Skałat, 36.

16. HI, PGC, 3469; also PGC, 4100; from Stanisławów, PGC, 2704.

17. HI, AC, 994.

18. The deterioration of economic circumstances of all classes of society needs to be taken into account as well.

19. HI, PGC, 7222.

20. HI, PGC, 1955.

21. GSHI, Polskie Siły Powietrzne Collection, Box 4, Ostrowski.

22. HI, AC, 6793.

23. HI, AC, 1686.

24. *Czerwony Sztandar*, Apr. 9, 1940.

25. HI, PGC, 3960, 8556, 10743. In Woropajewo village a group of young men who had successfully avoided arrest for some time were caught on March 17, 1940, when they reported to clear snow from adjacent railroad tracks, such service being a tax in kind routinely imposed by the Soviet authorities (HI, AC, 7527).

26. HI, AC, 6200; see also Czortków, AC, 3682.

27. HI, Poland. Ambasada USSR, Box 51, Pirożyński.

28. HI, AC, 1322.

29. HI, AC, 661.

30. HI, AC, 9810.

31. Szczuczyn, 35.

32. HI, AC, 6941.

33. HI, AC, 96.

34. HI, AC, 3686, 1397.

35. HI, AC, 6144, 6220, 6847.

36. HI, AC, 680, 137, 11222, 1252, 1196, 6823, 10991, 12696, 548, 4323, 1333, 3532, 2405, 8859, 8869.

37. HI, PGC, 3921.

38. HI, AC, 516, 1311, 1135, 3532, 523, 499, 508, 2402, 9411, 2375, 1545; Wat, *Mój Wiek*, 1: 324; HI, AC, 615, 1680, 1551, 549, 358, 548, 1255, 2375, 3678, 340, 518, 1252.

39. HI, AC, AWBD, doc. 62c, tables 26–c and 27.

40. HI, Poland. Ambasada USSR, Box 47, Moszoro.

41. HI, Poland. Ambasada USSR, Box 46, Maliszewska; HI, PGC, 8025.

42. "We could bring clean linen to the prison once a month. Who didn't live through it couldn't believe how we were persecuted. I left the house at 2 A.M. to stand in line in front of the prison. They opened at 8 A.M. and we all entered into a hall. The crowd was enormous, and in the window was one of ours who served the Bolsheviks—Kozdra—and he screams, there are no more masters, they are all in jail, and threatens imprisonment if anybody says anything. But worse, he wouldn't take the linen, so one stood without muttering a word and only prayed to God to shorten our misery. And so in the evening hours he took linen and on the next day one had to go there again to find out whether the loved one was still in this prison" (HI, Poland. Ambasada USSR, Box 46, Nowosielska [Lwów]). "Prisoners' families gathered in front of the prison every day waiting for some news about their folk, or pleading to hand in a

package. On the doors it was written that office hours begin at 7 in the morning. Very often, however, the door didn't open before 12, and freezing women and children were kept four to five hours outdoors where it was 40 C below zero (such was the winter in Poland in 1939/1940). Then, a 'commandant' appeared in the doorway, and if he was in good mood he accepted packages; otherwise he cursed us in nonparliamentary language and shut the door telling us to come back tomorrow" (Poland. Ambasada USSR, Box 48, [Białystok]).

43. HI, PGC, 4621, 8025.

44. HI, AC, 96, 550, 549, 2375, 4772; Wat, *Mój Wiek*, 1: 324; *Dark Side of the Moon*, p. 80.

45. HI, AC, 2402, 2375, 2510; *Dark Side of the Moon*, pp. 83, 87. In Lida prison there was no medical care for inmates. The sick were left in their cells until they either recovered or were about to die, when they were removed to a "death cell" (HI, AC, 9411). In Kowel a nurse visited the cells once a week. He called from the cell door for the sick to identify themselves, and from the crowd that surged forward he allowed a few, mostly those with visible wounds on their necks, faces, or hands, to step into the corridor where a doctor was waiting. Many died unattended in their cells. Our witness spent several days in the cell with a very high fever before he was taken to the prison hospital. He was brought there only because another prisoner fell ill with typhoid (it was the beginning of an epidemic during which dozens of prisoners died) and was screaming all the time, for he was suffocating. In the prison hospital both of them were put on the floor because the eight beds were already taken, and nobody paid attention to them anymore. His companion, Marian Dorosiewicz from Luboml, died the next night, leaving a young wife who had given birth to their child after his arrest. As the typhoid epidemic spread, sick prisoners had to be moved to the Kowel city hospital, which is how our witness survived (HI, AC, 2402). In the Brygidki prison in Lwów, a doctor walked around the prison periodically and treated in the corridor three to five prisoners from each cell. The guard at the door determined who would receive help. Our informant's cell constantly held about 20 very sick prisoners (HI, AC, 2375). Engineer Hełm-Pirgo witnessed the death of two fellow inmates in cell 33 of the same prison. Judge Janiszewski from Lwów and Captain Lifschutz died there of typhoid, unattended. How many died in the hospital is not known. Before corpses were removed for burial, they were kept in one of the two hospital lavatories, and it was almost always locked up (HI, AC, 1545). In the other large Lwów prison, at Zamarstynów, preventive shots were twice administered to the inmates. A nurse gave the anticholera vaccine to ten inmates in a row without changing the needle (HI, AC, 615). There were several epidemics of typhoid in the Białystok prison, the worst in January 1941 (HI, AC, 1311). In November 1940 a prisoner, a doctor by profession, clamored for the hospitalization of a few inmates who had fallen ill with typhoid in the Baranowicze prison. A Soviet woman doctor came, denounced him as an enemy of the Soviet state, and had him put in a punishment cell. When he returned to his

original cell, 20 inmates were already sick and were finally hospitalized, while the rest were deloused and disinfected (HI, AC, 11206). How many died in Białystok, Baranowicze, or in any other prison where there were similar outbreaks, we do not know.

46. HI, AC, 538, 548. In Nowa Wilejka, prisoners staged a hunger protest in one of the cells because older men were collapsing, unable to breathe. And they won: after a visit from the warden, they got permission to open the cell window for 10 minutes three times a day (HI, AC, 549).

47. HI, AC, 2375; *Dark Side of the Moon*, p. 78. In Stanisławów prisoners were taken for a 5- to 10-minute walk once a week (HI, AC, 340); in Lida, once a week for 20 minutes (HI, AC, 96). People in the NKVD prison at Sądowa Street in Lwów were never allowed to go for a walk (HI, AC, 352), and in the Wilno prison there were no walks from August to December 1940 (HI, AC, 1621).

48. In the basement cells of Nadworna prison the slop bucket was emptied only once a day. Consequently there were excrement and urine on the floor. For the first two or three days new prisoners might stand up around the clock, refusing to lie down at night, until they grew so tired they finally relented and went to sleep (HI, AC, 1680). In a cell in the Przemyśl prison inmates urinated on the floor or (a few bolder ones) through a crack under the door into the hallway, to upset the guards. They had a small wash bowl, not even a bucket, to use as a latrine (HI, AC, 1255). It was the same in the Kowel prison (HI, AC, 2402), and in the Dzisna NKVD prison feces were all over the prison floor due to the lack of adequate toilet facilities (HI, AC, 3999). Of course, prisoners hated to live in dung, so they tried to hold it in, which made them irritable and sick on top of everything (HI, AC, 1545).

49. HI, AC, 2402, 548, 1545.

50. As for the frequency of baths: in Przemyśl there simply were none; from June 1940 through January 1941 inmates of the Białystok prison were only once allowed a bath; in the Lwów Zamarstynów prison (where, we are told, hygienic conditions were far superior to those in the other Lwów prison, at Brygidki) baths were given in 1940 at roughly six-week intervals, and the same in Kowel. In Oszmiana a bath was allowed once every two weeks (though prisoners never shaved and had a haircut only once every two or three months), and in Wilno, at the Łukiszki prison, they bathed every ten days. HI, AC, 1255, 1135, 7759, 2402, 358, 6655; Wat, *Mój Wiek*, 1: 329.

51. HI, AC, 4772.

52. HI, AC, 1311.

53. The prison bath in Kowel had broken windows and only seven showers. Our witness's cell had 86 prisoners, so when all were brought at the same time, there were about 12 of them for each shower. The water was not kept on continuously but instead supplied in three rather short spurts (HI, AC, 2402). In Lwów, the water temperature was always extreme, either cold or hot (Wat, *Mój Wiek*, 1: 329).

54. The topic of delousing stations entered into conversations with the

Soviets repeatedly. As with many other items they regarded as enviable, they kept repeating "u nas vsyo iest" (we have everything) or "u nas etovo mnogo" (we've got plenty of this).

55. HI, AC, 2402, 1545; Wat, *Mój Wiek*, 1: 330.

56. HI, AC, 1311, 548, 6168, 93, 549, 1610; see also *Dark Side of the Moon*.

57. In Lida prison there was a special "educational cell," number 10. Originally designed to hold 12 inmates, at the time our witness (a 34–year-old engineer forester) was there it housed 96. A certain Falenty, a bricklayer from Łomża county, was in charge. He had worked briefly for the NKVD after the Soviet occupation but was eventually sent to prison, apparently for bribe taking. Falenty and his cronies, eleven sentenced Red Army soldiers and a thief from Lida named Więckiewicz or Więckowski, perpetrated a reign of terror in the cell. Prison authorities were in tacit complicity with them. Falenty had special rights: he could leave the cell whenever he pleased; he took property from other prisoners and divided it with his associates and the prison guards. Torture sessions inflicted on other prisoners were watched and openly enjoyed by the guards. Every new prisoner entering the cell was beaten into unconsciousness by Falenty's bullies—"hot buns" these receptions were called. The group introduced a variety of games to play with fellow prisoners. Hidden under imaginative names such as "windmill," "photographs," or "sawmill" there was always some sexual abuse and violence. A religious medal found on a young schoolboy from Lida was tied to his penis, and the boy was then forced to recite a blasphemous prayer. Individual inmates were chosen to lie on the floor and were forced to repeat an oath that the Western Ukraine and Western Belorussia would be Soviet forever, while convicted Red Army soldiers walked over them. Later, they were forced to carry an inscription, "Polish pig, enemy of the Soviet authority," pinned to their backs. Each evening, purportedly to fit everybody into the cell's cramped sleeping space, Falenty played "tin of sardines": he stomped all over lying inmates, beating right and left with the buckle of his military belt (HI, AC, 9411).

58. HI, AC, 358, 548; Wat, *Mój Wiek*, 1: 330.

59. HI, AC, 358, 2402, 523, 6283.

60. HI, AC, 1545.

61. HI, AC, 6263. It was not uncommon throughout the first months for Ukrainian prisoners to boast to their Polish fellow inmates of having lynched Polish colonists who settled in their area or stray Polish soldiers who ventured there in September 1939 (HI, AC, 1717, 2402).

62. HI, AC, 2402.

63. HI, AC, 8027.

64. Lectures were very popular in the prisons. The topics varied from "How to make preserves and ferment wine" in Białystok prison (HI, AC, 1311) to a systematic coverage of the political, religious, and economic problems of prewar Poland in a cell of the Dubno prison (HI, AC, 594; see also *Dark Side of the Moon*, p. 91).

65. Aleksander Wat (*Mój Wiek*, 1: 349) writes of one young, rabid Polish

nationalist who was brought into the cell and whose presence crystallized deeply antagonistic attitudes that until that time had been dormant, smoothed over by the prisoners' efforts to make life bearable. Fortunately, he was transferred after a short while, and the atmosphere improved.

66. HI, AC, 1311, 523, 2545, 2375, 7759.

67. HI, AC, 594, 661, 664, 1314.

68. HI, AC, 8027.

69. Each layer of clothing provided additional protection against blows; that was the reason to give prisoners, especially inexperienced ones up for their first interrogation, an additional sweater or a set of underwear. But that generosity sometimes backfired. A young Ukrainian girl was thus prepared for her interrogation by fellow inmates in the Lwów prison, only to be ordered by the NKVD man to squat-jump, with all her garments on, next to a hot stove (L.K. [Liuba Prokop], "U sorokovi rokovini protsesu 59–i," pt. 1, pp. 104–106).

70. HI, AC, 549.

71. HI, AC, 5842.

72. It is only fair to say, that the Soviet authorities had to overcome a sustained and well-organized resistance in the Western Ukraine and Western Belorussia.

73. More important yet, one might interpret the very phenomenon of privatization of the public domain (see Chapter 3) as the state's ultimate attempt to insert itself as a mediating term between any two individuals and thus become a party to all association.

74. See, for example, Umiastowski, *Russia and the Polish Republic*, p. 272.

75. Wat, *Mój Wiek*, 1: 345; Prokop, "U sorokovi rokovini protsesu," pt. 1, p. 88; HI, AC, 7472.

76. The highest-ranking officers of the ZWZ were, almost without exception it seems, interviewed by the chief of the NKVD, Lavrenti Beria, and his deputies. Many, concludes Major Bortnowski in a report dated August 13, 1941, fell under Beria's spell and were taken by his personality (HI, AC, 1576; UPST, File 3.3.1/5, Obszar Lwów).

77. Białostocki, 27.

78. Białystok, 64; mołodeczno, IV.3.

79. HI, AC, 3999.

80. Stryj, 41.

81. HI, AC, 594; also AC, 108. *Ugolovnyi kodeks RFSSR*, pp. 22–27.

82. "Since the majority of archives and personal files of the local administration, the state institutions, as well as social and political organizations, fell into Bolshevik hands, planned arrests and imprisonments of all who played any role in Polish public life began. Participation in Polish public life up to the 1939 war was considered by the Bolshevik authorities as counterrevolutionary activity, directed against the interests of the Soviet Union. This was used as an argument on every occasion, during arrests, investigations, and propaganda speeches. In all towns and villages prisons were so full of detainees of this sort that other quarters were taken over and turned into prisons" (HI, PGC, 2181).

This determination to arrest those who had participated in public life—that is, were active *outside* of the family circle—accounts for the overwhelming predominance of men among the arrested. See also Umaistowski, *Russia and the Polish Republic*, p. 271.

83. HI, AC, 1414.
84. HI, AC, 1551.
85. HI, AC, 4411.
86. HI, PGC, 4094.
87. HI, AC, 4411.
88. HI, AC, 2402.
89. Russell and his colleague Trant were in Lwów to arrange for the repatriation of a number of British subjects and Palestinian citizens who had been stranded in Soviet-occupied Poland. The quoted excerpt comes from Russell's memorandum summarizing their experiences (GSHI, Collection 82, Folder 29, ms. "Memorandum on conditions in the Soviet Occupied Areas of Polish Ukraine," p. 13). See also Wasilewska's testimony about the poor quality of Soviet personnel sent to the Western Ukraine ("Wspomnienia," p. 357). Yet one also finds in the higher echelons of the NKVD hierarchy brilliant, learned specialists, sophisticated and knowledgeable about their field. See, for example, Aleksander Wat's reminiscences of his interrogations in the Lubianka prison (Wat, *Mój Wiek*, 2: chs. 27–29).
90. Having scrutinized biographical information of 60 members of the state secret police party cell of the Western oblast who were subjected to questioning and screening in the course of the 1929 purge (which they all survived), Fainsod concluded: "A striking characteristic of this group was its youth" (*Smolensk under Soviet Rule*, p. 160). Here follows a reconstituted, though of course incomplete, roster of NKVD interrogators assigned to the Western Ukraine and Western Belorussia: Abrashkin, major from Pińsk; Aleynikov (Oleynikov?), lieutenant from Łomża; Artamoshin, from Święciany; Blinov, from Wilno; Baranov, nachalnik in Głębokie; Bobrov, lieutenant in Dzisna; Bobrykov, lieutenant from Wilno; Bondarenko, from Wiśniowiec; Bondarenko, colonel, nachalnik from Lwów prison at Sądowa Street; Borovikov, nachalnik from Lida; Brantzev, from Lwów; Brokovskij, from Równe; Bubnov, from Wilejka; Burchenko, from Kowel; Bykov, major from Wilno; Cherkashin, nachalnik of the railroad NKVD from Kołomyja; Chernogaev, nachalnik from Miadzioł; Chevichalov, from Lida; Doroshchuk, from Wilejka; Dymitrenko, lieutenant from Łomża; Fiedorov, lieutenant from the railroad NKVD in Tarnopol; Frolov, from Wilejka; Gorov, from Kowel; Gubarov, from Wilejka; Gumian, from the railroad NKVD in Łanowce; Gusiev, from Lwów; Ivanov, from Wilejka; Karch, captain from Wilno; Khabanov, from Dubno; Kharytonov, sergeant from Stanisławów; Khernyk, from Brody; Kiknadze, from the railroad NKVD in Kołomyja; Klepov, from Lwów; Klimiuk, sergeant from Równe; Kokovkin, from Białystok; Kosarev, lieutenant from Baranowicze; Kovalenko, nachalnik for Krzemieniec county; Kozlov, from Dubno; Kozlov, colonel (general), nachalnik from Wilno; Koźluk, from

Wilejka; Krasimenko, nachalnik from Żydaczówka; Krasnov, nachalnik from Lwów; Kudimov, from Równe; Kuzmienko, nachalnik from Słonim; Lavrov, lieutenant from Brody; Lazarevicz, from Białystok; Legaev, lieutenant from Lida; Lukianov, from Wilno; Makhardze, lieutenant, nachalnik from Tarnopol; Makieyev, from Żytomierz; Mamiedov, from Białystok, also from the railroad NKVD in Tarnopol; Nazarov, from the railroad NKVD in Tarnopol; Nieplokhin, from Żytomierz; Nudelman, from Białystok; Orlov, lieutenant from Stanisławów; Ostapishin, from Stołpce; Ovsiankov, lieutenant from Baranowicze; Pavlenko, from the railroad NKVD in Kołomyja; Pietrov, nachalnik from Drohobycz; Pobereźny, prison nachalnik from Przemyśl; Polimarchuk, from Przemyśl; Popov, colonel from Wilno; Popov, lieutenant from Nadworna; Popov, lieutenant from Sumy; Popov, major from Pińsk; Rakhlin, from Lwów and Rawa Ruska; Rozov, nachalnik from Włodzimierz Wołyński; Rybakov, lieutenant from Rafajłowo; Sazonov, lieutenant from Wilno; Sergeevski, nachalnik from Żytomierz; Sidorenko, major from Wilno; Sidorow, lieutenant from Kałusz; Siemionov, from Pińsk; Sirot, captain from Włodzimierz Wołyński; Smirnov, lieutenant from Łuniniec; Smolenskii, from Święciany; Sokolov, from Lubcza; Tiuleniov, *nachalnik* from Lubcza; Vinokurov (Vinokur?), nachalnik from Dubno; Vinokurov, lieutenant from Czortków; Volkov, from Wilno; Vykhovski, captain, nachalnik from Korzec; Yampolski, lieutenant from Wilejka; Zaporozhetz, from Wiśnowiec. See HI, AC, 549, 691, 765, 988, 1209, 1336, 1543, 1547, 1551, 1807, 2021, 2391, 2408, 2415, 2423, 3297, 3685, 3999, 4096, 4112, 4621, 4866, 5842, 6120, 6144, 7704, 7943, 8027, 8367, 8613, 9077, 9126, 9346, 9589, 9690, 9733, 10746, 10987, 12409, 12539, 12565, 12584, 12616, 12692; Poland. Ambasada USSR, Box 46, 47; krzemieniec, dodatek, 1; kowel, 58; kołomyja, 49; śniatyń, 47.

91. Wilejka, 45.

92. HI, AC, 549.

93. HI, AC, 4974.

94. HI, AC, 7472.

95. HI, AC, 7472, 107, 523, 2056, 6335, 9562, 10752; mołodeczno, IV.3; GSHI, A.9.III.2a/file 58; Wilno-Troki, 23; *Dark Side of the Moon*, pp. 87, 89.

96. Brasław, 24; Wilno-Troki, 22; łomża, 86; łuniniec, 43; HI, AC, 108, 392, 594, 7472, 7746, 7854.

97. HI, AC, 541; ostrołęka, 13; łuck, 63; łomża, 85; Wilno-Troki, 23; lida, 32; łuniniec, 43.

98. Oszmiana.

99. Pińsk, 63.

100. HI, AC, 499, 392, 7854.

101. HI, AC, 6259, 10570.

102. HI, AC, 3538. For a similar episode from Stanisławów, see GSHI, Polskie Siły Powietrzne Collection, File 6, Abczyński.

103. HI, AC, 107, 7472; kobryń, 44; sarny, suppl. 2.

104. In 1954 a Belorussian teacher from Wilejka, Vasil Misiul, told the U.S.

House Select Committee on Communist Aggression how, together with a few other members of the local community, he investigated the prison after the Soviets were routed from the area in June 1941: "In the yard we found something like a dugout, and there was a trail from it as if a body had been dragged along the ground. We went along that trail and into the cellar there, where we noted that the walls were spattered with blood, and there were holes in the walls as if from bullets. When we could see better in the darkness, after getting accustomed to it, we noted in one corner a large amount of dry blood. From the evidence it appeared to us that this was the place where many people had been murdered. Then we went along, following a trail of a body being dragged. This took us to another section of the yard of the prison and there we saw a long row of fresh earth. We decided to dig it up and see what was underneath. At a depth of about one foot we began to find bodies. . . . The condition of these bodies indicated that they had only recently been killed and buried. . . . The lowest layers were in such a condition of decomposition that they could not be touched, and those were not counted" (pp. 232–235). Still, they counted more than 500 bodies.

105. HI, AC, 392.

106. HI, PGC, 1393.

107. HI, AC, 2402; łomża, 86; sokółka, 44; oszmiana; mołodeczno, IV.3; Wilno-Troki, 22; drohobycz, 55; Przemyśl, 73; kostopol†, 114; kołomyja, 49.

108. There is reason to believe that at least some of these documents are already in Western archives. Hitler's special troops (*Einzatsgruppen*), which entered the area immediately following the Wehrmacht and were responsible for the mass murders of Jews and communist sympathizers, were also under orders to search for and secure NKVD files. They acquitted themselves with proverbial German diligence: the daily reports on their activities in the USSR, issued and distributed by the RSHA beginning on June 22, 1941 (Ereignismeldungen USSR, Bundesarchiv Koblenz, fol. 1–268), almost every day carry information about loads of Soviet documents seized for shipment to Berlin (see reports 3, 9, 10, 13, 14, 15, 21). Most of these were probably later destroyed when RSHA headquarters in Berlin burned down in 1945. But some survived, notably the so-called Smolensk Archive. Still other documents may be buried somewhere in the National Archives in Washington or held in CIA custody. In time they may surface—to confirm our worst estimates, I am afraid.

109. *Czerwony Sztandar*, Oct. 8, 1939; see also Umiastowski, *Russia and the Polish Republic*, pp. 272–273. A Lithuanian witness before the U.S. House Select Committee on Communist Aggression was kept as a warden in one of the largest Lithuanian prisons (he does not say which one) for three months after the Red Army took over Lithuania (through September 15, 1940). Prisoners who died during this time (we are not told whether they were victims of torture or of execution) "were buried in the night in the prison yard or in the forest near the city. When I suggested to the chief investigator that it would be quite humane to inform the relatives of the prisoners about their deaths and that this would raise the Bolshevik prestige, I was called a fool" (p. 275).

110. Liuba Prokop, "U sorokovi," pt. 2, p. 98; HI, AC, 10752; PGC, 8515.

111. Two scenarios were repeated with only minor variations: death in the forest, or in the prison cellar. "I want to tell how Poles were shot in the Wilno prison in 1940/41. The condemned prisoner was taken from the cell together with his belongings; he was brought to the prison office, where his personal effects and documents were returned; and then a decree of pardon was read to him. Afterwards he was taken to the main gate, where a few armed soldiers and some civilian agents came up to him and drove him to the nearby forest to be shot. The executed prisoner was then stripped of all his belongings and buried naked" (Wilno, 68). Another witness, a cook, states that in a period of three days he counted seventeen cars taking condemned prisoners to execution in the Belmont forest on Wilno's outskirts (Wilno, 68). How he could identify a car carrying prisoners for execution from any other car, we are not told; but apparently he thought he could. We have no choice at this point but to use evidence that is available. Only if mass graves of executed prisoners were unearthed and the circumstances of their deaths established through autopsy could we be more confident in our conjectures. Unfortunately, such discoveries have been made, and not exclusively in the ill-renowned Katyń forest.

112. Kołomyja, 49; Przemyśl, 71; Wilno-Troki, 22, 23; HI, AC, 661.

113. HI, AC, 3999; see also HI, AC, 499, 4342.

114. HI, AC, 110, 452, 9733.

115. HI, Poland. Ambasada USSR, Box 48, Pialucha.

116. I have one statement, though rather cryptic, from Lwów by a certain Głodowski: "On June 22, 1941, we were led out from a Lwów prison [he does not say which one] and we marched to Moscow. On August 28 we reached Moscow. On our way, whoever couldn't walk from exhaustion was pierced with a Bayonet and the guards checked his Pulse whether he had died, and if he hadn't they pierced him a second time" (HI, AC, 3101). I have seen no other indication that any of the Lwów prisons were evacuated and plenty of evidence to the contrary.

117. "My brother was living as an engineer in a small town in west Ukraine and was arrested in June—about June 20, 1941. He was put in the prison in Chortkiv [Czortków]. He was held in Czortków for about two weeks, and then with about 700 people, at least 700 people, they were forced to march about 300 miles through the country to Umań. . . . When they arrived in Umań the people saw them going into the prison, but nobody ever saw them coming out. . . . After a long search we found in Umań, behind the prison, a big hole for coal or wood for burning. We found that this was completely filled with bodies, which were covered by a special wood floor, and then it was camouflaged with scrap wood and lumber. After the people took all these bodies out of the big hole, one after another, they took them to a cemetery. It was my duty to investigate, because I was from the territory where the people had come from. I was investigating crimes like this for the newspapers. Then I established that all of the people were killed at a time in the night when a loud sound of motors could be heard by other inmates of the prison. Under the

cover of the sounds of machinery or motors like a large truck many people were shot and murdered. . . . [The victims] were from 14 to 60 years old. I found many small papers, written in the prison in Czortków, which identified some of the people, their birthdays, etc. . . . I found altogether 700–odd bodies. My brother was among them." Dr. Paul Turula gave this testimony before the U.S. House Select Committee on Communist Aggression in Chicago on October 18, 1954 (pp. 280–281).

118. *Lwów voivodeship*: Borysław, Bóbrka, Dobromil, Drohobycz, Komarno, Lwów, Sambor, Żółkiew. *Stanisławów voivodeship*: Nadworna, Ottynia, Pasieczna, Stanisławów, Stryj. *Tarnopol voivodeship*: Brzeżany, Busk, Czortków, Łopatyn, Przemyślany, Złoczów. *Wilno voivodeship*: Berezwecz-Głębokie, Nowa Wilejka, Wilno. *Wołyń voivodeship*: Dubno, Krzemieniec, Łuck. See Bundesarchiv, R 58/214, Ereignismeldung UdSSR, no. 9, 10, 14, 28; *ROU*, pp. 176–197; Rudnycka, *Western Ukraine under the Bolsheviks*, pp. 441–444, 477–492; testimony before the U.S. House Select Committee, pp. 112–113, 232–235; HI, AC, 2422, 5455, 15162, 15725, 15739; HI, Stanisław Mikołajczk Archive, Box 9, File "Correspondence, London, 1941"; UPST, B I/104; YV, 03/1323; interview with Jan Moldauer, Tel Aviv, Summer 1980.

119. There are many lacunae of this sort, all rather ominous. For example, we have several detailed testimonies about the massacre in the Brygidki prison in Lwów but no survivors' accounts from either Zamarstynów prison or from the NKVD prison at Łącki Street. We hear only about the piles of corpses found there after the Soviets left the city.

120. *ROU*, p. 177.

121. *ROU*, pp. 179, 183, 184, 185; testimony before the U.S. House Select Committee, pp. 112–113. In Dubno, prisoners were also machine-gunned in their cells. Both a male and a female survivor described these executions in depositions reported in a special appendix, "Bericht—über das Staatgefangnis Dubno und über das Blutbad vom 24 und 25.6.1941," to the Ereignismeldung UdSSR no. 28 (Bundesarchiv, R 58/214).

122. Testimony before the U.S. House Select Committee, p. 113.

123. We learn about this episode from indirect testimony. German planes caught up with the column that left the prison in Berezwecz near Głębokie at the crossing of the river Dźwina. "After the air raid, prisoners were divided into 'politicals' and 'criminals.' Then another air raid followed. When it was over, the escort shot all political prisoners with submachine guns. According to witnesses, over 1,500 people were killed. Criminals were then told to drag the corpses into roadside ditches and were set free" (HI, Poland. Ambasada USSR, Box 51, Hartman). Mr. Hartman learned these facts in conversations with "over twenty people," as he puts it in a sworn deposition before a Polish military investigating commission in Iran. He gives names of eyewitnesses but was not himself present at the scene.

124. Rudnycka, *Western Ukraine under the Bolsheviks*, p. 443.

125. *ROU*, p. 184.

126. *ROU*, p. 181.

127. Testimony before the U.S. House Select Committee, p. 113.

128. *ROU*, pp. 179, 182, 184, 185, 186, 187.

129. *ROU*, pp. 188–194, 197; HI, AC, 15725; Mikołajczyk Archive, Box 9, File "Correspondence, London, 1941."

130. Rudnycka, *Western Ukraine under the Bolsheviks*, p. 491. "In the vicinity of Dobromil an old, 80–meter-deep salt mine shaft full of corpses was discovered. In the immediate vicinity a 6 m by 15 m mass grave was also found. One can estimate that several hundred people must have been murdered in Dobromil" (Bundesarchiv Koblenz, R 58/214, fol. 1–268, Ereignismeldung UdSSR, no. 24). It was not unusual to leave the lower layers of corpses in mass graves; in the summer weather and with the bodies' advanced state of decomposition, they could have produced epidemics.

131. Interview with Jan Moldauer, Tel Aviv, Summer 1980; see also YV 03/ 1323. Confirmation of these practices may be found in a completely unrelated source. Edward Kuznetsov, a Lithuanian who kept a diary while interned in a Soviet prison camp in the 1970s, reproduces a petition written to the authorities by his fellow prisoner, Adomas Ludwikas Simutis. Its opening paragraph reads: "I was five years old when I was shown the corpse of my father. Half his face was swollen, blue, while the other half was covered in blood. His eyes had been gouged out. On his arms and legs the skin was white, peeling, scalded. His tongue had been bound with a piece of string. His sexual organs were crushed (I found this out later). Round him lay many other distorted corpses. I remember the sobbing of my mother and many people I didn't know. ... This was in June 1941, after the retreat of the Red Army" (Kuznetsov, *Prison Diaries*, p. 194).

132. HI, AC, 2103.

133. HI, PGC, Box 132, Józef Sołczyński; Box 234, Marian Nowosad; AC, 5455, 15162.

134. HI, AWBD, Dr. Tadeusz Wieliczko, ms. "Wilejka"; AC, 15223, 2921.

135. HI, AC, 15223. Dr. Tadeusz Wieliczko (pen name of Dr. Tadeusz Dymowski), author of a brief monograph about the Wilejka prison written for the Bureau of Documents of the Polish Army in the East, estimated that about 100 women were returned to prison from the train station and killed, while the rest were freed (HI, AWBD, Dr. Wieliczko, ms. "Wilejka"). But in this otherwise carefully documented text Wieliczko does not say what information led him to this optimistic assertion.

136. HI, AC, 5908.

137. HI, AC, 12558. "I didn't answer even though they called me several times, then they read some other names, and mine again, and I didn't answer. They didn't look for me in the crowd. They were in a hurry" (HI, AC, 392).

138. HI, AC, 12599, 2103.

139. HI, AC, 392. In any emergency or disturbance, the escort simply ordered prisoners to lie down (HI, AC, 2103, 12398).

140. HI, AC, 391, 1230, 1257, 2392.

141. HI, AC, 392, 1257, 12398.

142. HI, AC, 2103, 6467, 8499.

143. HI, AC, 2103, 3556, 8474, 12398.

144. HI, AC, 2103, 2582, 12398.

145. HI, AWBD, Dr. T. Wieliczko, ms. "Wilejka." Here follows a partial list of prisoners killed during evacuation of the Wilejka prison in June 1941. Unless otherwise indicated, names are quoted following Dr. Wieliczko's manuscript. Many others were killed, but they remain anonymous.

Prisoners killed in the Wilejka prison on June 24, 1941: Abakanowicz, railwayman from Zalesie; Apałko, forester; Bartoszewicz; Jan Bielewicz, high school student; Piotr Bonów; Bućko; Bułat, secretary of the court in Daniłowicze; Butrymowicz, peasant from Oszmiana county; Czernichow, attorney from Wilno; Hajbowicz, financial office clerk from Postawy; Stanisław Hassa, hospital administrator from Oszmiana; Wincenty Hurowicz (Gurowicz?); Jan Jankiewicz, high school student (policeman?); Jasiukiewicz; Kajro, peasant from gmina Miadzioł; Krupski; Konstanty Lemantowicz; Stanisław Małachowski from Górnica; Matyszczak, priest from Widze; Leon Michałowski; Edward Minkowski, policeman; Pankszteło; Witold Pietkiewicz, peasant from Oszmiana county; Franciszek Pisarczyk, engineer; Stanisław Pisarczyk, policeman; Michał Pulczuk (Pilczuk?); Józef Radecki from Miadzioły; Stanisław Stefanowicz; Franciszek Szymanel; Józef Urbanowicz, high school student; Waniurski from Głębokie; Wasilewski, son of a watchmaker from Oszmiana.

Prisoners killed during the evacuation march: Piotr Afronowicz (Achranowicz?), driver (HI, AC, 12558); Antoniewicz, peasant (HI, AC, 12558); Babicz, retired policeman; Stanisław Baryłko, teacher; Lucjan Boczarski, engineer; Piotr Bondar, peasant; Władysław Bondar, policeman; Wacław Bondarewicz, railwayman; Kazimierz Borowski from Wilejka (HI, AC, 1551); Józef Burdecki, court clerk; Jan Bychowiec from Oszmiana; Stefan Chorwat (Horwat?), manager of an estate; Chwoles (Chwolisz?), engineer from Wilno; Czechowicz, landowner; Daniłowicz, peasant; Dargiel (Dangiel?), sergeant from Brasław; Drobik (Drabik?), stationmaster; Ignacy Duchawski, voyt; Janusz Dziekoński, landowner; Witold Dziergacz, storeowner from Nistaniszki; Stanisław Fijałkowski; Stanisław Garnicki, attorney from Wilejka; Stanisław Gładysz, from Wilno railroad management; Sergiusz Grygoriew, captain (teacher from Święciany?); Hcyfec (Hcyfiec?), pharmacist; Józef Hranicki (Harnicki?), surveyor from Wilejka; Jan Jachondowicz, carpenter from Widze; Cezary Jamrzycki, high school student; Jan Jankiewicz, policeman; Stefan Janowicz, from Postawy county; Józef Jaroszewicz, director of farmers' chamber; Jaworski; Jan Juchniewicz, peasant; Józef Juchniewicz, financial clerk from Wilejka; Stanisław Kaczan, teacher; Ignacy Kamiński, colonist;

Józef Kanczanin, teacher from Łyntupy; Karcisz; Feliks Karolkiewicz, land-owner from Brasław; Karpowicz; Aleksander Kimbar from Wilejka; Kimbart, chairman of Stefczyk's Bank from Nistaniszki; Stanisław Kimber, peasant; Koblenc, merchant from Wilejka (HI, AC, 8474); Kornblum from Wilejka; Kosiak; Jan Kostrzewski, financial clerk from Święciany (HI, Mikołajczyk Archive); Stanisław Kowszon (Kowszyn?), village head; Stanisław Koziarz, from Oszmiana county (HI, AC, 12398); Kuczewski; Witold Lamprecht (Lam-parecht?), financial clerk from Wilejka; Łaps, locksmith from Daniłowicze; Jan Ławrynowicz from Mołodeczno; Teodor Lemontowicz from Mołodeczno; Jan Leskiewicz, shoemaker from Dołhinowo; Mikołaj Lipiński, surveyor; Lipski from Daniłowicze; Maciejewski, policeman; Antoni Maka-rewicz, railwayman from Łyntupy; Jan Małachowski, postmaster; Piotr Mar-czański, teacher from Święciany county; Jan Matusiewicz, policeman; Jan Matysiak, priest; Tadeusz Miczewski, policeman from Brasław county; Mi-razen, rabbi; Mironowicz, teacher from Wilejka; Roman Monid, peasant; Stefan Monid, railwayman from Zahacie; Muraszko, agronomist from agri-cultural school in Łuczaj; Jan Nadroszlański, landowner; Nagórski, deputy mayor of Wilno (HI, Mikołajczyk Archive); Niedroczlański, vice-voyt of gmina Świr (HI, AC, 6467); Niedrusztański, peasant; Nistomski (HI, AC, 4070); Władysław Olszewski, telegraph operator; Piotrowski; Pociejonek from Dzisna county; Hersz Rajchel, miller from Postawy; Bronisław Rakowski; Jan Raszkiewicz, peasant; Józef Raszkiewicz, NCO; Stanisław Romanowski, peasant (HI, Mikołajczyk Archive); Konstanty Roth (Rott?), engineer; Alek-sander Rusin, high school student; Józef Rynkiewicz, peasant; Walery Ryzon (Ryszon?), peasant; Józef Rzepko; Sawicki; Piotr Serdeczny, peasant; Siat-kiewicz; Siesicki, clerk (HI, Mikołajczyk Archive); Czesław Siwicki, high school student; Bronisław Skowroński, veteran of Piłsudski's legions; Józef Smolag, policeman; Bronisław Stachowicz, colonist; Stachowski, peasant; Apolinary Stachowski, deputy postmaster from Wilejka; Władysław Syrowiec; Alfons Szpiec, worker from Łyntypy; Antoni Szymański; Romuald Tarasiewicz, high school student (shot in prison according to AC, 2489); Edward Tomaszewicz, distillery worker from Łyntupy (HI, AC, 1282); Jan Tomaszewicz, distillery technician; Józef Tomaszewicz, electrician; Wacław Tomaszewski; Urbanek, peasant; Mieczysław Warakso, road guard (HI, AC, 12558); Bolesław Wasilewski, road technician; Wacław Waszkiewicz, policeman; Edward Wierzbicki from Wiszniewo (HI, Mikołajczyk Archive); Wojciechowski from Łyntupy; Stanisław Wojciechowski, peasant; Wojnowski, landowner (engineer?); Adolf Woroniec, cadet; Mieczysław Zaj-kowski (Sajkowski?); Ignacy Zawadzki; Zieliński, locksmith from Postawy; Zukowski.

146. HI, AC, 3223, 3479, 3366, 3837, 3929, 4298, 4967.

147. From Tarnopol, prisoners were first marched, with many killed, to the railroad station at Wołoczyska, and then sent further east by train on a journey

on which "many died." See HI, PGC, 8978; Box 132, Zenon Wcisło, ms. "Więzienie w Czortkowie"; UPST, B II, 589, 4; HI, AC, 489, 3477, 5134, 5592.

SIX: DEPORTATIONS

1. Ivan Serov, at the time people's commissar for internal affairs in the Ukraine, was Khrushchev's principal assistant in "the job of establishing Soviet power and normalizing the situation in the lands annexed from Poland" (*Khrushchev Remembers*, p. 143). Section 5 of Serov's strictly secret "Instructions Regarding the Manner of Conducting the Deportation of the Anti-Soviet Elements From Lithuania, Latvia, and Estonia" (see *An Appeal to Fellow Americans on Behalf of the Baltic States*, pp. 31–37) is entitled "Manner of Separating Deportee from His Family." "His" should be stressed, because Serov clearly emphasizes separate treatment for male heads of families; unlike the rest of the deportees, they "must be arrested and placed in special camps" (p. 35). Serov carefully describes the procedures that must be followed so that the designated future prisoners will not suspect that they will be treated differently. Clearly, not all heads of families were to be arrested. I have encountered only a few episodes in which such arrests were actually carried out, all of them during the June 1941 deportation. On the other hand, there is evidence that on several occasions families in transports were joined by fathers or husbands who had been arrested some months or weeks before.

2. HI, PGC, Box 117, Stefan Tabor; AC, 1379.

3. HI, AC, Dr. Tadeusz Wieliczko, "Polityka sowiecka na okupowanych ziemiach polskich."

4. HI, AC, 12403, 14458; PGC, 2090, 3534, 7612.

5. See note 14 in the Preface.

6. HI, Poland. Ambasada USSR, Box 46, Zofia Duch-Duniewska; also a woman doctor from Lwów, signature illegible; UPST, B I/3859, Dr. Jadwiga Mękarska; sambor, 49.

7. See, for example, *Czerwony Sztandar*, Mar. 9, 29, 1940; also HI, PGC, 10276.

8. HI, PGC, 4873. See also równe, 12; HI, PGC, 3194, 1137, 690; jarosław and lubaczów, 13; HI, Mikołajczyk Archive, Box 15, ms. "Czerwone rządy w Wilnie"; Gross and Gross, *War Through Children's Eyes*, doc. 63, 94; Gross and Gross, *W czterdziestym*, doc. 136, 138.

9. Gross and Gross, *War Through Children's Eyes*, doc. 63.

10. UPST, B I/3859, Dr. Józefa Mękarska.

11. HI, AC, 15550.

12. See also HI, AC, 10555, 12300, 15560; PGC, Box 131, Palestinian protocol no. 137.

13. *Czerwony Sztandar*, June 25, 1941.

14. Dobromil, 37.

15. *DPSR*, p. 180. The Serov instructions (see above, note 1) present the

general blueprint for organizing deportations but say nothing about which people were targeted.

16. An interesting article on the welfare apparatus of the Polish embassy in the USSR is Roman Buczek's "Działalność opiekuńcza Ambasady R.P. w ZSSR w latach 1941–1943." See also the memoirs of the Polish ambassador to the USSR at the time: Stanisław Kot, *Listy z Rosji do Generała Sikorskiego.*

17. Roman Buczek mentions a March 1940 and a May 1940 deportation ("Działalność," pp. 47, 48). But when he summarizes his findings, only the four deportations identified here are listed as distinct episodes. Maybe in a few areas the February and April deportations were dragged out. But unfortunately Buczek does not quote any specific reference for the March and May dates. In the individual depositions I have read, I have not encountered a single mention of a March or a May deportation, though of course there were transports of prisoners to the Soviet interior during these months.

18. Wilno-troki, 33; prużana, 39; kobryń, 50, 54; nieśwież, 68.

19. HI, PGC, Box 117.

20. See, for example, HI, PGC, Box 117, Stanisław Koziewicz; Box 119, Bronisław Andreasik; Poland. Ambasada USSR, Box 50, Lucjan Kwiatkowski, Józef Sukiennik; przemyśl, 92.

21. HI, PGC, Box 117, Stanisław Sypacz; Box 119, Czesław Jezierski; Box 120, Wiktor Buchorski, Kazimierz Adler; Box 122, Tadeusz Typrowicz; Box 123, Zbigniew Tatarczyk; Poland. Ambasada USSR, Box 50, Władysław Biełо, Jan Adamczyk; turka, 27; krzemieniec, 33.

22. Train size was much less frequently recorded and varies from reports of 15 cars to (a printing error, I think) 83 (przemyśl, 90; horochów, 54; krzemieniec, 33). A railroad employee from Baranowicze remembers that 60–car trains were put together prior to the February deportation. He says also that from the end of January freight cars were being outfitted for their new function. Sliding doors were nailed shut on one side, all other openings were covered or barred, and wooden boards were put inside with which to build bunks (HI, AC, 12674).

23. According to Leopold Bakalarczyk, at the time employed in the Baranowicze railroad station (HI, AC, 12674).

24. HI, PGC, Box 128, p. 3.

25. See, for example, horochów, 53; bóbrka, 33; lida, 47; jarosław and lubaczów, 44.

26. HI, PGC, Box 49.

27. Oszmiana; *Czerwony Sztandar*, Oct. 18, 1939. See also ostrów, 8; sokolski, 11; Białystok, 22–25; równe, 12, 13; brasław, 4; wilejka, 22, 23; kowel, 32; lida, 15; HI, PGC, 3926, 4633, 5723, 7261.

28. HI, Poland. Ambasada USSR, Box 46, doctor from Lwów, illegible name; PGC, 4085.

29. Łuniniec, 19; kobryń, 18; brasław, 8; wilejka, 17, 18; postawy, 14; zdołbunów, 10; kowel, 24; lida, 10; równe, 16; Gross and Gross, *War Through Children's Eyes*, doc. 46.

30. Both quotations are from HI, Poland. Ambasada USSR, Box 47, Helena Wypijewska. See also sarny, 24; dubno, 33; HI, PGC, Box 117, Edward Dudojc; Box 121, Marian Urbanowicz; Gross and Gross, W czterdziestym, doc. 133.

31. Zdołbunów, dodatek, 2; dobromil, 37; krzemieniec, 32; przemyśl, 90, 91; interview with Mirosłav Łabuńka, Philadelphia, Summer 1980.

32. Interview with Mirosłav Łabuńka, Philadelphia, Summer 1980.

33. Gross and Gross, W czterdziestym, doc. 111; sarny, 24; przemyśl, 68, 69, 92; szczuczyn, 47; jarosław and lubaczów, 45.

34. Równe, 38; zdołbunów, 28; horochów, 50, 51.

35. Czerwony Sztandar, June 9, 1940, published order no. 1 of the Lwów air defense authority calling for air raid drill readiness from June 10th on. See also Gross and Gross, W czterdziestym, doc. 137; HI, AC, 10565, 14513; Poland. Ambasada USSR, Box 46, Zofia Duch Duniewska; PGC, 8459.

36. See my references to this process in Chapter 1, based on Volodymyr Kubijovych's testimony.

37. Gross and Gross, 1983, W czterdziestym, doc. 137. See also HI, AC, 2168, 10584.

38. HI, Poland. Ambasada USSR, Box 46, Maria Czech; HI, AC, 14501.

39. HI, PGC, Box 131, Palestinian protocol no. 186. See also, for example, HI, AC, 10560, 12332, 12333, 12334. "Never in my life have I seen such a determined resistance as when Soviet authorities wanted to force the Jews to accept Soviet citizenship," wrote Lieber Gottlob. "How they defended themselves against this act of violence by moving from one apartment to another, or even changing towns. Their resistance defies description" (HI, AC, 12128).

40. According to Bolesław Jancewicz's deposition, Lithuanians (that is, local residents, not even refugees) were given a similar option in Wilno voivodeship and were also deported when they exercised it. "The Soviets announced that people of Lithuanian nationality could go to Lithuania with all their belongings. They wanted to test in this way the sympathy of the Lithuanian nation with Soviet rule. Those who signed up to go to Lithuania were deported to Russia." (HI, AC, 12574).

41. HI, PGC, Box 131, Palestinian protocol no. 148; also AC, 12300, 12301, 14015, 14017.

42. HI, AC, 10580.

43. HI, PGC, 5331.

44. HI, AC, 7989, 9672.

45. Wilno, 86; wilno-troki, I.33; prużana, 39; kobryń, 50, 54; nieśwież, 68; wilejka, 62; brasław, 32.

46. See note 1 above.

47. Gross and Gross, W czterdziestym, doc. 143.

48. Testimony before the U.S. House Select Committee on Communist Aggression, p. 40. See also An Appeal to Fellow Americans.

49. Nowogródzki, 50.

50. HI, AC, 12394.

51. Dolina, 75.

52. I know of only a few episodes of active resistance. A boy in Wasilków escaped through a window when they came to take his family in April. A militiaman shot and killed him as he fled. On another occasion in April, in Kałusz county, a Polish family already put on a truck by a Soviet escort was rescued by Ukrainian villagers. Another boy ran away from a transport on its way to the train station in February in Skałat county (Białostocki, 56; HI, Poland. Ambasada USSR, Box 49, Janusz Kułakowski; skałat, 42). See also dubno, 33.

53. Dolina, 73.

54. Wilejka, 62.

55. HI, PGC, Box 117, Maria Wilk. See also, for example, HI, PGC, Box 117, Kazimierz Pietraszewski, Henryk Połoszak; Box 119, Jan Marszałek, Czesław Jezierski; Box 120, Tadeusz Macheta, Kazimierz Adler, Stefan Janczyński; Box 122, Tadeusz Typrowicz; drohobycz, 68; Gross and Gross, W czterdziestym, doc. 19, 21.

56. Gross and Gross, War Through Children's Eyes, doc. 54.

57. HI, PGC, Box 120, Tadeusz Warzybok, Eugeniusz Łabędź; Box 117, Zygmunt Kotlarz, Leon Brucki.

58. Przemyśl, 91.

59. HI, PGC, Box 119, Czesław Jezierski; Box 120, Tadeusz Warzybok, Tadeusz Marków, Feliks Jarosz; Box 122, Bronisław Wawruszczak; lubaczów, 46; łomża, 111; kobryń, 53.

60. See, for example, HI, PGC, Box 117, Tadeusz Flasza, Henryk Połoszak, Stanisław Kaziewicz, Stanisław Sobolewski; Box 120, Tadeusz Macheta; stryj, 58; przemyśl, 90; postawy, 46; Gross and Gross, W czterdziestym, doc. 31. Serov recommended a month's supply for a family, but this instruction was rarely followed in practice.

61. See, for example, HI, PGC, Box 117, Stanisław Kaziewicz, Stanisław Sypacz; Box 119, Czesław Jezierski; Box 120, Kazimierz Adler; Box 122, Edward Markiewicz; Poland. Ambasada USSR, Box 50, Julia Łysoniówna, Zofia Mańkowska; mołodeczno, 18.

62. Postawy, 46; luboml, 14.

63. HI, Poland. Ambasada USSR, Box 50, Irena Kulikowska. See also, for example, dubno, 33, 34.

64. HI, PGC, Box 117, Edward Dudojc, Stanisław Matrejek; Box 120, Kazimierz Zasępa; nowogródzki, 50; Gross and Gross, W czterdziestym, doc. 56.

65. An Appeal to Fellow Americans, p. 34; jarosław and lubaczów, 45; HI, PGC, Box 117, Leon Borucki; Gross and Gross, W czterdziestym, doc. 63, 84.

66. Testimony before the U.S. House Select Committee, p. 40; HI, AC, 12394; Gross and Gross, W czterdziestym, doc. 85.

67. HI, PGC, Box 117, Stanisław Kaziewicz, Jerzy Trylski; kobryń, 53, 54; lida, 48; włodzimierz wołyński, 47; święciany, 40.

68. Postawy, 46. See also, for example, HI, Poland. Ambasada USSR, Box 50, Irena Kulikowska; PGC, Box 117, Henryk Połoszak; Box 124, Andrzej

Zajączkowski; gródek jagielloński, 33; krzemieniec, 32; Gross and Gross, *W czterdziestym*, doc. 4. "On February 10 I was at school at nine o'clock when three Soviet gendarmes walked into class with a list. They read names of students whom they ordered to go home. I was among them. I packed my books and bid farewell to friends, foreseeing what awaited me. The teacher and the students in class were all crying because about one-third of us were called out" (HI, AC, 14242).

69. Gross and Gross, *W czterdziestym*, doc. 16, 21.

70. HI, PGC, Box 117, Antoni Dudek; Box 123, Zbigniew Tatarczyk.

71. Dubno, 34.

72. Przemyśl, 93. See also HI, PGC, Box 117, Stanisław Resler; pińsk, 78, 79; nieśwież, 69.

73. HI, AC, 1379.

74. Pińsk, 78.

75. HI, AC, 3477, 8732, 9659, 11938; Poland. Ambasada USSR, Box 46, Stefania Gołaszewska, Czesława Maliszewska; Gross and Gross, *W czterdziestym*, doc. 136.

76. *The Tchortkiv District*, pp. 662, 754, 772; bóbrka, 34; pińsk, 78.

77. Luboml, dodatek, 8. See also HI, Poland. Ambasada USSR, Box 49, Janusz Kułakowski; Gross and Gross, *W czterdziestym*, doc. 39.

78. HI, PGC, Box 120, Tadeusz Macheta; Box 117, Mieczysław Omiotek; Box 118, Maria Stawarz.

79. See also HI, PGC, Box 117, Leon Borucki, Edward Dudojc; Box 119, Jan Marszałek; Box 120, Kazimierz Adler; Poland. Ambasada USSR, Box 50, Janina Strycharzówna, Maria Bargelówna.

80. HI, PGC, Box 117, Stanisław Sypacz, Stanisław Matrejek; Box 119, Czesław Jezierski.

81. See, for example, HI, PGC, Box 119, Stanisław Kucharski, Jan Marszałek; Box 120, Mieczysław Klimczyk, Tadeusz Macheta, Eugeniusz Łabędź, Tadeusz Markow, Feliks Jarosz; Box 122, Tadeusz Typrowicz; Box 124, Jerzy Pruszyński, Edward Markiewicz; Poland. Ambasada USSR, Box 50, Danuta Wilga, Jadwiga Lublińska, Janina Strycharzówna, Maria Bargelówna.

82. See, for example, łomża, 111; postawy, 47; kosów poleski, 43; bóbrka, 34; jarosław and lubaczów, 45; przemyśl, 91; łuniniec, 58; kobryń, 53; wilno-troki, 1.34; HI, PGC, Box 117, Kazimierz Pietraszewski, Stanisław Kaziewicz, Stanisław Sobolewski; Poland. Ambasada USSR, Box 49, Janina Adamarczuk; Box 50, Maria Bargelówna, Jadwiga Lublińska, Janusz Iwanowski.

83. Łomża, 112.

84. Its omission of major topics and its unbelievable treatment of others gave the publication a surreal quality. For example, one would not be able to tell from reading *Czerwony Sztandar* that half of Poland had been occupied by Germany since September 1939. The only news about the war came in the form of military communiqués, mostly German, describing the latest battle. In my mostly complete run of *Czerwony Sztandar* (only 30–40 issues missing), I

could find only one item about life in Warsaw under the German occupation. On July 27, 1940, a brief dispatch was reprinted in the paper after a TASS release. "The situation in Warsaw. The Berlin radio informs in today's communiqué about the situation in Warsaw. While at the beginning of the war the city had 1.4 million inhabitants, now its population has risen to 1.8 million. Reconstruction work is being done in the city." This is all. In other words, people were doing fine in Warsaw, and they could look forward to a comfortable future.

85. HI, PGC, 9419. See also Białystok, 91; łomża, 109; wilejka, 61; PGC, 8701.

86. Postawy, 46.

87. HI, Poland. Ambasada USSR, Box 50, Janina Strycharzówna.

88. Gródek Jagielloński, 33. See also, for example, HI, PGC, Box 117, Edward Dudojc, Leon Borucki; Box 119, Jan Marszałek.

89. Równe, 38.

90. Tłumacz, 21; lida, 47; mołodeczno, 18; łuniniec, 58, 89; drohobycz, 69; kowel, 70, 71; święciany, 39; zdołbunów, 28; luboml, dodatek, 8; brasław, 32; kałusz, 61; białostocki, 57; horochów, 54; łomża, 109; sarny, 24; łuck, 68; krzemieniec, 32, 33.

91. Gross and Gross, *War Through Children's Eyes*, doc. 23.

92. Oszmiana.

93. Kałusz, 61.

94. HI, PGC, Box 117, Stanisław Soboń. See also sarny, 24; białostocki, 57; drohobycz, 69; oszmiana; łuniniec, 59; turka, 27.

95. The only exception I found among thousands of personal recollections on the subject appears in a very thorough deposition concerning, among other issues, the April 1940 transport from Białystok. Bread and water were distributed there in an orderly fashion before the train reached the frontier (Gross and Gross, W *czterdziestym*, doc. 165).

96. HI, Poland. Ambasada USSR, Box 50, Maria Bargelówna; HI, PGC, Box 117, Edward Dudojc, Stanisław Kaziewicz; Box 120, Stefan Janczyński, Eugeniusz Łabędź; Gross and Gross, W *czterdziestym*, doc. 136, 160.

97. Such occasions were rare, usually only a few during a one-month trip. In Tadeusz Macheta's transport, people were allowed only once to dismount from the cars; in Kazimiera Pyrska's, once every three days; in Aleksander Lagota's, each day for three or four minutes, "but sometimes not at all" (HI, PGC, Box 120; Poland. Ambasada USSR, Box 50). See also Gross and Gross, W *czterdziestym*, doc. 1.

98. See, for example, HI, PGC, Box 120, Feliks Jarosz; Gross and Gross, W *czterdziestym*, doc. 141.

99. And dark they were indeed. "It took us three weeks to get wherever we were going. When we got there we all felt as if drunk because we hadn't seen light for all this time, as windows were boarded up in our car" (HI, PGC, Box 117, Mieczysław Omiotek). "Children were crying, it was dark as if under-

ground, and nothing to eat" (HI, PGC, Box 120, Tadeusz Warzybok). "It was dark and impossible to breathe in sealed cars" (HI, Poland. Ambasada USSR, Box 50, Irena Kulikowska). See also HI, Poland. Ambasada USSR, Box 50, Danuta Wilga; PGC, Leon Borucki, Mieczysław Ruchlewicz, Mieczysław Omiotek; Box 122, Bronisław Wawruszczak; białostocki, 55.

100. Jarosław and lubaczów, 45; postawy, 47; HI, PGC, Box 122, Tadeusz Typrowicz.

101. See, for example, HI, PGC, Box 119, Stanisław Kucharski; Poland. Ambasada USSR, Box 50, Julia Łysoniówna, Kazimiera Pyrska. Usually the trip took anywhere from two to four weeks.

102. HI, PGC, Box 117, Antoni Dudek. See also łuniniec, 58; kobryń, 53; HI, PGC, Box 117, Zygmunt Kotlarz, Stanisław Sobolewski, Edward Dudojc.

103. Doctors or nurses were occasionally assigned to transports, but apparently without medications or authority to help anyone. Stanisław Sypacz mentions one case of a medical intervention, the only one I encountered, when a deportee whose temperature was taken and showed him to be running a high fever was given two white rolls and a few candies by the medical orderly at the next stop (HI, PGC, Box 117).

104. HI, PGC, Box 124.

105. HI, Poland. Ambasada USSR, Box 50.

106. Gross and Gross, W czterdziestym, doc. 1, 42, 165.

107. Kobryń, 53.

108. See, for example, szczuczyn, 47; białostocki, 55; postawy, 47; HI, Poland. Ambasada USSR, Box 49, Zofia Jagodzińska; PGC, Box 117, Stanisław Resler, Stanisław Kaziewicz; Box 120, Kazimierz Adler, Mieczysław Klimczyk, Józef Jesionka.

109. Gross and Gross, W czterdziestym, doc. 165.

110. HI, PGC, Box 117, Jadwiga Lublińska; Poland. Ambasada USSR, Box 49, Zofia Jagodzińska.

111. Równe, 38.

112. Gross and Gross, W czterdziestym, doc. 165.

113. Oszmiana.

114. Wat, Mój Wiek, 1: 307.

115. Włodzimierz wołyński, 39; HI, Poland. Ambasada USSR, Box 47, Kazimiera Studzińska; Rudnycka, ed., Western Ukraine under the Bolsheviks, p. 82. For evidence about the deterioration of the general outlook of other cities immediately after the Soviet occupation, see also HI, Poland. Ambasada USSR, Box 46, Stefan Ogrodnik; PGC, 1789, 9037. Marian Epstein, a physician from Lwów, noted sententiously: "It is a rule which I have observed several times already, that wherever Russians appear, people inadvertently start 'camping' in railroad stations, hunger appears, stores are emptied, and lice show up" (HI, PGC, 3921).

116. HI, AC, 10718.

EPILOGUE: THE SPOILER STATE

1. Pospieszalski, *Documenta Occupationis*, pp. 244–247.

2. See Gross and Gross, *War Through Children's Eyes*, pp. 12–16. For more details about economic exploitation, consult documents published in that volume as well as in the Polish-language edition: *W czterdziestym*.

3. GSHI, A 9 III 1/1, "Działalność władz okupacyjnych ... 1.IX.1939–1.XI.1940," pp. 92–93.

4. *CSYP*, table 5, p. 33; table 12, p. 36; table 14, pp. 59–60.

5. Edward Homze quotes a somewhat disturbingly precise 1,007,561 for the number of workers and POWs from Poland employed in the Reich on October 1, 1941 (*Foreign Labor in Nazi Germany*, p. 65). For statistics concerning deportations from the Generalgouvernement, consult Pospieszalski, *Documenta Occupationis*, pp. 282–285); for data on resettlement from territories incorporated into the Reich to the Generalgouvernement, see GSHI, A 9 III 1/12, "Działalność władz okupacyjnych," p. 230.

6. In fact, the Germans provided somewhat better facilities at the time; for example, deportees might travel in regular passenger wagons. Just for illustration, let us consider the first experiment in deportation organized by Adolf Eichmann at the beginning of the war, almost exactly four months before the first Soviet-sponsored deportation wave swept through the Western Ukraine and Western Belorussia. Jews from Moravska Ostrava (Mährisch-Ostrau), Kattowitz, and Vienna were shipped to Nisko in the Generalgouvernement. Internal quotations in the following excerpt are from a documentary volume, *Nazidokumente sprechen*, edited by Rudolf Iltis (Prague, 1965), and from the personal archive of Jonny Moser, the author of the article. "The first transport from Märisch-Ostrau was loaded into railroad cars on 17 October 1939. The men spent 'the rest of the day and the next night' on the train, which had been shunted on a siding, and were not even able to get water. They were subjected to such terrible maltreatment that, as the daily report stated, many 'of the 916 Jews' had to be left behind because of illness. On 18 October, at exactly 8:20 A.M., the train left Mährisch-Ostrau with 901 Jews. 'The train consisted of twenty-two passenger cars and twenty-nine freight cars that carried construction materials, tools, and food' " (Moser, "Nisko," p. 11). On October 20 a transport of 875 men left Kattowitz in "twenty-two third-class passenger cars, two second-class cars, and five freight cars," and on the same day 912 men left for Nisko from Vienna (ibid., pp. 11, 12). Moser says nothing about the type of railroad cars used in the last transport; we are told, however, that in all three deportations only able-bodied men between 18 and 55 years of age were shipped. This was, I must repeat, *before* the Jews were transported in cattle cars to extermination camps.

7. Gross, *Polish Society under German Occupation*, p. 80.

8. For a description of the conditions of life in the Soviet settlements where Polish citizens were deported, see Gross and Gross, *War Through Children's Eyes*.

9. The figure of 100,000 includes the Jewish victims of German mass executions in the Western Ukraine and Western Belorussia immediately following the Nazi conquest of this territory from the Soviets in the summer of 1941. For numerical data, see Central Commission for Investigation of Crimes in Poland, *German Crimes in Poland*, 1: 145, 2: 50.

10. When mass graves were discovered in prison backyards in the summer of 1941, badly decomposed corpses turned up below the fresh layers of those killed during the prison evacuation, indicating that people were being killed and buried there months before.

11. For an interesting discussion of this problem, see Adam Michnik's essay "On Resistance," in his *Letters from Prison and Other Essays*.

12. Talcott Parsons, "Some Sociological Aspects of the Fascist Movements."

13. Let an episode from Bulgaria stand for illustration. Here follows a welcoming speech by a newly appointed factory director, as reported by Georgi Markov in his remarkable memoirs. "Frankly, I don't know why I'm here. I've no idea what you're doing, how you're doing it, and what it all adds up to. However, as they've sent me here, I'm going to stay. But I don't want us to tread on each other's toes. I shall be the director, but you will work in the way you're used to and as you think fit. Don't ask me questions because I can't tell you anything" (Markov, *The Truth That Killed*, pp. 37–38).

14. HI, PGC, 6466.

15. Quoted in Cohen, *Rethinking the Soviet Experience*, p. 114.

16. Boris Pasternak, *Doctor Zhivago*, p. 483.

17. Joseph Brodsky, *Less Than One*, p. 10.

18. Jakub Berman, one of the three most important party officials from the Stalinist period, uses a telling phrase when reminiscing about the consolidation phase of the Communist regime in Poland after World War II. He says that they attempted to "differentiate" (*zróżnicować*) various milieus that they considered to be hostile or independent. In other words, the Communist strategy was to undermine the solidarity of such a milieu, to make sure that it splintered, that people quarreled, that they turned disloyal to their associates. The strategy, then, was not so much to take over or to tap allegiance but, primarily, to destroy a social network that was already there. Torańska, *Oni*, pp. 184, 185, 188.

19. "Freedom when men act in bodies is power," wrote Edmund Burke (*Reflections on the Revolution in France*, p. 20).

20. Paulina Preiss, *Biurokracja totalna*.

21. Juan J. Linz, "Totalitarian and Authoritarian Regimes."

22. I am referring to Clifford Geertz's essay "Thick Description: Toward an Interpretative Theory of Culture," in his *The Interpretation of Cultures*, pp. 3–30.

23. For a thorough study of these endeavors, consult Michel Heller, *La machine et les rouages*.

24. Valery Chaldize, *The Responsibility of a Generation*.

25. For the best articulation of the ethical-political doctrine underlying the

Polish revolution, see Adam Michnik's *Letters from Prison and Other Essays*. Two valuable sources for English readers on the ethical inspiration and symbolism of the movement are Jan Józef Lipski's *Workers' Defence Committee*, and Irena Grudzińska-Gross's *The Art of Solidarity*. Jadwiga Staniszkis, in her important book, *Poland's Self-Limiting Revolution*, points to the affirmation of *dignity* as one of the most important inspirations of the Polish Revolution in 1980–1981 (see especially ch. 3).

26. Ernst Cassier, *Symbol, Myth, and Culture*, p. 254.

27. Roland Barthes, *Writing Degree Zero*, p. 24.

28. *Język propagandy*, pp. 61, 62.

29. Ibid., p. 3.

30. Pasqualini, *Prisoner of Mao*, p. 295.

31. Cassirer, *Symbol, Myth, and Culture*, pp. 148, 253–254.

32. The term "destruction" has been used, for instance, in *Język Propagandy*, pp. 27–28, and in Heinz Paechter's *Nazi Deutsch* (1944), p. 13.

33. Wanda Wasilewska once told Stalin that the word "patriot" was completely worn out in Polish. "He answered to me," she later recalled, "that every word can be given a new meaning and it is up to us what that meaning will be" (Wasilewska, "Wspomnienia," p. 383).

34. George F. Kennan, *Memoirs*, pp. 562–563. For a good statement of the problem, see Leszek Kołakowski's "Totalitarianism and the Virtue of the Lie."

35. Gorki, *Mother*, p. 145.

36. Gorki and Lenin, *Letters, Reminiscences, Articles*, p. 273.

37. Markov, *The Truth That Killed*, p. 16.

HISTORIOGRAPHICAL SUPPLEMENT: A TANGLED WEB

1. See Antoni Symonowicz, "Nazi Campaign against Polish Culture," in Roman Nurowski, ed., *1939–1945 War Losses in Poland* (Poznań: Wydawnictwo Zachodnie, 1960), 83.

2. Błoński's article was published in *Tygodnik Powszechny* on 11 January 1987, and Władysław Siła Nowicki's reply on 22 February 1987. Both texts, together with several other articles published in the follow-up of Błoński's essay, as well as a discussion on these matters held at a conference in Jerusalem one year later are published in English in a volume, *"My Brother's Keeper?" Recent Polish Debates on the Holocaust*, Antony Polonsky, ed. (London: Routledge, 1990). In the roundtable discussion in Jerusalem, Błoński specified his argument: "To put it most generally, Polish responsibility is, in my opinion, centered on indifference, indifference at the time of the Holocaust. Naturally not the indifference of everyone. There were those who were not indifferent and we pay tribute to them. The result of this indifference was that Jews died with a feeling of solitude, with a feeling of having been abandoned. This indifference was explicit, one could somehow feel it when one was a child" (Ethical Problems of the Holocaust in Poland. Discussion held at the International Conference on the History and Culture

of Polish Jewry in Jerusalem on Monday 1 February 1988, Błoński, *My Brother's Keeper*, 188).

For an analysis of letters to the editor of *Tygodnik Powszechny*, which the publication of Błoński's article engendered, see an unpublished MA thesis at the Institute of Sociology of Warsaw University in 1992 by Ewa Koźmińska—*Polskożydowskie rozrachunki wojenne. Wyzwania Holokaustu: Analiza listów do redakcji "Tygodnika Powszechnego" w odpowiedzi na dyskusję, Błoński-Siła Nowicki.*

3. Błoński, *My Brother's Keeper*, 46.

4. Ewa Koźmińska-Frejlak and Ireneusz Krzemiński, "Stosunek społeczeństwa polskiego do Zagłady Żydów," in *Czy Polacy są antysemitami? Wyniki badania sondażowego*, Ireneusz Krzemiński ed. (Warszawa: Oficyna Naukowa, 1996), 98.

5. Jan Józef Lipski's monograph entitled *Workers' Defence Committee*, published by the University of California Press in 1985, offers a wonderful portrait of Lipski's intellectual and political biography, as well as an aperçu of the entire milieu of the progressive Polish intelligentsia. My point is to take under scrutiny the views of a most enlightened individual from a libertarian, courageous, and unprejudiced milieu. If one can demonstrate that even the most open-minded approach to the issue addressed to a Polish audience does not confront what has actually happened we could be reasonably sure that the rest of the spectrum of views on this issues will be even less satisfying.

In addition to the article "Two Fatherlands, Two Patriotisms," Lipski addressed the issue of Polish-Jewish relations during the war in two speeches originally delivered at important anniversary celebrations. In March 1981 at Warsaw University, where a symposium was organized in connection with the thirteenth anniversary of the so-called March (1968) Events, Lipski read a long paper entitled "The Jewish Problem"; two years later he spoke at the fortieth anniversary of the Warsaw Ghetto uprising. All three texts, plus a few other essays on contemporary Polish politics, came out together (1985) in a book distributed by an independent publishing house, *Myśl*, entitled *Dwie ojczyzny i inne szkice*. The substance of all three of Lipski's statements on Polish-Jewish relations during the war is the same. Indeed, he uses occasionally identical phrasing. All quotes are from the 1985 *Myśl* edition. The English-language edition of his "Two Fatherlands, Two Patriotisms" can be found in *Between East and West: Writings from "Kultura,"* Robert Kostrzewa, ed. (New York: Hill and Wang), 52–71. All translations are mine.

6. Lipski, *Dwie ojczyzny*, 1985, 113–14.

7. Ibid., 34.

8. Ibid., 37.

9. Blackmailing hiding Jews and delivering them into Germans hands for a reward. The word itself comes from slang usage of the word *szmalec* (literally: lard) where it means "money," as in loot or dough.

10. Ibid., 36.

11. Dr. Ruta Sakowska, is an esteemed researcher of the Jewish Historical Institute in Warsaw now entrusted with the critical edition of the Ringelblum Archives. I am quoting from her doctoral dissertation originally published in 1953 and revised and republished in 1993—*Ludzie z dzielnicy zamkniętej* (Warszawa: Państwowe Wydawnictwo Naukowe), 239.

12. Lest I be suspected of flippancy and of underestimating the ferocity of German policies: in a myriad of individual, concrete situations many things had not been done in occupied Poland *because* of the fear of anticipated German repressions. And it makes perfect sense to say "we feared the Germans and therefore . . ." some delivery of underground newspapers did not take place there and then; a certain piglet had not been slain for black-market sale (all livestock was branded and had to be accounted for to the Germans); a Jewish acquaintance was told to go away and denied overnight shelter on a certain occasion. But the formula "we feared the Germans and therefore . . ." is not a sufficient explanation for general social phenomena characteristic of this period—or else, there would be neither the underground state, nor the black market, nor the Warsaw uprising, nor, in all likelihood, independent Poland at the conclusion of the war, since all the people would have died of starvation over the years on physiologically inadequate official food rations. Something else besides the fear of German sanctions motivated people to act one way or another—nothing mysterious indeed—namely their attitudes, norms, and the values they had been socialized to.

On another note, there is interesting evidence pointing out that the rescuers themselves did not perceive the risks involved as inordinately high. Nechama Tec interviewed several Poles who assisted Jews during the war for her book *When Light Pierced Darkness: Christian Rescue of Jews in Nazi-Occupied Poland* (New York/Oxford: Oxford University Press, 1986). In their opinion the risk of falling victim to random Nazi violence was so high that it almost equalized the presumed "calculable" risk of repression for actually breaking the German-imposed rules. "There was no guarantee whatsoever that one would survive, regardless of whether one followed the German directives or not" (Tomasz Jurski). "I felt threatened with and without the Jews. I could have been caught by the Germans during a raid for no reason at all" (Stefa Krakowska). Paradoxically, this may have induced people to violate German inductions: "if one could be punished for anything at all, or nothing, then one might as well do something worthwhile" (Stach Kamiński). "In fact," as yet another rescuer, Roman Sadowski, perceptively observed, "[m]aybe those who were engaged in some kind of anti-Nazi activity were less likely to be caught because they were more cautious, more aware. We were prepared and trained" (171). For a general argument along these lines with reference to involvement in the underground, see my *Polish Society under German Occupation—Generalgouvernement, 1939–44* (Princeton: Princeton University Press, 1979), esp. chs. 10 and 11.

13. Czesław Miłosz, *The Witness of Poetry* (Cambridge, Mass.: Harvard University Press, 1983), 84.

14. Readers are reminded of the public reaction provoked by Jan Błoński's January 1987 article.

15. For a general catalog of the Polish underground press, giving runs and duration of various publications, see Lucjan Dobroszycki, *Centralny katalog polskiej prasy konspiracyjnej, 1939–1945* (Warszawa: Wydawnictwo MON, 1962).

16. The term *Sanacja* refers to the ruling (post-1926 coup), regime in Poland. It is derived from the Latin root *sanus*, by reference to bringing "health," cleaning-up, to the political life of the country. For an excellent discussion of interwar Polish politics, see Antony Polonsky's *Politics in Independent Poland, 1921–1939* (Oxford, England: Clarendon Press, 1972).

17. A researcher at the Jewish Historical Institute (ŻIH) in Warsaw, Paweł Szapiro, spent a considerable amount of time culling *every* reference to "matters Jewish" in the wartime underground press. Thus a full record on this subject can be obtained. He also published a book, *Wojna niemiecko-żydowska: Polska prasa konspiracyjna 1943–1944 o powstaniu w getcie Warszawy* (London: Aneks, 1989), containing texts of all the articles published in the underground press about the April 1943 uprising in the Warsaw Ghetto. It is a sobering illustration of the point I have just made.

18. The manuscript of Karski's report can be found in the Hoover Institution archives (Stanisław Mikołajczyk Collection, box 12) with handwritten lines scribbled across the cover page: "Attention!! Pages 6 + 9 + 10 + 11 have double pages." Indeed, doubled pages paginated as 6a, 9a, 10a, and 11a are very carefully prepared. They begin and end exactly in the same place (once including a hyphenated word), for easy substitution. Karski was instructed, as he told me when I queried him about the document, to draft a sanitized version, omitting his description of the anti-Semitism prevailing in the Polish society, by a close confidant of then Prime Minister General Władysław Sikorski, Professor Stanisław Kot. Polish *raison d'etat* vis-à-vis the Allies required that the matter be covered up, he was told. For both versions of the document in their entirety, see *Mówią Wieki*, November 1992, 2–9.

19. See my *Polish Society under German Occupation: The Generalgouvernement, 1939–44* (Princeton: Princeton University Press, 1979), 184–86, for references to archival sources containing relevant documents.

20. See note 18.

21. See note 18.

22. It is some relief to know that the Polish boys got a thrashing at home when their parents learned about the episode from a woman the Jewish child told about it, and who knew his father. Władysław Bartoszewski and Zofia Lewin (eds.), *Righteous among Nations: How Poles Helped the Jews, 1939–45* (London: Earlscourt Publications, 1969), 411–12. As Michał Głowiński sadly commented in retrospect on his own childhood encounter when he was threatened with denunciation by three fellow boys from the orphanage where

his family placed him—"In the cruelty of children the cruelty of the epoch is concentrated and reflected. It mirrors swineries perpetrated in the grown-up world" (Michał Głowiński, *Czarne Sezony*) [Warszawa: OPEN, 1998], 116).

23. The standard word used in parlance of the common people in Poland when refering to Jews is "Żydek," instead of "Żyd." It is a diminutive with a derogatory connotation, not exactly a "kike" perhaps, though close. Hence I translate it as "Jew-boy." It would be used in reference to a grownup as well as a child. There are many much more directly pejorative terms to choose from as well. One would use "Żydek" as a matter of course, without a particularly vicious or ridiculing intent.

24. Michał Głowiński, *Czarne Sezony*, 93–96.

25. This, in any case, was the conclusion of a Dr. Schöngarth, commander of the SD in the *Generalgouvernement* who spoke as follows during one of the conferences on security problems with the governor general in 1941: "We must consider as members of the resistance movement not only those who actually belong to the organization. *Sicherheitspolizei* considers all the Poles as members of a resistance movement in the broader sense of the term" (Hans Frank, *Okupacja i ruch oporu w dzienniku Hansa Franka*, vol. 1, L. Dobroszycki et al., eds. [Warszawa: Książka i Wiedza], 366).

26. In Hochberg-Mariańska's introduction to a 1947 book of personal testimonies by Jewish children who survived the war, we read that several Poles who had helped Jews during the war requested anonymity for fear of hostile reactions in their own communities if their wartime deeds became known (Maria Hochberg-Mariańska's introduction to *Dzieci Oskarżają* [Kraków]: Centralna Żydowska Komisja Historyczna w Polsce, 1947). See also Nechama Tec's memoir *Dry Tears: The Story of a Lost Childhood* (New York: Oxford University Press, 1984). It is a fascinating theme—why those whom later we will honor as Righteous Among Nations were afraid of their neighbors should those neighbors find out that they had helped the Jews during the war. I have a hypothesis that somewhat anticipates what will be argued in this essay. In the first place, I believe, they feared becoming victims of robbery (see, in this respect, Shraga Feivel Bielawski, *The Last Jew from Węgrów* [New York: Praeger, 1991], 92, 147). In popular imagination, Jews were associated with money, and people were persuaded that those who sheltered Jews during the war must have enriched themselves as a result. But they also had another reason. Their wartime behavior broke the socially approved norm and demonstrated that they were different from anybody else and, therefore, a danger to the community. They were a threat to others because, potentially, they could bear witness. They could tell what happened to local Jews because they were not—neither by their deeds nor by their reluctance to act—bonded into a community of silence over this matter, a community of silence that shrouded the issue in many a place. As an illustration of this point I recommend a stunning documentary by a young filmmaker Paweł Łoziński entitled *Miejsce urodzenia* (The Birthplace), or a book by Henryk Grynberg, the film's protagonist, under the same title. Łoziński follows Gryn-

berg as he returns to a little village where he was hiding with his family as a child during the war. He comes on a quest to hopefully find the details of his father's death. One spring day in 1944, his father left the hiding place in the forest on a regular errand to get food for the family and never came back. To make a long story short, in the last sequence Grynberg's father's skeleton is dug out, together with a glass bottle the man always carried with him to bring milk to his children. All was known in the village—who killed him, why (over a cow he left for safekeeping and, as the end of the war was approaching, was likely to reclaim soon), and where he was buried—and was fearfully kept under wraps for forty years, and only reluctantly revealed at Grynberg's prodding.

In an identical circumstance, in which wartime murder of local Jews by their neighbors is a well-kept secret known to all in the community fifty years after the war, see Aharon Appelfeld's moving reminiscence from a 1996 return trip to his native village published in the *The New Yorker* (23 November 1998), as "Buried Homeland," especially p. 54.

27. See, for example, Tec's *When Light Pierced Darkness*, especially pages 58, 59, and chapter 10.

28. Zygmunt Klukowski, *Dziennik z lat okupacji zamojszczyzny* (Lublin: Ludowa Spółdzielnia Wydawnicza, 1958).

29. Ibid., entry of 23.9.1939.

30. Ibid., entry of 25.4.1940; see also pp. 113, 149, 183.

31. Ibid., entry of 12.8.1940.

32. Ibid., entry of 10.3.1941.

33. Ibid., entry of 13.4.1942.

34. Ibid., entry of 8.5.1942.

35. Ibid., entry of 17.5.1942.

36. Ibid., entry of 9.5.1942.

37. Ibid., entry of 24.5.1942 and 17.7.1942. In a bizarre coincidence members of the 101 Reserve Police Batallion would be tried after the war for these killings in Józefów, and Christopher Browning would use the trial records to write his pathbreaking *Ordinary Men: Reserve Police Battalion 101 and the Final Solution in Poland* (New York: Harper and Collins, 1992).

38. Klukowski, *Dziennik*, entry of 8.8.1942.

39. Ibid., entry of 21.10.1942.

40. Ibid., entry of 26.10.1942.

41. Ibid., entry of 26.11.1942.

42. Ibid., entry of 29.10.1942.

43. Ibid., entry of 4.11.1942. Similar conclusions can be drawn from numerical account of the activities of the Reserve Police Battalion 101 investigated by Browning: between July 1942 and November 1943 it killed in its area of operation a "minimum" of 38,000 Jews and it deported to Treblinka, between August 1942 and May 1943, the total of 45,200 Jews (Browning, *Ordinary Men*, 191, 192).

44. Before the war Jews made up somewhere around 9 percent of the total

population in the territories later occupied by the Red Army. They were scattered, amounting to no more than 5.2 percent in the Wilno voivodeship and reaching the high of 12 percent in the Białystok viovodeship. Being settled predominantly in urban areas, however, they were a more visible minority than these numbers suggest. If one adds to these figures some 250,000 to 350,000 war refugees who flocked into this territory from Western and Central Poland, one ends up with about 1.5 million Jews living there in 1939–41, about 11 percent of the total population. The number of Jews in some of the largest cities such as Lwów, Białystok, or Wilno, for example, is reported to have doubled within a month or two following the outbreak of the war. For various estimates, see Shimon Redlich, "The Jews in the Soviet Annexed Territories 1939–41," in *Soviet Jewish Affairs* 1 (1971) 81; Bernard Weinryb, "Polish Jews under Soviet Rule," in *The Jews in the Soviet Satellites*, Peter Meyeer, Bernard Weinryb, Eugene Dushinsky, and Nicolas Sylvain, eds. (Syracuse: Syracuse University Press, 1953), 331; Szyja Bronsztajn, *Ludność żydowska w Polsce w okresie międzywojennym: Studium statystyczne* (Warszawa: Ossolineum, 1963), 114; Dov Levin, *The Lesser of Two Evils: Eastern European Jewry under Soviet Rule, 1939–41* (Philadelphia and Jerusalem: Jewish Publication Society, 1995), 18.

45. Even among high officers of the Polish Army and functionaries of the administration—i.e., among those who were presumably best positioned to know what was going on—confusion was widespread. In Tarnopol county, prefect Majkowski urged the town population through loudspeakers to give a friendly welcome to the entering Soviet army. Posters signed by the mayor of Stanisławów and appealing for a calm, friendly reception were put up throughout the city on the morning of 18 September. In Równe the county prefect came out personally with a retinue of local officials to greet the spearhead of the Soviet column. He thanked the Red Army profusely for bringing help to Poles locked in combat with the German invaders. In Kopyczyńce a city official spoke from the town hall balcony: "Gentlemen, Poles, soldiers, we will beat the Germans now that the Bolsheviks are going to help us," while Red Army commanders embraced Polish officers. Soviet columns marched through Tarnopol and Łuck side by side with detachments of the Polish army, each giving way to the other at intersections (Hoover Institution [HI], Polish Government Collection [PGC], individual testimonies nos. 4102, 7568, 10015, 10204, 3435, 7557; Anders Collection [AC], 4307).

46. HI, PGC, Nieśwież, 13.

47. See, for example, the following county reports from the HI, PGC, białostocki, p. 3; białystok, p. 3, 4; sokolski, p. 9; mołodeczno, p. 5, 9; postawy, p. 5; dzisna, p. 4; brasław, p. 3; prużana, p. 2; nadworna, p. 17; łuck, p. 5; lida, p. 2, 3; szczuczyn, p. 1; nowogródzki, p. 10, 11; horochów, p. 2; sambor, p. 6; kowel, p. 7.

48. HI, Poland. Ambasada USSR Collection, Box 46, Stanisława Kwiatkowska; Box 47, Alicja Sierańska; PGC, 3194, 4060, 7508; nieśwież, p. 13; postawy, p. 5; wilejka, p. 5; sokolski, p. 9; kołomyja, p. 22; kostopol, p. 5.

49. Yad Vashem [YV], 03/2309, 03/1791; PGC, drohobycz, p. 2; PGC, Box 131, Palestinian protocol no. 187.

50. Interview with Celina Konińska, who at the time was a member of the Communist Youth Organization (Tel Aviv, summer 1980).

51. To continue Konińska's account: "First contact with the Russians, I mean with the Soviet soldiers, struck us as something strange and unpleasant. We thought that every soldier was a communist and therefore it was also obvious to us that each must be happy. So their comportment, their behavior, struck us as queer. First of all their looking after things, after material objects—watches, clothing—with so much interest and so much rapacity. We waited for them to ask about life under capitalism and to tell us what it was like in Russia. But all they wanted was to buy a watch (we met those who wanted to buy, not those who just took it). I noticed that they were preoccupied with worldly goods, and we were waiting for ideals." Or take the case of this left-wing Zionist, who also must have sensed that something was amiss when he asked a newly met Soviet officer about the prospects of emigration to Palestine and heard in reply that the Soviet authorities would gladly create Palestine for Jews, but . . . "right here . . . One of them, himself a Jew, said to us, 'You want to go to Palestine? Fine, l'shana habaah b'Yerushalayim—next year we shall be all in Jerusalem. The Soviets will be there too'" ([Hashomer Hatzair] *Youth Amidst the Ruins: A Chronicle of Jewish Youth in the War* [New York: Scopus, 1941], 88, 90).

52. When "anarchy" began in Drohiczyn county, "everybody hoped that some pacification detachment would come—it didn't matter whether ours or foreign—and restore order." Józef Użar-Śliwiński, a Polish military settler who wrote these words, fled to Drohiczyn where "the Soviet authorities and the military had already arrived." Only after three weeks did he dare return to his village (HI, Poland. Ambasada USSR Collection, Box 47). A forester from Dolina county recalls that he "had to leave the house and all posessions and hide with the whole family in the forest until the Soviets came" (HI, Poland. Ambasada USSR Collection, Box 47; see also PGC, 2432, 8764; AC, 1078). For a more general discussion of the anarchy and civil war in this area, see my *Revolution from Abroad: The Soviet Conquest of Poland's Western Ukraine and Western Belorussia* (Princeton: Princeton University Press, 1988), 35–45.

53. HI, Poland. Ambasada USSR Collection, Box 48, Barbara Lejowa.

54. For some preliminary statistics, see Szymon Datner's "Zbrodnie Wehrmachtu w Polsce w czasie kampanii wrześniowej," in S. Bronsztajn, ed., *Ludność żydowska w Polsce*, 269.

55. HI, PGC, Box 131, Palestinian protocol no. 85; see also Palestinian protocols nos. 120, 124, 182, 188; AC, 10559, 15526.

56. For ample evidence indicating the absence of Jewish functionaries, see chapter 2 of my *Revolution from Abroad* where I quote lists of names of local functionaries on the basis of testimonies preserved in the Hoover Institution Archives. One may also consult recently opened Soviet archives for

confirmation. See, for example, *Okupacja sowiecka (1939–41) w świetle tajnych dokumentów: Obywatele polscy na kresach północno-wschodnich II Rzeczypospolitej pod okupacją sowiecką w latach 1939–1941*, Tomasz Strzembosz, Krzysztof Jasiewicz, and Marek Wierzbicki, eds. (Warszawa: Instytut Studiów Politycznych, PAN, 1996). In a contemporaneous Soviet document on the establishment of temporary authorities and peasant committees in Western Belorussia, the following individuals are listed as operating within the jurisdiction of the War Council of the Belorussian Front: "Brykov, Babayev, Otvalko, Kotovitch, Kushtel Joseph Antonovich, Bogdanovitch Vladimir Benediktovich, Puzyrevski Mikhal Adamovitch, Tomko Leon Igantevitch, Kirilenko Iosif Antonovitch, Leisha Vasili Dominikovitch, Gasiul Boris Martinovitch, Lukianov Matviey Grigorevitch, Bielski Joseph Antonovitch, Yefimov Nikifor Ilitch, Sherstnev Pavel Grigorevitch, Yurkevitch Andrei Andreievitch, Zilberman Moysey Borysovitch, Gaukshtel Nikolai Frantzevitch, Boronov Dimitri, Pazurevski, Gradkovski Kazimir Adamovitch, Titovich Aleksander Antonovitch, Parfenov Yevstigenij Fedorovitch, Pitiukevich Wilhelm Walerianovitch, Lysenok Nikifor Andreyevitch, Rafalovitch Aleksander Mikhailovitch, Sharanovich Motel Leibovitch, Leonard Mikhailovitch Dubickij." Among the twenty-eight persons listed above, perhaps three or four, judging by their names, might be Jewish (*Okupacja Sowiecka*, document no. 1, 49–55). For further evidence see also document no. 49, 194–97; document no. 50, 198–99; document no. 52, 205; document no. 53, 207.

57. HI, AC, 12128. See also HI, AC, 10560, 12332, 12333, 12334; PGC, Box 131, Palestinian protocol no. 186.

58. *Khrushchev Remembers*, Strobe Talbott, ed. (Boston: Little Brown, 1970), 141.

59. Chaim Hades (*sic*!) from Brześć wrote the following: "I stood long hours in line and I finally got the authorization card for departure, which was considered at the time a pot of luck. A German officer turned to a crowd of standing Jews and asked: 'Jews, where are you going? Don't you realize that we will kill you?'" (HI, PGC, Box 131, Palestinian protocol no. 148).

60. Dov Levin, in his important recent study, puts it as follows: "Over time, however, the sense of relief dissipated and the Soviet regime wore out its welcome. Passive resistance increased, and some Jews actively opposed the arrangements imposed by the new regime. They refused to work on the Sabbath, adhered strictly to religious customs, crossed the borders between the annexed areas, maintained contacts with foreign countries (even transferring information), and criticised the regime (behind a smokescreen of jokes and other devices). This unwillingness to acquiesce was especially prevalent in groups and organizations that previously had been known for nonconformism. Some of these now merged into new underground frameworks in order to continue inculcating their ideologies and values. . . . Zionist groups did not reject the fact of the annexation of their areas of residence. Even so, their positions and behavior in response to Soviet anti-Zionism constituted acts of

organized resistance, however passive most of them were. . . . In due course, the very term underground became a specific synonym for clandestine Zionist activity of various kinds by Jews in the annexed territories" (*The Lesser of Two Evils*, 235–36).

61. HI, PGC, Box 588, "Obliczenie ludności polskiej deportowanej do ZSSR w latach od 1939 do 1941." For a more recent estimate of the national composition of the deportees, excluding labor camp inmates, see Grzegorz Hryciuk, "Zasady i tryb deportacji: Liczebność i rozmieszczenie zesłańców," in *Życie codzienne polskich zesłańców w ZSRR w latach 1940–46*, Stanisław Ciesielski, ed. (Wrocław: Wydawnictwa Uniwersytetu Wrocławskiego, 1997), 31. According to Hryciuk's data about 23 percent of the deportees were Jewish, while 63 percent were of Polish nationality.

62. Shimon Redlich, "Jews in General Anders' Army in the Soviet Union, 1941–42," *Soviet Jewish Affairs* 2 (1971): 97. Klemens Nussbaum, following Anders, quotes an even smaller number of four thousand evacuated Jews ("Jews in the Polish Army in the USSR, 1943–44," *Soviet Jewish Affairs* 3 [1972]: 95).

63. YV, SH, 191–2131, quoted after Ben-Cion Pinchuk, *Polish Shtetl under Soviet Rule* (in manuscript), 56.

64. HI, AC, 14528.

65. Dov Levin, *The Lesser of Two Evils*, 141–42; 29–30.

66. On the eve of the 1940–41 school year, in the summer of 1940, there were 1,003 Ukrainian-language schools, 314 Polish-language schools, 7 Russian-language schools, and 20 Yiddish-language schools in the Lwów district (*Czerwony Sztandar*, 20 August 1940). About 10–12 percent of the population in the area was Jewish, the rest more or less equally divided between Poles and Ukrainians. These numbers do not reflect the influx of refugees, predominantly Jewish, who dramatically swelled the population of Lwów and other towns in the district. By January 1941 the total number of Yiddish-language schools in the Lwów district had been further reduced to fourteen (*Czerwony Sztandar*, 5 January 1941). Naturally, the Yiddish-language Bund-sponsored school system, TSISHO, as well as the Zionist-sponsored Tarbut, were both closed.

67. Dov Levin, *The Lesser of Two Evils*, 143–46.

68. Pinchuk, *Polish Shtetl*, 68.

69. Ibid., 68.

70. The dispatch was authored by the son of General Januszajtis and may be found in the archives of the *Studium Polski Podziemnej* in London (3.1.2.1).

71. In the first two thousand individual statements collected from survivors of the Holocaust immediately after the war by the Jewish Historical Commission and now deposited, over seven thousand of them, in the Jewish Historical Museum in Warsaw (Relacje indywidualne, collection no. 301), one may find details about such pogroms in Bolechów, Borysław, Borczów, Brzeżany, Buczacz, Czortków, Drohobycz, Dubna, Gródek Jagielloński, Ja-

worów, Jedwabne, Kołomyja, Korycin, Krzemieniec, Lwów, Radziłów, Sambor, Sasów, Schodnica, Sokal, Stryj, Szumsk, Tarnopol, Tłuste, Trembowla, Tuczyn, Wizna, Woronów, Zaborów, and Złoczów. A concise article with summary data on this subject was presented by Dr. Andrzej Żbikowski at a conference on the *Holocaust in the Soviet Union* held at Yeshiva University in New York in October 1991 and entitled "Local Pogroms in the Occupied East Poland Territories, June–July 1941."

72. Lublin is the name of the city where, since 1 August 1944, the Committee for National Liberation (PKWN) established in Moscow on July 20 took seat, as a temporary executive authority for liberated Polish territories. It published a "Manifesto" on July 22 (known as the "July Manifesto") denouncing the London government in exile and declaring itself as the only legal authority in Poland during the period of liberation.

73. Let me also point out that the numbers at stake in our case—a few dozen names altogether—are trivial given the total Polish population of around 27 million at the time.

74. For a recent study of the Central Committee of Polish Jews and its politics, see David Engel, *East European Politics and Societies*, vol. 10, 1996.

75. Żydowski Instytut Historyczny (ŻIH), Centralny Komitet Żydów w Polsce (CKŻP), Komisja Specjalna (KS), box no. 3–7, "Sprawozdanie z działalności CKS przy CKŻP," pages 1, 3, 4. CKS files are deposited in two boxes numbered "1–2" and "3–7."

76. The pogrom, which lasted for almost an entire day and involved the participation of hundreds of Kielce inhabitants, resulted in the murder of forty-two Jews. It began with the made-up accusation of a young boy who, at the instigation of his father, declared that he was held captive for a few days in the basement of a house where Jewish returnees lived in Kielce (the house, incidentally, did not have a basement). A squad of Citizens' Militia was then dispatched to search the house and investigate the matter, and the pogrom started. Both militia and uniformed soldiers were involved in the killings. There was certainly massive incompetence on the part of security forces and the way they responded to unfolding events, maybe even foul play. The main preoccupation among Polish historians and journalists addressing the subject (such as there was, for the matter was considered taboo) was mostly about whether this was a deliberate provocation by the security police. The best study of the Kielce pogrom can be found in Bożena Szaynok's *Pogrom Żydów w Kielcach 4, 7 1946r.* (Warsaw: Wydawnictwo Bellona, 1991).

77. The episode is described in Yitzhak Zuckerman's *A Surplus of Memory: Chronicle of the Warsaw Ghetto Uprising* (Berkeley: University of California Press, 1993), ch. 15. Zuckerman does not mention Edelman in this context, but Marek Edelman, the Deputy Commander of ŻOB during the Warsaw Ghetto uprising, recollects that they both went to Kielce (personal communication).

78.

On the third of October [1946] at seven in the evening I boarded a train from Warsaw to Cracow. I was accompanied by my husband, Henryk Liberfreund, and Amalia Schenker. We rode in a compartment with a couple more passengers, including a nun. A candle was burning. We traveled peacefully until we reached Kamińsk station near Radomsko. In the meantime the candle burned out and passengers were sleeping in darkness. During the train stop in Kamińsk a man in civilian clothes, wearing a cap with an eagle sign and toting a submachine gun, entered the compartment. He checked the passengers one by one with a flashlight. When he reached my sleeping husband, he pulled the coat covering him and said "I got you, kike, *heraus, heraus, aussteigen.*" My husband drew back, unwilling to get off the train, and the man pulled him by the arm but could not budge him. Then he whistled and immediately another man appeared, whom I did not see very well, accompanied by the train conductor. I started screaming terribly, and then the first assailant pushed and pulled me using the words "*heraus, aussteigen.*" I pulled myself away; in the meantime the train took off, and the assailant pushed my husband off the train and jumped after him. I continued to scream and I don't know what happened afterward. I wish to add that nobody's documents were checked, not even my husband's. Other passengers and the conductor did not pay much attention to the whole episode; quite the opposite, they laughed and behaved rather improperly. One man sitting next to my husband was accosted by the assailant with the words "you Jew." But he stated that he could show documents that he was not a Jew, and he was left alone.

The following, unusually detailed description—for the most part murders on the railroad leave little trace in the archives—is supplemented by an unsigned memorandum entitled "Information," dated three days after the event:

On the Cracow-Warsaw line, trains go through Kamińsk about fifteen minutes after Radomsko. Railroad line cuts through this village situated in a wood, with houses built along the track. Inhabitants of these houses before the war, during the war, and now, for the most part live off the passing trains. This applied especially to coal transports that passed thereby. Almost all the people in the vicinity made a living from coal pushed off these trains, especially at night. In two of these houses, one right next to the station and the other a one-story house farther down, there lives a bunch whose central figure is a woman of dubious reputation. . . . They party at night and drink and from time to time they stake a passing train in expectation of some spoils. Jewish passengers are now victimized by these bands, for they can be easily scared with a gun, taken off a train, robbed of cash and possessions in a forest, where all of this is taking place, and then they can be made to disappear, and thus one gains an easy living for oneself and one's companions. This area should be carefully watched and put under observation.

Whether anything noteworthy was observed I cannot tell, but the circumstances of Liberfreund's disappearance were not found out (ŻIH, CKŻP, CKS, box 1–2, pages 156–58).

79. The phrasing of this document is somewhat oblique and awkward in Polish as well, State Archive in Cracow (SAC), Urząd Wojewódzki (UW) 2, File 1073.

80. I.e., local agendas of the Central Committee of Polish Jews established in several localities with sizeable Jewish populations.

81. SAC, UW 2, File 1073, memo from the County Jewish Committee in Chrzanów to the Sociopolitical Department of the Cracow Voivodeship dated 11 July 1945.

82. SAC, UW 2, File 1071, Card 183, "Stan liczebny poszczególnych narodowości w chwili obecnej."

83. ŻIH, CKŻP, CKS, box 1–2, "Komisja Specjalna w Krakowie, Oświęcim," 27.1.1947. On 20 October 1945 deputy commander of the Soviet counterintelligence agency SMERSH, Nikolai Selivanovsky, who in 1945–46 was serving as advisor to the Polish Ministry of Public Security, sent to Lavrentii Beria in Moscow a lengthy "Report on the Situation of the Jewish Population in Poland." The document can currently be found in the "special files" (*osobye papki*) of Molotov and Stalin in the State Archives of the Russian Federation (GARF), *fond* 9401, *opis* 2, *delo* 104, pp. 81–89. He described in it, among other things, an episode illlustrating anti-Semitic attitudes of employees of the Ministry of Public Security. "In the Ministry of Public Security," writes Selivanovsky in his report, "there is a box for suggestions to improve the work of this authority. In the box there were found two anonymous letters with the following contents: 'Why does democratic Poland exist only for the Jews? Why do only they have power there and everything is for them? Why do they all have high positions, why are they the *kierowniki*, the bosses? Why can they use their diamonds and gold to gain the ranks of colonels, lieutenant colonels, majors, in short all kinds of officers, rather than we rank and file' " and more in a similar vein. Excerpts from this and other NKVD reports from Poland contained in Stalin's "special files" were recently published in Poland as *Teczka Specjalna J. W. Stalina. Raporty NKWD z Polski 1944–46*, Tatiana Cariewskaja and others, eds. (Warszawa: Rytm, 1998). Selivanovsky's report also offers a telling example of anti-Semitism among the personnel of the Citizens Militia—forty militiamen were arrested for participation in the anti-Jewish pogrom in Cracow in August 1945. I am grateful to Natalia Aleksiun for sharing with me the entire text of the October 20 report.

84. SAC, UW 2, file 1073. As I read only Cracow voivodeship archives all my examples are from that area. But I want to stress again that the hostility of local authorities was a general phenomenon. In a recent article Ewa Koźminska-Frejlak quotes yet another reprimand sent out from the Ministry

of Public Administration—in that case to the Kielce voivodeship authorities: "In Jędrzejów the county head (*starosta*) Feliks turns down all cases presented by Jews. The same situation prevails in Chęciny and Chmielnik. The city Council in Ostrowiec called representatives of the Jewish committee and requested that all Jews be sent to work in a mine." See Ewa Koźminiska-Frejlak, "*Polska jako ojczyna Żydów—żydowskie strategi zadomowienia się w powojennej Polsce (1944–49),*" in *Kultura i Społe-czeństwo*, vol. 43, 1 (1999): 131.

85. Padraic Kenney, *Rebuilding Poland: Workers and Communists, 1945–50* (Ithaca: Cornell University Press, 1997), 111, 114, 115.

86. SAC, KWZ, file 14, p. 87.

87. SAC, UW 2, file 173, Pismo Żydowskiego Zrzeszenia Religijnego w Krakowie do Obywatela Wojewody Krakowskiego, 25, 7, 1945.

88. ŻIH, individual statements, collection no. 301, doc. no. 1582, Hania Zajdman.

89. See a very moving recollection by Michal Głowiński, entitled "It Is I Who Killed Jesus Christ," in which he describes an anti-Semite priest who taught religion and hatred against Jews in his primary school immediately after the war, and a beating he suffered as a result from a fellow student (Głowiński, *Czarne sezony* 144–55).

90. ŻIH, CKŻP, CKS, box 1–2, folder 1, p. 114, notatka do MBP dated 6.11.1946.

91. SAC, UW 2, file 905, p. 26.

92. SAC, UW 2, file 914, "Sprawozdanie z powiatu bocheńskiego," dated 21.8.1945.

93. ŻIH, CKŻP, box 3–7, p. 107, "Sprawozdanie KS przy WKS w Warszawie."

94. ŻIH, CKŻP, CKS, box 1–2, p. 282, Komitet Żydowski w Nowej Rudzie do Urzędu Bezpieczeństwa w Nowej Rudzie, Doniesienie; 8.12.1946.

95. ŻIH, CKŻP, box 1–2, p. 317. See also Andrzej Friszke, "*Żydzi w szkolnych podręcznikach,*" *Więź*, vol. 42, 1 (1999): 23–36.

96. Natalia Aleksiun-Mądrzak recently published a multipart article on the subject in the *Biuletyn ŻIH*.

97. On the scandalous treatment, or rather neglect, of this subject in primary- and high-school history textbooks, read the special issue of the quarterly *Biuletyn Żydowskiego Instytutu Historycznego* (no. 3-4, 1997) devoted to the analysis of coverage of "Jewish Subjects in School Textbooks." Thirty-nine different textbooks approved by the Ministry of Education and published between 1994 and 1997 are reviewed in this issue.

98. Lewis Namier, *1848: The Revolution of the Intellectuals* (New York: Doubleday and Co., 1964), 58.

99. I wish to end on a positive note, however, in recognition of a number of great authors in Poland who always spoke on this subject with audacity and wisdom—Jerzy Andrzejewski, Jan Błoński, Czesław Miłosz, Zofia Nałkowska, Stanisław Ossowski, or Kazimierz Wyka—and a new generation of

scholars who in recent years have taken on the subject with critical and open minds: Natalia Aleksiun-Mądrzak, Alina Cała, Barbara Engelking-Boni, Ewa Koźmińska, Paweł Szapiro, Bożena Szaynok, or Andrzej Żbikowski. We are on the verge, I believe, of a major reassessment of the epoch by Polish historiography, and a new sensitivity and awareness concerning all matters Jewish among the Polish public.

BIBLIOGRAPHY

Archives

Bundesarchiv, Koblenz.
General Sikorski Historical Institute Archives, London.
Hoover Institution Archives, Stanford, California.
Piłsudski Institute of America, New York.
Public Record Office, London.
Sukiennicki's Archive (private collection).
Underground Poland Study Trust, London.
Yad Vashem, Jerusalem.

Documents and Newspapers

Armia Krajowa w Dokumentach. Edited by UPST. Vols. 1 and 2. London: n.p., 1970, 1973.
Central Commission for Investigation of German Crimes in Poland. *German Crimes in Poland.* 2 vols. New York: Howard Fertig, 1982.
Concise Statistical Yearbook of Poland, September 1939–June 1941. Glasgow: Polish Ministry of Information, 1941.
Czerwony Sztandar, Lwów, October 1939–June 1941.
Documents on German Foreign Policy. Vol. 8. Edited by R. J. Sontag. Washington: Government Printing Office, 1954.
Documents on Polish Soviet Relations, vol. 1, *1939–1942.* Edited by GSHI. London: Heinemann, 1961.
Eksterminacja Żydów na ziemiach polskich w okresie okupacji hitle-rowskiej. Zbiór dokumentów. Edited by T. Berenstein, A. Eisenbach, and A. Rutkowski. Warsaw: Żydowski Instytut Historyczny, 1957.
Główny Urząd Statystyczny (GUS). *Mały Rocznik Statystyczny.* Warsaw, 1938.
———. *Polska—dane skrócone.* Warsaw, 1937.
———. *Okręgi hodowlane, produkcja i spożycie mięsa w Polsce.* Warsaw, 1933.
———. *Statystyka Druków, 1931.* Warsaw, 1932.
———. *Zagadnienia demograficzne Polski. Ruch naturalny ludności w latach 1895–1935.* Warsaw, 1936.

Izvestia (Moscow).

Nowe Widnokręgi (Moscow and Lwów), no. 1–4 (1940–1941).

Pospieszalski, K., ed. *Documenta Occupationis.* Vol. 6. Poznań: Instytut Zachodni, 1958.

Pravda (Moscow).

Ugolovnyi kodeks RFSSR. Moscow: OGIZ, 1935.

U.S. House Select Committee on Communist Aggression, 83rd Congress, 2nd Session, 8th Interim Report. Washington: Government Printing Office, 1954.

ARTICLES AND BOOKS

Amsterdamski, Stefan, et al., eds. *Zeszyty Towarzystwa Kursów Naukowych.* Vol. 6: *Język propagandy.* Warsaw: Niezależna Oficyna Wydawnicza, 1979.

An Appeal to Fellow Americans on Behalf of the Baltic States. New York: Lithuanian American Information Center, 1944.

Arendt, Hannah. *The Human Condition.* Chicago and London: University of Chicago Press, 1958.

Babel, Isaac. *The Collected Stories.* New York: New American Library, 1974.

Babii, B. M. *Vozzyednanya Zakhidnoi Ukraini s Ukrainskoyu RSR.* Kiev: Vidavnitstvo Akedemii Nauk Ukrainskoi RSR, 1954.

Barthes, Roland. *Writing Degree Zero: Elements of Semiology.* Boston: Beacon Press, 1967.

Berger, Tuvia. "My Visit to Grodno." In *Encyclopedia of the Jewish Diaspora,* vol. 9, ed. Dov Rabin, pp. 510–518.

Bilii, D. "Bolshevitske pridooshivania religiinykh proiaviv u drogobitskikh shkolakh." In *Drohobychchyna—Zemla Ivana Franka,* vol. 2, ed. Luke Luciw, pp. 60–62. New York, Paris, Sidney, Toronto: Sheuchenko Scientific Society, 1978.

Blitzka, Hasia. "Zionist Youth Maintains Contacts." In *Encyclopedia of the Jewish Diaspora,* vol. 9, ed. Dov Rabin, pp. 507–509.

Bonatt, Edward. "International Law and the Plebiscites in Eastern Poland, 1939." *Journal of Central European Affairs* 5 (1946), pp. 378–398.

Borwicz, Michał. "Inżynierowie dusz." *Zeszyty Historyczne* no. 3 (1963), pp. 121–163.

Boyarin, Jonathan, and Jack Kugelmass, eds. *From a Ruined Garden: The Memorial Books of Polish Jewry.* New York: Schocken, 1983.

Brodsky, Joseph. *Less Than One: Selected Essays*. New York: Farrar, Straus, Giroux, 1986.

Buber Neumann, Margarete. *Under Two Dictators*. New York: Dodd, Mead, 1949.

Buczek, Roman. "Działalność opiekuńcza Ambassady R.P. w ZSSR w latach 1941–1943." *Zeszyty Historyczne* no. 29 (1974), pp. 42–115.

Burke, Edmund. *Reflections on the Revolution in France*. Garden City, N.Y.: Doubleday, Dolphin Books, 1961.

Cassirer, Ernst. *Symbol, Myth, and Culture: Essays and Lectures of Ernst Cassirer 1935–1945*. New Haven: Yale University Press, 1979.

Chalidze, Valery. *The Responsibility of a Generation*. New York: Chalidze Publications, 1981.

Chudy, Władysław. "W sowieckim więzieniu w Brześciu nad Bugiem." *Zeszyty Historyczne* no. 61 (1982), pp. 11–128.

Cohen, Stephen F. *Rethinking the Soviet Experience: Politics and History Since 1917*. New York, Oxford: Oxford University Press, 1985.

Conquest, Robert. *The Harvest of Sorrow: Soviet Collectivization and the Terror-Famine*. New York: Oxford University Press, 1986.

Dark Side of the Moon. London: Faber and Faber, 1946.

Davies, Norman. *God's Playground: A History of Poland*. 2 vols. New York: Columbia University Press, 1982.

Davies, Robert W. *The Socialist Offensive: The Collectivization of Soviet Agriculture, 1929–1930*. London: Macmillan, 1980.

Ehrenburg, Ilya. *Memoirs, 1921–1941*. New York: Grosset and Dunlap, 1966.

Fainsod, Merle. *Smolensk under Soviet Rule*. New York: Random House, 1963.

Gafencu, Grigore. *Prelude to the Russian Campaign: From the Moscow Pact (August 21st 1939) to the Opening of Hostilities in Russia (June 22nd 1941)*. London: Frederick Muller, 1945.

Geertz, Clifford. *The Interpretation of Cultures*. New York: Basic Books, 1973.

Gorki, Maxim. *Mother*. Moscow: Progress Publishers, 1949.

Gorki, Maxim, and V. I. Lenin. *Letters, Reminiscences, Articles*. Moscow: Progress Publishers, 1973.

Gross, Jan Tomasz. *Polish Society under German Occupation: The Generalgouvernement, 1939–1944*. Princeton: Princeton University Press, 1979.

———. "W zaborze sowieckim." *Aneks* no. 22 (1979), pp. 16–44.

Gross, Jan Tomasz, and Irena Grudzińska-Gross. *War Through Children's Eyes*. Stanford: Hoover Institution Press, 1981.

Gross, Jan Tomasz, and Irena Grudzińska-Gross. *"W czterdziestym nas matko na Sybir zesłali...."* London: Aneks, 1983.

Grossman, Vassili. *Tout passe....* Paris: Stock, 1972.

Grudzińska-Gross, Irena. *The Art of Solidarity*. Special issue of *International Popular Culture*, vol. 3. New York, 1985.

Gubarev, V. *Syn*. Moscow: Molodaya Gvardia, 1940.

Hakehillot, Pinkas, ed. *Encyclopedia of Jewish Communities, Poland*. Vol. 2: *Eastern Galicia*. Jerusalem: Yad Vashem, 1980.

[Hashomer Hatzair]. *Youth Amidst the Ruins: A Chronicle of Jewish Youth in the War*. New York: Scopus, 1941.

Heller, Michel. *La machine et les rouages: La formation de l'homme soviétique*. Paris: Calmann-Lèvy, 1985.

Hindus, Maurice. *Red Bread*. London: Jonathan Cape, 1939.

Homze, Edward. *Foreign Labor in Nazi Germany*. Princeton: Princeton University Press, 1967.

Horak, Stephen. *Poland and the National Minorities*. New York: Vantage Press, 1961.

Jędrychowska, Anna. *Zygzakiem i po prostu*. Warsaw: Czytelnik, 1965.

Kennan, George F. *Memoirs*. New York: Bantam Books, 1967.

Khrushchev, N. S. *Khrushchev Remembers*. Edited by Strobe Talbott. Boston: Little, Brown, 1970.

Kołakowski, Leszek. "Totalitarianism and the Virtue of the Lie." In Irving Howe, ed., *1984 Revisited: Totalitarianism in Our Century*, pp. 122–135. New York: Harper and Row, 1983.

Kosharnyi, I. Ia. *U suziri sotsialistichnoi kulturi*. Lviv: Vidavnitstvo pri Lvivskomu Derzhavnomy Universiteti, 1975.

Kot, Stanisław. *Listy z Rosji do Generała Sikorskiego*. London: n.p., 1956.

Kowalski, Józef. *Trudne Lata*. Warsaw: Książka i Wiedza, 1961.

Kubiiovych, Volodymyr. *The Ukranians in the Generalgouvernement, 1939–1941*. Chicago: Mykola Denysiuk Publishing Co., 1975.

Kubiiovych, Volodymyr, ed. *Ukraine: A Concise Encyclopedia*. 2 vols. Toronto: University of Toronto Press, Shevchenko Scientific Society, 1971.

Kugelmass, Jack, and Jonathan Boyarin, eds. *From a Ruined Garden: The Memorial Books of Polish Jewry*. New York: Schocken, 1983.

Kuznetsov, Edward. *Prison Diaries*. New York: Stein and Day, 1973.

Lewin, Moshe. *The Making of the Soviet System: Essays in the Social History of Interwar Russia.* New York: Pantheon Books, 1985.

Linz, Juan. "Non-Competitive Elections in Europe." In Richard Rose, Guy Hermet, and Alain Rouquié, eds., *Elections Without Choice,* pp. 36–65. New York: John Wiley and Sons, 1978.

———. "Totalitarian and Authoritarian Regimes." In Nelson Polsby and Fred Greenstein, eds., *Handbook of Political Science,* pp. 175–412. Reading, Mass.: Addison-Wesley, 1975.

Lipski, Jan Józef. *Workers' Defense Committee.* Berkeley: University of California Press, 1985.

Lubachko, Ivan S. *Belorussia under Soviet Rule, 1917–1957.* Lexington: University Press of Kentucky, 1972.

Malia, Martin. *Comprendre la Revolution russe.* [Paris]: Édition du Seuil, 1980.

Mann, Reinhard. *Zur Soziologie des Widerstandes in nationalsozialistischen Deutschland.* Cologne: Institut für Angewandte Sozialforschung, 1979.

Margolin, Y. "The Days of Soviet Occupation." In N. Tamir (Mirski) ed., *Sefer Pinsk,* vol. 2. Tel Aviv: Association of the Jews of Pinsk in Israel, 1966.

Markov, Georgi. *The Truth That Killed.* London: Weidenfeld and Nicolson, 1983.

Michnik, Adam. *Letters from Prison and Other Essays.* Berkeley: University of California Press, 1986.

Moser, Jonny. "Nisko: The First Experiment in Deportation." In *Simon Wiesenthal Center Annual,* vol. 2, pp. 1–30. White Plains, N.Y.: Kraus International Publications, 1985.

Naszkowski, Marian. *Lata próby,* Warsaw: Książka i Wiedza, 1965.

Nots, Moshe. "Beitar." In *Encyclopedia of the Jewish Diaspora,* vol. 9, ed. Dov Rabin, pp. 509–510.

Ostrovskii Nikolai. *How the Steel Was Tempered.* Translated by R. Prokofieva. Moscow: Progress Publishers, 1964.

Paechter, Heinz. *Nazi Deutsch: A Glossary of Contemporary German Usage.* New York: Frederick Ungar, 1944.

Pasqualini, Jean (Bao, Ruo-Wang). *Prisoner of Mao.* New York: Coward, McCann and Geoghegan, 1973.

Parsons, Talcott. "Some Sociological Aspects of the Fascist Movements." *Social Forces* no. 21 (1942), pp. 138–147.

Pasternak, Boris. *Doctor Zhivago.* Translated by M. Hayward and M. Haravi. New York: Pantheon, 1958.

Polskie Siły Zbrojne w Drugiej Wojnie Światowej. Vol. 1. London: Instytut Historyczny im. Generała Sikorskiego, 1950.

Preiss, Paulina. *Biurokracja totalna*. Paris: Institut Littéraire, 1969.

Prokop, Liuba [L.K.]. "U sorokovi rokovini protsesu 59–i." *Suchasnist* no. 9 (1981), pp. 83–108; no. 10 (1981), pp. 81–98.

Rabin, Dov. "Two Years of Soviet Rule in Grodno." In *Encyclopedia of the Jewish Diaspora*, vol. 9, ed. Rabin, pp. 503–508. Jerusalem, 1973.

Raeff, Marc. *Understanding Imperial Russia*. New York: Columbia University Press, 1984.

Redlich, Shimon. "The Jews in the Soviet Annexed Territories, 1939–1941." *Soviet Jewish Affairs* no. 1 (1971), pp. 81–90.

Rigby, T. H. "A Conceptual Approach to Authority, Power and Policy in the Soviet Union." In T. H. Rigby, Archie Brown, and Peter Reddaway, eds., *Authority, Power, and Policy in the USSR: Essays Dedicated to Leonard Schapiro*, pp. 9–31. New York: St. Martin's, 1980.

Rudnycka, Milena, ed. *Western Ukraine under the Bolsheviks, IX 39–VI 41*. New York: Shevchenko Scientific Society, 1958.

Russian Oppression in the Ukraine. London: Ukrainian Publishers, Ltd., 1962.

Scott, John. *Duel for Europe: Stalin vesus Hitler*. Boston: Houghton Mifflin, 1942.

Sefer Sokolkah. Jerusalem, 1968.

Shohat, Azriel. "World War II until the Nazi Occupation." In V. Z. Rabinovitsch, ed., *Sefer Pinsk*, vol. 1, pp. 287–292. Tel Aviv: Pinsk-Karlin Association, 1977.

Smirnov, E. *Pavlik Morozov—pomoshch pioniervozhatomu*. Moscow: Molodaya Gvardia, 1938.

Staniszkis, Jadwiga. *Poland's Self-Limiting Revolution*. Edited by Jan T. Gross. Princeton: Princeton University Press, 1984.

Studnicki, Władysław. *Polska za linią Curzona*. London: n.p., 1953.

Sukiennicki, Wiktor. "The Establishment of the Soviet Regime in Eastern Poland in 1939." *Journal of Central European Affairs* 23 (1963), pp. 191–218.

The Tchortkiv District. Ukrainian Archive, 26. New York, Paris, Sidney, Toronto: Shevchenko Scientific Society, 1974.

Torańska, Teresa. *Oni*. London: Aneks, 1985.

Turauskas, Eduardas. "Communist Diplomacy Exposed." *Lithuanian Information Service* (New York), bulletin 2 (February 1941).

Turlejska, Maria. *Prawdy i fikcje*. Warsaw: Książka i Wiedza, 1968.

Ulam, Adam. *Expansion and Coexistence: The History of Soviet Foreign Policy, 1917–1967*. New York, Washington: Praeger, 1968.

Umiastowski, Roman. *Russia and the Polish Republic, 1918–1941.* London: "Aquafondata," n.d.

Vakar, Nicholas P. *Belorussia: The Making of a Nation.* Cambridge, Mass.: Harvard University Press, 1956.

Vincenz, Stanisław. 1966. *Dialogi z Sowietami.* London: Polska Fundacja Kulturalna, 1966.

Vyshinskii, Andrei Y., ed. *The Law of the Soviet State.* New York: Macmillan, 1948.

Wasilewska, Wanda. "Wspomnienia Wandy Wasilewskiej (1939–1944)." In *Archiwum Ruchu Robotniczego*, vol. 7, pp. 339–432. Warsaw: Książka i Wiedza, 1982.

Wat, Aleksander. *Mój Wiek.* 2 vols. London: Polonia Books, 1977.

Watowa, Ola. *Wszystko co najważniejsze.* . . . London: Puls Publications, 1984.

Weissberg, Alexander. *The Accused.* New York: Simon and Schuster, 1951.

Żarnowski, Janusz. *Społeczeństwo Drugiej Rzeczypospolitej.* Warsaw: Państwowe Wydawnictwo Naukowe, 1973.

Zawodny, Janusz. *Death in the Forest: The Story of the Katyń Forest Massacre.* Notre Dame, Ind.: Notre Dame University Press, 1962.

INDEX OF NAMES
AND PLACES

INDEX OF NAMES AND PLACES